Becoming Modern

The Industrial Exhibi
Shaping of a Late Victorian Culture

North American cities of the late nineteenth century, grappling with the effects of industrial capitalism and urban growth, were subject to a succession of massive social transformations. Scientific and technological advances were shifting the balance of cosmopolitan power, and people faced the challenge of comprehending and adapting to the rapidly changing social environment. In *Becoming Modern in Toronto*, Keith Walden shows how the Toronto Industrial Exhibition, from its founding, in 1879, to 1903 (when it was renamed the Canadian National Exhibition), influenced the shaping and ordering of the emerging urban culture. Unlike other studies of its kind, it fully integrates experiences on and off the fairground by viewing the fair as a microcosm of developing structures in the city and surrounding rural areas.

The book is arranged around seven thematic elements – order, confidence, display, identity, space, entertainment, and carnival – each of which concerns the way the Exhibition contributed to a search for definition in the face of innovation. The efforts to divide existence into logical, unambiguous categories and to promote controlled conduct was, however, constantly frustrated by the novelty of the fair itself. The Exhibition presented fairgoers with new perspectives and information, while the exhibits simultaneously denied and invited their participation. Though the fair seemed to glorify professional accomplishments and legitimate élite leadership, it also implied that the fruits of industrial capitalist society were not exclusive. Walden concentrates on these ambiguities, revealing how the status quo was both confirmed and challenged at the fair.

Becoming Modern in Toronto takes into account a variety of social tensions and concerns that pervaded late Victorian culture. It will be compelling reading for historians, sociologists, and cultural anthropologists, as well as for those interested in the symbolic and social meaning of public festivity and its regulation.

KEITH WALDEN is a professor of history at Trent University, and the author of a cultural history of the Canadian Mounties.

KEITH WALDEN

Becoming Modern in Toronto

The Industrial Exhibition and the Shaping of a Late Victorian Culture

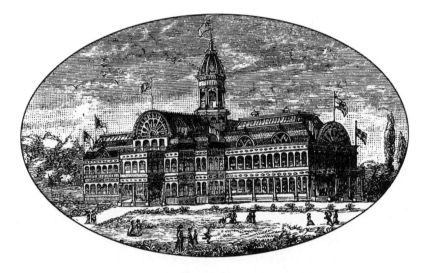

UNIVERSITY OF TORONTO PRESS
Toronto Buffalo London

© University of Toronto Press Incorporated 1997
Toronto Buffalo London
Printed in Canada

ISBN 0-8020-0885-2 (cloth)
ISBN 0-8020-7870-2 (paper)

∞

Printed on acid-free paper

Canadian Cataloguing in Publication Data

Walden, Keith, 1948–
Becoming Modern in Toronto : the Industrial
Exhibition and the shaping of a late Victorian culture

Includes index.

ISBN 0-8020-0885-2 (bound)   ISBN 0-8020-7870-2 (pbk.)

1. Toronto Industrial Exhibition – History.
2. Exhibitions – Social aspects – Ontario – Toronto.
3. Fairs – Social aspects – Ontario – Toronto.   I. Title.

T940.B1W34 1997   306   C96-932288-7

University of Toronto Press acknowledges the assistance to its publishing
program of the Canada Council and the Ontario Arts Council.

This book has been published with the help of a grant from the Humanities
and Social Sciences Federation of Canada, using funds provided by the
Social Sciences and Humanities Research Council of Canada.

To my mother,
Eleanor Walden,

my father,
Norman Walden (d. 1979),

and my sister,
Carol Gerein

Contents

Preface

This is a cultural history of the Toronto Industrial Exhibition from its founding, in 1879, to 1903. After this first quarter century, the fair became known as the Canadian National Exhibition.[1] The name change represented neither a sudden metamorphosis in the character of the show nor a formal expansion of status, but simply the ambitions of organizers and the fact that no other fair in the country was big enough to challenge the claim. Despite its original title, the exhibition was never just a showcase for manufactured products. Industry was meant in the broad sense of 'useful effort.' Agriculture and the fine arts shared the pedestal, though the latter was much the weakest sister. As well, like most fairs, this one was an occasion for many sorts of commercial activities, leisure entertainments, and socializing. It was not the only fair in nineteenth-century Ontario, but it was the largest, bringing together a broad segment of the population from Toronto and the surrounding areas. For farm people, it was something of a harvest festival. For the city's élite, it marked the end of summer, cushioning regrets at leaving cottages and resorts. For ordinary urban folk, it offered a regular injection of excitement, exotic novelty, and sometimes inconvenience to punctuate the tedium of routine. By any measure, the fair was a distinct and important component of life in Toronto.

To approach the exhibition from the perspective of cultural history requires some brief comment. The study of culture has evolved substantially in the last few years. Long ago, the narrow focus on great artists and thinkers, and their influence, was supplemented by more-embracing anthropological notions that understood culture to include everything people do and think. Their relationships, activities, and world views became targets of investigation, not simply their concrete productions; any human creation was relevant, not just those accorded high prestige; all individuals and groups were significant, not just the most technologically and artistically developed. For scholars beyond anthropology, this broadened conception stimulated investigations of marginalized groups and mass pastimes, legitimizing the study of such things as Native culture, Black culture, working-class culture, and popular culture.[2]

Until recently, most analyses dealt with the structure of social organizations or the content of beliefs. Now, this approach has begun to be complemented by more interest in how meaning is constructed through active human practices. Growing concern with different forms of cultural domination has directed more attention to dynamic processes rather than static elements.[3] Indeed, structures themselves seem to be merely convenient shorthand for never-ending interactions. Content is unceasingly negotiated. Even language has become destabilized as deconstructionists like Jacques Derrida have undermined presumptions that precise vocabulary can lay bare fixed qualities about the world. Naming, it now seems, is always provisional and contingent.[4] For many investigators, then, discovering how meaning is debated and disseminated, rather than uncovering any specific meaning, has become primary.

Historians have not been immune to this development. From various quarters, calls have been sounded to pay more attention to the processes of representation. 'The project of cultural history,' says Catherine Belsey, 'is to identify the meanings in circulation in earlier periods, to specify the discourses, conventions and signifying practices by which meanings are fixed, norms "agreed" and truth defined.' The most pressing question in cultural history today, argues Roger Chartier, 'is that of the different ways in which groups or individuals make use of, interpret, and appropriate the intellectual motifs or cultural forms they share with others.'[5] By taking the construction, propagation, and contestation of meaning as its major focus, cultural history has suddenly moved from the sidelines to the forefront of historical writing. As Richard Fox and Jackson Lears noted in the introduction to a recent collection of essays on cultural themes in American history, the higher profile is due partly to a broadened definition that includes many analyses formerly slotted as 'social' and 'intellectual,' but it also reflects the impact of postmodern sensibilities. Cultural history, they suggest, 'is the rubric under which a massive doubting and refiguring of our most cherished historical assumptions is being conducted.'[6]

As an effort to respond to these challenges, this book is an exercise in what Lynn Hunt has labelled 'new cultural history.' Although this approach, she suggests, has no rigid methodology or model, it is characterized by a tendency to apply insights from anthropology, cultural studies, and linguistic theory to close examinations of localized social productions and activities.[7] This study conforms to that description. My intent has not been to survey the contents of the fair for their own sake. I have not paid much attention to the exhibition's beginnings or administrative development. I have not tried to catalogue every feature offered up for edification and enjoyment. Rather, I have tried to explore how, once established, the exhibition helped shape understandings in a society being altered profoundly by industrial capitalist production, technological developments, and new ideas and values, including consumerism. This is not a history of an institution, but an attempt to understand how certain cultural dispositions formed around an institution.

The 'Ex' has long been recognized as one of Toronto's primary attractions. Celebratory volumes have appeared at regular intervals,[8] but there has been no detailed assessment of its impact. This imbalance is not unusual. Considering the prevalence of modern local fairs, the absence of scholarly investigations of them is surprising. Popular histories abound; sustained, critical studies are scarce.

There are exceptions. Sally Alexander's short pamphlet *The St. Giles Fair, 1830–1914* is very suggestive about the evolution and social meaning of entertainments at an Oxford event. Anne Lincoln Fitzpatrick, in *The Great Russian Fair*, is mainly interested in the market at Nizhnii Novgorod as a case-study of commercial modernization in the nineteenth century, but she does pay considerable attention to the disruption it created.[9]

Closer to home, Wayne Neeley's *The Agricultural Fair*, now more than half a century old, is still the only broad survey of American institutions that, he claims, were important agents of socialization. Ted Ownby, in *Subduing Satan*, suggests that turn-of-the-century fairs in the American south were instruments of modernization and centralization, breaking down rural isolation, broadcasting evangelical moral and domestic ideals, and, via the midway, introducing a version of urban decadence. In tracing the evolution of the Iowa

State Fair, Chris Rasmussen pays particular attention to the tension between amusement and instructive features. As befits a historian of material culture, Karal Ann Marling approached the Minnesota State Fair like an artifact, trying to understand 'the ways in which a culture sees and what it chooses to observe.' The survey of activities lends itself to an extensive use of photographs, but her sophisticated appreciation of the nuances of the fair experience makes this much more than a coffee-table book for aficionados. Even if studies of fairs abounded, this would be a useful one.[10]

In the Canadian context, David Jones's insightful *Midways, Judges and Sharp-Tongued Fakirs* emphasizes the desire to use western Canadian fairs in the Progressive era to promote economic development and community life. Elsbeth Heaman's recent PhD thesis on central Canadian fairs and Canadian displays at international exhibitions in the nineteenth century takes a broad look at their role in economic development and in the creation of a public sphere. Elwood Jones's *Winners: 150 Years of the Peterborough Exhibition*, on the other hand, provides a more focused depiction of how a specific show became more urban, more commercial, and more formulaic in its attractions.[11]

Compared with the paucity of materials on local events, the secondary literature on world exhibitions is positively voluminous. Robert Rydell's historiographical essay in *The Books of the Fairs* documents its broad range of themes. Singly or together, expositions have been looked at in relation to such themes as nationalism, international peace, trade, women's participation, popular culture, art, architecture, and technology. At present, interest is especially keen in their use as justifications of imperialism and racism, in their role in reorganizing society around capitalist production and mass consumption, and, as a corollary, their influence on the development of museums, department stores, and other institutions of modern industrial society. There is no need to duplicate here this exhaustive review.[12]

American cultural historian Neil Harris has divided recent works into two basic categories. The nostalgic school of 'urban sentimentalism' revels in the decorative exuberance of these events and emphasizes their aspirations for human progress. The 'revisionist' school strips away benign facades to find not idealizations of harmony and abundance, but revelations of unequal distribution of wealth and power; not innocent entertainments, but ideological weapons to impress particular world views.[13] My own slant on this material is not dissimilar. For me, the key distinction is whether these events are seen as mirroring or as moulding culture. The line is not hard and fast, but individual analyses have tended to lean heavily towards one side or the other.

The 'snap-shot approach,' as the former might be termed, is implicit in older studies in which culture is viewed as finished artifacts, and has been used more recently by historians seeking concrete markers for phenomena not easily pinned to conventional political chronology. Exhibitions represent dense nodes where complexly interwoven currents can be dissected. Thomas Schlereth uses the American fairs of 1876, 1893, and 1915 as time-specific anchors for discussions of broad aspects of everyday Victorian life. Deborah Silverman suggests that the Paris show of 1889 'crystallized' the confrontation between advanced technological structures and bourgeois liberalism stemming from the Enlightenment. These authors do not necessarily believe that the effect of expositions was entirely passive, but this impression is a by-product of the way they have made use of them.[14]

For some scholars, however, freezing time is not simply a convenient analytical tool but the whole point of the actual shows. Reid Badger's explicit goal in studying the Columbian Exposition was to determine what light it shed on the overall psychological or emotional condition of American society in the 1890s. He concludes that it had 'far greater significance as a reflector of the general culture than as an influence upon it.' Robert Muccigrosso's centenary reexamination of the same event acknowledges that the show led to new directions in architecture, design, and social reform, but maintains it was more fundamentally 'an expression of what Americans had accomplished, were accomplishing and promised to accomplish.' Dwelling on those accomplishments allows him to downplay allegations of 'racism, class and gender domination, social control and cultural regression' that, to him, 'ring hollow.'[15]

The second approach is less interested in defining the character of specific eras than in understanding how and why exhibitions were used to shape attitudes in and towards industrial capitalist society. For Alan Trachtenberg, the 1893 extravaganza was a ruling-class device to 'win hegemony over the emerging national culture.' The White City was intended to show how places like Chicago might look and be governed, and to prove that business, political, and cultural élites knew how to fashion a modern industrial society better than workers, farmers, women, and immigrants did. For Paul Greenhalgh, the great expositions were the principal means by which governments and private bodies presented their visions of the world to the masses. They were instruments to define national identity, marshall support for imperialist policies, and persuade ordinary folk that the harshness of life was being dispelled. To Burton Benedict, fairs were sites where those with power and those reaching for it competed for ascendancy and legitimized their social dominance. They were display cases to sell both ideas and mass-produced goods. Industrial products on view did not merely cater to middle-class taste but helped to form and validate that taste. People were taught what to buy and how those purchases defined their social niche. According to Robert Rydell, in the period up to the First World War, exhibitions were used to make the social world comprehensible and to organize the direction of society from a class perspective. Fairs, he says, were triumphs of hegemony that deeply influenced many individual and collective beliefs, particularly with respect to ideas about race and progress. In a more recent book, he characterizes depression-era fairs as exercises in 'cultural and ideological repair work,' representing 'a drive to modernize America by making it an ever more perfect realization of an imperial dream of world abundance, consumption, and social hierarchy based on the reproduction of existing power relations premised on categories of race and gender.' Neil Harris is probably the most positive of those in this stream, pointing out that fairs improved the status of local institutions, contributed to the beautification of urban landscapes, helped identify new local leadership, stimulated support for local improvements, and generally legitimized the urban idea. However, he too acknowledges that they reinforced prevailing notions of cultural hierarchy, generated class and ethnic tensions, and became giant advertising organs.[16]

Notwithstanding their different shades of emphasis and angles of approach, all these works in the second stream hook into the same complex of assumptions: fairs were instruments of hegemony, used by élites to generate support for a culture dominated by white, male, middle-class values, and organized increasingly around capitalist production and the possibilities of consumption thus provided. In fostering and reinforcing hierarchies of taste, gender, and race, they shaped class identities, social spaces, and public policies. This book shares these premises. What can it contribute that is new?

First, it is focused on an annual fair, a relatively neglected kind of event, qualitatively different in some ways from world's fairs. Although it resembled these prestigious but short-term shows in many ways, and wished the similarities were greater, the Toronto Industrial Exhibition was more local, more firmly integrated into yearly routine, more concerned with corporate than national identities, more oriented to immediate commerce than encyclopedic presentations of human accomplishments, and more devoted to readily available and mass-produced commodities than to exotic products from distant lands.

Though annual fairs may not have admitted as many people in any given year as world expositions, it is arguable that they had a greater impact on visitors, who often returned time and again. The opportunities for moulding were more sustained. There is little point, however, in trying to measure degrees of influence. What is obvious is that the Industrial Exhibition, and other annual fairs like it, were significant institutions, highly successful over a long period, and deeply connected to the emergence of an urban, industrial, consumer society. They deserve more notice.

Second, this study attempts to integrate more fully experiences that occurred both on and off the fairground. Most analyses of exhibitions and local fairs view them as self-contained, almost insulated, environments. The Columbian Exposition, says Trachtenberg, set itself off against what lay beyond its gates. It enforced its lessons by contrast. World's fairs, according to Benedict, built idealized cities within their walls. His gaze on these fantasy environments is directed internally. Even James Gilbert's *Perfect Cities*, which draws attention to other utopian presentations in Chicago outside the fairground – the experimental community of Pullman and the 'evangelical metropolis' conjured by Dwight Moody's revival – treats them as coexistent but discrete realms. It is not clear how they intersected in individuals' consciousness or experience.[17]

What has to be remembered is that the fair represented a time as well as a space. For out-of-towners, the show itself was only one part of a total experience. What happened in a hotel or a store could be just as significant as what happened within the gates; who was encountered on the street could be just as memorable as who was noticed in a pavilion or sideshow. For city residents, as well, fairtime was different from the rest of the year. Even those who chose to abstain from the actual event had trouble ignoring crowds and the conditions they created. This study, then, assumes that understanding the impact of the Industrial Exhibition requires consideration of what was happening in Toronto as a whole.

Third, following from a focus that is external as well as internal, this analysis tries to comprehend more broadly how the fair experience shaped understandings of modern urban culture. Unlike previous works that have attempted to document the effect of exhibitions on popular perceptions, this one does not deal only with deliberate messages intended by formal displays but, rather, tries to show how these messages intersected and competed with others, inside and outside the grounds, that were contradictory and subversive.

The analytical scaffolding used to explore meaning is ritual. Other scholars have also noticed the applicability of this concept to exhibitions. Warren Susman argued that fairs served as rites of passage for American society, generating acceptance of new technologies, new possibilities of consumption, and large capitalist organizations. Burton Benedict described world's fairs as 'a series of mammoth rituals' in which all sorts of power relations were expressed. Rydell suggested that fairs provided 'symbolic universes' which 'ritualistically affirmed fairgoers' faith in American institutions and social organization, evoked a community of shared experience, and formulated responses to questions about the ultimate destiny of mankind in general and Americans in particular.'[18] For all these authors, rituals are understood as consistent statements or ceremonies that coherently express the values of those who direct them. My notion of ritual, derived from anthropologist Victor Turner's concept of liminality and from Peter Stallybrass and Allon White's discussion of transgression, refers to situations when ordinary structures are dissolved and cultural elements are allowed to interact and combine in ways normally prohibited. Fairs were useful for exploring the meaning of modern urban society not because they were thoroughly stable, but because they were in some ways highly unstable, and so allowed exceptional perspectives.

It is all very well to investigate the creation of meaning, but this presupposes some way of determining exactly what elements of culture are worthy of scrutiny. In the recent past, much debate has centred around Robert Darnton's analysis of the 'Great Cat Massacre' in eighteenth-century Paris. Darnton described how a group of printers' apprentices and journeymen expressed dissatisfaction with conditions in their own workplace and with decreasing opportunities for advancement within their trade by subjecting neighbourhood felines to mock trials and executions.[19]

As a number of critics have pointed out, by assuming that symbolic forms have transparent meanings, Darnton felt free to assign a greater measure of importance to some actions and metaphors than to others.[20] His criteria for deciding what was worthy of notice and what was not lay beyond the text and was ultimately subjective.[21] I acknowledge the same flaw. My themes, and the examples used to support them, are not the only ones that could have been selected. I have no hesitation in arguing the significance of these choices, but I do not pretend to have used any scientific or objective method in isolating them.

My experience of the Victorian fair probably duplicated that of many contemporary visitors who discovered too much going on to assimilate it all, even with repeated trips. Forced to be discriminating, I lingered in the places that most aroused my own curiosity. I spent much more time in the Crystal Palace than in Machinery Hall, was more intrigued by the midway than the animal barns, found more to contemplate in the crowd than on the walls of the Art Gallery. Others, with different priorities, will think I missed the most important parts. They will have to make their own excursions.

Acknowledgments

This book has taken a long time to materialize, and many debts have been incurred in the process. It has been published with the help of a grant from the Humanities and Social Sciences Federation of Canada, using funds provided by the Social Sciences and Humanities Research Council of Canada. Earlier, the research was facilitated by grants from the Trent University Committee on Research and from the Social Sciences and Humanities Research Council. I am grateful to all these bodies, and to the people of Canada whose taxes were the ultimate source of these monies.

The staffs of the Metropolitan Toronto Reference Library, City of Toronto Archives, Metropolitan Toronto Police Archives, National Archives of Canada, Archives of Ontario (particularly Carolyn Heald and Leon Warmsky), and Robarts Library at the University of Toronto were unfailingly helpful. At the latter institution, Judy Young Chong, Joan Links, Iqbal Wagle, and Mary Ann Wilson in the Microtext Department merit special thanks for their courtesies over a protracted period and for helping so often to get the microfilm copier into better focus. I am deeply grateful to Linda Cobon at the Canadian National Exhibition Archives. Since most of the nineteenth-century records of the fair have long since disappeared, that repository had much less material than I anticipated, but Linda was always considerate in making available the sources that did exist and, later, in arranging for photographic reproductions.

Other individuals also contributed in specific ways that deserve mention. Joe Muldoon, of the Trent University Office of Research and Graduate Studies, did much to ensure the success of my SSHRC application. With insight and enthusiasm, Liz Wilton, my research assistant, scoured small-town Ontario papers for references to the exhibition. Peter Bailey first drew my attention to Stallybrass and White's *The Politics and Poetics of Transgression*, a book that became critical to the analysis that follows. Elsbeth Heaman generously shared many useful leads to studies about exhibitions and exhibiting and allowed me to read her recently completed PhD thesis on nineteenth-century central Canadian fairs. Joan Sangster read an earlier draft of chapter 3, while another colleague, Doug McCalla, commented with great tact and charity on a longer and more tedious version of the introduction. Pam Johnson forsook valuable bicycling time to read a number of chapters at early stages; her interest was much appreciated and her encouragement greatly sustaining. At the University of Toronto Press, it has been a pleasure to work with Gerry Hallowell, Emily Andrew, Karen Boersma, and Darlene Zeleney, and a privilege to have Rosemary Shipton as copy editor.

Many people helped in ways that were less direct but no less significant. For accommodation, hospitality, comfort, advice, intellectual stimulation, and other forms of support, I especially would like to thank Holly Benson, David Churchill, Ken Dewar, Bob Gerein, Carol Gerein, Margaret Hobbs, Colin Howell, Peter James, Pam Johnson, Laura Macleod, Doug McCalla, Alison Melville, David Monod, Tamara Myers, Diana Pederson, Joan Sangster, Colin Savage, Donald Smith, Eleanor Walden, and Liz Wilton.

George Rawlyk, the first person to read the entire manuscript, died while it was in final preparation. He had previously commented on early drafts of several separate chapters, so the bound version bears the firm imprint of his astute critical eye. I had looked forward to a time when I could offer some small token of appreciation for his unstinting support by presenting him with a copy of the book. Not being able to enjoy that moment has detracted significantly from the satisfaction at completing the project. George was a good friend, and I miss him very much.

Becoming Modern in Toronto

Introduction

On 2 September 1892 Hannah Heron was struck by one of Toronto's new electric trolleys in a downtown residential neighbourhood. The sixty-one-year-old woman from Scarborough, at the city's eastern edge, had been staying with an aunt. Shortly before 3 p.m. she was being escorted to the Church Street car by her host's companion, who saw the trolley approaching. As they stood on the northeast corner of the intersection, Heron was told she had to board at the southwest. She raced into the street, intending to cross diagonally. Recognizing the danger she was in, the driver rang a warning bell, but the noise disoriented her. She stopped in the middle of the street. Too late to brake now, the motorman started to shout, increasing her bewilderment. Finally, she darted in front of the car, which knocked her down and passed over both her legs below the knee. She was carried back to her aunt's house, where she died five hours later.

An inquest held the next day revealed that the two motormen were almost as unfamiliar with the capabilities of the modern trolley as Heron was. The cars had been introduced to Toronto less than three weeks before, and workers were being trained during regular service. The actual driver, with only one day's experience on the vehicle, was under instruction from the other, who himself had yet to pass an examination for competency. Neither had read the manual outlining operating instructions, though one had had it read to him. They were unsure of the speed of the car, of the most effective braking techniques, of stopping distances once the brakes were applied, and of official procedures for emergency situations. They and the victim were assigned equal blame for the tragedy,[1] which was soon forgotten as the city went on adapting to the tumultuous transformations of the late nineteenth century. However, for those involved, the incident was a sobering example of the problem of meaning in a dynamic society. This book is about that problem.

The extent of change in the late Victorian Western world was staggering. None of it materialized abruptly out of thin air, nor was there any dramatic turning-point that marked the arrival of modernity, but by the closing years of the century even those most insulated from overt effects and most determined to resist intrusions could sense that Western society was shifting its axis. Cities grew inexorably; powerful new business organizations announced their presence with high-rise office towers and sprawling factories; bureaucratic centralization and regulation became more pronounced; migrations from distant parts of the globe snowballed; medical breakthroughs abounded; scientific discoveries spawned startling new theories; and bicycles, automobiles, dry-process photographs, halftones, movies, tractors, electric lights, typewriters, telephones, and other marvels of technological sophistication appeared with dizzying regularity. The list could be extended for pages and still not begin to capture the full effect of the innovations. The world seemed to have speeded up, to have become more complex. Change itself was in the saddle. Nothing, it seemed, was immutable. As so much gave way, as so much was pushed together, people were required to re-establish the comprehensibility of their physical and intellectual environments. The necessity was obvious, though precise meanings to be ascribed were not.

Meaning is never self-evident. Nothing in the world is straightforwardly 'given.' Human beings create reality by interpreting and relating some elements of a universe whose totality can never be completely comprehended. How they make sense of existence invariably reflects where they are situated within a given social structure and historical continuum. What is designated as 'natural' or 'true' varies considerably – across cultures, within a specific culture over time, and within a specific culture at any given moment.[2]

Meaning is established through hierarchies of value that are complex and fluid. Language in itself is inherently incapable of pinning down reality.[3] What is understood as 'high' has significance only in relation to what is considered 'low.' What is 'big' or 'fast' depends fundamentally on what is simultaneously perceived as 'small' or 'slow.' These spectrums are never completely separate, discrete categories. According to Peter Stallybrass and Allon White, the 'fundamental basis to mechanisms of ordering and sense-making in European cultures' is the intersections of high/low oppositions in four main symbolic domains – the human body, social order, geographical space, and psychic forms: 'Divisions and discriminations in one domain are continually structured, legitimated and dissolved by reference to the vertical symbolic hierarchy which operates in the other three domains. Cultures "think themselves" in the most immediate and affective ways through the combined symbolisms of these four hierarchies.'[4] Change in one category has consequences for all the others. Not only is the entwining of scales conducive to infinite permutations and combinations, but rankings on any given spectrum are affected by a wide assortment of factors, including race, class, gender, and age, to mention just some of the most obvious.

Meaning, consequently, is always contested. It is continually debated by different groups and individuals, each attempting to assert its own understandings, derived from its own assessments of interests. Not all versions of reality have the same authority or are propagated as widely. These cultural productions are regulated by the same relations of power that govern all social interactions, though the ability to influence meaning is not just a straightforward reflection of wealth or numbers: marginal groups can sometimes exert disproportionate influence, at least in some fields. Those disadvantaged by a particular sort of interpretation, however, resist to whatever extent, in whatever ways, they can. Often, enough overlap and intersection exist to allow some more commonly accepted version of reality to emerge, but rankings and connections are constantly negotiated and refigured in the context of specific circumstances. Meaning is always rooted in concrete situations, is generated at all social levels, and invariably remains unstable.

When Hannah Heron stepped into the middle of Church Street, she was articulating a particular understanding of what a Toronto roadway meant – of the nature of the vehicles likely to be encountered there, of the dangers that needed to be considered, of appropriate ways of moving through that space, of the status of a human body relative to all these things. Unfortunately, her understanding, based on past experience, was contested by the street railway company, a much more powerful entity, which wanted to run cars at speeds faster than had been possible with horse-drawn wagons. By changing just one element in the situation, the entire web of signification had to be reknit. Whether individuals or trolleys should have precedence, who was responsible for regulating encounters, what space should be occupied by pedestrians – such questions, which went to the heart of the meaning of the street, bodies, machines, and citizenship, all had to be renegotiated because hierarchies of speed and power had changed.[5]

The effort to communicate by both parties in this confrontation was intense, yet the gap between what each was trying to say – through bells, shouts, or expressions of abject terror – and what actually came out was, to risk a pun, striking. Nor was the significance of the encounter fully understandable without precise knowledge of who had been hit, who had charge of the car, where and how the accident occurred, and so on. A different configuration of bodies, locations, and movements would have produced a very different message – as another incident, just three days after Heron's death, confirmed.

Harris Weise from Orangeville, fifty miles to the northwest, was almost run over in downtown Toronto by an electric tram. He ran into the roadway to catch a horsedrawn car, oblivious to a trolley coming from the other direction until he was standing on the track. He dived headfirst out of the way onto a pile of mud, gathered himself up, and 'guessed' he would walk to the exhibition grounds.[6] Both encounters pointed up public inexperience with streetcars and the consequent dangers, yet their social meanings varied profoundly. An energetic male was judged differently from an elderly female. A rustic tourist was not the same as the close relative of an affluent city resident. Mortification did not call for the same response as mortality.

As examples of contestations, these run-ins between citizens and streetcars were all too concrete, but they demonstrate how, as old formulations began to corrode, as new technology began to appear, as industrial capitalism reshaped structures and expectations of modern existence, the problem of meaning became more insistent.

Meaning could not simply be imposed from above. It was generated and contested at every level, in ways that were conscious and unconscious, formal and informal, carefully considered and spontaneous. Nevertheless, many agents and agencies, recognizing the extent of cultural fluidity, were anxious to shape responses favourable to their own projects. In many cases, they hoped to shuck away the inertia of routine, the stasis of inherited conceptions, to make people more receptive to new ideas, new commodities, new patterns of behaviour. They sought physical and mental spaces where consciousness, or certain ranges of it, would be more acutely susceptible to revision. The impulse to propagate new messages, in other words, stimulated the creation of new sites of public discourse and the transformation of older ones – among them, fairs.

This book explores one specific site in the late Victorian period – the Toronto Industrial Exhibition – and tries to suggest how it contributed, intentionally and unintentionally, to the shaping of understandings of modernity. The show's impact was rarely straightforward. As was often the case, the increased intensity of efforts to mould perceptions encouraged more pronounced reactions. The fair could never generate universal acceptance of its preferred messages, but it could, and did, illuminate significant areas of social concern.

The establishment in Toronto of an Industrial Exhibition that devoted considerable attention to farming interests made perfect sense. In the late nineteenth century the city was metropolis to a hinterland that was markedly agricultural in character, with a growing industrial base. In 1871, 78 per cent of slightly more than 1.6 million Ontarians lived in rural areas, the vast majority in the eastern and southwestern regions. Only thirteen places had more than 5000 people, representing less than 11 per cent of the population. These ratios began to change quickly as urbanization took hold in the last three decades of the century. By 1911, only 47 per cent of the now more than 2.5 million residents were classified as rural.[7] Farm people worried about their declining influence, but, well into the 1930s, agriculture remained the keystone of the economy. If the proportion of rural people was declining, their absolute numbers were not. Ontario farms were not depopulated in this period. According to census data, 309,000 people were gainfully employed in agriculture in 1901, 78,000 more than three decades earlier.[8]

Most farms were family owned and operated and were relatively prosperous, though obviously there were exceptions.[9] By the 1870s the shift from growing wheat for export to mixed production for local urban markets was well under way.[10] Along with fruit, vegetables, meat, and dairy products, farms also sent to the city much of their excess population. Some family members who were unable to acquire land in traditional settled areas took up homesteads in the West, but many were attracted to industrial and white-collar employment in cities. Their departure allowed the rural sector to escape constricting poverty from overpopulation, and meant that, instead of supporting large numbers of indigent relatives with nowhere to go, surpluses could be used to modernize operations and to purchase consumer goods.

As agriculture was restructured, industry matured. Throughout the 1860s, much of it, such as implement manufacture, butter and cheese making, and milling, had been farm centred. In the 1870s production became much more diversified, with many firms much larger than those that had existed previously.[11] Some industries recorded impressive advances. The gross value of baked goods and confectionery rose from $3 million in 1870 to more than $14 million in 1910. Agricultural implement production in the same period went from $2.3 million to more than $19 million. Clothing went from slightly more than $4 million to over $30 million.[12] Clearly, industry was supplying new needs, not just more people.

Although the performance of the provincial economy as a whole in the late nineteenth century was not spectacular, it was 'creditable.'[13] At a time when population growth was comparatively sluggish, as in the 1870s and 1880s, or virtually non-existent, as in the 1890s, when many Ontarians emigrated to the United States, this was perhaps the most that could be expected.[14] Despite occasional downturns, there was no general depression, and expansion in most respects was uninterrupted from one decade to the next.

The beneficiary of much of this development was Toronto. By the 1870s, when industrialization began to take off, its well-developed entrepôt structure, as well as its reserves of capital and labour, rapidly attracted scores of enterprises, including foundries, metalworking plants, furniture workshops, clothing sweatshops, distilleries, piano manufactories, and slaughter houses. In 1870, 11 per cent of the province's industrial employment was located in Toronto. By 1910 the figure had risen to 27.3 per cent.[15] Other places also grew, sometimes at rates that outpaced Toronto's.[16] None, however, had the same range of industrial activity, and most came increasingly under Toronto's control, especially in the 1890s and after, when the city's investment tentacles began to stretch. By the end of the First World War, when Toronto was rivalling Montreal as a national metropolis, the nickname 'Hogtown' was only partly attributable to its flourishing meat-packing plants.[17]

With industry came other economic activity. Factories, office buildings, and houses were erected in a series of construction booms.[18] Streets, sewers, and utility infrastructures were set out. The railway system was overhauled and expanded, tightening the city's grip on central and southwestern portions of the province and extending its transcontinental reach.[19] Retail trades, already well established, grew even more. In 1871 the city had 71 dry-goods dealers; in 1891 it had 119, including several large department stores.[20] These shops were important sources of jobs for women, as were expanding government and business bureaucracies, where more and more clerical workers were needed. Economic dominance inevitably produced cultural influence. Toronto became headquarters for religious bodies, labour groups, professional organizations, and voluntary associations, not to mention legal, medical, and educational institutions.[21]

Naturally, economic growth was reflected in population changes, which, though not nearly as dramatic as in places like New York and Chicago, were still impressive. In 1871 there were 56,000 residents, a few more than twice the number in the next largest Ontario centre, Hamilton; by 1911 there were in excess of 375,000, more than four times the number in Ottawa, now the closest provincial rival. Even through the general deflation of the 1870s, 1880s, and 1890s, Toronto grew by 270 per cent; the province as a whole, in comparison, increased by less than 35 per cent. In 1871 the city accounted for 3.5 per cent of the entire provincial population. By 1911 it represented 9.5 per cent, and the proportion was increasing.[22] Some of this boom was due to the annexation of adjacent villages, but most was the result of natural increase and immigration. No other urban place in Canada rivalled it as a destination for newcomers. In the 1890s, more than a third of Toronto residents were not native born.[23]

The most remarkable thing about Toronto's mushrooming population in the late Victorian period was its homogeneity. Not only did rural emigrants from the surrounding hinterland come from Anglo-Celtic stock but so did the majority of those from abroad. From the middle of the nineteenth century to its end, no more than 6 per cent of residents were characterized as 'foreign born.' The rest came almost entirely from the British Isles.[24] A significant component were Irish Catholics, sometimes viewed with hostility by Protestants, but the linguistic and ethnic differences so apparent in many American cities at this time were largely absent. By the 1890s even Orange–Green antagonisms were subsiding.[25]

All this sameness made at times for a large degree of conservatism and smugness among the better off. Many working people continued to struggle at the margins of subsistence, often protesting strenuously about intrusions of industrial capitalism into their traditional

practices.[26] Affluent burghers, on the other hand, easily overlooked
the pockets of slums, emphasizing instead the number of shady
streets, comfortable houses, large churches, and substantial public
buildings. Theirs, they believed, was a 'British' city – God-fearing,
loyal to Queen and Empire, and, particularly compared with centres
south of the border, moral. Boosters painted it as a progressive, go-
ahead kind of place, full of evidence of civic-mindedness and material
progress.[27] 'The industrial and social evolution of Toronto, especially
within the last two decades, is so remarkable as to be almost without
a parallel in the history of the communities of the New World,' rhapsodized publisher and man of letters G. Mercer Adam in 1891, as the
city approached its centennial.[28]

A year later, Adam moved to the United States. Toronto, it
seemed, was not the only centre of opportunity. Nor was it as distinctive as Adam maintained. Notwithstanding its ethnic homogeneity,
it was in many respects a typical North American provincial city:
though it was not not in the first rank of urban places, it was ambitious to prove that it belonged there and was convinced that it would
soon arrive. It was a little too impressed by its own sophistication, a
little too insistent about its own virtues. Though every city is unique
in some respects, Toronto was not really unusual, and one indication
was its annual fair.[29]

Fairs are ancient institutions. The impulse to suspend routine,
exchange goods and information with those from beyond, and enjoy
extraordinary entertainments seems deeply rooted in human experience. Certainly by the Middle Ages, fairs had become an integral
part of Western culture.[30] Some were connected to particular
moments of the annual round, such as harvest or pre-lenten carnival
celebrations. Others were mainly market opportunities and occurred
much more frequently. While appreciating the commercial possibilities of fairs, authorities were often wary. From their perspective,
acceptable levels of civility, order, and deference all too often went by
the boards as crowds caroused, miscreants of various sorts plied their
trades, and outsiders such as travelling actors introduced dangerous
notions – particularly about the failings of those on top. There was
often good reason to be suspicious. St Bartholomew's at Smithfield,
for example, was a 'raucous, free-spending fortnight' during which
thousands gorged, drank, gambled, and brawled. This oldest and biggest of London's fairs acquired a reputation for riot and lewdness

that persisted long after it was abolished in 1855.[31] From the seventeenth century on, respectable elements in many areas joined forces to suppress, moderate, or transform traditional shows that they considered excessive. This process became easier as middle-class mores gained ascendancy and as the commercial importance of many events was undermined by the increase of permanent retail shops.[32] Shows that evolved into largely entertainment occasions became much harder to defend.

Paradoxically, festering intolerance towards some fairs in the nineteenth century was accompanied by the creation of all sorts of new fairs.[33] Two currents fed this resurgence of respectability and acceptance – the commitment to scientific agriculture and the success of international expositions. With the agricultural revolution of the eighteenth century, advances in farming became tied to fairs where new techniques and implements could be demonstrated, and where competitions were used to foster the improvement of crops and livestock. The notion that shows almost automatically stimulated the impulse to do better became conventional wisdom. 'He must be a very thick-skinned and out-of-date farmer, indeed,' declared the editor of *Farming* at the 1895 Toronto event, 'who does not feel incited by the sight of so many fine farm animals brought together, to try, in a small way, to emulate those breeders in improving his own stock.' The dissemination of improvements proceeded along many other avenues, but fairs sponsored by local agricultural societies became a key avenue of advance.[34]

The deep roots of the Toronto show were often traced to this sort of commitment to progress: to be precise, to a $40 prize purse donated by Lieutenant Governor John Graves Simcoe to the Niagara Agricultural Society in 1792. This commitment was interpreted as proof of an enlightened approach to agriculture from the province's very start, though not until 1830 did the Upper Canadian government make a systematic effort to encourage district agricultural societies and their shows by giving legislative recognition and small grants.[35] Although this support seems to have been about a decade earlier than the revival of interest in agricultural societies in the United States, it was not until 1846, five years after the first New York State Fair, that the newly formed Provincial Agricultural Association and Board of Agriculture for Canada West, set up as a coordinating body for local societies, organized the first provincewide fair, held in Toronto that fall. The site of the Provincial Fair, as it came to be known, moved from year to year, eventually settling into a rotation among London, Kingston, Hamilton, Ottawa, and Toronto.[36]

By 1878, when its turn came around again, Toronto had hosted on seven previous occasions, and local leaders were anxious to secure the fair as a permanent attraction. After obtaining a long-term lease on a portion of the Garrison Common, federal land reserved for military purposes, the city erected a number of substantial buildings, hoping that provincial exhibition directors would recognize the desirability of reusing the facilities. These worthies heaped praise on the 1878 organizers, then promptly picked Ottawa for the next fair. Toronto responded by forming a separate Industrial Exhibition Association and, in direct challenge, mounting its own show a year later.[37] As the name of the new organization indicated, urban manufacturing and business interests were now extensively involved. They had long attached themselves to agricultural shows to advertise and sell, but their interest in this sort of venue was reinforced by the other, more urban, current that rehabilitated fairs in the nineteenth century – the phenomenal popularity of international expositions.

Although London's 1851 Exhibition is usually considered to have inaugurated the era of great international shows, the British merely expanded on a concept that had been evolving for at least six decades.[38] After the resounding success of the Crystal Palace exhibition hall, the popularity of such extravaganzas spread like wildfire. Between 1855 and 1914, an event involving more than twenty nations was held somewhere in the world on an average of once every two years, and these exhibitions were supplemented by many smaller ones. The French were probably the most ambitious sponsors, having decided to use expositions to establish their cultural pre-eminence. The great Paris shows of 1867, 1878, 1889, and 1900 set glittering standards for others to follow. Americans were relatively slow in getting started, but the Centennial Exposition at Philadelphia in 1876 inaugurated a long succession of grand fairs, including the largest and most successful at Chicago in 1893, the Columbian Exposition.[39]

The character of international exhibitions evolved quickly. By the early 1870s organizers discovered that straightforward presentations of technology and manufactured goods were no longer sufficient to attract visitors. Space was given increasingly to other things, including natural history, science, agriculture, and educational methods.[40] The two most important additions were fine art and popular amusements. The latter brought in more people, but the former had a higher symbolic status. A dominant theme in most fairs was the union of new forces of industrialism with the great traditions of art. For the most part, conservative juries chose staid, academic works, creating striking contrasts between the new, innovative, and unsettling, represented by industry, and the reassuringly familiar, represented by art. As Paul Greenhalgh has pointed out, the juxtaposition encouraged perceptions of a wide gulf between high and popular culture, between the functional and the ethereal, but the presence of art also conferred prestige on the whole proceeding. Without it, 'an exhibition became just a trade fair.'[41]

The first amusement additions were fairly innocuous landscape attractions long featured in pleasure gardens – lawns, mazes, grottos, lakes, islands, fountains, and the like. As with fine art, part of the motivation was a desire to set industry into a more humanized, pastoral context.[42] Before long, other respectable entertainments were allowed, especially after working people were targeted as visitors. The Crystal Palace show had been inaccessible to anyone who was not at least in the prosperous artisan class, but Napoleon III deliberately opened the 1867 Paris show to the masses as a way of winning their loyalty.[43] Allowing amusements brought in more revenue, permitted authorities to monitor popular entertainments more closely, and kept tourists out of more dangerous dens elsewhere in the city.[44] Of course, middle-class people were just as eager as workers for light frolics – and far more able to pay. Altogether, the attractions of the grand expositions were exceptionally diverse, making them unusual social phenomena. As Neil Harris has pointed out, in an age when many cultural institutions were carving up and dividing social spheres, the exposition was bringing them together.[45]

The Toronto fair was never an international exposition, though it constantly aspired to be one. Talk of getting official accreditation began as early as 1880 and continued throughout the century.[46] Although the formal designation was never attained, many supporters claimed that the Industrial was little different – 'Not a World's Fair but Nearly So,' as the 1893 program cover put it. The disappointed took consolation in the permanence of what Toronto had. Recent expositions at Chicago and Buffalo, 'efflorescent and beautiful as they might be,' said the *News* in 1903, 'were yet evanescent, a dream prolonged over half a year.' The Industrial's glory would grow and last.[47]

Whether the Toronto fair rivalled international events or not, it was viewed as part of the same tradition. The 1851 Crystal Palace show had marked 'an era in the history of the humanities of the world,' wrote a *Globe* columnist somewhat obscurely, and from it came all the smaller ones, 'our own amongst the number.' In fact, association managers did keep a close eye on exposition innovations, adapting features of demonstrated popularity or utility according to their own budgetary constraints. Organizers were most interested in American expositions, which were not only more accessible but had audiences and exhibit priorities that more closely resembled their own.[48] The 1893 Chicago show had not closed its gates, for example, before some of its star attractions arrived in Toronto. Individual exhibitors likewise were sharply attuned to developments elsewhere and quick to adopt them. Again, influences from Chicago in 1893 soon pervaded Toronto. 'On every side,' wrote *Mail* columnist Kit Coleman in 1894, 'one could see that we had profited by certain teachings. Goods were better set out, practical workings of machinery and the different trades were better operated, harmony of form and coloring more closely studied with beautiful effect than ever before. The Exhibition was fuller, broader.'[49]

The impact of the Columbian was profound, but it was not the only exposition to which Torontonians paid attention.[50] Nor were world's fairs the only models from which they drew. Amusement parks, vaudeville theatres, museums, trade shows, and department stores all became sources for general ideas and specific features. In the Victorian period, distinctions among these institutions were often fuzzy, which was not surprising. All were shaped by the same basic conditions, including more disposable income in more hands, more leisure time, better transportation, and more commodities that had to be sold. Inevitably, a certain sameness was evident in spectacle environments of all kinds, and fairs specifically took on a 'generic likeness,' as a European visitor noted in his diary after seeing the 1883 Toronto show.[51]

However desirable it might be to tag onto the broad exposition tradition, pride and ambition ensured that the Toronto production would be viewed as something more than the local version of an international phenomenon. The Industrial was special, maintained boosters, because, of all annual shows, it was the largest. The editor of the Orillia *Packet* called it 'the chief exhibition on this continent.' The editor of *Farming* was convinced there was nothing like it in North America or Europe.[52] Such language was hyperbole. As North

American fairs went, Toronto's was one of the biggest, but it was similar to many state fairs and other regional Canadian shows, such as the Central Canadian Exhibition in Ottawa and the Western Fair in London. With larger audiences and greater revenues, Toronto could draw more exhibitors and offer more attractions, but they were not significantly different ones.

According to the *Mail and Empire* at the turn of the century, the modern era had become the 'age of the exhibition.' 'Recent times have been so fertile of new processes and of economies that there has been a veritable profusion of improvements. To get to know anything about these at first hand we must have specimens of them assembled at some one point of observation.' A decade earlier, *The Week* had insisted that exhibitions 'have done and are doing very much in the way of stimulating enterprise and giving fresh impulse to ingenuity and effort in almost every department of human activity.'[53] For both agriculture and industry, fairs were seen as essential tools of progress, necessary both to comprehend and to continue it. The effect of these assertions, and countless others in the same vein, was to obscure the fact that they were also instruments of hegemony, intended to further the goals of specific interests.

The exhibition was designed to engineer consent, to legitimate the leadership of particular interests. The most effective kind of consent, as Gramsci explained, derives from structures of understanding that are common in a culture. Where traditional Marxists emphasized the coercive clout of the state to enforce compliance with élite projects, Gramsci highlighted the socializing power of the civil sphere in turning élite biases and values into 'common sense' perceptions of day-to-day existence. Relations forged here appeared to exist apart from the potentially menacing state and from the often bitterly contested realm of production.[54] Although promoters were of course unfamiliar with Gramsci's insights, they recognized the fair's utility for inserting self-interested predispositions and values into the fabric of ordinary life.[55] Farm and factory interests backed the Industrial, not just for immediate monetary gain but for the favourable light it cast on their pursuits. Other groups had less transparent but still impelling objectives. For Torontonians trying to extend the influence of their metropolis, for the city's industrial capitalist élite trying to prove itself, and for a growing middle class trying to solidify its identity and secure its hold, the great show was a valuable lever.

In an immediate sense, its power lay in the hands of those who administered it. The Industrial Exhibition Association was composed of delegates elected or appointed annually from various political bodies and from societies representing agricultural, manufacturing, horticultural, commercial, and educational interests throughout the province. The fair began in 1879 with fifty-three representatives from eighteen organizations. By 1883 it had expanded to seventy-three members from twenty-six organizations, ranging from the Toronto City and York County councils to the Canadian Institute and the Ontario Beekeepers' Association. About half these groups, including the Toronto Horticultural Society and the Toronto Board of Trade, represented strictly local interests; the rest had broader geographic bases, though many were headquartered in the city as well, such as the Ontario Department of Education and the Ontario Society of Artists. The Toronto City Council, with thirteen seats, and the Toronto Electoral District Society, with twelve, had by far the most influence. Except for the Manufacturers' Association of Canada, with five seats, and the Ontario Association of Mechanics' Institutes, with three, none of the other organizations sent more than two representatives.[56] From this larger body, a twenty-person board of directors was elected to advise the general manager on the planning and operations of the show.[57] The directors had the real clout.

Although some effort was made to choose proportionally from the various societies, virtually all directors were Toronto residents. This, in itself, suggests how the fair was used to normalize Toronto's metropolitan dominance. What has to be remembered is that this preeminence was relatively new and, for many people, disturbing. As Robert Wiebe argued in a now classic study of the Progressive era, one of its major features was the gradual demise of the 'island community.'[58] With improved transportation and communications, and the reorganization of production on a continental basis, the isolation of small centres scattered throughout the hinterland eroded. Many hamlets and crossroads became redundant and disappeared.[59] The rest were pulled increasingly into new orbits by such things as telegraph and telephone wires, travelling salesmen, railway tracks, and mail-order catalogues. Communities with traditions of relative self-sufficiency and autonomy were not happy at the prospect of becoming mere satellites. The refusal of smaller Ontario cities to permit Toronto's monopolization of the Provincial Exhibition was one example of resistance to the process, although Hogtown's assumption of pre-eminence was an indication that it was well under way by the time the Industrial was founded.

For Toronto, then, the fair was a useful way of persuading the periphery to acquiesce with minimal resentment to increasing centralization. People in the hinterland came to the Industrial Exhibition because it was more impressive than local shows, but also because it claimed to be more than just a Toronto venture. Representation on the overall governing body of groups, such as the Eastern and Western Dairymen's Associations, the Fruit Growers' Association of Ontario, and the Dominion Grange, disguised the effective control by city interests.

Of course, power was exercised by specific individuals, not simply by anonymous agents. Who were these men? The initial cohort of twenty directors was typical of those who served during the first quarter century. In fact, over half remained directors for a decade or more, and two for the entire period. The large majority were prominent business figures. John Withrow, president of the association for more than twenty years, owned a construction firm, developed real estate, and was president of the Canadian Mutual Loan and Investment Company. W.F. McMaster, nephew of a prominent dry-goods dealer, had himself been involved in numerous retail enterprises, was a promoter and director of the Toronto, Grey and Bruce Railway, and eventually became secretary of the Bureau of Industries in the Provincial Agricultural Department. John Hallam, 'one of Toronto's most prosperous citizens,' was a hide, wool, and leather merchant, and Robert Barber, of Barber and Company, was an agent for woollen manufacturers. William Christie presided over a well-known biscuit company that produced for the national market. Both James Fleming and William Rennie owned seed-growing companies with large retail divisions, while George Leslie operated a highly successful nursery. Joseph Davids and W.H. Doel had drug businesses. W.H. Howland took over his father's milling business and from there become prominent in other financial, insurance, and electrical enterprises. W.B. Hamilton manufactured boots and shoes, and Samuel Wilson, cigars. George Booth ran a copper and brass foundry, and Patrick Close was a wholesale grocery, wine, and spirit merchant.

Of the remaining five directors, at least two could be described as professionals. Dr Andrew Smith was principal of the Ontario Veterinary College and president of the Ontario Veterinary Association. D.C. Ridout, trained as a civil engineer, was a patent solicitor. Both had close connections to the business sphere, as did James McGee, identified in the City Directory as a bookkeeper. Lucius O'Brien, a distinguished painter, might also be considered a kind of profes-sional. As founding president of the Royal Canadian Academy, he was a central figure in establishing an accreditation organization for fel-low artists. The occupation of the final director, Alex McGregor, was unspecified in city directories, though he lived in a fashionable dis-trict and, like ten of the others, served on the Toronto City Council.[60]

What does this heavy business presence suggest about the fair as an instrument of social power? Why were these people willing to give it a considerable portion of their energies? Individual ambition played a large role in determining specifically who came forward for service. The only material rewards for their labour were free lunches on the grounds while the show was in progress, but directorship con-ferred a significant measure of prestige, which some may have hoped would translate into other advantages.

However, the homogeneity also suggests that these individuals represented not simply private interests, but a particular social and economic constituency that was attempting to flex its muscles. As J.M.S. Careless has pointed out, political and social power in late nineteenth-century Toronto was shifting from 'old families,' whose prominence was rooted in land ownership and patronage connec-tions, to new men whose claims lay in industrial and mercantile suc-cess.[61] Merchants, factory owners, railway entrepreneurs, and contractors – precisely the sort of men who served as directors – were emerging as the city's most influential element. In the initial cohort, even the two with ties to the older élite – Ridout, whose family had long been socially prominent, and Howland, whose father had been lieutenant governor of the province – were firmly enmeshed in the new business culture. There was no sharp antagonism in the transi-tion; the values of the two groups were close. Still, a general snob-bishness towards the newly rich by the old made it clear that the process was not completely uncontested,[62] and the eagerness of the former to gain municipal office suggests that their priorities were not identical. This was an élite committed to capital as the vital coordi-nator of social organization.

The fair was invaluable to the new men in asserting their claims. Running it successfully gave them a chance to demonstrate their competence to the wider public, suggested they were motivated by ideals of community service, and allowed them to bypass the partisan quagmire of regular politics. Through the Exhibition Association and its board, they not only inserted themselves into dominant positions in an alliance with agricultural and cultural organizations but they heightened the impression that they deserved support, not because they were wealthy or because they wore a particular party stripe, but because they stood for honest, efficient administration of public affairs. Though many were appointed to the board because of their positions as aldermen, thereby ensuring that the city's concerns were carefully considered, the ostensible arm's-length relationship, as well as the participation of individuals who did not hold political office, implied that the fair was operated on principles far different from the patronage and self-interest that seemed to underlie the older élite's approach to public service.[63]

If the directors represented a new business élite trying to legitimate claims to civic leadership, they also represented more generally the middle class, the large body of respectable citizens whom Careless described as the 'balance-weight' of late Victorian Toronto.[64] This was a group in ascent, but also in considerable flux, and not just in Hogtown. Some would say that this class had been rising since the dark ages, but in nineteenth-century North America its situation did, in fact, change dramatically. The merchants, professionals, and more prosperous artisans who made up the 'middling sorts' in its early decades were relatively few, and not far removed from the mass of people in the lower orders. They soon became more numerous and, at least initially, more distinct.

The stimulus, according to Stuart Blumin, was the growing distance between manual and non-manual labour. Previously, both kinds of activities were carried out in close proximity, with no great differentiation between the status of the two. Many business proprietors themselves plied a craft beside their employees. Economic specialization, concomitant with the increasing size and complexity of enterprise, drove a wedge between those who worked with their hands and those who did not. More and more, the former tended to earn hourly wages in rough, utilitarian environments, while the latter were paid salaries for wearing more presentable clothing in finished, centrally located offices and stores, well separated from the sweat and grime of production.

As the number of non-manual workers swelled and the status of manual workers declined, the former became more intent on shaping a distinct identity. They began to live, as well as to work, apart, and they used these spaces to nurture new values. The domestic sphere became, in Mary Ryan's words, 'the cradle of the middle class.' Protecting the sanctity of the family, honouring its rituals, preserving its genteel accoutrements, and supporting agencies that extended its influence, such as evangelical religion and voluntary reform societies, became the central focus of efforts at self-definition.[65]

By the closing decades of the century, with the growth in professions, bureaucracies, and sales forces, this class had swollen enormously. In addition to those whose wealth and education placed them firmly in its ranks, it encompassed many who thought they belonged there by virtue of self-employment, acceptance of bourgeois ideals, or aspirations to positions of affluence and responsibility. As late as 1905, according to Jurgen Kocka, about 50 per cent of American retail clerks saw their positions as an apprenticeship before they began their own businesses; the public saw them as potential future store owners as well. This ideological identification with businessmen was not unique to sales clerks or to men. Many working women, themselves ghettoized in menial jobs, believed with good reason that they could achieve higher status through marriage. Nor was it exclusively urban: prosperous farm families, not to mention village notables, also saw themselves as something other than lowly labourers.[66]

Needless to say, the internal cohesion of this class should not be exaggerated, not just because the collar line was really a murky zone but also because the effects of industrial capitalism cut across middle-class interests and sensibilities. Not everyone welcomed the arrival of experts, large enterprises, and commercial values. Not everyone felt comfortable with the urbanization, mass immigration, and deskilling of jobs that sank the status of workers.[67] Still, there was broad unanimity within the middle class in the pursuit of two far-ranging projects: to ensure their leadership of society as a whole, and to define more precisely their own class characteristics. The fair was a useful tool for both objectives, because it was embraced at all social levels.

The fair's popularity was indisputable. Over the quarter century after its founding, paid attendance rose from 102,000 to 527,000. In only four of those years did admissions drop from what they had been the previous season. In 1881, 125,000 people passed the turnstiles – equivalent to 6.5 per cent of the provincial population. In 1901, 439,000 official entrances amounted to 20 per cent of the provincial population.[68] It is hard to know precisely what these figures represent, since multiple visits became more common as the show got larger, but it seems safe to assume that participation more than kept pace with immigration and natural increase.

If contemporary reports can be believed, the entire social spectrum was attracted. 'People of all sorts and conditions of life are here found in promiscuous confusion, the bootblack bustling elbows with the millionaire,' commented a *News* reporter in 1883. The following decade, a Guelph editor remarked on 'the delightful mingling once a year of the rich and poor upon the same level, the elbow to elbow contact of aristocrat and plebeian.'[69] Such comments were no doubt accurate as far as they went, but whether the fair drew in the same proportion from every constituency is harder to assess.

Excursion trains from outlying parts, 'crowded with passengers as thick as they can hang on,' as one contemporary put it,[70] testified to the interest of small-town and farm folk. Probably a higher percentage of the former came, since they were less encumbered with day-to-day chores, but diaries indicate that even in this harvest season many farm people managed a visit, often by alternating days on which family members were freed up.[71] They were sometimes torn between conflicting local and metropolitan pulls, and not always at ease in the city, but they were ideologically at home on the fairground.

Were working people equally enthusiastic? A good number of firms hoped they were and actively promoted attendance. In 1881 the Compton Corset Company actually provided tickets for employees.[72] The city and the Exhibition Association encouraged these gestures. In 1880 Mayor Beaty issued a special request asking employers to grant a half holiday on the first Saturday of the fair so workers would have a chance to visit.[73] 'Citizens' Day,' as it was designated, quickly became an annual feature, proclaimed by council each year in response to petitions from some of the larger companies, including the Massey agricultural works, the Gurney stove factory, the Heintzman piano factory, and the Morse soap works.[74] By the end of the decade, except for operators of essential services and for merchants reluctant to turn away visitors with money to spend, most employers were conceding the holiday.[75] Their generosity may not have been entirely altruistic. Firms like Massey and Morse, which mounted large displays, had an interest in generating excitement by boosting attendance, and they may have preferred to shut down production on a planned basis than to cope with unpredictable patterns of absenteeism.

As well, they may have appreciated that the fair was a more effective instrument of working-class subordination than moralistic hectoring or outright coercion. By cultivating a labourer's tastes, counselled a *Dry Goods Review* editorial in 1894, his desire for more and better goods would increase. 'His bare floors must be carpeted, his windows curtained, his furniture covered, his walls papered, his bookcases replenished, and his wardrobe enlarged.' With the props of bourgeois domesticity in place, the corresponding sentiments would follow. Although there was some danger that the fair might kindle resentment, its overall effect was thought to work more consistently in the other direction. The coming together of manufacturers, mechanics, and labourers for a common purpose at the fair, preached Rev. Theodore Parr to a Toronto congregation in 1892, was an important instrument in educating the population for carrying out the duties of citizenship. Putting goods out for mass display not only provided tangible proof of the advantages of class cooperation but seemed to suggest a commitment to making them available to all, regardless of station. Show the worker that he can be cultivated and educated, and still pursue a calling that was honest, said the *Dry Goods Review*, and 'bitter feelings will be removed from the hearts of those who under very adverse circumstances come to hate capital, government and the social structure.' Such ideas about the utility of exhibitions were long standing. From the Crystal Palace show on, fairs were deliberately intended as antidotes to class conflict.[76]

Did working people take the bait, on Citizens' Day or any other time? Notorious congestion on the official holiday suggests that many did, as do other snippets of evidence, the most compelling of which come from labour bodies that sometimes found the fair too much competition. The Toronto *Star* summarized the problem in 1903, when some unions considered petitioning to change the date of Labour Day:

> There are only two propositions to work upon to celebrate the day. If it is decided to go to the Exhibition the individuality and distinctive characteristics of the day are lost sight of in the magnitude and national character of the Exhibition, and the social features of the day are entirely set aside. If it is decided to go to the Island or elsewhere, the Exhibition as a counter attraction on the only holiday during the Fair makes it almost impossible to bring the workers together to celebrate labour's holiday.

Organizers spoke from experience. In 1896, for example, when labour festivities took place on Toronto Island, only two hundred people had gone to hear the speeches. The problem was never resolved in the Victorian era. Toronto unions waffled from one approach to the other, sometimes meeting on the grounds, sometimes not. When they did not, many in the rank and file opted for solidarity with the middle class.[77]

As a bourgeois influence, the Industrial had a big advantage. Because it was a new institution, no traditions of rough conviviality, no long-standing working-class rights, had to be accommodated. This independence became abundantly clear in 1898 when the Exhibition Association cancelled a commission arrangement with the local Trades and Labor Congress on Labour Day admission tickets sold to its members. Union officials were furious. 'Shall we calmly submit to this ignoble insult thrown at us by this practically irresponsible body,' asked the secretary in an open letter, 'or shall we rise indignantly and prove that we can, when occasion demands, give the lie to those who tell us we will not work unitedly to assert our dignity and influence in the community.'[78] Labour Day was celebrated that year at a skating rink rather than at the fairgrounds. The congress preserved its dignity, but only by boycotting the show. Similarly, three years later, when the Knights of Labor objected to the association's refusal to cancel a coal contract with a non-union employer, their recourse was a resolution not to attend.[79] Workers' organizations protested from a distance, without disturbing the symbolic coherence or the festive mood of the actual grounds. When working people did come, they had to conform to acceptable standards of behaviour, or risk being ejected.

While the fair supported bourgeois hegemony, it also helped the middle class to explore and fix its own identity. This was not a settled constituency. More and more people were working with their brains than with their hands; more and more were achieving levels of economic comfort well beyond mere subsistence; more and more believed they could achieve some reasonable degree of gentility. By the end of the century, according to Eric Hobsbawm, this group was larger than the working class itself. As the number of white-collar positions at the lower end proliferated, the obscurity of class boundaries produced enormous confusion and anxiety. The urgent need to create comprehensible markers resulted in much greater attention to the signifying power of knowledge and to lifestyles.[80] The fair fed into both, especially the latter.

In an economy that put increasing emphasis on managerial and technical expertise, an intensification of formal accreditation was not surprising, but it also served desires for social exclusivity. According to Robert Wiebe, two main tracks towards proficiency emerged. One stressed professional education at universities, in fields such as medicine, law, administration, and economics; the other, consultation and cooperation among those grappling with common problems in areas such as business, labour, and agriculture. For individuals in both groups, 'identification by way of their skills gave them the deference of their neighbors while opening natural avenues into the nation at large.' Class boundaries were protected by increasingly rigorous training requirements and the 'shared mysteries' of occupations.[81] The 'People's University,' as the Industrial was sometimes called, offered no degrees, but it continually reinforced the prestige of specialists, from agricultural scientists, through mechanical and electrical engineers, to professional display designers. The very composition of the Exhibition Association, with its high proportion of representatives from breeder and producer organizations, indicated that status, not just progress, derived from professional cooperation.

Although visitors were exhorted to learn from the fair, a studious demeanour was not necessary to demonstrate bourgeois inclinations. Simply being there went some way towards that end because it indicated an ability and a willingness to indulge in leisure, a sphere that became central in the definition of class boundaries. Having the wherewithal and the time to play sports, take vacations, and patronize commercial amusements were luxuries much less available to working people, though in the case of the fair, with a relatively modest twenty-five cent admission, exclusivity was not the point. Rather, mass accessibility universalized a middle-class standard, suggesting that rational recreation was not a wasteful extravagance but a normal expectation. Those who did not participate were eccentric or inferior. Those who did found at the show a secure field where constraints of class and ethnic background interfered less with the practice of new ways of being.

Leisure was an important part of the bourgeois lifestyle, but not the only component. Although that culture was becoming homogenized, its forms were not preordained. What it meant to be middle class was something to be defined and promulgated, in the home and on the street as well as at work. Language, dress, domestic accoutrements, public deportment – all such important mechanisms for grounding identities had to be debated, ranked, tested, propagated, normalized. As much as anyone else, middling sorts had to decide the meaning of what was new in modernity, and had to integrate it into their ordinary existence. For them, the exhibition was an extraordinary site not because of its commercial functions, but because it laid out with unusual comprehensiveness the hierarchies of taste around which class consciousness took shape.[82]

What made the fair so effective a catalyst in helping people handle new arrangements and possibilities was its ritual quality. It may seem strange to think of ritual as a device for encouraging openness to alternatives. After all, many prominent rituals are marked by rigid schedules and strictly prescribed behaviour. For some observers, this is their essential characteristic. Ritual is a declaration of form against indeterminacy, say Sally Moore and Barbara Myerhoff. It must be orderly because it 'veils the ultimate disorder, the nonorder, which is the unconceptualized, unformed chaos underlying culture.'[83] Repetition and order disguise the contingency of being, permitting cultures to function on fairly stable foundations at a cost of discouraging inquiry.

According to anthropologist Victor Turner, this understanding, typical of those observing from the outside, is incomplete. From the perspective of serious participants, a ritual looks very different. Its essence is liminality – a condition 'betwixt and between' ordinary existence when 'anything can or even should happen.' Turner suggested that a participant in ritual crosses a threshold, leaving behind the ordinary realm, and enters one where everyday forms and conditions are dissolved. Here, things are able to interact and combine in ways that are inconceivable in regular life. Not that they necessarily do combine, but they may. Anything is possible. The ritual concludes when the participant recrosses the threshold to ordinary existence, sometimes having been changed in the process.[84]

An outsider observing a religious congregation, for example, might see a group of people who assemble week after week in the same spot to perform a series of unvarying activities. True believers have a different sense of what is transpiring. For them, the space is an access point to the primary forces of the cosmos. Through methodical ceremonies, they are attempting to become more attuned to the presence and purpose of those powers. The House of God is a place 'betwixt and between' mundane reality, where anything can or even should happen. If the proper connection is made, miracles are possible. New ways of being that are learned here can be carried back to normal life, though there is no guarantee that substantive change will occur during any particular session.

Ritual, in other words, permits 'a heterodox merging of elements usually perceived as incompatible.' The quotation comes from Stally-brass and White's description of fairgrounds, and, indeed, their conception of this transgressive space, where high/low oppositions in all domains have the greatest freedom to intersect and upset usual hierarchies, fits comfortably with Turner's notion of liminality. It is this tolerance of the 'radically hybrid' that makes ritual so effective for investigating meaning.[85] From this perspective, its rigidity derives not from a desire to stifle imagination, but from a recognition of the need to tread warily where so many protean possibilities exist and the effect of powerful forces is unpredictable.

In rituals, then, there is usually a continual tension between prescribed forms and formlessness, between structure and what Turner called anti-structure. Those who preside make some effort to control the encounter by organizing the context where it occurs, mediating between participants and forces that may be unleashed, and directing responses into appropriate channels. Toronto burghers were comfortable with the amalgam of extraordinary creatures, bizarre objects, and aberrant behaviour at the Industrial Exhibition just because its external scaffolding seemed so stable. Its firm administrative structure kept it a step or two removed from the hurly-burly of party politics. Its spatial structure, set off from the rest of the city and enclosed, allowed more careful regulation and protection of what was inside and buffered the ordinary world from disturbing influences. Its temporal structure, two or three weeks that began and concluded with unambiguous precision, ensured that any transgressive overflow would be of limited duration. With these reassuring constraints, abnormalities produced by the fair could be viewed as playful experiments rather than as challenges to prevailing hierarchies.

Though most rituals invented by industrial capitalism were not understood at the time in these terms, they were crucial in forging transitions to modernity. To a large extent, they defined the modern. In an expanding consumer culture, where many groups had an interest in proliferating messages about abundance and the possibilities of material gratification, liminal environments which suggested that anything could or should happen were central. The innovators of department stores, advertising pages, billboards, and display windows who attempted to expand the import of consumption were just as intent on awakening expectations about the possibilities of existence as those who presided over more traditional religious ceremonies. They, too, sought to mediate encounters and channel responses while they extended horizons. Though older rites were not necessarily abandoned, modern culture was shaped as people participated in these new rites, then integrated perceptions gleaned from them into other spaces of their lives. It is impossible to comprehend the acceptance of industrial capitalist culture without grasping the role of rituals like the Toronto Industrial Exhibition.

Before embarking on an extended discussion of how the fair influenced meaning, it is important to have a realistic expectation of what can actually be charted. Many people of all ages and from all levels of society went to the Industrial; few bothered to record what they did there, let alone what they thought of it. Aside from odds and ends of municipal records, administrative reports, photographs, cryptic diaries, and the like, information about the fair in the Victorian period is available only from the press, mainly Toronto daily newspapers. Canadian trade periodicals, like the *Canadian Grocer* and *Electrical News*, sometimes commented on exhibits and issues relevant to their particular readers. Papers in smaller cities and towns occasionally contained columns by special correspondents or reports by staff writers on their own visits, but their coverage was sporadic, probably because metropolitan papers, teeming with news of the Industrial, circulated widely in the hinterland.[86] Though ideally it would be otherwise, Toronto newspapers are the single detailed source of information about what happened on and off the fairground.[87]

Like most large cities in the late Victorian period, Toronto supported an abundance of daily papers – a minimum of five by the early 1880s, six by the end of the decade, and seven between 1892 and 1895. The *Globe*, *Mail*, and *Empire*, the last founded by the Conservative Party in 1887, when the *Mail* started to stray from the party line, and then amalgamated with the *Mail* in 1895, were more staid and expensive, at two or three cents an issue. The *Telegram*, *World* (founded in 1880), *News* (founded in 1881), and *Star* (founded in 1892) were shorter, more spritely, and cheaper, at one to two cents an issue.

Though political leanings varied in sort and in degree, and though,

according to Thomas Walkom, readerships were more sharply delineated by class during the 1880s and 1890s than before or after,[88] all
these journals had remarkably similar attitudes towards the exhibition. The *Globe* and the *Mail* offered more exhaustive coverage. The
penny papers generally tried to capture more of its colour and excitement. Occasionally one organ or another mounted a high horse to
berate the fair's administration for some failing. Every one, however,
strongly supported the exhibition as a municipal institution, and all
had fairly uniform ideas about the significance of its features.

In part, consistency was due to the commercialization of news
occurring in this period. As papers began to compete more intensively for readers to pay for more expensive printing equipment,
quality journals like the *Globe* and the *Mail* reached out more deliberately to the lower classes, while the penny presses tried to appeal
to wealthier readers. Class conflict was downplayed across the
board.[89] The older emphasis on political commentary and partisan
advocacy declined. Instead, the press concentrated more consistently
on serving the commercial needs of the business community, which
bought advertising, and making the rapidly changing, increasingly
diverse urban milieu more comprehensible. Instead of merely reporting on already transpired political events, reporters went out to
gather news, looking for sensation and 'human interest' stories that
they delivered in vivid, exciting prose.[90] The exhibition became a natural target for extensive coverage, though it took on a homogeneous
tone.

The other reason for consistency was the fact that all the Toronto
dailies were city boosters. Paul Rutherford has argued that the
entire Canadian daily press in the Victorian period had a uniformly
bourgeois outlook which stressed progress, nationality, democracy,
order, and social harmony.[91] Hogtown editors certainly saw the
Industrial as a progressive, popular institution advancing Canadian
economic and social possibilities, but, more particularly, they saw it
as a key part of what made Toronto notable and successful. Since
their own fortunes depended on the prosperity of the metropolis as a
whole, they were not inclined to dwell on the shortcomings of an
important civic project. Quite the contrary. Coverage of the fair,
depicted as a shining example of local capabilities, was overwhelmingly positive and bright.

Although Toronto papers contain an enormous amount of material
about the fair and fairtime, the information is problematic. It is

impossible to tell who produced much of it. Some appeared with bylines, but the bulk was churned out by anonymous scribes who revealed almost nothing about their age, class origin, ethnic background, and sometimes even gender, although, fortunately, a substantial part of fair coverage was supplied by female columnists. Ultimately, meaning is achieved by individuals whose perceptions are affected by complex personal situations. With the information available, analysis at this level is seldom possible.

As well, the information is not disinterested. Reporters and editors worked for instruments tied closely to the city's dominant economic forces. A few had slightly more scope for personal expression, but all spoke as journalists, not Orange Protestants, migrants from small towns, children of unskilled parents, or any other peculiarity of identity. Direct voices of many significant groups – farm people, workers, ethnic minorities, children – are hard to come by. What can be heard from them has been filtered through other ears – how accurately is hard to know. In any event, press reports were regularly distorted. Negative impressions were often muted and expressed long afterwards. Some things were interpreted too generously. Contexts for evaluating observations were sometimes obscure. What did saying the fairground was 'relatively free' of drunkenness, for example, really mean? These failings are disappointing. Homogeneity of perspective and interpretive warping make it difficult to discover diverse readings and plural uses of symbolic elements. However, although the circumstances that created the records produced certain kinds of uniformity, the event was so large and complex that completely consistent responses across the board were impossible. Aggravations, anxieties, and competitions among values and purposes could never be entirely submerged.

What do these sources reveal, then? Though offering at best a one-sided view of its contestations with subordinate groups, they provide important insights into the attitudes of an urban middle class in a fairly typical North American provincial city during the emergence of the culture of consumption. Although the evidence may not always be accurate in describing actual conditions, the distortions are themselves indications of how late Victorian, bourgeois Torontonians wanted to make sense of their world. Since this was the hegemonic class, its interpretations of everyday, mundane experience spread to other segments, establishing the norm against which non-conformity was measured.

However, bourgeois understandings of industrial capitalist society were by no means definitive or monolithic. What these sources indicate most acutely is the urban, middle-class desire to impose meaning in a culture that had become remarkably fluid, and how problematic that goal was. What they allow, for the most part, is an analysis of some of the ways that this group tried to erect and test its hierarchies of value. What they highlight are not crisp, straightforward assertions about what was, but troublesome issues arising from the circumstances of modern existence. As a mechanism to engineer support for metropolitan, middle-class leadership, the fair was relatively successful; as a device to provide absolute reassurances about the anxieties of modernity, it was much less effective. Its messages were ambiguous and contradictory, pulsing first in one direction, then in another. Determining with any degree of sophistication the impact of the Industrial Exhibition on the consciousness of specific individuals is impossible. It would have been impossible at the time. What can be described is some sense of the competing force fields created by the fair through which many Victorian Ontarians oscillated into a different world.

The themes examined in the chapters that follow were not necessarily new concerns, but that did not make them less troubling. 'Order' deals with one of the fundamental intents of the whole exposition enterprise – the effort to arrange existence into logical, comprehensible categories and to promote controlled behaviour – and with the continual failure to accomplish this goal. It describes an alternating current that characterized almost every dimension of the fair experience: the effort to use the show to impose rigid hierarchies, and its tendencies to challenge and undo hierarchies already formed. 'Confidence' likewise tries to explain how a major goal of the fair, persuading people that modern existence was workable, was undermined by the show's very success. 'Display' suggests how the creation of meaning involved the interplay of different hierarchical domains. Specifically, it shows how manufacturers and retailers, trying to find ways to let mass-produced goods 'speak for themselves,' were compelled to tie meanings of commodities to different sorts of human bodies. 'Identity' looks at two significant social groups who participated in the fair, women and farm people, demonstrating that this environment was capable of both unsettling and hardening social stereotypes. 'Space' relates perceptions about the layout of the grounds to middle-class anxieties about urban growth. As a pleasure garden and as a miniature city, the fair's arrangement spoke to widespread concerns about the separation of social classes, and reflected a belief that architecture and landscaping could be used to reassert a sense of community. 'Entertainment' argues that what distinguished commercial amusements inside the gates was their relative detachment from a morally suspect male sporting culture. Because it did not have to contest against disreputable elements, the middle class was able to use fair diversions to debate among itself standards of taste. At the same time, the increasing popularity of these features pointed up challenges to the prestige of producer groups in a culture of leisure and consumption. Manufacturers had more success than farm interests in trying to restrict sideshows, but even they had to acknowledge the power of the midway. 'Carnival' discusses the actual experience of fairtime in Toronto, trying to assess the extent to which it represented a carnivalesque overturning of regular social conditions, and whether any part of it was carried back into ordinary life. Although these themes have been isolated for analytical convenience, they merge and overlap. Many discussions, many pieces of evidence, could have been inserted just as easily into other sections. Certainly, these topics did not exist as neat compartments in the minds of actual fairgoers.

For most people, the establishment of meaning at and around the fair was not as abruptly conclusive as it was for Hannah Heron in her encounter with the streetcar, nor was it as painful. There were many ways to discover what modern society was all about. The one described here brought enjoyment to millions of people, just as it affected them profoundly in countless ways.

1

Order

Every year, it seemed like something of a miracle. As soon as the gates of Exhibition Park opened on the first day of the fair, a line of wagons and workers backed up a quarter mile or so streamed onto the grounds, fanning out to different buildings to get the show ready by the next morning. Roads were crowded all day with lorries and carts, and sidewalks were covered with masses of packing crates, wrapping paper, display apparatus, and construction materials. Grounds staff put final touches to flower beds and lawns. Concession holders provisioned their stands. Anxious exhibitors, after hunting down officials to discover if goods had arrived, where displays should be erected, and whether more space could be procured, hurriedly put together stands and started laying out wares in eye-catching arrangements. They worked with furious intensity, 'too busy to do more than exchange a hurried word of greeting to the interested passer-by.'[1] Articles were placed in position, inspected, and adjusted, often with an eye to what was being done by a competitor across the way.[2] If comparisons were unfavorable, the whole creation might be dismantled and erected anew. The curious few who ventured down to inspect the activity, though fascinated by the sight of 'so many people in such a comparatively small space, up to their eyes in business which they feel must be finished at once,' often despaired that the show would ever open on time.[3]

It always did. Every year, confusion abruptly resolved into coherence. Buildings virtually empty at the start were filled with masses of valuable goods, set out in clever, enticing ways. This transformation 'from vacancy to chaos and from chaos to order' was an annual source of surprise and delight, striking testimony to the power of human agency. 'Where all worked with a will, order was ultimately restored and by evening what appeared chaos in the morning began to look like order.' The spectacle of 'hundreds of deft hands and organizing brains' engaged in countless tasks, but all working together for a common project, had a powerful resonance in Victorian society.[4]

For North Atlantic societies in the latter part of the nineteenth century, where unprecedented rates of industrialization and urbanization seemed to be unravelling a centuries-old fabric of behaviour and belief, concern about the nature and possibilities of order lay at the heart of most social endeavour.[5] People in all classes sought assurances that order existed or could be made to exist. Much of the Victorian enthusiasm for expositions derived from their power to suggest that life had stability and pattern.[6] In carving up the natural and human realms into logical arrangements for display, fairs presented an image of an ordered world, creating a stage where élites symbolically presided over crafted presentations of the best their societies could produce. But while these events created and reaffirmed cultural hierarchies, they also provided a space where accepted categories could be playfully transgressed. This ability simultaneously to confirm and question the categories of existence gave fairs like the Industrial Exhibition much of their appeal.

Although the fair represented a powerful affirmation of order, Toronto authorities took pains to guard their show from disruptive elements that continually threatened it. The sad fact was that as much as the fair gratified longings for order, it also produced disorder. Protection of the fair as a privileged site required concerted action, not just within the grounds but throughout the city. Both private and public organizations marshalled their resources to hold in check the disruptive inclinations of those in attendance. Their activities became an important part of the discourse on order created by the show, helping to define in concrete terms the nature of authority in late Victorian Toronto. Inevitably, these efforts were never entirely successful. Accidents, violence, and crime could not be banished from the grounds, nor could the profusion of things brought to the fair be neatly slotted into its limited categories. Even in its most contrived manifestations, order remained an elusive ideal.

～✓～✓～✓～✓～✓

Countless things about the exhibition, from designating a day to honour Americans, through giving out free passes to members of the press, to determining where washrooms would be located, involved the imposition of categories on the seamless web of existence. Though these divisions were largely appropriated from the logic of common perception, requiring no great exercise of imaginative powers, they did reinforce the legitimacy of many of the cultural divisions of everyday life.

The most obvious ordering task for those in charge of the fair was determining the categories of official exhibits. 'Once inside the grounds,' marvelled a *Globe* reporter in 1890, 'you are lost in wonder at how an exhibition can be organized and run.' It was scarcely possible that a small group of individuals could 'arrange, dispose, allot, distribute, methodize, systematize, catalogue, tabulate and index everything – and, in short, reduce everything to order.'[7] In truth, the job was probably not as onerous as it seemed. Exhibit categories for animals and crops which had been devised long before for local and provincial agricultural fairs were easily modified as rural interests changed. For arts and manufactures, basic priorities and systems of classification had been worked out for the great international expositions;[8] it was not difficult to adapt them to local circumstances. Such influences were apparent in decisions about the themes of specific buildings and parts of buildings. Where Philadelphia's Centennial Exposition in 1876 had a category for 'motors and transport,' Toronto had a Carriage Building; where Philadelphia had a category for 'tools, implements, machines and processes,' Toronto had an Agricultural Implement Hall.[9] However, even with an eye cocked to precedents set by grander shows, it did not take a genius to realize that with Ontario's economy, special attention had to be given to such things as carriages, agricultural implements, and stoves.

Still, the *Globe* reporter's reaction was understandable. There did seem to be a bewildering variety of classification principles. Things were divided according to geography, history, race, gender, species, age, residency, use, material, ownership, and scores of other criteria. A quick perusal of the prize list left no doubt about the intricacies of human and natural existence. The Ladies' and Children's Department in 1891 encompassed seven classes, with a total of 179 sections. Class 131, 'Painting on China (for amateurs only),' delineated the activity according to eight types of dishes and six styles of decoration. Considering all 136 classes, with more than 1700 sections, not to mention numerous things not entered for prizes, it did seem overwhelming.

The exhibition's power as a symbolic ordering agency derived from more than specific divisions of activity. More fundamentally, it rested on the belief that the whole of existence could be arranged into logical taxonomies, which together provided a comprehensive, unified compendium of all creation. The goal of seeing life in universalist, ahistorical terms had been inherited from the Enlightment by the big European expositions.[10] The Toronto fair never encompassed as much as those events, but it shared their aspiration to present an overview of an ordered world. What the fair conveyed through its elaborate system of classes and sections was an impression that total inclusion and perfect arrangement was attainable, even if some things at present were left out or misplaced. What it suggested about the possibility of order was much more gripping than the specific categories it established.

The taxonomic frame of mind was apparent in the value put on the 'completeness' of displays. Exhibits in the Natural History Department were especially prone to this principle of evaluation. John Notman's mineralogical display in 1879 was notable because it contained '53 specimens of iron showing ore in its various stages from clay iron stone to the finest Bessemer.' Mr Herring's ornithological collection shown in 1882 was praised for including 'specimens of almost every known description of duck.' At the 1888 fair, the insect displays were commended for being 'very complete,' while the fossil exhibit, with only a half-dozen examples, was 'miserable.'[11] The *Mail* reporter covering the 1892 dog show complained about an excessive number of classes, many for little known and scarce breeds. The absence of entries in twenty-eight categories could have been predicted when the prize list was being drafted. Why, he wondered, were large purses offered where only one or two dogs were competing, while that for fox terriers, with the largest number of entries, had only ten dollars.[12] The judges may have been trying to attract participants from further afield, but they also may have had a deeper understanding of the cultural preferences of their audience; even if achieving completeness was impossible, recognizing its desirability, defining its parameters, and establishing a normative hierarchy of values were laudable aims.

In the age of Darwin, when answers to troubling religious and social questions seemed to hinge on comparisons of species and varieties, 'completeness' in exhibits relating to the natural world had a special resonance. Yet this criteria was applied much more broadly. The exhibition of 1887 deserved attention, according to the *Globe*,

because it was 'far more complete than ever.' Going to the fair, it suggested on more than one occasion, was the next best thing to an
extended tour of the country – 'as if one could take ... in a few hours
time, a trip from Montreal to Windsor, and from Toronto to the
wooded north, acquainting himself with the life of field and mine and
factory.'[13] There was no better way to appreciate how the region's
social and economic components fit together into a prosperous whole.

Affirmations of order were also conveyed through individual displays. Nearly all exhibitors understood the attraction of neat, coordinated arrangements, but none appreciated the popular fascination
with order more than those who demonstrated gizmos based on
precision movement. Complex mechanical devices, such as 'The
Little World' that appeared in 1884, invariably drew large crowds. It
featured about one hundred figures performing 'all the operations
required in the carrying on of the leading industries of the day.'
There was a railway train with a conductor who stepped on a platform and raised his hand when it stopped at the station, a steamboat
that arrived at a river landing just as the train moved on, a bicycle
ring, a honeymoon scene, and animated depictions of house building,
wood sawing, blacksmithing, and mining.[14] It was the biggest drawing card on the grounds; some people endured half an hour of crush
to get into the tent where it was set up. The apparatus appeared
again for the next two years and was replaced in 1887 with the 'Automatic City and Musical Carnival,' which offered miniature boats,
trains, grain elevators, and pile drivers, all engaged in busy activity
while a twenty-seven figure mechanical orchestra, run by an 'Orches-
trion' underneath, kept time.[15]

These devices and others like them, all based on elaborate systems
of clockwork, offered an attractive contrast to the human realm that
too often seemed incomprehensible and uncontrollable. If small combinations of gears and levers could produce such charming animation, surely more complex combinations of technology and planning
could create a coordinated, predictable, efficient society. The chaos
produced by industrialization could be banished, these novelties
seemed to promise; irritating delays and disruptions could be eliminated. Social harmony was simply a matter of extending the familiar
mechanism of the common pocket watch. It was reassuring to learn
that 'The Little World' had been constructed by a blacksmith, and
the 'Automatic City' by a young man who 'built it in his hours after
work.'[16] Imposing order was not beyond the reach of ordinary people.

The attractions of precision movement were equally apparent in demonstrations of human coordination. Marching drills, executed by all sorts of groups including military regiments, fraternal societies, and brass bands, were always received enthusiastically. Fancy manoeuvres were popular enough to be included in regular grandstand entertainments. The Streater Zouaves from Illinois, whose intricate exercises done at double quick step with a precision that was 'nothing short of marvellous,' were received so well in 1899 that they were engaged again two years later.[17]

Some of the most popular drill displays were performed by local schoolchildren. In the first such demonstration, on Children's Day in 1886, the Wellesley Street senior class, wearing red rosettes, competed against the unadorned Ryerson School boys. The contest was repeated the following year, with four schools taking part. Teenage cadets in 'neatly made Glengarry caps and dark suits,' carrying wooden weapons, shared the spotlight with a younger troop of fourteen girls and seven boys from the George Street School who did callisthenics, and a much larger contingent from the Whitby Collegiate Institute who did fancy field movements, callisthenics and Indian club exercises. The drawing power of this kind of display was apparent, noted a Whitby editor, when a third of the fifteen or twenty thousand spectators scattered after it was over, 'notwithstanding the fact there were horse races to come off.'[18]

Even if many in the audience were relatives, duty-bound to watch, these demonstrations were compelling because they were performed by those at a stage of life considered unruly.[19] The successful channelling of youthful exuberence into safe, patriotic activities provided encouragement that other disruptive groups could be disciplined. Participation in the 1889 competition by a team from the Mimico Boys' Reformatory was doubly instructive. Like all the other displays and the classification systems employed at the fair, drill exhibitions spoke to the possibilities of order as much as its real accomplishment.

꙼꙼꙼꙼꙼꙼꙼

Because the fair was a vast assemblage of symbolic representations of order, it was useful for élites who espoused the virtues of hierarchy, authority, discipline, and stability. Usually these people were well aware of their own symbolic dimensions, recognizing the utility of presenting an example for others. For them, the exhibition was a logical stage on which to perform in public roles. A few possessed sufficient stature to become headline attractions, but claimants to political and social leadership at all levels recognized that the grounds could be a reciprocal force field where their attendance augmented the stature of the fair while its success amplified their standing.

The exhibition was regularly graced with visits by the governor general, whose office represented the apex of political and social life in Victorian Canada. These occasions always generated a good measure of excitement, though none more than the initial visit in 1879 when Torontonians got their first look at Princess Louise, 'the favoured daughter of our beloved Queen,' whose husband, Lord Lorne, had just begun his term.[20] Their activities, including a thorough inspection of the Crystal Palace, often called the Main Building, were followed with intense interest. Every acquisition made by the vice-regal entourage was carefully reported, especially Louise's purchase of engraved glass and inlaid woodwork. In subsequent days, many ordinary people consciously set out to examine what the royals had considered worthy of attention, aided in their quest by firms whose publicity insisted the couple had lingered at their booths.[21]

The response to subsequent vice-regal appearances, including a return by Lorne and Louise in 1883, was less frenzied but essentially similar: enthusiastic turnouts to welcome the visitors, detailed interest in what had caught their eye, and much self-congratulation by those so favoured. The Exhibition Association understood well the drawing power of the governor general, but more was at stake than a chance to ogle the results of selective breeding. These rituals of approval by members of the most prestigious élite in the land not only affirmed the importance of the city and the quality of local industry but also suggested that Canadian progress was profoundly related to the stability and order engendered by the British constitution and the empire it sustained. If the governor general was not available to embody the link, the Ontario lieutenant governor was often called upon. During its first quarter century, the fair was opened nine times by the lieutenant governor and once by the lieutenant governor's wife. Even when the monarch's representative was not on hand, the symbolism of empire and order was sustained by frequent military parades and concerts on and off the fairgrounds.

A number of other groups took advantage of the exhibition to see and be seen. For politicians, it was a logical place to gladhand.

Municipal officials were always about, but some members of parliament and cabinet ministers usually showed up, and occasionally the
prime minister, too. John A. Macdonald was about to open the 1889
show when a member of the provincial legislature pre-empted him by
resting his hat on the sensitive switch. Wilfrid Laurier did the
honours without mishap in 1901.[22]

Toronto high society, eager to align its own prestige with that of
the invited celebrity, turned out in numbers for the opening ceremonies. For the ambitious, the ritual provided an excellent opportunity
to hobnob with 'all that Toronto has of beauty, wealth, and ability.'
Mackenzie King, never a wallflower when there was an opportunity
to advance his interests, buttonholed the lieutenant governor and his
wife at the 1897 proceedings. Those who were more secure also
appreciated the chance to demonstrate pre-eminence. Handsome carriages and elegant clothes provided visual confirmation of status.
Militia officers in dress uniforms hinted that social primacy was
closely linked to public service. Reserved seating in areas closest to
the official party revealed clearly who had social clout.[23] Considering
that speeches were entirely predictable, not to mention inaudible to
all but those in close proximity to the speakers, these rituals were
enormously successful in affirming élite hegemony. Ordinary visitors
flocked to witness the ceremonies and the coincident ascendancy of
Toronto gentry, sometimes packing the grandstand almost a full
hour before the official party was due to arrive.

Many other groups profited from the fair as well, including the
business community and men in general. J.W. Bengough's sketches
in *Grip* of 'Representative Exhibitors' – all men, all business leaders
– demonstrates as well as anything how assumptions about the class
and gender prerequisites of social order permeated the exhibition
and were reinforced by its success. What made the fair such an
attractive site for groups that claimed to represent the foundations of
stability and progress was not just that it provided visibility and that
it posed these groups on the same stage, allowing élites from different realms to merge claims to authority. The fair also allowed them
to intersect with the ordered representations on display, weaving
their pre-eminence tightly into the strands of ordinary material
existence. A lieutenant governor or a prime minister who turned the
key to start all the machinery, while surrounded by the city's first
citizens, offered suggestive intimations of the essential unity of order
in all its manifestations.

Although caricaturist J.W. Bengough's scrawl was difficult to decipher, the meaning of his oversized, mature, male heads in this 1880 cartoon was not.

While fairgoers were eager to witness confirmations of order, they
also delighted in tinkering with some of the structures that ordinarily bound their lives. It was a natural inclination in a society
becoming increasingly regulated, routinized, and regimented. Upsetting normal codes was a way of probing the logic of conventions, of
exploring the legitimacy of assumptions on which they were founded,
of demonstrating that human beings need not be arbitrarily constrained by existing categories. Little experiments were done everywhere, but some of the most dramatic occurred on the exhibition
ground, where disturbing implications of transgressive behaviour
could be safely contained within the fairground fences.

One of the simplest and most pleasurable ways of loosening the
bonds of everyday reality was to alter ordinary scale. Fascination
with 'The Little World' was due as much to its miniaturization as its
automation, a fact recognized by many other exhibitors. The Massey
display of 1890 featured a 15-foot-long electric model of the train that
carried their agricultural implements to market. A much admired
miniature farm in the 1893 North-West Territories display included
machinery, stock, and humans, all reduced to appropriate size. A
real stuffed duck placed beside it, which to one observer appeared to
be on the verge of devouring the figures, suggests how these reductions allowed spectators to play with conventional assumptions
about the order of things.[24] The appeal of miniaturizations was echoed in the sightseeing proclivities of visitors who eagerly sought high
vantage points from which to peruse their surroundings, such as the
balconies of the Crystal Palace and the cars of the Ferris wheel.[25]

The search for overviews was not confined to the grounds. Among
the most popular city attractions were buildings with towers – University College and, after 1898, the new City Hall, or, later on, high-
rise structures like the Canada Life building. The spire of St James
Cathedral, a perennial favourite, required 'the somewhat tedious
climbing of the winding stairs,' but offered a spectacular vista over
the city and lake, as well as an opportunity to examine the mechanism of its great clock.[26]

By the late nineteenth century the panorama was an essential
component of the urban tourist gaze.[27] It drove home the new
immensity of urban scale, but, at the same time, created an image
of the city as a comprehensible whole, displacing the profusion of

sensory experience, as John Kasson put it, 'with the cold, distant grasp of the eye' and subjecting the city to the beholder's privileged inspection.[28] The grand perspective worked to fix what the city already was by establishing more clearly the relationship of various parts, yet, as a reporter who ascended in a balloon at the 1885 show discovered, simultaneously engendering impressions of fragility, malleability, and radically different possibilities: 'The thousands of upturned faces visible in the grounds when the balloon first began to ascend were blurred and indistinct, while their owners seemed dwarfed to the dimensions of Lilliputians. The public buildings in the city shrank into comparative insignificance, and the island itself looked so small that the finger of one's hand seemed to cover it.'[29] Power to behold was also power to imagine alternatives.

Like these shifts in perspective, disruptions of normalcy sanctioned by the fair were not outright rejections of order but manipulations of its normal parameters. Usually they involved juxtaposing categories normally kept separate, or playing with conventional expectations, or both. Sometimes the results were predictable. Children's donkey races invariably produced gales of laughter when obstreperous little beasts threw riders, resisted attempts to remount, and lay down on the track. Featured as a change of pace between horse races, they were both a parody and a contrast, and highlighted skills demonstrated in more serious events.[30] On other occasions, as in the race between a dog and a horse in 1889, there was genuine uncertainty about the outcome. One of the most memorable apposition of categories occurred when a curious boy threw a stray dog into a pit of alligators. To no one's surprise, the dog was devoured, but there was much amazement at how quickly it disappeared.[31]

Not all transgressions were acceptable. There were no hard-and-fast criteria about such things, and opinions differed as to what was appropriate, a fact made abundantly clear in 1884 to Miss Drew of Oshawa. When she approached the stand to be weighed for the Farmers' Premium horse race, judges were thrown into a quandary because of her sex. They professed an unwillingness to take responsibility for the dangers involved, but she insisted on the right to participate, pointing out that her registration had been accepted without comment the previous day. After another huddle, the judges decreed her ineligible because the rules stipulated that riders had to be farmers or farmers' sons. For them, direct female competition with men in an athletic contest represented too significant a violation of social categories, yet the clerk who enrolled her apparently thought otherwise.[32]

Indirect gender comparisons were less threatening, as the enthusiasm for drill exhibitions by schoolgirls revealed. In 1888, only two years after boys had started to perform before the grandstand, a contingent of girls from Victoria Street School, ranging in age from seven to fourteen, appeared in white frocks with dark red caps. Except for officers, who had tin swords, each girl carried a long-handled corn broom, and on her back, like a knapsack, a bright new dustpan. The 'broom brigade' went through a variety of regulation parade-square exercises while the crowd cheered with delight. The contingent returned the following year, accompanied by female classes from Cottingham School, in blue and white costumes, and Sackville School, dressed as Zouaves. By 1890, when uniformed corps of girls from ten public schools showed up, their routines had completely upstaged the boys'. The demonstrations, said a visitor from Guelph, 'were a feature of the day that could not have been replaced by anything more pleasurable.'[33]

These performances involved significant transgressions of normal social categories: female children mimicked the actions of adult males; women displayed a marked ability at military activities; implements of housekeeping were juxtaposed with dangerous weapons. Still, all this was far from a simplistic rejection of order. There was a kind of alternating current at work: the routines simultaneously affirmed the desirability of training and challenged fundamental precepts of societal organization. For many of those involved, both participants and spectators, the activity was only a charming diversion, a temporary suspension of norms. For others, it may have embodied aspirations to change stereotypes, redefine expectations, reshape categories, and realign existing hierarchies. For everyone, it raised questions about the logic of everyday assumptions and posited alternatives to the way things were.

~~~~~~~~~~

Nothing about the Industrial Exhibition generated more local pride than the orderly behaviour of its visitors. Torontonians frequently congratulated themselves on the absence of the 'boisterousness and exuberant gush' characteristic of similar events elsewhere. A *Globe* editor, describing the crowd of 'comfortably-dressed, well-fed, intelli-

gent, interested, orderly, perfectly sober visitors' as the best feature
of the show, suggested that a whole day could be spent on the
grounds without hearing a rude voice or seeing an angry gesture. 'No
country but Canada and no city but Toronto,' pontificated the *Telegram* on another occasion, 'can produce or exhibit crowds so thoroughly satisfying to the believer in our higher human nature.'[34]
Despite perennial reprises on this theme, the innate goodness of
those at the fair was never taken for granted. Perhaps because the
grounds were a site where unusual degrees of transgression were
permitted, a variety of agencies, both public and private, made special efforts to maintain high standards of rectitude. Among the most
prominent were religious groups, temperance advocates, and, of
course, the police.

Though many local clergy attended the fair, often courtesy of free
passes, no specific denominations proselytized on the grounds.[35]
Acrimonious religious debate was considered out of place, but a few
ecumenical organizations did attempt some outreach. The Upper
Canadian Bible Society handed out tracts and sold cheap editions of
the New Testament from a booth that displayed the Holy Book in
over a hundred languages.[36] The more ambitious Young Men's Christian Association erected a large tent where, in addition to tract distribution and Bible sales, daily services and prayer meetings were
conducted. In 1884 twenty-five meetings held over nine days drew an
estimated 2500 worshippers. In 1893 demand was sufficient to warrant three prayer sessions a day, and seemed to be equally strong the
following year. Services were intended especially for 'those whose
business keeps them on the grounds,' and for many harassed exhibition workers a quiet moment of prayer may have been a welcome
respite.[37]

The Y itself recognized the importance of serving practical needs,
erecting a drinking fountain, publishing Exhibition Bulletins that
included a map of the grounds,[38] and, especially, offering its tent to
visitors as a place to relax when services were not being held. A writing table supplied with pen, ink, and paper was provided at no
charge. Other reading desks along the sides were stacked with newspapers, magazines, and religious weeklies. A city map, city directories, railway timetables, and a clock were also available.[39] Probably
the greatest attraction for the foot weary, however, was simply a
chance to sit down.

The Y had aspirations to build a permanent structure on the site, partly to establish a more imposing presence but also to avoid the inconveniences of autumn weather. Their tent blew down in wind storms in 1879, 1882, and 1884, the last occasion described by a *News* reporter as the biggest scheme in tract distribution ever tried. Despite wide agreement that the need for moral and religious influence was 'never more strongly experienced than during absence from the restraints of home,' the Y never had sufficient funds to attempt the project.[40]

The Woman's Christian Temperance Union, on the other hand, did acquire a permanent structure by adopting a profit-making approach to the elimination of vice. The first formal appearance of the WCTU at the Industrial seems to have been in 1887 when, on a day designated in its honour, a large meeting of temperance workers assembled to hear Mrs Letitia Youmans, national president, deliver an address. The organization returned the next year, this time with a tent for regular meetings which, like the Y's, was opened at other times to those seeking relief from fatigue.[41]

By the early 1890s the WCTU was offering considerably more than tracts, talks, and a place to sit. It had entered into the refreshment business. The inspiration may have been local, but the change coincided with increasingly emphatic calls from the organization's national executive to undertake 'fair work.' Ellen C. Rugg, superintendent of the Department of Exhibitions and Fairs, was one of its most vociferous advocates. 'The W.C.T.U. have found out,' she declared, 'that these Fairs are open doors through which to push forward their work for God and Home and Native Land.' Part of the strategy was to 'save days of time and miles of travel' by taking advantage of the concentration of farmers at agricultural shows to lobby for temperance and feminist goals, especially when elections or plebiscites were in the offing. The other part was to provide refreshments as a means of undercutting the desire for 'that which is a snare and cannot satisfy,' facilitating the distribution of WCTU literature, and raising funds to forward the cause of righteousness. Some 'croakers' disparaged this work, Rugg warned. They were wrong. 'Sisters, beloved,' she exhorted, 'while evangelistic work must be the backbone of our W.C.T.U., Fair Work is a most important member with a mission all its own.'[42]

The Toronto chapters obviously agreed. By 1892 they were dispensing coffee and tea and running a parcel check. In 1894, when sales of coffee, tea, milk, sandwiches, cake, and ice cream netted a profit of about four hundred dollars, their tent was so crowded with diners that gospel meetings had to be abandoned. Two years later, $1678 was invested in a permanent pavilion that included a large kitchen, serving room, spacious dining-hall, and reception room. The debt was almost completely paid by the end of the next season after an estimated fifteen hundred to two thousand people had been fed at each meal during the seven busiest days of operation. Thousands had been turned away; organizers believed they could have filled a building twice the size. The whole operation was a testament to the dedication of local volunteers, bragged the executive, since the only hired help were dishwashers, sandwich makers, and one woman to assist in making tea and coffee. As profits accumulated year by year, the menu was expanded and more facilities were added.[43]

The comparison with the Y's experience is striking. Services provided by the Y may have been much appreciated by visitors, but once its tent was set up, there was no heavy labour to do. WCTU volunteers worked hard every day. From one perspective, they simply extended regular household obligations of cooking and cleaning up to a wider field. From another, they demonstrated in convincing fashion that, in the public marketplace if not the private home, housework did have monetary value. At the fair, the work of volunteer women brought in more than enough funds to build a permanent pavilion, while the work of volunteer men could not. This was yet another example of the transgressions permitted on the fairgrounds. It is unlikely that the WCTU, or any other body of middle-class women, could have gotten away with operating a regular lunchroom downtown – though, for that matter, it is unlikely they would have wanted to try.

Executives were clearly delighted with the financial success, and they were also pleased with what was gained for their spiritual and social causes. The contest between diners and gospellers was resolved by erecting a gospel tent adjacent to the dining-hall, and from both locations anti-alcohol and anti-tobacco pledges were solicited, foster parents enlisted for the Children's Aid Society, and thousands of tracts distributed. 'So much good must result from the seed sown,' sighed a tired but satisfied participant after the 1900 show, when seventeen-hundred pages of literature had been passed out and thirty boys and girls had signed the pledge. However, the fair's ground could be remarkably stoney; taking advantage of a cheap, wholesome meal was no indication of sympathy with WCTU goals.[44]

Kit Coleman, one of those who ventured into the dining-tent in 1894, thought it reminiscent of pioneer days or 'quaint tales of Cape Cod fisher folk.' Her initial relief at escaping the 'glare and clamour' outside was punctured by a 'lank and melancholy-looking individual' sitting nearby, reading his Bible while awaiting lunch. 'No doubt this was a good and a pious thing to do,' she acknowledged, 'but a wild feeling of revolt took me, and if our own luncheon hadn't appeared that same moment, there is no saying but I would be up for assualt and battery this very morning. It was too much religion. And at the fair too! Still, the luncheon was a good one.'[45] Kit's ambivalence might have given volunteer agencies dedicated to moral reform a sobering indication that no amount of resources put into the fair could produce an ordered environment, but apparently her column had no impact on the union's strategy.

The heaviest responsibility for maintaining order on the grounds inevitably fell on the police. Initially, the force provided daytime security only, while private guards hired by the association were granted powers of arrest to handle problems after the gates were closed. When a nightman was beaten up in 1880 by a group of toughs reluctant to leave the park, it was decided that irregulars did not inspire sufficient fear, and police assumed round-the-clock responsibility.[46]

As at ordinary times, the force was charged with a wide variety of tasks, including patrolling fences, looking out for suspicious characters and activity, supervising lost children, directing the confused, maintaining order among the crowd, clearing the horse ring, tending the ambulance, and, occasionally, regulating the association itself. In 1888, for example, Detective Reburn forced a grandstand ticket vendor to shut down when overselling had created such a jam that patrons could not get into the stands. As soon as Reburn left, the vendor resumed operations.[47]

As this incident revealed, the fair contingent of mounted men, plain-clothes detectives, and uniformed constables and officers on foot and was utterly stretched at peak times. The number of uniforms assigned to the site increased from fourteen constables and two officers in 1879 to at least thirty men and four officers by the turn of the century.[48] The grounds were considered a temporary division while the show was in progress, with several regular beats laid out and a small station in the same building as the men's toilet. By the end of the 1880s the post had acquired a wooden holding cell, so obstreperous detainees no longer had to be locked to iron rings on the outside wall. It had a second floor where off-duty men could sleep, a necessity since they were not allowed to live at home for the duration. Complaints about poor conditions, especially foul smells emanating from the washrooms, were incessant, but dismal accommodation was just one of the things that made fairtime a trying period for members of the force.[49]

No one understood better than the police that the exhibition experience extended far beyond the perimeter of the fairgrounds and that it was equally prone to manifestations of disorder as order. The combination of city folk in high spirits and country residents released from regular labours and the scrutiny of neighbours produced significant increases in ordinary misdemeanours like rowdyism, drunkenness, and prostitution which were rife even during more somnolent periods. The presence of unusually large numbers of people, many carrying more than ordinary quantities of valuables, meant that temptations to more serious crimes were also greater. The police were expected to keep a lid on all of it.

Complaints of 'rowdyism' reeked of class bias. Groups of working people who socialized in public areas, especially young men, and at night, were viewed with suspicion by respectable sorts, even when they exhibited no overt disrespect.[50] They simply created a bad impression. The *News* got upset in 1887 with a gang of 'impudent, loud-talking, ill-mannered, profane, filthy youths' who congregated on a downtown corner, making it a place 'to be shunned by strangers arriving from the Union Station.'[51] Police could do little except order offenders to move on, knowing they would probably regroup as soon as the constable continued his beat.

If an example could be made, it was. In the aforementioned case, Andrew Goodwin, a newsboy, was fined a dollar or six hours in the cells for jostling pedestrians off the boards. On another occasion, vowing 'to stop rowdyism if I can,' Magistrate Denison handed out steep penalties of ten dollars or thirty days to two men for the same offence. Deliberately blocking the sidewalk was one of the most common forms of horseplay at fairtime, done more commonly by locals than visitors. Whether inspired by impulses to show off, assert territorial pre-eminence, express contempt for those unfamiliar with the city, or augment the general spirit of fun, it sometimes took on more serious proportions. In 1882 residents of the area near the streetcar terminus closest to the grounds complained that drunkenness and ruffianism were so prevalent there during the fair that 'peaceably disposed citizens had to organize themselves into special constables for their mutual protection.'[52] Ordinarily, street hooliganism was much less threatening. Its connection with drinking, though, was nothing unusual.

In Toronto, as elsewhere, a culture of alcohol was tightly woven into working-class existence and into the sporting male culture that transcended class lines.[53] In the mid to late 1880s the city probably had one legal liquor outlet for every five hundred people, not to mention unlicensed blind pigs, widows' kitchens, and bootlegging cellars.[54] Needless to say, these places were concentrated in less respectable neighbourhoods. While no one so inclined needed an excuse to drink, the exhibition seemed to encourage exceptional indulgence. Even those inured to it were struck by the increase in drunkenness during fairtime. A *World* reporter, on a short walk from his office at the height of the 1884 show, saw no fewer than four street fights and eleven 'reelers,' a number he professed was 'something astonishing.'[55]

Many city residents, including a *Saturday Night* columnist, attributed the increase to 'Young Hayseed,' who arrived with half his savings in his pocket and 'the all-absorbing idea of seeing the sights and painting the town a bright vermillion.' Corroborating examples of the stereotype were not hard to find. Police-court reporters frequently remarked on the number of strangers brought up on drinking charges, thereby deeply offending some rural folk. J.C. Speer of Mono Road contested such an allegation by the *News*, claiming to have been present through the entire docket at issue, when not more than one in five cases involved a country person. The *News* stuck to its guns, repeating that four-fifths of the twenty-two inebriants came from outside. Some of the most outraged rural denizens were those who faced the magistrate, such as three country people who came up in court on the same day in 1889. Mindful of reputations back home, each stoutly defended his innocence. Angus McKellar said he was picked up for no good reason, James Lockhart of Wellington insisted he slipped on a banana peel, and James Goodfellow of Bolton explained he was a strict teetotaller overcome by fumes during a tour of the Gooderham and Worts distillery.[56]

Some non-Torontonians were willing to acknowledge the disruption caused by visitors. 'Citizen' from Port Hope, who dismissed the whole Industrial as just 'a big drunk,' complained to a local paper about the 'otherwise respectable young fellows' from his town whose 'orgies' on returning excursion trains had to be endured by other passengers.[57] No one pretended that city residents did not participate in the revelry. Though often it was difficult to distinguish between habitual and exhibition-induced inebriation, the festive mood certainly had an impact. A vivid example of holiday spirit occurred in 1885, when a merchant and a tailor 'borrowed' a barrel-organ and spent a day testing the profitability of the street music business. By midnight, after each had bailed the other out of jail, they had accumulated $8.75, a damaged shirt donated by women in a garment factory after an impromptu concert, and an indeterminate number of drinks. In police court the next day, in consideration of previous good records, they were let off with a warning to stay out of the music trade.[58]

These would-be organ grinders were not the only ones who tried to take advantage of increased street congestion during the fair. For prostitutes, it was a golden opportunity. According to 'G.H.,' protesting to the Telegram in 1882, 'frail women' thronged the streets at night, 'thinking it a rare turn to practice their calling unmolested.' The seduction process was rather more physical on occasion. Margaret Mevoney was arrested in 1881 as she tried to manhandle a grey-headed rural denizen into a low dive on Queen Street. Aggressive marketing was perhaps necessary considering the competition. An Empire reporter investigating vice in 1891 was shown ten street-walkers during a short stroll along King Street and was approached by six women in ten minutes as he stood in a particular alleyway. During the very first Industrial, four ladies rode along King Street in a cab, throwing business cards into the street.[59]

Undoubtedly, prostitutes were attracted to the city by the fair. On a Sunday morning during the 1879 show, eleven ladies of suspect character landed from a single boat. Of seven women swept up one night in 1888, three were lately arrived from a country town. Three women arrested a year earlier in a Richmond Street brothel were from south of the border. The found-ins on that occasion also had an international cast; they included a Boston traveller and a Buffalo clerk, as well as a clerk and a broker from Toronto.[60]

Long conditioned to drunkenness and soliciting, most respectable city residents were much more alarmed about the possibility of crimes to property. Anxiety was fed by police and press reports of organized gangs about to descend on the city and by constant warnings to keep track of valuables. There was sometimes a sense of helplessness about the situation. 'Do what they can,' lamented the *Mail* in 1888, 'it is impossible for the police to keep their eyes on the large influx of thieves who annually appear at this time.' Some years earlier, the paper had expressed resentment at the number of constables drawn off for exhibition duty. 'The homes of the people require not less but greater protection when promiscuous visitors, some of them with sinister intent, come amongst us.'[61]

In fact, theft was much more likely to occur where visitors congregated. The heart of criminal activity was York Street. Running north to Queen Street from York Quay and Union Station, it was a main thoroughfare connecting transportation facilities with the downtown core. Some large, entirely legitimate businesses were located there, including Macdonald's Wholesale House and the Rossin House Hotel, but the less reputable also recognized its commercial potential. Pelham Mulvany, commenting in 1884 on its dichotomous character, thought the section north of King Street might be one of the most beautiful of streets, but its eastern side was blighted by dingy, rotten shanties which, from 8 p.m. until midnight, were 'alive with ... wretchedness.'[62]

According to an 1879 exposé, York Street was to Toronto what the Bowery was to New York. The stretch between King and Queen streets contained ten known brothels where robberies were almost daily occurrences, several houses of assignation, eight unlicensed groggeries that supplied 'maddening liquor to the depraved classes,' and a number of eating houses equally bad. The report failed to mention the numerous second-hand dealers who, as in many cities, had a reputation for receiving stolen goods and hiding whiskey sold in adjacent liquor dens. The arrangement suggests that Toronto's underworld possessed a degree of community solidarity that might have been encouraging to those troubled by urban alienation, but most citizens worried about 'the opinion of strangers who are dumped from the train into one of the most disreputable streets that ever existed in any city.'[63]

It was a dangerous place for the unwary and the unwise, both in oversupply during the exhibition. Innocent visitors who wandered up from the train, and not so innocent ones who overindulged in the dives, were often victimized. William Smith was robbed there of thirty dollars in 1883 while drunk. John Teefy of Pickering was mugged by a group of ruffians in 1886.[64] Those who escaped outright violence still had to endure intimidating knots of locals who sized them up. By 1885 extra constables were being assigned to patrol York Street while the fair was under way, but they did not eradicate the problems. A year later, the *Telegram* called for more police patrols to disperse crowds of loafers who insulted passers-by and made themselves generally disagreeable.[65]

Criminals were attracted to York Street not just by the likelihood of encountering victims, but also by the location there of an infrastructure that served their needs. Crime occurred throughout the downtown area and beyond, but after it happened, perpetrators were likely to return to York Street to fence their loot or celebrate their gains. When police went looking in 1883 for two women who stole a drunken farmer's watch, they soon found the culprits in a York Street bar.[66]

That theft typified much of the crime that took place during the exhibition season. Victims, often inebriated, were selected spontaneously by members of the underclass, also often under the influence. Prostitutes took advantage of clients, muggers lured strangers into dark alleys, and drinkers kept careful watch on other patrons whose condition could be exploited. Memory loss and embarrassment worked strongly in favour of criminals, as did lack of familiarity with basic city procedures. George Richardson of Aurora, assaulted and robbed on Queen Street in 1892, had to be persuaded by a friend to report the matter.[67] All this meant that visitors were much more likely to be targeted than residents.

Not all theft during the exhibition was committed by local petty criminals. Though fears of organized gangs were highly exaggerated, outsiders were attracted by the prospect of crowds with holiday cash. Hotel thieves, for example, tended to be professional operators 'on tour.' With unfamiliar faces and decent wardrobes, they were hard to spot. Proprietors were on constant alert at fairtime. When a man entered the Clyde Hotel at five o'clock in the morning and shouted fire, the owner grasped immediately what was happening and chased him out.[68]

Most thieves of this sort preferred a quieter approach, practising their arts while victims slept. This too had risks. Ed Hunt, alias Mick Moran, got nine months when the Palmer House staff noticed him

York Street contained some eminently respectable buildings, including the Rossin House Hotel, but its notorious reputation stemmed from 'dives' like these, captured in a photograph from around the turn of the century.

skulking around the corridors in the wee hours. Another thief had to make a precipitous dash when the victim unexpectedly woke up. He escaped into the corridor, collided with a housemaid, and rolled to the bottom of the stairs – but still he managed to get away.[69] Lots of practitioners were all too successful, manifesting a dexterity that suggested extensive experience. An English tourist had his pocket-book lifted from under his pillowcase. Four ladies from the country sharing a room at the St James Hotel dozed contentedly while money was taken from under each of their mattresses.[70] With so much coming and going, and so many strangers to absorb suspicion, chances of escaping detection were high, and, soon, both crook and victim were gone.

Exceptional levels of criminal disorder in the city core were an integral part of the exhibition experience, though there is no way of measuring its occurrence in quantitative terms, since much of it went unreported. A Markham Township man, robbed of a gold watch and two hundred dollars by a stranger who put him up for the night, refused to complain. Given the magnitude of the loss and the known residence of the thief, it seems clear that the victim desperately wished to avoid closer investigation. John Waite, a Grimsby farmer, denounced in bitter terms the man who took his silver watch and chain, but would not give information to the police for fear of being ridiculed when he got home.[71] For every case like these, there must have been dozens in which losses were sufficiently small or time constraints so tight that victims just shrugged off their misfortune.

Most people were resigned to disorderly conduct in the heart of the city, even at the best of times. It was more disappointing to find disorder at the fairground. Because the site was enclosed and intensively organized, expectations of behaviour there were much higher. Frequent comments about the low incidence of crime at the Industrial Exhibition were intended to reassure nervous visitors, but they also embodied aspirations for a genuine spirit of community.[72] Despite perennial optimism, fences could not create a *cordon sanitaire*. Most types of urban disorder, from littering to indecent exposure, seeped into the 'city by the lake.' Some, like the accidents that occurred regularly, were reminders that human existence, no matter how stringently organized, was never perfect, while others, like fighting and theft, underlined character deficiencies that seemed equally permanent.

The most spectacular accidents occurred in front of audiences. A jockey who fell underneath his horse in a collision broke his ribs 'with a snap that could be heard fifty feet away.' Ben Laydell miscalculated a double somersault on the trapeze and crushed his back. He died four days later, the same day another rider was thrown and seriously injured.[73] The fair was also dangerous for visitors. Carelessness and disregard of rules produced predictable misery. One man broke his leg while scrambling down from a cattle-shed roof where he had been watching horse races. Enthralled by the inflation of a balloon, a seven-year-old boy was killed as he ran across the horse-ring track, smack into the middle of a race. In many instances, however, people were injured through no fault of their own except being in the wrong place at the wrong time. Mrs Jolly was wounded when a mortar used to launch fireworks blew up, sending metal fragments clear across the horse ring. When stairs leading to the spectators' stands at the zoo collapsed, a score of people were precipitated into a 'screaming, struggling mass,' and ten of them sustained significant injury. Elizabeth Pollock had several ribs crushed when the crowd pressed her into the fence during an evening show.[74] The vast majority of cuts, scrapes, burns, and bruises, of course, were simply too trivial to report.

Though little permanent damage was sustained by participants, the frequency of fighting on the grounds was symbolically disappointing. Almost all of it involved males, but occasionally women vented their feelings in physical ways. One young boy was stabbed in the thigh with a long hat pin by a well-dressed middle-aged lady, irritated at having to make room for him to pass out of his grandstand seat. Most confrontations were more predictable. John Wilkinson of Aurora thrashed a stranger who had interfered with his wife. James Kyle refused to get down from a railing in the grandstand and got into a tussle with a man whose view was blocked. Another dispute began as a debate about the merits of two horses, progressed to angry words, and ended in blows, including one to the head with a monkey wrench. The set-to attracted such a crowd that police could not get in to break it up, a circumstance demonstrating that not everyone was demoralized by a good, old-fashioned brawl.[75]

The same tolerance did not extend to theft. Both exhibitors and visitors were victimized. Since product displays and refreshment-stand merchandise were meant to be alluring, temptation was natural. Most pilfering was done by children whose filching was impulsive and small scale.[76] If caught, they tended to be treated leniently; authorities were more intent on scaring than punishing. James Anketell, who crawled under the fence and stole a tumbler of honey, was told he was a bad little boy and discharged. Ed Hopkins, fourteen, pleaded guilty to the theft of a silk handkerchief, but was given over to his mother when she promised to guarantee his future good behaviour. On the other hand, George Brown, a Black youth, got a month in jail for stealing an umbrella.[77] As ever, class and race were important factors in the disposition of cases. Undoubtedly, so was gender. No young females appear to have been charged with this sort of offence, which suggests not just that they tried it less, but that, if caught, they were not officially reported.

Some youthful depredations were clearly premeditated. In 1882 a gang of boys and youths staged a night raid on a beehive to get honeycombs. The same year, four boys, two of them fourteen and one of them twelve, were jailed for prying open a case of rare coins and walking off with about seventy-five of them. Nobody, including patrolling guards, noticed what they were doing, in contrast to the experience of three adults who tried to rob a coin collection the following year. One man broke the case and moved off into the crowd while two associates waited for the watchman to be drawn off. The guard had noticed the three hanging about together and did not move.[78] Security may have been increased after the 1882 episode, but, more likely, diminutive size and stereotyped assumptions of childhood goodness were assets not available to adults, who were probably less willing anyway to take large risks for the sake of trifles.

The greatest concerns about theft on the grounds involved pickpocketing. It infected the whole city at fairtime, to the extent that authorities felt compelled to post gloomy signs reminding people to 'beware.'[79] A periodic pat of pocket or purse became instinctive, part of the habit of suspicion that increasingly characterized urban life. Constant attentiveness, though, was difficult, especially in an environment of sensory overload.

Pickpockets thrived in crowded situations where congestion and external distractions provided maximum opportunity and cover – along parade routes, in front of arresting window displays, on train platforms, and, of course, at the fair. Within the grounds, they operated most frequently in front of sideshows, at the streetcar stop, and in the Crystal Palace, where narrow aisles and high densities produced abnormally close contact,[80] but they could be found wherever knots of people formed. Of serious crimes at the show, pickpocketing was the most common.

Wallets and loose cash were not the only targets: watches and chains, jewellery and small parcels were also routinely taken. Most gains were modest. The three cases reported on 1 September 1898 amounted to a total loss of six dollars. A thief caught red-handed in 1883 was about to make off with sixty-five cents. Joseph Lapointe escaped charges because there was nothing in the pocket of his intended victim. However, some hauls were lucrative. On the same day in 1886, one lady lost twenty-five dollars while admiring Japanese crafts, and another, fifty dollars, in front of a candy stand.[81]

According to Chief Constable Grasset, the majority of victims were women. Open pockets, gaping handbags, watches and jewellery pinned to delicate lace pockets made for easy work, but, as well, women were less likely to hurt or hold an operator caught in the act.

Country people, both women and men, also figured frequently among fairtime targets, because, as travellers, they tended to carry more cash and, like G.H. Storey of Sherbrooke, they were less wary of urban dangers. Storey learned an expensive lesson about big city morality by leaving his wallet on a washroom table.[82]

Most people probably assumed that the 'light-fingered gentry' were adult male professionals from outside the city.[83] Criminals of this type were active. David Moore of Buffalo, caught with Frank Williams of Cincinnati in possession of the contents of a woman's changepurse, was wearing a coat with a slit cut near the pocket, allowing him to use a hand that appeared to be innocently tucked away. Charles Johnson, a middle-aged man from Hamilton with seven children, already had fourteen convictions when he was observed in 1897 putting his hand into nine different ladies' pockets. Joseph Huddle, a 'mollbuzzer,' specializing in female victims, was arrested in Toronto in 1892 and sent out of the city, arrested a week later at the London fair but released on a technicality, and arrested finally at the Barrie fair, when he was sentenced to a year in the Central Prison. By 1894 he was back on the exhibition circuit.[84]

Not all who practised the craft were transients. John Connor, caught in the act in 1894, tried to establish his innocence by explaining that he worked every day at the Gurney stove exhibit. Police reminded him that he was charged with pickpocketing, not vagrancy. Local origin was especially common in the case of children, who constituted a significant proportion of those involved. Richard Rowe, fifteen, described as a 'small boy,' claimed that he inadvertently grabbed a purse for support while ducking under a horse and that he was afraid to return it. He got ten days. Sam Jessop and Herman Kuskey, both about fifteen, incriminated each other during interrogation. Joseph Isaacs indiscreetly bragged that he and several equally young associates had tapped over two hundred pockets during the 1891 exhibition. A year later, he was serving a three-year term in the Industrial School.[85]

Whether these youths were supervised by adults or operated on their own is not clear. Professionals usually worked in teams, the standard configuration calling for three operatives – one to deflect attention, one to make the grab, and one to escape with the goods. It is striking that many young offenders were arrested in pairs, but this does not mean necessarily that they operated in tandem, using sophisticated diversionary ploys taught by more experienced practitioners. Some children, however, were employed in professional gangs. Joseph Huddle, who himself relied on a youthful, innocent appearance to get out of scrapes, worked with his twelve-year-old half-brother.[86]

The obvious advantages possessed by young pickpockets were available in almost equal measure to women. Far fewer women were arrested than men, an indication perhaps that fewer were involved, but, again, that they were less noticed and more easily excused. Chief Constable Grasset once complained that juries would not convict female pickpockets, even though they were responsible for a high proportion of those crimes.[87]

There were exceptions. The respectable-looking Mary Wren tearfully proclaimed her innocence as she was led away to the cells for thirty days, but refused to provide details of her identity or offer a defence. Jessie Thompson, on the other hand, was known all too well. She was born in Simcoe County in 1867 but moved to Toronto, ostensibly to work as a domestic. Tall and thin, with long, slim fingers, according to a police description, she became one of the city's most proficient purse snatchers. She married Charlie Thompson, another regular in the trade, and they prospered after a fashion, though not without discord. At one point, she sued Charlie for half interest in a house, telling the judge it had been purchased with the proceeds of pickpocketing and that she had picked just as many pockets as her husband. The case was thrown out of court.[88]

Fair season was a busy period for Jessie. Her arrest during the 1890 show gives some idea of its intensity. That year, she achieved unusual notoriety while trying to free her husband and two male associates who were being escorted to Toronto in police custody. All four, recently released from jail in Berlin, where they had worked the music festival, had decided to try their luck on the crowded excursion trains headed for the Industrial. When her partners were apprehended yet again, she put her skills of deception to a different end:

Hoping to divert attention from the passengers to herself, she pretended to be ill with a violent epileptic fit. She commenced to screech and howl like a maniac, and acted like a person in convulsions, and the moment the passengers rushed to her assistance the prisoners made a break for liberty, first smashing the constable over the head. His cry alarmed the already startled passengers and they gave the prisoners a terrible pummelling.

The incident is instructive for what it suggests about the persistence and loyalty of professionals, the greater likelihood of women escaping detection, and what the public thought of pickpockets.[89]

It also suggests Jessie's wily resourcefulness, a quality the exasperated police would have readily acknowledged. When arrested, she usually elected to go before a jury and wept incessantly during the trial, especially while her lawyer delivered his summation. The tactic wore thin. In the spring of 1893 she was committed to Kingston Penitentiary for three years, but went back into operation as soon as she was released, ongoing proof that not all fairtime criminals were adult males from away.[90]

It was ironic that an event intended to foster order created conditions so amenable to disorder, just as it was ironic that so much of that disorder, including its most serious varieties, was attributable to women and children, groups that were thought to possess the most innate goodness. As authorities tried to keep a lid on the potential for disruption, they generated more paradox and ambiguity. Not unreasonably, they assumed that the chief sources of disorder were alcohol and crime. When they tried to eliminate alcohol from the fairgrounds, they discovered there were different standards of order and very different ideas about what was required to maintain it. When they tried to police the city, they decided the most effective way to maintain order was to bend, if not break, some of the most fundamental precepts of the law.

One of the clearest indications that some people saw the fairgrounds as a symbolic terrain where higher degrees of order should prevail was the effort of temperance advocates to prevent the consumption there of alcohol. Needless to say, there was no agreement about the desirability of this goal, nor was there consensus about what constituted an intoxicating beverage. The process of applying provincial liquor legislation at the Industrial Exhibition and the ongoing disregard of the law by some parties represents a typical example of the processes of contestation and resistance that mark any effort to erect and maintain standards of order.

When the fair began in 1879, provincial legislation prohibited the sale of alcohol on the exhibition grounds and within a 300-yard radius. The association decided, however, that the provision of lager beer for thirsty visitors was entirely reasonable. Refreshment booth concessionaires were advised that no interference with the supply of lager to the grounds was anticipated. Legal action would be taken only if an outsider laid a complaint, in which case the law would have to be enforced, but fines would be minimal. Kegs rolled in. Even before the official opening, stands were doing a thriving business. Some breweries put in telephone lines to the grounds so fresh supplies could be ordered quickly when stocks got low.[91]

Early in the second week of the show, liquor inspectors arrived on the grounds and began to issue summonses, prodded by prohibitionists and some of the licensed victuallers in the city who resented the competition. When the charges were heard after the show ended, the police magistrate handed down fines ranging from forty to fifty dollars plus costs.[92]

The concessionaires were taken aback at the size of the fines. They complained that it would have been impossible to recoup rental charges from the sale of lemonade and tea only, that the booths had not been fitted up with facilities to make tea or coffee but had been provided with fixtures for glasses, that making fires in the booths had been expressly prohibited, that booths had been leased to several breweries, and that the directors themselves had ordered beer for one of their lunches.[93] They also pointed to the popular demand for the beverage, arguing that, in fact, it was a temperance drink. C.R. Beswetherick, leasee of the dining-room concession, insisted he was 'totally opposed to the unrestricted sale of spiritous liquors,' but that lager beer was 'perfectly harmless and non-intoxicating.' Temperance could best be promoted by admitting lager, 'thereby weaning thousands from whiskey who are daily filling our gaols and hospitals.'[94]

Booth operators found the lager trade hard to resist. They were back at it the next season, selling collectively about a thousand barrels a day. Though more wary of liquor inspectors, several concessions openly advertised the availability of lager, and the dining-hall advised that wine and liquors could be obtained at an adjoining bar. When the fair was over, sixteen leasees were each fined twenty dollars and costs, a token that may have encouraged some the following year to peddle hard liquor, advertising only by word of mouth.[95]

The directors, meanwhile, were attempting to regularize the sale of liquor on the grounds. After a motion to legalize the sale of lager was defeated by City Council, they obtained a hotel licence for the dining-hall, once again upsetting the Licenced Victuallers' Association, which protested official willingness to see a hotel where only a restaurant existed. What particularly aroused the ire of both victuallers and prohibitionists was the way the dining-hall permit was stretched to include eight refreshment booths under the grandstand. One incensed teetotaller suggested it represented the most open and flagrant violation of the province's liquor act since its passage. The *Globe* shared his apprehension that the exhibition would become 'an occasion for widespread drunkenness,' but took a more moderate position, advocating the closure of two-thirds of the booths and strict insurance that only 'light' drinks would be sold at the rest.[96]

Visitors spoke with their pocketbooks. Booth holders maintained that they sold five times as much lager as anything else. Even with stronger potions sold surreptitiously at some stands, intoxication remained within acceptable limits. A reporter for the Port Hope *Guide* thought arrangements for selling 'strong waters' on the grounds 'as reprehensible as well could be,' but admitted 'there was not so many drunk as might have been expected,' though the number in that condition was still too high.[97]

Encouraged by assessments like this, the association adopted the same strategy in 1882, assigning the hotel licence to Mr Bingham, the dining-room leasee, who then sublet eight grandstand booths included in the contract. Once again, booth operators connived to sell the whole range of alcoholic drinks, dispensing them from bottles with innocuous labels. The liquor inspectors, obviously under pressure, were less accommodating. Bingham was informed his licence applied only to the dining-hall, and concessionaires were told that instead of adjourning liquor cases until after the fair, as in the past, any alcohol found in booths would be confiscated. Since Bingham continued to insist his licence covered the whole grounds, tenants like Benjamin Tomlin found themselves in a difficult position. Licence commissioners refused to allow him to dispense alcohol, while Bingham refused to refund the nearly three-hundred dollars paid for the concession, and refused to supply another site where the sale of non-alcoholic drinks would be more profitable.[98]

True to their word, inspectors kept close watch. Though they do not seem to have confiscated liquor, they appeared on the grounds both weeks of the fair, issuing summonses that resulted eventually in fines of twenty dollars for first offences and thirty for second. Temperance supporters still viewed the penalty as tantamount to a small licensing fee, but so much confusion now existed that the directors decided a new approach was necessary. In 1883 the dining-room concession was given to the Toronto Coffee House Association, a temperance organization, while grandstand booth operators were reminded that the sale of hard liquor was absolutely forbidden. Native wine and lager only could be sold.[99]

Prohibitionists applauded the change, but remained disturbed by the extent of drunkenness. Strong drink, they insisted, was still being sold. Several people who became mysteriously intoxicated claimed that the native wine had been fortified. Others alleged that hard drink was being dispensed under the counter. The *Globe* later described the grandstand booths as a 'plague spot' that drew all the disreputable souls on the grounds to a focus. Responding to temperance concerns, the provincial government amended the licensing act in 1884 to prohibit the sale of alcohol completely at the Industrial.[100]

Thinking the question had been resolved, 'drys' were chagrined to learn that the association had applied for the transfer of a dominion licence from Mrs Mead's hotel on Toronto Island to the grounds. The licence was good for one spot only, and a half-dozen beds had to be set up to satisfy the legal definition of a hotel, but the request was approved. Had no licence been obtained, the directors insisted, liquor would be sold on the sly anyway, but they had an eye on the value of concession rentals as well.

Drinkers did seem to be considering alternative sources. Some loaded up before entering the grounds. Little Johnnie's Hotel, close to the eastern entrance, advertised itself as the perfect place for a glass of the finest lager on the way to the exhibition. Other visitors brought their own. Police on the grounds confiscated twenty-five 'loaded' canes during the first three days. Some prohibitionists still were not mollified by the increasing difficulty of getting a drink at the Ex. Some, like 'Simcoe,' stayed home in protest, but others, like James Thompson, secretary of the Temperance Electoral Union, went to monitor activity at the booths, laying charges as private citizens that resulted in twenty-dollar fines for thirteen defendants.[101]

Again, the penalty was a trifle. The association and the concessionaires probably would have repeated the strategy had the federal government's licensing law not been declared unconstitutional. Thinking the jurisdictional confusion resolved, the *Mail* confidently asserted that no liquor was available at the 1885 fair. It was wrong. The Oaklawn Dairy's Swiss Cottage was selling koumis or milk champagne, 'the much praised health beverage' that contained anywhere from 1 to 4 per cent alcohol. No one seemed to care. There was concern, however, about the ever resourceful booth holders who now offered what was labelled conspicuously on kegs as 'temperance beverage.' After liquor inspectors confiscated samples from each stand, they concluded that the liquid tasted very much like lager beer, sent specimens off to be analysed, and laid over seventy charges.[102]

One case was selected as a test to be tried before the police magistrate, and each side summoned scientific experts to sustain its position. Professor Ellis testified that the two samples he tested contained alcohol levels of 1.96 per cent and 2.11 per cent, respectively. Professor Shuttleworth found 2.97 per cent and 3.75 per cent in the same batches. Neither was prepared to swear that the beer was intoxicating. Doctors W.B. Nichol and George Wright and Professor Hayes of the Toronto School of Medicine testified for the defence that while beer containing 5 or 6 per cent alcohol was intoxicating, that with only 3 per cent was not. Doctors McCully and Ogden, for the prosecution, maintained that beer with 2.5 per cent alcohol was intoxicating if a person was not in the habit of drinking. After listening to all this, Magistrate Denison was inclined to acquit, but felt it advisable to convict so the matter could be heard at a higher level. The test case was given a twenty-dollar fine, though Denison told the licence inspectors he did not hold himself bound to be consistent in convicting other blue-ribbon beer cases.[103]

The higher courts took another two years to determine that blue-ribbon beer was intoxicating, but, after 1885, concessionaires seem to have stopped selling it at the fair. Temperance advocates enthused about the improved atmosphere. 'When we see Prohibition working so well among the thousands who flock to the Exhibition,' said Inspector Stephens in a typical assessment, 'it ought to convince us that we should have the same Prohibition all over the country.'[104]

Not everyone was persuaded. Old habits of conviviality were hard to break and there was money to be made in the defence of tradition. Already partly underground, the liquor business simply dug deeper. The number of smuggled 'growlers' apparently increased, as did the number of bootleggers who operated both inside and outside the grounds. One opportunist who panicked as inspectors approached his operation outside the Dufferin Street gates left behind a ten-gallon jug of whiskey as well as his tent. Charles Lyne, a Pickering farmer, was fined fifty dollars for selling booze from the cattle sheds, and Thomas Riddle, a city resident who rented a horse stall, was caught

SHORT-HORNS AT THE FAIR.

(EXHIBITED PRIVATELY).

Bengough's 1888 depiction of another kind of 'representative exhibitor.'

serving half a dozen men when Inspector Hastings suddenly jumped over the partition. This small-scale commerce was difficult to stop, especially in the animal barns where alcohol was easily hidden and customer trustworthiness quickly ascertained. A man arrested for selling liquor to Indians in a Wild West Show was nabbed only through the services of an informer, who agreed to work for the police if charges stemming from his arrest in a brothel a week before were dropped. How much of this activity went on is impossible to determine, but a 1888 *Grip* cartoon suggests it was not uncommon.[105]

Neither was the continued sale of alcohol from refreshment booths. Year after year, concessionaires were charged for violating the liquor law, but it was worth the risk.[106] Greater precautions were taken, of course. Illicit stocks were smuggled in when officials were presumed to be off duty. A variety of methods were used to screen customers, including passwords, tickets, and on-the-spot character references. Those already drunk were probably turned away.[107]

Still, it was not hard to get served. A waiter at Mike McGarry's booth in 1892 gave a drink to Inspector Hastings himself. McGarry immediately jumped over the counter to wrench away the glass but failed, just as he failed to prevent Hastings from getting behind the bar. As police arrived to reinforce the liquor inspectors, a protesting clientele withdrew, throwing bottles at the stand to express displeasure at the discovery of their oasis.[108]

In 1894 the *News* tried to raise a public outcry at what it claimed was the Exhibition Association's indifference to the surreptitious consumption of liquor at refreshment stands. The practice continued because management winked at it. The *News* probably was right. So long as no significant disorder resulted, the directors were content to ignore a situation that produced higher concession rents.[109]

At least they were consistent. There is evidence to suggest that neither the *News* nor the liquor inspectors were. Two years before, during efforts to dislodge the Canadian Manufacturers' Association from its quarters in the Press Bureau, allegations were made that the room had been used in the past as a storeplace for liquor and a place where liquor was consumed. The association secretary quickly blamed a former caretaker.[110] Neither press nor police was inclined to question why a simple custodian would leave an excess of booze in a lounge for sophisticated businessmen, or why none of those community pillars reported him.

Temperance supporters were successful in convincing the provincial government that the consumption of intoxicating beverages at the fair produced too much disorder, but it took them a while and they were never able to eliminate alcohol or drunkenness entirely. Different opinions remained about what was necessary to maintain social harmony, just as they remained about what was necessary to have a good time. Once the issues were decided by the courts, contestation by many turned into resistance by a few. The level of disruption on the grounds created by alcohol was reduced to a point that satisfied the majority, and standards of public order were defined as much in practice as in law.

The inability to stop alcohol sales at refreshment booths throws into perspective the gargantuan task faced by police as they tried to control the whole range of illegal activities whose practitioners did not advertise. Given the tremendous additions to the population, including the criminal population, during fair periods, it is logical to assume this was the busiest time of year for the force. It probably was, though this was not always reflected in arrest statistics.

Indices of police activity, such as monthly tabulations of warrants in the first instance and daily records from the Police Magistrate's Court, indicate that relatively high numbers of charges were laid during the fair but not necessarily greater than in other periods of the year. Certainly they were not in proportion to the increased number of people being supervised. In 1898, for example, a total of 440 charges came before the Magistrate's Court during the thirteen days of the fair. During a period of the same duration but a month earlier, 357 charges were heard. In 1899, however, there were 406 charges during the show and the same number during the control period, and the following year, 453 charges during the fair and 479 a month before. The only specific offence that increased dramatically during the influx, predictably, was being drunk and disorderly, although larceny, vagrancy, and prostitution numbers generally increased as well.[111] Although more people probably made more trouble during the Exhibition period, slight manpower additions to the force were not sufficient to allow police to keep them under wraps.

Perhaps the statistics that best reveal the police strategy of enforcement are the Reports on the Patrol Signal System. In 1892, for example, 14,116 calls were received during September, compared with 14,824 for August. Yet September showed the highest number of alarms responded to, 268 compared with 258 for August, and the highest number of arrests resulting from those responses, 287 compared with 276. This pattern was not invariable. In 1894, September was only the fourth highest month both for alarms responded to and arrests resulting. However, in the period from 1890, the first full year for which these statistics were kept, until 1903, September showed the highest rate of response in eleven of the fourteen years, and the highest rate of arrest in nine years and the second highest rate in three years.[112] These figures suggest that during the show, police overlooked more infractions than normal, but responded with alacrity and firmness to situations judged to be serious.

This reactive approach had two inherent problems. It was ineffective against crimes not immediately apparent, and it threatened to escalate the seriousness of criminal activity. If offences were overlooked, more would be committed; if more were committed, increasingly serious ones would have to be ignored. Police realized that preventative action was the crucial ingredient in maintaining an acceptable level of order.

Some efforts were made to shut down illegal booze dens and brothels. In 1888, for example, a number of dives in the Ward, the city's most prominent slum, were raided on the Saturday evening preceding the opening. On this occasion, police were lucky; liquor was confiscated at several places. Frequently, they came away empty-handed, as they did a week later when the same area was invaded. An official noted several years later that police made many raids 'which never amount to anything, for the simple reason that the keepers of a dive or room receive assistance in many cases from neighbours in the secretion of the liquor.'[113]

It was much the same story with prostitution. In 1890 'the usual Exhibition raids' involved descents on three brothels, probably the limit for effective surprise. News spread quickly, alerting other houses to be on guard. Police activity, though, could be disruptive. Rumours in 1883 of a general raid created a stampede of disreputable women. Livery stables were busy until three in the morning carrying them to railway stations, boarding houses, and nearby villages. However, it was easy to slip back, to change premises, to lie low until police were more preoccupied. A trade so decentralized was impossible to root out. Moreover, if authorities were too assertive, they risked unleashing a backlash even more disruptive than the initial offence. When Nellie Diamond's establishment was raided in 1888, a large crowd assembled and threw stones at the police, another indication of differing standards of public order and of a self-help ethic that operated within working-class neighbourhoods.[114]

A preventative strategy had the most chance of success, authorities concluded, if it targeted individuals rather than activities. Using a broad definition of 'vagrancy,' they tried to sweep troublemakers off the streets before mischief was done. Sometimes charges were preferred because of suspicious behaviour. Fred Thornton, a 'notorious character,' was picked up for trying to sell a silver watch. Charlie Thompson, the pickpocket, got collared when he was seen among the crowd at Parkdale Station.[115]

In many cases, arrests were entirely anticipatory. Joseph Dalton and Harry Shine, 'two old penitentiary birds,' were 'jugged' in 1886. Two homeless girls from Parkdale were given ten days in 1888 'to keep them away from the fair.' Joseph Rooke, 'well-known westender,' was grabbed in 1890, and Jessie Thompson was put away in 1896 'on general principles.' Minnie Lessard was taken in at the turn of the century 'because police believed that she was not a fit and proper person to be associating with Exhibition visitors.' She managed to walk away from custody after being sentenced, but was recaptured five hours later. In a few instances, charges were preferred simply for cosmetic reasons. Richard Clayton, described as intelligent looking but dirty, was sent down in 1881 'to get him out of the way.' Three years later he was arrested again. 'He is not dangerous,' admitted the *Mail*, 'yet everyone who sees him feels compelled to keep a civil distance from him.'[116]

The number scooped up each year is hard to verify. In 1888, when vagrancy arrests were particularly high, a *Mail* reporter claimed to have seen a detective's notebook with a list of forty local criminals to be detained; press reports from the fair period mentioned only twenty. Some of the targeted may have been charged with other offences. Most seasons, the number put away seems to have been between five and ten, including people from out of town.[117]

Clearly, not everyone with a record was incarcerated during the show. The local jail could not have held them all. Most of those arrested on this basis were kept for the duration of the fair, usually a week or two depending on when they had been found. William Williams was put away for fifteen days in 1888 and a week in 1896, his release on both occasions coinciding with the end of the show. However, incarceration periods varied considerably and were related to individual assessments of risk. In the same session of the Police Court in 1887, P. Naven was sent down until the fair was over, but three others also hauled in for vagrancy were remanded until called on, or basically released on good behaviour. At the other extreme, Sam Pillow, rounded up in 1883 shortly after the fair opened, was remanded to the cells for an additional week after it closed, perhaps to keep him away from other shows.[118]

This tactic probably was not limited to the fair season. In many cities, vagrancy laws were used as tools of intimidation whenever the need arose, and it is unlikely that Toronto was an exception. However, in Hogtown, these sorts of arrests were closely associated with the fair, a routine part of civic preparations for the influx. When four 'idlers' were locked up in 1883, the *Mail* simply noted 'the benefit of having a good reputation is now being made manifest.'[119]

Taking local offenders off the streets was a relatively straight-

SIDETRACKED !

In this 1897 *Star* cartoon, which gave an approving nod to the annual fair-time incarceration of criminals, the policeman has become a con artist, slyly shunting gullible crooks towards the city jail.

forward matter. Using preventative tactics against unknown criminals from outside was much trickier, especially if their outward
appearance was respectable. Stool-pigeons within the city's criminal
circles were pressured to provide what information they could, but the
identification of transient felons depended mainly on effective police
organization. Some cities sent mug shots of criminals thought to be
heading towards Toronto, and, occasionally, personnel. As early as
1880 Detroit dispatched a detective to help spot thieves; the Toronto
force reciprocated a week later at the Michigan State Fair. The following year, Hamilton sent one detective, and London sent three. In 1886
officers came from Hamilton, Detroit, and Buffalo. Interforce cooperation extended beyond municipalities. Detective Cooper of the Barnum Circus agreed in 1885 to stay over a few days to point out
criminals. Railway security kept city counterparts informed about
suspects who detrained in the area. These forces, too, were often augmented for the fair season. In 1887 the Grand Trunk hired detectives
from St Catharines and Windsor to watch for thieves at Union Station.
Three years later, Special Constable Donnelly of Point Levis, 'who
knows the crooks of Montreal and Quebec,' was stationed there.[120]

These efforts required close and constant observation, a strategy
also adopted by Toronto's own detectives. They kept an eye out for
known felons, of course, watching for transients who had been in the
city before as well as for local fugitives who could not resist a visit to
the fair. Bella Rogers, wanted for almost a year on theft charges, was
nabbed in 1892. Four years later, Stephen Nagle, another robber,
was captured.[121] City police, however, tried to maintain a careful
watch on anybody who acted suspiciously and, to do this, they positioned themselves in places most likely to attract criminal activity.

While the fair was in progress, two men were assigned to keep an
eye on the leading hotels. Two detectives were sent to Union Station
and, as of 1889, two more to Parkdale Station, where malefactors
often detrained to avoid detection downtown. One man made a daily
check of pawn shops and second-hand stores, concentrated on York
Street, while another patrolled the bank district until closing time at
3 p.m., after which he usually reinforced the hotel contingent. Others
took up positions at the fairground, normally at the gates and in the
Main Building. Detectives put in long, exhausting days during the
exhibition, and at night some were ordered to sleep at hotels to keep
up surveillance and to be on hand if needed. In 1895 eleven hotels
were billeted, more than double the number from five years earlier.[122]

Known or obvious malfeasants who strayed into the police net were usually encouraged to leave town forthwith. Four thieves recognized as they stepped off a train in 1881 were persuaded to get right back on. An elderly man intercepted in Union Station in 1889 with a wheel of fortune was given the choice of leaving or going to jail until the fair was over. Unidentified suspicious characters were often shadowed to determine whether action was required. Generally, assessments were made quickly. Professor Waters, professed magician and ventrilo-quist, was sent packing as soon as police concluded he was in league with pickpockets who worked his audience. John Gunther, vendor of a corn cure 'concocted in the most filthy manner,' was given a day to disappear. On the other hand, stylishly dressed H.L. Howard of New York spent a week ingratiating himself with local sports before being hauled in for questioning. Detectives had noticed him when he first registered at a leading hotel, but left him alone until they were sure he was not an ordinary tourist. Howard was allowed to leave town, as were Patrick Davis of St Louis and Edward Maust of Chicago. Detec-tive Reburn followed them for two days before deciding they were up to no good. They were given eight hours to leave the city, providing they allowed themselves to be photographed.[123]

Getting suspects to leave town was a convenient way of saving police time and public money, but it was also a safe way of dealing with respectable-looking people who had committed no crime. Albert Field of Montreal and Frank Howard of Cleveland had merely seemed overly anxious while changing a number of American bills into Canadian currency. They were charged with vagrancy, though they had more than three hundred dollars between them. The uncomfortable magistrate set a modest bail, hoping they would take the opportunity to depart. They did, just before the arrival of a tele-gram from the States indicating that one was a well-known bank sneak and the other was wanted in Milwaukee.[124]

Not everyone was given an option. Two known thieves from Detroit picked up in 1883 begged piteously to be allowed to leave, but were held until the end of the show. 'Doc' Stothers of Brantford and John Moran of upstate New York claimed to be honest businessmen, but were locked up as suspected gamblers. William Easton wanted to return to Brown's Corners, where he claimed he could get work, but authorities were unwilling to take a chance.[125] Decisions were obvi-ously highly subjective, much depending on appearance, demeanour, past records, and information from elsewhere.

Authorities seemed quite satisfied with their system for handling unwanted residents and visitors. Police bragged that criminals shunned Toronto at fairtime to avoid a week or two of jail. There was probably some truth in this claim. Locked up in 1887, Charlie Thompson made a point of calling on police a year later to say he was leaving the city until the show was over. Four Hamilton pickpockets intercepted at Union Station in 1902 insisted they were merely passing through. 'We know too much about your town to touch it.'[126] How effective the strategy really was is impossible to tell, but it is hard not to question the police assessment when every year it was necessary to post pickpocket warnings.

Criminal opinion of police tactics was divided. Leaving town was often entirely acceptable to both parties. Miles Gillespie, a Detroit thief recognized on the grounds in 1882, was not the only person who quickly offered to depart, if, as he put it, that was all that was wanted. Some of those run out of town, like Fred Davis in 1889 and Joseph Lyner in 1896, tried to slip back unnoticed into the city a day or two later, but many moved on gratefully to work elsewhere, including the four thieves dismissed on one day in 1888 who simply headed for the Provincial Fair in Kingston. On the other hand, those incarcerated often protested being locked up for no specific reason, and a few were outraged at police harassment. Joseph Silvey, insisting he was not a vagrant, told the Court he was followed about the city and bothered at every turn. When he managed to find a job, detectives interviewed his employer, who promptly fired him. The magistrate ordered an investigation and meanwhile held him on remand.[127]

Walter Johnson, arrested in 1893, took the unusual step of hiring a lawyer, who demanded a trial. The crown attorney agreed to proceed, calling Inspector Armstrong, who testified that the prisoner had no peaceable occupation, associated with thieves, and lived off the proceeds of crime; under cross-examination, however, he admitted that the defendant had never been convicted. Acting Detective Vernet testified that the accused had been convicted of housebreaking, which Johnson from the dock vigorously denied. The magistrate refused to listen to hearsay evidence that Deputy Chief Stewart wanted to present, but instead remanded Johnson for a week to allow further testimony to be gathered. Bail set at two hundred dollars effectively ensured that the accused remained in jail until the fair ended, even though the case against him was obviously flimsy. In a sense,

Johnson was lucky to have gotten any sort of hearing. Normally, the Crown asked for a delay right off the bat.[128]

For the most part, Toronto citizens were content with fairtime policing. Now and then, when innocent burghers were mistakenly subjected to these arbitrary measures, there was a twinge of discomfort. Thomas Tegart was handing out cards for the Davies Ferry Company when he saw a friend heading for the train. They were chatting when Detective Reburn arrested him for interfering with travellers. Ignoring requests to send for character references, the officer took him off to the cells. Tegart persuaded a small girl playing on the sidewalk outside the cell window to take a message to his employers, but everyone had gone to the exhibition. It was 10 p.m. before anyone came, too late to get bail, so he remained locked up all night 'among the dirty blackguards.' In court the next morning, Reburn was getting set to prove the charge when one of the lawyers recognized Tegart as a respectable citizen who 'shouldn't be here at all.' He was released, but as the *Globe* commented, 'after a night of the degradation that such confinement entails it is no satisfaction to an innocent man merely to be discharged by the magistrate in the morning.'[129]

For most middle-class Torontonians, occasional instances of over-zealousness were a small price to keep the dangerous classes in check. The *Labour Advocate* once complained about the 'needless harshness and brutality' that police ordinarily used to enforce the law, but it noted sadly that 'the majority of our citizens rather like that sort of thing, when other people are the victims, so we suppose there is not much use in protesting.' It was especially true at fair-time, when an inspiring standard of enforcement seemed to be set. If police could clear a city for a fortnight for the safety of visitors, asked *The Week*, why not do it permanently for residents?[130]

It was a logical question, though the answers were obvious. Police did not have enough energy to maintain such a tight lid on a constant basis. Incarcerating people who had committed no specific crime was a serious violation of civil rights – and expensive to boot. Forcing criminals out of town, rather than stopping disorder, dispersed crime into jurisdictions that had fewer resources to cope. It was a strategy that worked only for limited periods in a limited area. Even *The Week* recognized the legal difficulty of locking up people for an extended time on nothing more than vagrancy charges. It wondered, though, about establishing a penal colony somewhere in the North to which criminals could be removed. Thus the exhibition inspired a vision of permanent social harmony, by banishing to a wicked city those who did not fit into the righteous one.

~~~~~~~~~~~~~~~

Was anyone surprised that accidents, fighting, and crime occurred at the fair? Not likely. More unexpected was the persistent confusion of exhibit organization. Visitors assumed that the overall arrangement of things was more insulated from individual peculiarities, perfect-able through the ongoing application of rationality and consistency. Yet the project that promised to catalogue existence and present it in a logical fashion never quite met the test.

The directors professed entire satisfaction with the official division of exhibits. Others were often puzzled by the principles of inclusion. Class 82 at the 1881 show, styled 'Economic Minerals and Industries Relating Thereto,' also contained medals, coins, and, more mysteri-ously, Indian relics. A *Mail* reporter described it as 'an accumulation of valuable matter lacking discrimination in its distribution and clas-sification.' Even the judges baulked at evaluating a stamp collection slotted into the category. Nor was it clear in 1887 why the poultry class contained ferrets, Guinea pigs, and peacocks, or the chemical class surgical instruments and artificial limbs. A disgruntled artist in 1903 wondered why the prize for watercolours of fruit had been awarded to a picture of a jar of onions.[131]

The placement of goods was more confusing. A *Globe* reporter once promised that each building would be devoted solely to the class of goods for which it was intended, so visitors would have a better chance of seeing everything on view. In practice, it rarely worked that way. The Carriage Building in 1879 contained 'a perfect medley of exhibits' – candies, row boats, axel grease, beer kegs, refrigerators, bricks, shutters, and wheelbarrows, 'with a coffin intervening here and there.' Machinery Hall was well filled in 1882, but 'not with the class of goods that properly come under the head of machinery.' The Dairy and Apiary Building in 1891 featured 'various non-descripts unconnected, but interesting,' including taxidermy. Those wishing to inspect the Nicolle double-flushing odourless closet in 1899 had to go to the Bicycle Building.[132]

Nothing matched the eclecticism of the Crystal Palace, crowded with 'an almost infinite variety of exhibits of the most miscellaneous character.' Exhibitors themselves condemned 'the utter failure on the part of management to arrange the goods even in a small degree according to classes.' An exasperated *Mail* reporter at the 1885 show concluded it would be hard to find a more diverse collection of goods than those on the ground floor of the Main Building. Wedding cakes were placed near tin ware, refrigerators close to pianos, firearms and artificial flowers lay side by side, as did fishing tackle and condensed milk, organs and edge tools. In some cases, random placements created disorienting juxtapositions of association and mood. A reporter in 1880 berated management for putting pork products 'in a building usually used for the display of more fancy articles.'[133]

Perhaps the most disappointing aspect of exhibit arrangement was the scattering of goods in the same class. Part of the 1880 furniture display was located just inside a door of the Crystal Palace, but a climb to a far corner of the upper gallery was required to see the rest. The following year, the *Mail* complained about the diffusion of building material displays, some of which were in the Main Building and some in Machinery Hall, adding that the 'same want of attention to order is seen in other matters.' Most ironware in 1884 was in the Crystal Palace, but some was scattered in other buildings. Some bicycles in 1885 were in the Carriage Building, 'but unfortunately, others of these much discussed items [were] in the Main Building.' And on it went.[134]

The problem was not confined to manufactured goods. Reporters expected to produce coherent accounts of animal classes were driven to the end of their tether trying to identify entries in the jumble of stalls. 'The confusion of breeds and breeders is simply appalling,' wrote one frustrated scribe in 1885, and, to make matters worse, many pens had no information cards posted, so it was impossible to tell what was inside. 'In pen after pen – in fact, in the majority of pens,' echoed a farm journal some years later, 'it would be impossible for a visitor, unless he was either previously well informed, or else particularly inquisitive, to get any proper idea of the exhibits.'[135] Advising visitors to make better use of time by 'doing the show according to system' was patronizing twaddle. Truth was, as one reporter admitted, any ordered plan of seeing everything was almost out of the question.[136]

Without doubt, space shortages contributed to the confusion. No matter how much additional accommodation was created, there never seemed to be enough, and planning was further complicated by the tendency of exhibitors to put off requests until the last minute. Too many of those who lived some distance away neglected to apply until they arrived with their goods, and then they expected to secure choice positions. On occasion, latecomers had to be turned down flat. In 1887, a particularly difficult year, one of the largest machinery manufacturers who belatedly decided to show had to be refused. However, officials did their best to get everyone a place, sqeezing here, cutting there, quickly reassigning allotments if exhibitors failed to appear on the first day. All this meant, of course, that articles got placed wherever there was room, irrespective of their class.[137]

Some exhibit confusion was impossible to control, but much was deliberate. Enterprises intent on making sales needed sites where traffic flows were heaviest. Well-known companies wanted prestige spaces commensurate with their public image. Some firms insisted on parity with competitors. Was it coincidence in 1886 that the Gutta Percha and Rubber Manufacturing Company was just inside the eastern entrance of the Main Building, while the Canadian Rubber Company was just inside the west door?[138] Other businesses desired distance from their rivals, not necessarily just to escape comparisons. Musical instrument makers were a case in point.

Probably no class of manufacturers had to reconcile such contradictory imperatives as piano and organ builders. Initially, they were placed together in the Crystal Palace, so customers could easily find and compare the options. This orderly grouping of the class produced a complex overlay of sounds that some listeners found 'simply amazingly beautiful,' but others, excruciating. In 1882, at the suggestion of a music judge, keyboard instruments were spread through the building to reduce noise interference and to disperse harmonies more widely. It did not make much difference. Noise rebounded through the building, fusing the sound of pianos with knitting and sewing machines, fire gongs, telegraphic apparatus, voices, and much else.[139]

Management wrestled with the problem for over a decade, scattering the instruments some years, clustering them in others. Either way, key pounding was required to make them heard. The cumulative impact was debilitating. Indiscriminate mixing of waltzes, mazurkas, polkas, ripples, and hymns, according to a *Globe* reporter, was 'not without its peculiar effect on the teeth.'[140]

In 1893 piano and organ companies were moved from the Main Building to the Annex Building. An improved comfort level in the

Crystal Palace was offset by the din now experienced in the 'pande-
monium pavilion.' Even the booth manager for the R.S. Williams
Company admitted that 'no musical instrument of merit can be
exhibited with any degree of enthusiasm.' Firms tried to establish a
schedule that allotted exclusive time to each competitor in turn, but
it was hard to tell potential customers not to test an instrument during a rival's slot. The building remained 'as noisy and less enticing
than the Cave of the Winds.' When the new Hall of Manufactures
opened in 1903, piano makers moved to a series of alcoves along its
north and south walls. It provided a more reasonable balance
between the contradictory desires to centralize music displays, yet
eliminate noise interference. However, a cavernous building full of
babble and buzz was not the ideal spot to listen for sound qualities,
though perhaps manufacturers of cheaper brands saw advantages in
this arrangement.[141]

Devising logical classes and placing exhibits in harmonious relationships should have been some of the things most under management control, but these types of order were often just as elusive as
others. There were always too many awkward angles and bulges in
what was brought to the fair. It never did fit together into a tidy
package.

Still, the scope of the exhibition as an ordering agency was impressive. Competition categories, prize values, space allocations, apparatus displays, and entertainment spectacles, to mention just a few
things, set out in concrete, visible form the hierarchies of value, networks of connection, and visions of coordination. These were never
perfectly realized, but there was a hovering impression that, over
time, defects might be eliminated. If the standards employed in
Toronto were not original, they did help to merge the specifics of local
culture into wider metropolitan webs of signification.

Exhibitions, like the Industrial, were not the only Victorian institutions that aimed to define, promulgate, and sustain structures of
order. In a complex, rapidly changing environment, the impulse to
devise categories, establish inventories, shape norms, and affirm the
possibility of harmony was strong. Museums, libraries, symphony
orchestras, and department stores all embodied the same desire to
systematize the particulars of existence, and all featured arrange-

ments of reciprocal credibility with political and social élites in their regions.

The fair was not necessarily more influential than other institutions, but it was different in some respects. It was more inclusive, more so even than department stores, which did not have space to accommodate farm equipment, heavy machinery, or horse races. It was more regularly a site of transgression, where normal social categories and boundaries were inverted and rearranged, tested and questioned. Museums, libraries, and symphonies were more concerned with protecting cultural standards than with experimenting with their validity. Finally, the fair was thought to require extraordinary use of the state's apparatus of repression, at least in Toronto. The operation of Eaton's and Simpson's was never assumed to depend on the stakeout of Union Station or the incarceration on 'general principles' of members of the city's underclass. Playful dissolutions of order within the fairgrounds were accepted, it seems, because of more insistent efforts to affirm order outside. In a recent study of burlesque, Robert Allen argued that power is more rooted in ordination – the dictating and internalizing of cultural classifications – than in subordination through physical coercion.[142] The exhibition experience in Toronto suggests that the two processes were crucially linked.

Was there resistance to the order established at and by the fair? Of course, though little of it aimed to pull the whole arrangement down. The seriously disaffected stayed away. Most who contested were concerned with specific aspects and had a vested interest in the success of the enterprise as a whole. Even the petty criminals most harassed by the police benefited as long as they stayed out of jail. Some, like refreshment booth concessionaires who sold booze, were engaged in disputes about where lines should be drawn. Others posited different kinds of order that reflected alternative values. Teams of pickpockets who targeted specific types of victims were threats to order from one perspective, but from another were compelling evidence of the advantages of organization. Fistfights established rankings just as effectively as prize lists did.

The ordering potential of the fair was subverted far more fundamentally by contradictory impulses than by overt resistance. Toleration of competing scales and transgressive behaviours meant that human existence could never be absolutely fixed. Instead, ordering currents continually alternated. The exhibition experience knit, cast, arranged, and steadied, but simultaneously unstitched, corroded, disturbed, and upset. Both sorts of processes were revealing. Through its ambitious effort to bring together so much of life, the inversion and disruption it stimulated, and the alternative types of order it attracted, the fair did offer exceptional insights into the logic and efficacy of the categories, rules, and values that gave meaning to everyday existence.

2

Confidence

Within a few days of her arrival in late August 1882, Madame Henault had Toronto in an uproar. Each afternoon, decked out in Turkish trousers, silk gown embroidered with cabbalistic characters, red-leather boots turned up at the toes, jewelled tiara, and fistfuls of diamond rings, she drove a golden chariot, three horses abreast, up Yonge Street to a platform erected in a vacant lot close to the commercial district. There, interpreter on one side, uniformed attendants on the other, with a band 'dressed up swellishly' behind, she donned a large black apron and offered the crowd her skill as a healer, which was free, and her wondrous curative, 'le parfum chinois,' which was not.[1]

Dentistry was her specialty. On a typical afternoon she treated perhaps a dozen people, using a jackscrew forceps to draw as many as twenty-five teeth. As the instrument was applied, the band struck up a stirring tune to distract the patient, cover any discomforting indications of pain, and herald the triumph of surgical skill. However, this was only part of her repertoire. She also attended to the deaf, blind, and crippled, usually by massaging the afflicted parts, then swabbing them with copious amounts of the Chinese elixir of life. No more than five such cases were dealt with on any one day, but Madame Henault was adept at extracting a full measure of performance value from each. Emphatic gestures, humorous antics, and constant patter about the suffering of the person being examined and her own prowess, all relayed to listeners by a Black interpreter, Dr Biddoux, kept the crowd enthralled.[2]

The exact nature of her manipulations was never very clear. Even spectators within six feet of the platform could see little when, as often happened, Madame's retinue formed a protective shield. Delicate cases were treated in the chariot, behind a curtain, from which she emerged periodically with reassurances that all was going well. Though uncertain of the process, the audience was electrified by some of the results. A woman in her early twenties, who had suffered for fourteen years with a disabling hip disease, was handed up to the chariot. The screen was drawn. Half an hour later, after the crowd had been requested to clear a passage, the young lady proceeded to walk back to her own vehicle. When the cheering abated, Madame promised a complete cure in fifteen days. This demonstration was not unique: scores of crutches were left behind by owners who apparently had no further use for them.[3]

Those desperate for cures thronged to the vacant lot to get close to the 'wonderful woman,' as the press had dubbed her. Attempts to intercept her elsewhere were fruitless. Sessions were conducted only in public beside the chariot. So, each day, increasing numbers of people, some from as far away as Niagara Falls and Syracuse, buffeted themselves into a perspiring pack trying to get close to the golden wheels, while thousand of others suffering mainly from curiosity came to inspect the pathetic display. One reporter confessed that he had never realized how many deformed children lived in the city.[4]

By the beginning of September Madame Henault had become a principal topic of conversation in Hogtown and beyond,[5] partly because so little about her was known. Rumours abounded: municipal authorities had run her out of Glasgow; priests had attacked her in Quebec; she was a Gypsy healer of a type commonly found in Italy; she had been consulted by Mrs Gooderham, doyen of Toronto society; Ned Hanlan had invited her to stay at his hotel free for as long as she wished; the Grand Trunk Railway was going to run cheap excursions from every station on the line so the sick could reach her.[6] All these suggestions were probes towards an answer to the overriding question on everyone's mind: Was she legitimate?

There was every reason to be suspicious. In the late nineteenth century medical charlatanism was a high art – and a familiar one.[7] Yet in this instance the evidence was confusing. Reports said that local dentists were inundated with cases of ulcerated mouths, root fragments, slivered jaws, and other problems resulting from her botches.[8] On the other hand, a *World* reporter saw her draw twenty-five teeth in a row, each clean and unbroken. Patients who had

SOME HARD CASES FOR THE FEMALE DOCTOR.

Bengough's depiction of the crowd around the golden chariot features an
array of contemporary politicians in need of miracle cures.

requested as many as seven or eight extractions testified that they
had experienced no pain and wanted to go back for more. Harry
Webeck, resident of Bay Street, was delighted with the removal,
'done instantaneously and with very little pain,' of a decayed tooth
that several regular practitioners had refused to touch.[9] Who should
be believed?

The same question arose from her other treatments. A young boy
inspired to walk home without his crutches had immediately gone to
bed and was still unable to get up days later. Another lad, whose
crutches were broken by Madame Henault in front of the crowd, had
to have a new pair made the next day. The experience left him 'much
worse than ever.'[10] On the other side, Hattie Newman of Yorkville,
incapacitated through most of her thirteen years with a knee injury,
was able to walk after a quarter hour in the chariot. For the previous
fifteen months she had been entirely dependent on crutches; now she
could go up and down her front steps without aid, something she had

never been able to do before even with support. A long-standing hip displacement, aggravated by a serious fall, had caused running wounds on the leg of twelve-year-old Eliza Phillips, forcing her onto crutches. These had been abandoned immediately after treatment, and five days later she was still walking without external support and without pain. Her sores had begun to heal.[11] Many cases were simply ambiguous. The young woman with hip disease, whose dramatic return to her own carriage had astounded onlookers, had been able to walk before. Had her condition really changed? Mrs Taylor of Albion Township thought she could hear better, but was this wishful thinking?[12]

The same kind of confusion surrounded the identities of those who were treated. Some were local characters, well known or easily checked out. The man who sold apples at the corner of Front and York streets maintained that his rheumatism of thirty years had disappeared. Thomas Hazelhurst, a former *Globe* typographer, announced that his head wound sustained in the Civil War had been cured. Captain Brown, whose four-year-old daughter was treated, was the eminently respectable proprietor of a stationery business. Others, though, were more mysterious. Mr Graham, who described great improvement in his hearing, claimed to be postmaster of Sheridan in Halton County. Why could his name not be found in Lovell's provincial directory? Why was someone else listed as the postmaster of Sheridan?[13]

No wonder public opinion was sharply divided. To some, Madame Henault was 'a miracle worker,' 'a public benefactor,' 'too clever' for local doctors.[14] To others, she was a quack, a fakir, a charlatan.[15] For them, the sticking point was the Chinese perfume. The many supplicants who failed to gain access to the chariot were advised to undertake their own cure by purchasing a supply of the medicine at a dollar a bottle. Many did. Estimates of the value of sales ranged as high as two thousand dollars a day; while the actual figure may have been half that, a substantial amount of cash was changing hands. And from what reporters could see, most was coming from the pockets of those who could least afford it.[16]

When the press began to raise doubts, Madame responded vehemently. She was no ignorant Gypsy, she boasted, but the daughter of the most celebrated physician in Italy. She was, in fact, the seventh daughter, who alone of all her sisters had inherited the healing gift. She had diplomas, which she could show, proving she was a medical doctor, well versed in the theory of her art, and no one in Toronto could equal her practical skill in the extraction of teeth: she would give a hundred dollars to anyone who came close. All the hurtful innuendo circulating about her past, all the aspersions on her methods, were the result of professional insecurity and gender bias. 'Parce que je suis femme,' was her explanation to the crowd; 'because I am a woman, they are jealous of me.'[17]

About two weeks after her arrival, she decided to close shop. Whether motivated by fear, exhaustion, satisfaction with the take, or something else is not clear. Public explanations were garbled. One report said she was indisposed, another that she had given birth to a baby boy. Either way, the public was told on Saturday that treatments would resume on Monday, but she never reappeared. Instead, leaving the golden chariot behind for repairs, she and her entourage boarded the train and headed west.[18] The *Telegram*, in full crusade against conniving fraud, was reluctant to let go of her. It found people she had treated who now professed to be worse than before. It tracked down a local man who, while working for the show, claimed to have witnessed dozens of instances of bungled dentistry. It discovered that many purchases of Chinese perfume were bogus, bought by confederates who returned the bottles on the sly. It had the mysterious substance analysed by a doctor, who determined it contained five cents worth of methyl alcohol, tincture of cinnamon, and glycerine.[19] The *Telegram* made a powerful attack, undoubtedly motivated in part by concern for the public welfare. Yet the fact that the Hattie Newmans, Harry Webecks, and other satisfied patients received no attention suggests that Madame Henault may have possessed genuine therapeutic abilities and raises questions about why she inspired such vehement denunciations. Perhaps her explanation, 'parce que je suis femme,' was close to the mark.

While Madame Henault was clearly exceptional, the broad problem she embodied for many people was all too common. She underscored the difficulties of distinguishing what was legitimate, sincere, and beneficial from what was not. She highlighted an endemic anxiety about confidence, an anxiety that was particularly acute in constantly shifting, anonymous urban environments, but one that few people anywhere in the late nineteenth century could avoid. In a variety of ways, the Industrial Exhibition was established precisely to alleviate these sorts of concerns. It was intended to be an assertion, a forum, an engine of confidence. However, while it assuaged tensions to some extent, it also sidestepped and, worse, exacerbated them. Madame Henault was not the only slick operator attracted by large crowds primed to spend. Nor was she the only one who tried to evade too close a scrutiny. The fair did not solve problems of confidence, then, but it did help to shape a response that in the long run suited the requirements of corporate capitalist production.

⌇⌇⌇⌇⌇⌇⌇⌇⌇⌇

While no society in any historical period has been immune from concerns about confidence, urban and industrial growth in the nineteenth century created a context that made them extraordinarily pervasive. Human relationships in the hamlets, towns, and walking cities of the pre-industrial period were conditioned by familiarity. In most places, smallness of scale provided stable foundations of individual identity. Face-to-face dealings in markets, churches, and political and social meetings continually reinforced knowledge about those beyond the family circle. Who others were, where they lived, what they did, what they thought, who had to be shown respect, who would provide assistance – such things were simply known. Difficulties of dramatically altering economic circumstances made for relatively resistant social structures. Strangers were quickly identified and integrated if they stayed. This was a world in which privacy was a luxury and secrets were hard to keep.

The growth of industrial organization and technology increasingly eroded this situation. As travel got easier, as economic opportunities in distant parts began to be more common, as the reorganization of production undermined existing social structures, people started to move. When they left farm and village, they left behind cultures of intimacy and began to encounter problems involving confidence. The very decision of where to go required judgments about the prospects of places whose futures were far from certain, and, once migration began, it was sometimes hard to make permanent commitments. High rates of transiency throughout the nineteenth century in both rural and urban areas suggest that many people remained unsure about where best to settle,[20] while legions of boosters preaching the inevitable progress of whatever burgs they happened to be in did their best to stifle doubts, including their own.

If confidence about places was problematic, confidence about people was even more troubling, especially for those who ended up in large industrializing cities. Here, for older residents and newcomers

alike, massive influxes created social worlds much bigger than anything most of them had ever known, worlds that kept getting more
and more complex. Some doubted whether it was possible for so
many people to live together successfully in such close proximity.
How could essential services be supplied efficiently on such a grand
scale? How could the significance of so much and such varied animation be comprehended? As John Kasson has pointed out, major
centres, almost bursting with activity, presented such 'compressed,
tangled, contrasting, chaotic, and often opaque surfaces as to be
simply unintelligible in terms of any earlier coherent system of
signs.' More worrisome was the sense that older social restraints
were fraying. So many people seemed to be adrift from the steadying
influences of family and community. So many seemed to be in the
thrall of commercial values. In the city, suggested a *Telegram* editorial in 1890, where neighbours were unknown, 'money bought such
aid as friendship offered in more sparsely settled communities.'
Could one survive and prosper in a seething cauldron of humanity
where everyone had an eye, it seemed, only on self-interest?[21]

Even the optimistic could not ignore the fact that they were
surrounded by strangers – strangers who made demands, strangers
who asked for their trust, strangers on whom their own welfare
depended, strangers whose professions of identity could not always
be substantiated. According to Karen Halttunen, the new city presented a serious problem. 'How could one identify strangers without
access to biographical information about them, when only visual
information was available?' That visual information, moreover, was
increasingly ambiguous. As traditional attitudes of deference weakened, as mass production made clothing more uniform, as anonymity
became more of a social goal, it was increasingly difficult to distinguish not only inferiors from superiors, but counterfeits from the
legitimate. Though in day-to-day interactions it had to be maintained, the old assumption that manners and appearance were outward clues to inward character was understood to be tenuous.[22]

The most disturbing aspect about this breakdown in the familiar
was that the quality of strangeness wormed its way back into the
self. Cut off from family, friends, and an environment in which one's
place was secure, it was difficult to be sure of personal identity.
Could sufficient strength of character be maintained to avoid temptations that continually threatened body and soul? Would the will
and wherewithal always be available to perform the countless rituals

in everyday existence necessary to convince others, equally wary, that one was worthy and safe? What did it mean that confirmation of the self depended on the judgments of others, the very strangers whose motives and sincerity were hard to fathom? When emotions, attitudes, and patterns of behaviour varied widely according to company and location, how could one be sure which represented the true self? Was there, in fact, a single, coherent personality, or did one simply don a succession of masks?[23]

As if coping with bigger places and more bodies was not enough, concerns about confidence were also generated by an expanding, aggressive market economy. When businesses grew to encompass regions and continents, relations of trust became increasingly problematic. Many organizations could no longer operate only with family members or small numbers of closely supervised workers. Identifying employees who were stable, honest, and efficient, especially if they operated at a distance, became an important task. Determining the reliability of investors, suppliers, and customers became harder as relationships were conducted more and more on paper. In the late nineteenth century, when so many business initiatives came to naught and the spectre of business failure was ever present, anxieties about such matters were inevitable.[24]

Insecurities pervaded the consumer end of the economic spectrum as well. As individuals and families became less self-sufficient, figuring out which goods represented true value and which were produced by unscrupulous or incompetent operators became a priority. Would an expensive sewing machine hold up with heavy use? Was a shirt actually made of high-quality cotton, or simply treated with sizing that would soon wash out? Was a can of corned beef full of ptomaine? For masses of people who no longer knew who produced what they used, what they wore, what they ate, questions of confidence arose at every turn.[25] Advances of the modern age seemed to multiply uncertainties. Maybe Madame Henault had stumbled on a miraculous elixir. With the exploration of remote corners of the globe, who knew what wonders were being discovered? Who could predict what secrets were being unlocked by science?

As new technology changed familiar habits, as industrial capitalism uprooted people and required choices about an unprecedented variety of things, the creation of confidence became a central concern at all levels of society, in all places. Obviously, not everyone was affected in the same way, at the same time, and to the same degree; this brief, generalized description cannot do justice to the complexity of the developments summarized here. Nor should it be forgotten that anxieties were balanced by faith in the reality of progress.[26] However, the magnitude of this crisis of confidence is apparent from the extent of the measures developed to deal with it. All sorts of techniques, instruments, and codes were invented and refined in efforts to decrease the risks and control the uncertainties – from the establishment of credit agencies and regulatory commissions, through the professionalization of occupations, to the transformation of the domestic parlour into a theatre where dress and behaviour could be scrutinized.[27]

The exhibition, as a Victorian institution, was simply one of these devices. It was useful because it allowed people to present themselves, their organizations, and their goods and services more coherently, to scrutinize things presented by others more closely, and to test assumptions and structures in unusually intense conditions. In the case of the Toronto fair, and probably typically, the matters of confidence that were addressed ranged enormously: the effectiveness of local élites, the sturdiness of animal stock, the power of military forces, the efficiency of fire companies, and the durability of machinery were just a few of the things that might be mentioned. It would be pointless to talk about all of them. The discussion that follows will be limited to three brief examples: confidence about local, national, and imperial existence; confidence about the sociability of crowds; and confidence about manufactured goods. The remainder of the chapter will suggest how an institution honed so keenly to concerns about confidence was regularly blunted.

〜〜〜〜〜〜

From its inception, the exhibition was an expression of confidence in Toronto, and it quickly came to be seen as a key element in the city's, and the nation's, ongoing success. Dramatic forward strides evident at the fair evoked frequent expressions of nationalistic pride and made it a logical place to boost the settlement of hinterland areas. At the fair, visitors could see what material progress meant and how it was being achieved.

The city's decision to abandon its place in the existing rotation for the Provincial Fair was an assertion of local pre-eminence that other centres thought arrogant, but soon their shows were scheduled so as not to conflict with Hogtown's.[28] For Torontonians, fairtime became an occasion to pontificate expansively about present conditions and future prospects. They were especially appreciative when visitors, like Colonel Blair, master of the Dominion Grange in 1881, confirmed their own assessments that the Queen City, 'from its geographical position and the resources which it and the country surrounding it possess,' was destined to be 'the banner city' of the whole dominion.[29]

If the success of the fair was heavily attributed to Toronto's extensive transport connections, plentiful hotel accommodation, and wide range of sight-seeing attractions,[30] the 'extraordinary growth and large measure of prosperity' enjoyed by the city was correspondingly linked to the fair. The condition of the two were so interwoven that 'the one cannot suffer without injury to the other.' It was no coincidence that each year more of the space between downtown and the exhibition grounds was filled in with handsome new industrial buildings. It was no surprise that the needs of the fair became an onoing rallying cry for better hotels, improved streets, dependable water systems, and more handsome parks.[31]

One of the clearest indications of municipal progress was the annual improvement of the fairground itself. For some, this was an accurate gauge for measuring civic development in all its aspects. Since its first establishment, claimed the *Globe* in 1891, the exhibition 'has been a reliable barometer of the city's growth in numbers, wealth and refinement.' Each year, the press detailed what new buildings had been added and what old ones had been renovated, often adding that requests for exhibit space still could not be met entirely and that failure to provide the fair with the resources it needed would be an injury not just to the city, but 'in no small measure to the country at large.'[32]

Indeed, many Torontonians and others saw the show not just as a local asset but as a national one. Bringing together what one banquet speaker described as 'representative men' from all over the dominion created national unity and confidence. Lieutenant Governor Robitaille of Quebec, on the same occasion, agreed that the power of the Industrial Exhibition to promote the great and glorious future of Canada was unrivalled, particularly because it could suppress interprovincial and interracial hostility. 'Men engaged in commercial, industrial and agricultural pursuits coming here from different provinces learn to know and esteem each other, and thus a feeling of sympathy is created amongst all.'[33]

If the fair predicted future greatness, it also demonstrated how far

THE GREATEST WONDER OF THE FAIR:
"How Toronto has Grown!"

Bengough's cover illustration for the 1889 fairtime issue of *Grip* personified Toronto as a carnival freak, but captured the widespread feeling that the exhibition was deeply connected to current and future civic greatness.

the nation had come in its short existence. Lecturing beneath a 'monster map' of Canada, Principal George Grant of Queen's University asked the grandstand audience to 'look at this wonderful exhibition, and then ask how long has it taken for all this to grow together.' The same message in concrete form was evident to reporters covering almost every department. Hot-air furnaces on display in 1886 spoke of the 'increasing culture and wealth in the country where such poetical combinations of iron, steel and tile work are possible.' A decade later, the agricultural implement department was 'an object lesson setting forth the material development of this great country'; comparisons with things shown only ten or fifteen years before were 'cause for the most profound gratification to patriotic Canadians.'[34] The same was true of livestock. The *Empire* reporter in 1889 was gratified that cattle prizes were no longer swept by imported animals. Thanks in large measure to knowledge gained at the exhibition, the winners now were Canadian bred, and they compared well with the best at leading English shows. The improvement in pigs was so thorough, according to the *Mail and Empire* in 1898, that the most popular breeds of a decade ago were fast disappearing.[35]

For business and governments, this optimistic milieu was an obvious place to promote settlement of frontier agricultural lands. Not only did the exhibition attract large numbers of rural people, the chief emigrant prospects for new tracts, but also the proximity of the best animals, most impressive crops, and most advanced technology was more likely to inspire positive visions of what could be achieved. Success was made to seem virtually automatic. After seeing a Manitoba government display in 1880 which included locally grown vegetables, cereals, and animal feed, as well as soil and grasses taken from every district, a *Mail* reporter concluded that almost the entire province consisted of a rich, black loam, well mixed with clay.[36] A decade later, a *Saturday Night* columnist, overwhelmed by images of 'grand proportion, gigantic enterprise, boundless possibilities, and a glorious future of success and prosperity' at an exhibit of Canadian Pacific Railway photographs, turned to a stranger and blurted impulsively, 'Plenty, plenty, plenty, everywhere! Isn't it a grand country! I never realized what the C.P.R. had opened up before!'[37] Some thus persuaded to relocate on the prairies may eventually have felt misled, but they could have done worse. The Ontario government promoted agricultural settlement in the Shield areas of Muskoka and Algoma with similar techniques.

Fair visitors who saw the evidence of Canadian achievement with their own eyes could not fail to return home 'with a more vivid impression of the continued advance of our country in all the arts which go to make up a great nation and a powerful community.' However, it was a matter of some regret that this awareness could not be disseminated more widely. Reports of the proceedings sent abroad could alert the world to the capacity of Canada, and thereby stimulate trade and immigration, but that was not the same as having outsiders marvel at first hand. If the Industrial could be transported bodily to the Colonial Exhibition in London, suggested the *Telegram* wistfully in 1886, it would open the eyes of many people who had no idea that the dominion was so advanced.[38] Like most colonials, Torontonians longed for metropolitan recognition; in their eyes, the achievement and potential evident at the Industrial proved they deserved it. Unfortunately, when it came to progress, the fair could be a mirror, a prod, even a crystal ball, but it was not a moveable feast.

If the city was seen as an economic and cultural unit, it was simultaneously viewed as the habitat of unprecedented numbers of people who did not all share the same values. Inevitably, uncertainties about mass behaviour were intensified. Respectable folk had long been wary of the malevolent power of the crowd and what seemed to them its propensity for irrationality. Individuals in crowds cast off inhibitions to the same degree that authorities lost the ability to subdue them. It was the crowd that perpetrated the worst excesses of revolution, the very notion of which was bound up with paralysis of legitimate order by mob intimidation. This was one reason why the increasing use of collective action by workers in the latter part of the nineteenth century inspired apocalyptic visions of social breakdown. Even without revolution, the anonymity, visual cover, and obstructive protection provided by masses of bodies allowed bad apples to vent frustrations in riot, or to disguise calculated criminal acts. When cities began to attract more and more people, therefore, concerns about the destructive potential of human agglomerations heightened. 'In a crowd keep your hand on your jackknife' was the advice of the editor of the Port Hope *Guide*.[39] There was a measure of small-town paranoia here, but that is not to say that many long-time urbanites did not have equally strong fears – of inadvertent crush and claustrophobia, if not deliberate lawlessness.[40]

From this perspective, the fair was something of a social gamble because its whole point was to draw a multitude. Theoretically, visitors were dispersed among a number of features, their consciousness safely steered into celebratory channels. However, when large numbers gathered in a relatively restricted space, the potential for mob behaviour was never absent. 'There is no way of knowing what may happen in a crowd,' warned the Accident Insurance Company in an 1879 advertisement for special policies covering a day at the fair.[41] As noted earlier, reporters continually stressed the good-natured, orderly character of the exhibition crowd, but the frequency of these assertions underscored a hypersensitivity to possible dangers. For them, and many others, the fair provided an unfolding reassurance that extraordinary gatherings were not a social danger. One of the most notable 'experiments' occurred in 1882 during the destruction of the 'Arabi Pasha.'

Exhibition organizers had arranged with local military authorities for a demonstration of modern warfare. A derelict Great Lakes sailing vessel was fitted out to resemble a war ship, with makeshift masts and logs mounted like guns. Around these were grouped a number of dummies, with another at the stern to represent the commander, nicknamed Arabi Pasha after the nationalist leader then threatening British interests in Egypt.[42] The plan was to tow the hulk to a spot two thousand yards off shore from the exhibition grounds, from which point it would be shelled by artillery and finally blown up with gun powder placed along the hull to simulate the effect of torpedoes.[43] The intent was to demonstrate not just the sophistication of modern military technology, but also Canadian military proficiency and the inexorable power of the British Empire. This was to be an assertion of confidence in imperial might and will.

All went well until the last stages of preparation, when a passenger steamer heading for the grounds ran over the insulated wire connecting the explosives with the detonator on shore, chopping it into more than a dozen pieces. These fragments had then to be fished up and soldered together. The resulting five-hour delay meant it was after 3:00 p.m. when the Toronto Field Battery started shelling, and after 5:30 p.m. when the explosion finally occurred.[44]

As a dramatic presentation, the performance rather flopped. The first shells fired had percussion fuses activated by impact. They could be seen bursting, initially in the water, then, once the distance had been established, against the ship. The remainder were shrapnel-filled with timers, meant to go off in the air above the target. The results could not be seen from shore, so it was impossible to gauge their accuracy. Many spectators assumed the gunners had missed.[45] The explosion was surprisingly flat. The centre of the vessel rose a little, and a rush of water and debris fell in a shower around it, but the sound was barely audible and the commotion subsided very quickly. To an audience half expecting the Crystal Palace to shatter, this promised glimpse into the nature of modern warfare, not likely to be experienced again in fun or in earnest by this generation or the next, was disappointingly brief and unspectacular. 'What did it all amount to?' asked a *Telegram* reporter, whose answer probably represented majority opinion:

The cannon made plenty of rattle, but I couldn't see anything hit.
It wasn't the least like a battle, and that I think all will admit.
Of course, there is nothing too hard meant, but really I cannot applaud.
You may call it a splendid bombardment – I call it a common place fraud.[46]

Although the advertised attraction fizzled, the spectacle of the crowd compensated. Because of the delay, more people were able to attend than otherwise would have been the case, and the effect of extraordinary, unanticipated degrees of fatigue and frustration could be appraised.

The volume of mail enquiring about the date of the bombardment, and a half holiday granted to most of the city's factory hands and many of its clerks, had primed officials for a large turnout, but even they may have been surprised by the numbers. 'Never in the history of a Toronto crowd has such a gathering been got together as that which assembled in and around the exhibition grounds yesterday,' reported the *World*, though its estimate of thirty-five thousand individuals was conservative. The *Mail* put the total at somewhere between fifty and sixty thousand, far more than the forty thousand Oddfellows who had assembled in the city two years before. Whatever the actual figure, everyone agreed that the extent of the assembly was remarkable. On the lawns in front of the Crystal Palace, packed bodies made it 'utterly impractical for anyone desiring a change of position to make his way through,' while roofs on the grounds were 'black with people.' Thousands of others lined the shores at Parkdale to the west and at Toronto Island, or watched the proceedings from boats.[47]

The event affirmed the difficulties of controlling large assemblages. Around the artillery pieces, in particular, mostly male spectators continually surged forward to inspect the instruments of destruction. Gunners used abusive language and horses to drive them away, knocking down several men and boys in the process. The antagonized audience cursed them right back and did what it could in the way of reciprocal torment, mainly pressing in so close that riders got caught up continually in gun traces, flagstaff ropes, and each other's spurs. One sergeant, in the midst of an extended oath, suddenly found himself being launched from the saddle when his horse was prodded with a thistle. Police finally pushed their way to the scene where, with 'a few sharp decisive words or a smart repartee,' they managed to cool tempers. They were much less successful in stopping thousands of people from trespassing onto the grounds, or from demolishing the western fence near the waterfront. As this went on, according to the *World*, the police were 'completely demoralized and could not cope.' The association's treasurer claimed that 20 per cent of the entire body of spectators had entered the grounds illegally.[48]

Despite these problems, the firm consensus held that this was 'a good humoured, holiday-making crowd' that posed no social danger. It was overwhelmingly respectable, so much so that the *World* claimed it consisted mainly of 'what would be called in English caste slang, the middle class.' Indeed, it was not a faceless agglomeration at all, but a gathering of the wider community whose discrete elements remained clearly visible: 'Private citizens of Toronto and farmers from the surrounding country, Catholic priests and Protestant clergymen, soldiers and lawyers were all to be seen among the excited throng. Women and children were there in thousands, and in innumerable instances, whole families down to the baby in arms were present.' There was nothing approaching disorderly or riotous conduct, concluded the *Mail* reporter who penned the previous observations.[49]

The event could have been interpreted as typical mob unruliness, but was not. Why were the destruction, the trespassing, the kerfuffles, not to mention lots of minor incidents of fainting and alcoholic excess, downplayed? A variety of factors were at work, including the patriotic atmosphere and the presence of large numbers of females. The predisposition to see this crowd in a favourable light was obviously related to the assumption that this was a safe occasion to gather. In turn, that assumption derived to no small degree from the fact that the event was sponsored by the Exhibition Association. Its high social prestige had mitigated an extraordinary range of transgressive lapses.

The point is not that this one incident suddenly overturned pathological fears of mobs, but that it was part of an ongoing process through which positive crowd experiences became a more normal expectation of urban life. The fair, among other spectacles, represented a festive, seemingly non-partisan situation that provided reassurance about the intentions of large gatherings and made people eager to participate, despite inconveniences. Once those situations were established, they helped authorities learn how to handle crowds, helped individuals adapt to being part of large public assemblies, and helped demonstrate that these occasions could occur without undue disruptions. There was always an awareness of the potential power of the mass. 'Legions of police could not have restrained the crowd had there been any disposition to riot or panic,' commented a reporter who obviously contemplated those possibilities at a particularly packed grandstand show in 1890. Apprehensions about crowds were not eradicated, but they were reduced considerably.[50]

No aspect of the attempt to build confidence at the fair was more important than the efforts of manufacturers to demonstrate the quality of their products. Without their participation, the Industrial would have been a much diminished affair, with much less cultural prestige. Business supported the show partly because of its potential for actual sales, but also because of its ability to enhance positive impressions of products and organizations.

The fair was so connected to the process of generating confidence that many companies took pains to justify their absence. A Toronto undertaker announced that he had no display at the 1882 show in deference to popular opinion that reminders of death did not belong there. Two years later, a sporting-goods dealer explained that alterations to his premises kept him away. Companies regularly tried to turn non-attendance to advantage by claiming to be too busy filling regular orders. One manufacturer told a trade publication that he would not dare to look any of his waiting customers in the eye.[51] This was a clever ploy, but firms that did show up naturally had a wide range of confidence-boosting tactics to draw on as well. The chief strategy, exhibit display, will be addressed at length in chapter 3, but here brief mention will be made of some of the other prominent techniques used to create positive impressions of goods and their creators – namely, advertising, opening windows to corporate existence, providing free samples, offering demonstrations, conducting tests, and displaying awards.

The most obvious way to extend the reach and impact of a fair presentation was to advertise it in newspapers. Up to 1884, both the *Mail* and the *Globe* approached exhibits as news, attempting to provide coverage of all significant booths. Though likely instructed to pay particular attention to regular purchasers of space, reporters had some leeway to emphasize what had genuinely impressed them. After 1884, reviews of individual displays were restricted almost entirely to paid 'Exhibition Notices.' Now, at fairtime, as one cynic put it,

> The business editor doth ply his trade,
> The puff is written and the price is paid.

The *Canadian Manufacturer* complained that while all other parts of the show were covered free, businesses were charged twenty-five cents a line. This was unfair to the companies and unfair to consumers, since unscrupulous operators could pay to have poor products praised lavishly. Perhaps that was the point. Even exhibitors expecting positive reviews valued increased control. They could determine the extent of coverage and express exactly what they wished to get across. A blurb for the Gutta Percha and Rubber Manufacturing Company in 1886, for example, indicated where the display was located, the range of products made by the firm, why these goods were superior to the competition, and who would be on hand to talk to visitors. These notices were deliberately constructed to look and read like real news. Penned for the most part by regular newspaper staff who used a conventional reporting style, they were integrated into the other coverage of the fair and set in exactly the same type. There were many ordinary ads that made no pretense to objectivity, as well, but the 'notices' were particularly credible because the evaluations seemed disinterested.[52]

The most popular advertising materials were handouts distributed at displays. According to a *News* reporter in 1886, the tons of paper given away every year were one of the marvels of the fair. The visitor who took everything offered was soon downright encumbered. The content of this matter varied widely. The Canada Oil and Paint Mills complemented a display of linseed and derivative products with an instructive four-page pamphlet on the refining procedures and uses of flaxseed, illustrated with a handsome bird's-eye view of its factory on Front Street. Some companies, not just piano manufacturers, gave out sheet music. In 1895 the Hyslop bicycle booth was besieged for copies of 'Blooming on the White-Rimmed Wheel.' Other firms gave away fans, calendars, perforated mottoes, and trade cards, many chromolithographed in gorgeous colours. Company products or activities involving their use were sometimes depicted on these print products, but many images and texts were completely extraneous to what was being promoted. Pastoral landscape scenes, sentimental views of women, children, and animals, and inspirational thoughts abounded, such as Nestlé's Psalm of Life offered to mothers at the 1880 show. So did patriotic motifs. One of the most prized cards at the 1886 show was a portrait of the queen given out at Ruse's Temple of Music.[53] These souvenirs, carried home and hung on walls or pasted in scrapbooks, could leave an ongoing impression of a company's prosperity, importance to the nation, and determination to satisfy customers. A fair was not the only place such materials were distributed, but probably nowhere else could so many be collected in so short a time. The competition may have pushed companies to produce special things that would stand out.

A few concerns tried to impress by encouraging consumer contact with actual workplaces and workforces. In 1891 both Samuel May and Company, maker of billiard tables, and the Heintzman Piano Company extended open invitations for factory visits. Less willing to cope with unpredictable intrusions, the *Globe* held an annual 'at home' so subscribers could see how the paper was produced. At the 1899 event, carpets and palms were rented to brighten the premises, and an orchestra was hired to entertain seven thousand people who came to inspect the giant presses and typesetting machines.[54]

For some businesses, it was easier to bring workers to customers. Company bands, for example, were almost certain to draw appreciative audiences. On Grangers' Day in 1881 the two musical groups that entertained in front of the grandstand were both work related. The Upper Canada Furniture Company Band from Bowmanville made an impressive appearance in blue uniforms with yellow facings and shako hats with white plumes. The Massey Company Cornet Band played just as well without elaborate costumes, though the difference in appearance may have rankled. Five years later its twenty-four members were resplendent in dark-blue uniforms with tricolour braid and helmets surmounted by red and white plumes. These manifestations of corporate culture had a double-edged advantage for a company: they enhanced the loyalty and satisfaction of workers and they boosted the confidence of consumers, who assumed that orderly, disciplined employees participating in a firm's voluntary activities also cared about the quality of goods they produced.[55]

A more common confidence-building strategy, less disruptive to the production process, was the distribution of free samples. Sometimes they were dispensed in highly imaginative ways, such as the packets of Old Chum tobacco thrown from a balloon in 1903. Most giveaways were comestibles. It was a standing joke that a little patience could procure a square meal at no cost: 'After a lady has had a cup of tea, a cup of coffee, a cup of cocoa and a cup of some patent substitute for all three, together with a bit of cream cheese, six samples of various breakfast foods, a little jelly, a pickle or two, and perhaps a cracker, it is doubtful whether she takes home much appetite for dinner.' Of all the senses, taste probably requires the most trust for experimentation. For new, unfamiliar products, including the beverage made by the Kaoka Manufacturing Company, prepared samples, made correctly by trained staff, were an astute way of breaching consumer resistance. For more generic commodities, such as baking powder, trial-size packages to be taken home, sometimes with printed recipes, fostered label identification and loyalty.[56]

Companies whose products did not lend themselves to free sampling often favoured demonstrations instead. Since one of the best ways to impress potential buyers was to show them products in actual use, pianos, sewing machines, lathes, and farm machinery were in fairly continuous operation, often in unusual ways to attract audience attention. Goldie and Lambert promoted its band saw with a worker who cut cubes of black walnut into thirty or forty pieces, then invited onlookers to fit them back together. Another concern used two dogs to run its small threshing machine. Some demonstrations were more in the order of special events, staged for maximum dramatic effect. This technique was a favourite of fire-fighting equipment manufacturers. In 1884 a company that made hand-grenade-type extinguishers set ablaze a temporary fence in the middle of the horse ring, then doused it in a few seconds with three of its devices. Several years later the Waterous Company of Brantford put on a similar show with a steam-powered fire engine.[57]

No demonstrations seemed more persuasive than head-to-head competitions between similar commodities. Results of tests arranged by individual firms were usually suspiciously decisive. Ed Lawson, operator of a baking concession on the grounds, made breakfast cakes from samples of different baking powders provided by the W.D. McLaren Company. All who tasted the results agreed that the ones made with 'Cook's Friend' brand were superior. Curiously, 'Cook's Friend' was distributed by McLaren. Some competitions, however, were clearly legitimate, including an 1883 contest between two new writing machines, the typewriter and the caligraph. All three judges agreed that the latter was simpler in its construction and better at producing multiple copies, while the former required less effort and produced cleaner-looking letters. Two rated the caligraph slightly higher, while the other leaned towards the typewriter to the same degree. An 1880 comparison of portable engines that took a week to complete, supervised by impartial experts, also produced no clear winner.[58]

Inconclusive results from real tests like these were hard for the public to assess and hard for companies to use to advantage, even if they showed up relatively well. Much more satisfying for both parties were awards, which conveyed unambiguous impressions of superiority. A weighty medallion with an impressive crest made abundantly clear that something was worth a closer look. Firms with sizeable collections of prizes from various fairs often made them a focal point of presentations. The Dominion Piano and Organ Company had a large case of gold and silver medals in its Temple of Music. Renfrew and Company, furriers, showed eleven gold medals and a number of diplomas. The Ayr Agricultural Works exhibited an awesome fifty-five medals won in recent years by its binder.[59]

In terms of what was available within Canada, probably no awards had more prestige than the ones given out at the Toronto Industrial, or so said Minister of Agriculture John Dryden in 1892. As at international expositions, some commendations were given to unique products in recognition of high quality, ingenuity, or consumer benefit. In 1884, for example, Professor Vernoy of the Electro-Therapeutic Institute on Jarvis Street won a first prize and medal for his electro-medical battery, a device that 'harmonizes with nature and anastimoses with the nerve currents of the system, assisting nature in a way superior to any other curative principle, and in a manner altogether different.' Clearly, nothing else directly compared with it.[60]

Even a single bronze medal had lasting advertising value. King & Co. incorporated theirs into the firm's logo.

Most awards did involve some real competition, and the way triumphs were publicized indicates that they were extremely useful in the crowded marketplace. 'Reindeer' brand took out a full-page ad in the *Canadian Grocer* to celebrate an 1895 medal for condensed milk. The Ontario Beekeepers' Supply Company depicted an 1884 prize on the back cover of its catalogue. R.W. King and Company, makers of power knitting machines, incorporated its 1882 award into the firm's letterhead.[61] As rewards, medals were far more valuable to industry and commerce than token monetary prizes, simply because they were easily reproduced in two-dimensional advertising images.[62]

In the art and agricultural departments, cash and ribbons were more meaningful, but success was just as coveted. The same impulse to boost confidence was evident in other parts of the show. In everything from breeding stock to oil paintings, producers had the same aim: to persuade buyers that their particular merchandise represented top value and ought to be acquired. Techniques used to impress varied, but in every sector this goal was a priority, and judgments by impartial experts were highly persuasive.

While awards boosted confidence in winning entries, they also boosted confidence in the fair itself. These trophies, after all, pointed to one of the most important rationales of expositions – to identify what was best in current artistic, agricultural, and industrial production; to reward the hard efforts of winners; and to inspire losers to better efforts. Most of the individual strategies to build confidence could be used elsewhere, but only the fair seemed to provide an honest assessment of accomplishments, based on wide, easily accessible comparisons. That was the theory. Practice often fell far short.

For producers in all categories, a lot was riding on competitions. Winning was fine, but falling short bruised egos and perhaps did significant damage to public confidence in things on which livelihoods depended. Inevitably, complaints about the competence of judges and the processes of adjudication abounded, and some organizations, deciding the risks were too great, simply declined to be considered for awards.

On occasion, losers or their supporters protested winners' tactics. The runner-up in the 1880 medical appliances class, who insisted the winning entry had been imported and was thus ineligible, had his own award taken away when the charge was disproved. The association seemed determined to discourage frivolous sniping, although, in 1899, directors did hold back prize money after the sudden death of eight milk cows on the grounds was attributed to 'manipulation' of their udders.[63] It was usually safer to cast aspersions on judges than on other exhibitors.

Some charges of incompetence may have been justified. In 1880 the judge of railway 'frogs,' used in switching, apparently had no idea what they were, while a stove judge adamantly insisted that heat could not radiate from a coal-oil stove, even though an adjacent thermometer showed a temperature of 208 degrees. Several years later, an irritated breeder pointed out to the *World* that a prize-winning lamb had two permanent incisor teeth, which appear only after fourteen months.[64] In the Ladies' Department, alleged ineptitude was often described as bad taste. 'A Non-Exhibitor' in 1880 felt that the rewards in those classes had gone to the most hideous submissions. Similarly, at the end of the century, 'Onlooker' protested that the prize in raised gold work had been given to an uninspired bonbon-nière, whose gold embellishment consisted only of dots in circles, rather than to a tray of 'decidedly artistic design with exquisitely modelled flowers and leaves.' The unfairness had ruined her enjoyment of the whole ceramic exhibit.[65]

A few critics trying to comprehend bizarre decisions alleged outright bias rather than ignorance. Only rarely were judges accused of direct conflict of interest,[66] but there were many charges of favouritism. According to the *Farmer's Advocate* in 1882, first prize in Aylesbury Ducks had gone to a broken-down bird worthless for breeding purposes, but owned by an influential member of the association. When two prizes for fruit won by the Hamilton Horticultural Society were switched without explanation from a first and a second to thirds, the *Hamilton Spectator* wryly noted that the new winner, a prominent exhibitor of fruit wine, invariably returned from the show with numerous cases of empty bottles.[67] Whether these gripes had substance is impossible to say, but regular suggestions of mechanisms to eliminate bias, from appointing judges who came from outside Toronto to shielding the identification of exhibitors prior to competitions, suggest widespread concerns. Judges, for their part, often tried to protect themselves by splitting prizes and multiplying honours, much to the dissatisfaction of the fair's management.[68]

The more important disputes about judging involved philosophical principles rather than subjective deficiencies. Not all points at issue were worthy of deep consideration. Probably few others shared Ed Shrapnel's indignation that second prize in oil paintings of dead game in 1879 had been given to a picture of a salmon. On the other hand, it was legitimate to ask whether the prize for the best milk cow should be given for the quantity of milk obtained or the value of the products that could be made from the milk, whether beef prizes should go to animals loaded with fat or sleeker entries preferred for breeding, and whether awards for industrial products should go to specially made exhibition pieces or to regular production models. If these discussions sometimes verged on the metaphysical, as in the suggestion of a cheese maker that 'taste' be included with 'flavour' rather than treated as a distinct quality,[69] they did underscore the fact that excellence, no less than beauty, was in the eye of the beholder.

When these substantive questions arose, the goal of critics was not simply to vent at stupid judges but to rationalize and clarify the criteria on which decisions were based. This approach was taken especially in the agricultural sector, where competition was considered essential to progressive farming and where a bad showing was not financially devastating. As one reporter put it, 'the awarding of a prize for wheat, for instance, to one farmer, is not calculated to injure the trade of his neighbour who shows, but does not get a prize. The prize has rather a salutary effect upon all farmers, and encourages them to emulate one another in the growth of a superior class of produce.'[70] It was farmers, therefore, who were most preoccupied with reforming the judging system. Two of the most popular suggestions – using single judges to eliminate the confusion created when prizes were decided by committee compromises, and judging by points with scorecards to encourage consistency in evaluations and to give exhibitors a better idea of where improvement was needed – had been introduced by the turn of the century, though they did not end dissatisfactions by any means.[71]

In industrial and commercial categories, where a bad showing could be financially injurious, the tendency was not to reform but to bypass the uncertainties of competition. 'Let the Ladies Judge,' urged the proprietor of the Great Housekeeper's Emporium on Yonge Street, in an ad feigning indifference to awards in the house furnishings department. 'We want no Silver or Bronze Medals, but something more lasting, more worth having, *the patronage of the ladies*, and to obtain that we devote our whole time and business abilities.' The Gananoque Carriage Company brought thirty wheeled vehicles and ten sleighs to the 1888 show, but competed for no prizes; the object was simply 'to meet their many customers.' The linseed products of Elliott and Company were exhibited as samples only and not for competition, though care was taken to emphasize that they were recognized as equal to the best anywhere in the world.[72]

Of course, when a firm refused to put this kind of assertion to the test of independent assessors, competitors pounced on its credibility. The Waterous Company hung a sign on one of its engines at the 1881 show, announcing it was not entered for awards because judges could not distinguish between specially built models and models in regular production. Haggert Brothers responded immediately with a sign advising that their engine was in the competition because it feared no rival. To avoid losing or looking bad by sidestepping competition, some companies decided not to show at all. The attendance of only four manufacturers of boots and shoes in 1881 was attributed by a *Mail* reporter in part to the general rush of business, but also to concerns about the prize process. 'If a hundred show in any one class,' he pointed out, 'only three men of the hundred will leave the exhibition satisfied, and they are the three who take the prizes.'[73]

The preferred course of many exhibitors was to do away with prizes altogether. Manufacturers in several classes had exercised this option at the very first show, requesting that judges recognize only recent improvements that were noteworthy.[74] The Exhibition Association quickly realized that this approach eliminated a great deal of discontent and increased industrial participation as well. The annual report after the 1879 show strongly recommended the discontinuation of prizes in nearly all classes of manufactures. 'Your directors find that this is the desire of a large number of exhibitors, as no matter how much care is taken in the selection of judges, it is impossible to give satisfaction and in many cases an injustice is often unintentionally done to the exhibitor.'[75]

The association was quick to implement the recommendation whenever manufacturers in a particular class requested it with relative unanimity, and it justified the decision however it could. In 1883 and after, it announced that prizes had been done away with in textile classes, so each mill could display its whole product line together. In 1881 it lamely explained that prizes would not be offered for billiard tables because no 'practical men' could be found to judge the class. Presumably, any number of 'impractical men' would have volunteered.[76]

By 1883 prizes had been stricken off for cotton and woollen goods, wearing apparel, hosiery, furniture, and bookbinding. More were discontinued in subsequent years until finally, in 1888, all prizes in manufacturing departments were abolished, 'a course which, while not acceptable to some few exhibitors, your Directors have reason to believe gave satisfaction to the much larger number of exhibitors.' The association reserved the right to award medals or diplomas to exhibits of outstanding merit that seemed to call for special recognition, but this appears to have been done rarely.[77]

Most companies remained hostile. As late as 1900, representatives of the Canadian Manufacturers' Association affirmed their opposition to prizes in industrial departments, 'as they consider that wares displayed under such conditions do not always fairly represent the merit or quality of the goods placed on the open market by the various exhibitors.'[78] Such barking may have been necessary periodically to restrain enthusiastic exhibit committees, but manufacturers had effectively drained their sections of the prize system in less than a decade.[79]

Professional artists had succeeded even more quickly and thoroughly. In 1880, after just one year's experience, most had declined to send in productions, and the exhibit of art that year was not impressive. The artists let it be known that they favoured the elimination of the prize list, with the money being used instead to cover shipping costs. It was demeaning, they suggested, to evaluate art according to crude monetary standards. Its qualities could not be tallied the same way as a stock animal or a piece of machinery. The *Mail*, however, was blunt in suggesting that their real fear was being shown up, possibly by amateurs.[80]

The next year, when the Ontario Society of Artists was given complete control of the art department, including the appointment of judges, it promptly abolished prizes for professionals. The exhibit would be much better than before, it claimed, because the reputation of the organization was at stake; its members would exercise considerable care in selecting items for display so the department would not look ridiculous, as it had at the previous show. Art, it seemed, could be judged, and that was the point: with the possibility of public humiliation removed, members were persuaded more easily to submit their work. The society's Annual Report noted a marked improvement in the quality of the exhibit. Though the show was not 'of a character to prove directly remunerative to the artists concerned,' it was 'a source of great pleasure to many people and if continued, will exercise a powerful influence in cultivating a taste for art.' At subsequent shows, management of the Art Department passed back and forth between the society and the Exhibition Association, but the professionals continued to abstain from the contests for paltry cash sums. Instead of having their work evaluated by others, they took the view that they were teaching the public 'correct ideas on art matters.'[81]

The unfettered competition of all commodities, evaluated by impartial experts, was conceived as a powerful instrument for stimulating progress and creating public confidence. Yet for understandable reasons, producers who were more impressed by what could be lost than gained quickly dismantled many of its pieces. Even in the agricultural sections, where the apparatus was most firmly grounded, suggestions of skewed results and complaints about the calibre and criteria of judging were constant. Still, by putting goods on display, in or out of competition, producers gave the impression that they were encouraging the most searching examinations and comparisons. Despite the retreat from competition, an aura of confidence about material progress and increasing technical competence continued to permeate the fair. After all, the evidence of advance was there to be seen, year by year.

~~~~~~~~~~~~~

The problem with the fair as an instrument of confidence in modern life was not simply that it did not meet expectations but that, in some ways, it actually intensified anxieties. The most obvious manifestation was the appearance during fairtime of some of the most powerful symbols of the lurking perils of urban existence – confidence men and women.[82] The exhibition attracted not just honest citizens looking for pleasure and excitement, but astute sharpers intent on fleecing the gullible and unwary.

By no means was their presence in Toronto limited to the few weeks of the show, but this period was particularly suited to their endeavours. Chances of remaining unnoticed were greater where so many visitors were congregated amid the general movement. More people in town meant more potential victims, including ones inexperienced with city ways and determined not to be seen as naive or unsophisticated, and ones who would soon return to homes far from scenes of crimes. The fair drew confidence men and women like a magnet, and the newspapers were full of accounts of their activities.

Most crimes of this sort were small scale, unsophisticated, and perhaps even spontaneously conceived. Many tricks, such as befriending rural folk and then taking advantage of them, were perpetrated by members of the poorer class on individuals who also came from modest circumstances. John Love, a 'quiet farmer' from St Andrews, struck up a conversation with several men on York Street who took him on a tour of the city. Shortly after they left him on the Esplanade, he noticed that his wallet was gone. William Campbell from Aurora was taken on a saloon crawl by two new friends, and then to a vacant house on Berkeley Street where all three collapsed in a stupor. When he woke, his friends were missing along with his watch and cash. He had no idea who they were. David McNeilly, a farmer from Jarvis, was being shown the town by several men who beat and robbed him as soon as they reached a secluded spot. John McFarlane of Vaughan, picked up by two strangers at Union Station who rowed him to a lonely spot on Toronto Island, was a little more astute. When he got suspicious and refused to leave the boat, they threatened to blow his brains out if he did not hand over his money, but he chased them off with a pocket knife.[83]

Occasionally, hicks got the better of locals. In 1882 two innocent-looking girls who rented a room on Ontario Street during the 1882 show departed with a number of family valuables, while an older man, 'whose clothing had a provincial cut about it,' got very drunk on other people's money by flashing a roll of bills as he headed into a King Street dive. The swarm of vultures who treated him eventually discovered that the wad was composed of advertising flyers.[84]

Passing phoney money was, in fact, a staple confidence activity. Hardly a year went by without some public warning to be wary of 'the queer.' Sanford Johnston, a pedlar arrested in 1901, carried a variety of bogus bills, including a $5 Bank of Toronto note, a $10 Molson's Bank note, and three different $5 American notes. Even clumsy counterfeits were easier to get rid of during the fair, when business was brisk. John Sheehan's poorly executed $2 bills confiscated in 1893 had a plug for a clothing store on the reverse side. A $10 Molson's Bank note in circulation in 1900, made by a photographic process, was very poorly done, but still took in a grocer on the Danforth.[85]

The other advantage of fairtime for counterfeit frauds was that the city was full of visitors from distant places whose possession of unfamiliar looking currency was plausible. Saloon keeper Angus Kerr gave $3.95 in change for a bill from the non-existent Bank of Western Canada, but it was not even necessary to fabricate materials, since paper from institutions that had gone belly up was easily obtained. At a time when notes were issued by many private banks, it was hard to keep track of which were sound and which were not. In 1892 the *World* published a list of twenty-nine defunct Canadian banks whose bills were worthless. This came in the aftermath of the energetic activity of Chauncy W. Riggs of Buffalo, who spread a large number of notes from the failed Bank of Prince Edward Island around the fairground. A decade earlier, Henry Stewart and George Musson, professionals from Detroit, were nabbed with a sizeable sum of Confederate money.[86]

The ready availability of this material was a temptation even to amateurs like the Haliburton County man, eventually released for previous good character, who obtained $200 in Confederate paper from an Indiana firm for only $2.50. At least he got the goods he paid for. Actual chances of delivery on a somewhat similar offer circulating in 1892 were dubious. This one took the form of a letter from a man claiming to have been superintendent of steel engraving for twenty-eight years at one of the largest bank-note companies in America. During that time, it claimed, he had forged duplicate plates that could not possibly be distinguished from the real ones. Now seventy-five and too weak to operate on his own, he sought trustworthy accomplices. Partners could invest no less than $200, which would buy $1000 in bogus bills, and no more than $5000. He was, he admitted, taking 'a dare-devil chance' to secure the confidence and cooperation of a stranger. If the proposition was objectionable, he trusted that the recipient 'will not be so heartless as to betray one who is willing to be your friend and benefactor.' It is doubtful if many in Toronto tried to take advantage of the offer, but not because people were honest or the story too far-fetched. Rather, though allegedly an exclusive offer, the letter was mailed extensively throughout the city and became public knowledge. Although the perpetrators offered to arrange meetings where samples could be examined, the timing just prior to the fall fair season might have indicated a hope that some recipients would act quickly to take advantage of approaching opportunities.[87]

Some con artists preferred to work with real money. In the slip-change scheme, the thief made a purchase with a large bill, getting a number of smaller ones back. Tucking one of these surreptitiously into a pocket, she or he would then ask the proprietor to make up the apparent mistake. A variation was to pay for an inexpensive item, such as a nickle cigar, with a large bill, then produce a coin and ask for the return of the original bill, having already extracted a portion of the change. Another ploy was to fold a bill so it was counted twice. These flimflams were hard to detect if done in busy places and if the take was modest. Once the transaction was over, no concrete evidence of criminal activity remained, and even if detected in the act, a perpetrator could pretend to have made an honest mistake. Still, people did get caught. Manuel Firsch, alias Solomon Goldstein, was nabbed in 1893, perhaps because the two victims who complained were cheated of ten and fifteen dollars, relatively high amounts, and perhaps because they were more inclined to press charges against a Jew.[88]

Promises of work could also be effective confidence lures. A man who advertised in the *Telegram* for five employees needed during the exhibition, offering to provide details for three cents, had very modest ambitions. Less than three weeks later, however, the operator of a phoney labour bureau collected two dollars each from two hundred men as a deposit for sending them to jobs on the West Coast, and then he disappeared. Hugh Clark, a recent arrival in the city, put down a returnable deposit of twenty-five dollars in response to a classified ad offering both instruction in the art of window lettering and help in finding a job. His suspicion was kindled the first day when he and another applicant were left to dither with paint brushes and bits of glass, so when thirty more men appeared the next, he asked for his money back. The 'manager' retreated to a back office for the cash, and disappeared through a window. William Morrison, from Port Hope, met two men who promised to pay his fare to England if he looked after some cattle on board ship. He was persuaded to float them a short-term loan of three hundred dollars, which would be returned when arrangements were made. Morrison quickly realized he had been cheated and led police to one of the culprits, but the other with the money, and therefore the evidence, could not be found.[89] These employment-related scams were probably tried at all times of year, but fairtime was perhaps especially lucrative because of the presence of so many people from outside, including agricultural labourers nearing the end of harvest who had to think of finding other positions, and people hoping to remain permanently in the exciting urban environment.

One of the most common instruments in confidence operations was the watch, partly because it was easily disguised and partly because it had symbolic as well as monetary value. A good timepiece was a mark of wealth, respectability, and social importance. The ability to demarcate time precisely was an indication of being attuned to modern ways and values, of being integrated into the complexly scheduled fabric of urban life. It is not surprising that rural people tended to be especially interested in acquiring impressive ones.[90]

Union Station at fairtime seemed to be perennially full of near-destitute travellers compelled to hawk valuable chronometers for next to nothing. John McManus, a Peterborough area man, waiting for his train in 1887, was approached by a sad gent asking directions to a pawn shop where he could get money for a ticket home by selling a magnificent-looking gold watch and chain. McManus was examining the articles, at his own request, when a jeweller just happened along, spied the objects, and appraised the chain alone at forty dollars. Falling for the bait, McManus traded for it with his own watch and a dollar. After having his new acquisition appraised, he complained to authorities. This confidence team of George Cain and Jacob Levi had already stung a Parry Sound youth, who exchanged his watch and ten dollars for what was purported to be a gold chain with a large nugget of raw gold attached. The lump of smelted brass into which a few pebbles had been pressed evoked general laughter when shown in Police Court. Cain had spent much of the previous fair period in the Toronto jail for similar activities.[91]

Watches were not the only commodities used to conjure expectations of windfall profits. One of the most unlikely but successful scams was executed in 1893 by a mysterious stranger claiming to be an escaped Siberian exile with thirty-five pounds of gold to sell. An interested buyer was found, who, after a complex series of negotiations and tests, and after being fed a hint that the gold had been stolen from an American bank, was persuaded it was genuine and with a market value of eight thousand dollars. He paid less than half that, for a suitcase full of brass.[92]

Notwithstanding the importance of realistic props, the success of any scheme depended fundamentally on persuading the victim of the perpetrator's trustworthiness. At fairtime in Toronto, there seemed to be three main ways to win this confidence. The most common was to manipulate prevailing expectations about ethnicity, gender, and class. The second was to demonstrate personal knowledge of the victim. The third was to convey an impression of integrity and stability by operating out of a fixed, seemingly legitimate location. In the case just described, which involved Jewish pawnbrokers, bonds of race and perhaps language were crucial in establishing a connection to the victim and a context in which the willingness to part with gold for less than half its value was believable. An even clearer example of the effectiveness of ethnicity in cementing credibility took place in the Italian community in 1891.

Pietro La Mantia, a fruit and cigar store owner on Queen Street, was victimized by a stranger who initially claimed to be looking for more palatable fare than was served in regular Toronto eateries. Building on the intimacy of a shared cultural background and shared meals, the traveller confided that he carried a quantity of gold coins he was afraid to leave at his hotel. La Mantia not only agreed to keep the horde in his own hidden strongbox but gave away the key. A day later, the stranger was gone – and so was nine hundred dollars of La Mantia's money.[93]

The expectation that one would not be betrayed by a fellow countryman who shared the difficulties of an alien, hostile culture was obviously strong. So was the assumption that modestly behaved females were entirely moral. This too was a useful tool for breaking down suspicions. An elderly woman travelling by train to Toronto was taken in by a well-dressed younger lady who boarded shortly before Cobourg, sat down beside her, and struck up a conversation. At Cobourg, where they went out together for some air, a gentleman appeared who was introduced as the younger woman's husband. At the last minute, he remembered he had forgotten to cash a cheque and had no money to buy a ticket. The older woman loaned him twenty dollars and watched the couple head inside to the wicket. They never returned.[94] It was a clever racket, because victims were unlikely to disrupt travel arrangements by lodging complaints immediately, when the pair were still close by. Gender stereotypes about men could be used just as effectively. The befriending and waylaying of rural males, for example, relied heavily on shared assumptions about masculine behaviour.

As both Pietro La Mantia and the lady coming through Cobourg found out, class expectations were also manipulated. Where middle-class victims were intended, and where large bills or supposedly expensive goods were involved, a facade of affluent respectability was a prerequisite. Some criminals used things like clerical collars and medical bags to insinuate the right impression, but usually it was enough to appear in the right clothes. A young Samaritan who offered to help a Belleville man loaded down with luggage, then promptly ran off with his coat, was granted immediate trust because he was well dressed. James Doyle, a well-off farmer from West McGillivray Township, was stung because he automatically assumed that a presentable stranger was on the up and up. Doyle was waiting at Union Station for his train to depart when he began talking with someone who identified himself as a Chatham merchant, in to see the fair and secure his fall stock. A few minutes later, an authoritative looking official arrived, notebook and pencil in hand, demanding money for excess baggage. Since the merchant had no cash, Doyle loaned him more than seven hundred dollars on the understanding it would be returned with 'a good shave' at Chatham. The men went off to attend to the loading, and disappeared.[95]

The circumstances of this case suggest that the thieves knew quite a bit about their mark before approaching him – where he lived, when he was leaving town, and how much money he carried. To what extent they used personal knowledge of him in establishing their credibility is unclear, but this kind of information was very effective in building trust. Obviously, more preparation was required to track specific victims, but more elaborate schemes with the chance of larger takes were possible.

Alexander Begg, a merchant from Orillia, was the intended goat in a phoney lottery ticket scam, an old standby in the confidence trade.[96] He encountered a well-dressed young man on King Street who professed to know him, his family, and his town. Begg immediately took a shine to his new friend, who soon remembered he had an American lottery ticket and wanted to see if he had won. They entered a room over King Street, where another stylishly dressed young man indicated that the ticket was worth $2000, but required a deposit of $270 to secure the prize. The winner, without the necessary cash on hand, asked Begg for a loan. Begg had only twenty dollars to spare, but agreed to write a cheque for the rest. No sooner was the ink dry than the attendant disappeared. Begg got suspicious and hurried over to his bank, where much to his relief he found that the manager had refused to hand over such a large amount to an unfamiliar customer. By the time police got around to the King Street room the birds had flown, though later that day Charles Ross Henderson, alias Bunco Charlie, and two associates were arrested.[97]

James Stoughtenburg, not so lucky, was snared in a trap that called for even more coordination. While visiting the exhibition from Markham Township, he likewise encountered someone who claimed to know him and who gave him a twenty-five-dollar cheque towards the construction of a new Methodist Church in Victoria Square Village, the cheque to be negotiated at Kent Brothers Jewellers on Yonge Street. About 6:30 in the evening, as Stoughtenburg was leaving the store with the money, he was hailed by a man in a buggy parked directly in front who asked if he was not staying at Lemon's Hotel. The driver had seen Stoughtenburg there that morning and offered him a ride back, since he was going that way.

By the time they passed over the Don River, Stoughtenburg realized he was far from the hotel. When asked about his direction, the driver replied he had to make a short call a little further on, then would turn back. As Stoughten started to complain again, a chloro-formed handkerchief was stuffed in his mouth and two accomplices suddenly appeared who knocked him unconscious. He awoke the next morning in a marsh, relieved of five hundred dollars, including the donation to the church. The thieves were well prepared or thor-ough, because much of the cash was not in pockets but distributed in secret places in his clothing.[98] In this case and the previous one, respectable appearance was important, but more so was affirming the individual identity of the victim. By seeming to possess personal knowledge, the perpetrators took advantage of the sense of being alone in a place far from home, flattered the desire to be recognized as a figure of consequence, and lessened inclinations to question their own motives. Acknowledgment of the victim's social identity was a scaffolding that carried much of the weight of their own invented ones.

The third technique for creating trust, operating out of premises that seemed legitimate, was in some ways the most disturbing because it was used so brazenly, notably by fake auction houses that sprang up just before fairtime throughout the commercial district, particularly in the vicinity of York and King streets. Operators rented premises on short-term leases, brightened facades with flags and banners, took out temporary auction licences, and set about to bilk the public. Some specialized in fake Oriental carpets, cheap sil-verware, or shoddy oil paintings, but the most common goods passed off were watches, generally culls covered in thin gold wash and got up to look expensive.[99]

Some sales were made across the counter, but the auction format was preferred, with a pitch that this was bankruptcy stock that had to be sold without reserve bids to the public rather than the trade. Touts on the street hustled unwary passers-by inside, where bogus bidders feigned excitement and pushed up prices. At one spot investi-gated by a *News* reporter in 1895, 'the tool at the door signalled to the man of the hammer whenever a "jay" was approaching and instantly that gentleman began his solicitations. When Ruben Glue was gone the auctioneer invariably sat down and relighted his cigar until the next relay of victims arrived.'[100] City residents were not immune to the flash of these places, but rural customers were the main targets, not necessarily because they were less discerning consumers but because they were likely to be further away when the gold wash wore off or the mechanism broke, and they were probably less sure of themselves in seeking redress.

This was not always the case, but even when complaints were lodged they were not taken very far, as Mary Ann Weatherly, a farm wife from Bruce County, discovered. In town for the 1890 fair, she wandered into the auction rooms of one A. Curtis Roebuck at 112 Yonge Street. The auctioneer, Henry Hyam, showed her a watch that, he claimed, was solid gold worth $60.00, and of such quality that he would guarantee it for fifteen years. The price was a mere $4.25. She could take it to a jeweller, and if it was not as represented, her money would be refunded. She paid, went immediately to a legitimate store, where she was told it was no good, returned to the auction room, and asked for a refund. Hyam refused, saying he did not do that kind of business. When she continued to press, he passed her on to another man who ordered her off the premises and commenced to sprinkle the floor near her with water, forcing her to retreat out the door.

Probably few disgruntled customers, especially if they had trains to catch, pushed the issue beyond this point. Weatherly did. She went to the police, who sent a detective with her to interview the auctioneer. He offered $10.00 to settle the matter, but she declined. A summons was issued for obtaining money by false pretenses and the case was heard in Police Court the next day. After Weatherly told her story, the defence lawyer suggested she be refunded the original purchase, a resolution the magistrate urged her to accept. He heard another witness, James McCuaig, a grain merchant on Front Street, tell substantially the same tale, and held that case over, but he warned that charges would likely be dismissed since it was almost impossible to establish *prima facie* guilt.[101]

Obviously, some people fared far worse than Mrs Weatherly. They not only got saddled with bad watches but paid outrageously for them in rigged bidding processes. One farmer forked out $9.00 for something worth about $1.50. Two women spent $18.00 and $21.00 for watches that together did not cost $5.00. Another victim, pushed out the door by an 'ex-pugilist' when he returned to complain, put up $22.50 for a mechanism appraised at less than $4.00.[102]

Even people with no intention of buying got badly swindled. One farmer who entered an auction room just to observe saw a refined-looking elderly gentleman bid on the lot being held up. The auction-

eer refused to accept the offer and denounced the man as a Yonge
Street jeweller trying to obtain stock more cheaply than he could
through a wholesaler. Claiming to be under firm instructions to sell
directly to the public, the auctioneer requested the jeweller to leave.
The old man complied with an injured air, but motioned the farmer
outside, where the latter was enlisted as an agent to obtain a particular consignment. Bid as high as $20.00, the farmer was told; the
jeweller would wait to reimburse him, with a generous consideration
to boot. Once the watch was secured, the jeweller was nowhere to be
found. What struck the reporter covering this case was the 'superior
appearance' of the nefarious pair. The 'old rascal' looked like a scholarly gentleman, and the auctioneer, a typical city man of business. It
was no wonder, he concluded, that inexperienced strangers were
deceived by such smooth operators.[103]

There was widespread indignation that these places were allowed
to operate. For a mere fifty dollars, the city seemed to be granting
licences to defraud. Suggestions that auction permits for anything
less than a year be disallowed were not taken up. Perhaps the city
needed revenue; perhaps it was pressured by landlords who preferred short-term occupants to none; more likely, it could not prove
deliberate fraud and could define objectionable practices only in
terms so broad that legitimate vendors were also hampered. And so
the rooms remained, visible reminders for those who recognized the
true nature of their business that cupidity and deception were all
about.[104]

The pigeon taken by the bogus Yonge Street jeweller got his money
back. When the gold began to wear off three days later, he went back
to the auctioneer and then to the police. He was unusually persistent
and lucky. Probably only one victim in ten tried to get a refund, and
of those, only one in ten was successful. The year before, several men
stung for ten and twenty dollars in similar schemes were observed
around King and York streets trying to unload their purchases for a
dollar. They had decided to chalk up the losses to experience, but
other recourses had probably come to mind. No wonder auctioneers
surrounded themselves with toughs, though one at least did not
carry protection far enough. In 1903 Herbert Bedford was arrested a
few days after arriving in the city. He was charged with robbing
Henry Hyman, keeper of an auction room on York Street – probably
the Henry Hyam who had dealt with Mary Ann Weatherly. Hyman
was waylaid after closing up, beaten (with the loss of three teeth),

and relieved of $8.20. The incident had all the markings of consumer protest.[105]

Undoubtedly, many more confidence crimes occurred than were reported in the press. Victims, especially if their losses were small, often kept silent rather than suffer the added indignity of appearing foolish and perhaps immoral to others. Yet it also seems apparent that the threat posed by confidence men and women was exaggerated. Of the thousands of people in the city at fairtime, only a small percentage were led astray through arts of practised deception, including those who wandered into jewellery auction rooms. Inspector Stark of the Toronto Police was only being sensible when he advised visitors to the fair, and others, to 'fight shy of all strangers who display any unusual tendency to cultivate speedy acquaintance,'[106] but the exercise of such prudence led mostly to diminished social interaction with ordinary citizens, not the warding off of hidden criminal danger.

For women, the injunction to maintain distance from strangers was especially strong and isolating. Don't make acquaintances on cars or in hotels, and don't sit alone in public parlours, was the advice of the *Christian Guardian* to 'Girls Travelling Alone'; 'better be alone in your room and read than make yourself an object of comment.'[107] Men who had adapted to urban ways were also wary, for navigating the shoals of confidence was not simply a matter of repulsing others but of restraining the self. Any show of enthusiasm, any gesture of good will towards a stranger, might be misinterpreted, causing embarrassment or worse. One reporter related the agitation he experienced while purchasing a travel ticket from an ordinary clerk. On the surface, the exchange was entirely proper: 'Yet all through I felt the influence of a strange repulsion. He treated me exactly as a policeman treats a prisoner in the dock – as a suspicious character who has to be guarded against, and who may cheat, lie, steal, or murder, on the slightest opportunity.'[108] Clearly, even small indications of public suspicion could be disconcerting.

Stark's warning, then, had a powerful resonance. There was a deep popular fascination with the doings of the reprobate yet intelligent scoundrels who victimized through masquerade, a fascination primed by a long-standing advice literature on the dangers of false-hearted strangers[109] and sustained by the eagerness of newspapers to relate the most recent depredations. The stereotype of the confidence criminal was a fixture in Victorian discourse, its meaning, at a superficial level at least, clear: not everyone was what he or she appeared to be. People in the most elegant clothes, with the most polished manners, exuding the greatest candour, charm, and sincerity, with the most respectable connections and the most expensive possessions, could turn out to be hardened villains. They misrepresented themselves and they misrepresented their things. It was impossible to tell from surface impressions who was legitimate and who was not, especially if the circumstances of acquaintanceship were fleeting. Constant wariness, constant public reserve, were advisable.

There were enough real confidence criminals to give the stereotype credibility, but its cultural power was produced not so much by the damage they did as by the social anxieties they highlighted. The confidence man or woman was a symbol of the difficulties of identifying the real, the genuine, the trustworthy, the substantial, the reliable in an anonymous, mobile society, full of wondrous new scientific discoveries, technological marvels, industrial profusion, and entrepreneurial exuberance.[110] Making accurate determinations was a vexing problem, one that the Toronto Industrial Exhibition, along with hundreds of other fairs and expositions, was designed to redress. It was not a perfect instrument. Integrity, excellence, and worth often turned out to be highly subjective qualities. Moreover, while the show assuaged some anxieties about confidence, it simultaneously attracted to the city a larger number of the very criminals who intensified concerns about it. Yet this failure may have suited almost perfectly the needs of an evolving industrial capitalist system.

What the fair experience tended to do was persuade people that they could feel reasonably confident about the possibilities of material progress, about the effectiveness of established political and social institutions, and about goods – not all goods, but ones that were mass produced by large, brand-name manufacturers who could afford extensive advertising and who sold through reputable dealers. They could feel confident about the quality, ongoing availability, and affordability of these goods. They could not feel as confident about other individuals, at least not ones who existed apart from institutional and corporate roles. As people became more alienated from each other, material objects became more attractive to them. To sooth their growing solitude, to alleviate their uncertainties, to demonstrate their own trustworthiness, people reached out for goods. In an expanding industrial, corporate economy, it was a useful response.

3

Display

Modern urban culture was, and is, a culture of the eye. It was not simply that visual images, especially photographs, became increasingly important in the representation of reality, but that in the actual interactions among people and things the power of other senses weakened. In a crowded environment of anonymous neighbours and paper-work jobs, touch and taste tended to become private pleasures, while smelling and hearing were overwhelmed by the density of competing sources and diminished by the growing reticence to provide outsiders with clues to identity. Increasingly, understanding was rooted in seeing, the most magical, according to Roland Barthes, of all the senses.[1]

As ratios of perception began to shift, the desire to see and the need to see became more acute. One indication was the proliferation of fairs and exhibitions, many, like the one in Toronto, organized around transparent Crystal Palaces that symbolized aspirations for vision. With the growing primacy of the eye came a corresponding emphasis on display, on the presentation of things in manners calculated not just to impress, but to elicit specific types of responses. By the time the Industrial Exhibition was inaugurated, ambitious Victorians were already sensitive to the possibilities of display. The overstuffed middle-class parlour, full of furniture and bric-à-brac in intensively decorative styles, testified to a conviction that status was grounded in the display of possessions whose appearance counted far more than their substance. Machine-made objects with clawed feet, clusters of fruit, scroll work, or other imitations of aristocratic models were designed to demonstrate social worthiness on the basis of refinement of taste.[2]

The impulse to display was not new, but it began to enter the public realm in unprecedented ways. Those who wanted to communicate to the public increasingly turned to visual means, and no one desired to communicate more than makers of consumer goods. In the old commercial world, relatively small-scale producers had greater opportunity to speak to buyers in human voices. With the advent of mass production, allowing single firms to supply hordes of customers spread over vast reaches, such dialogue was impossible. Marketers, through the development of sophisticated display venues and techniques, now worked towards making goods speak for themselves. Their goal was not simply to broadcast the availability and virtues of specific products but to generate increased demand by reformulating the whole cultural meaning of consumption. Their project was one reason why exhibitions proliferated so quickly in the late nineteenth century and why fairgrounds became dynamic places, though controlling meaning in such liminal environments was extremely problematic.

If commodities became subject to display, so did people. Reticence towards strangers intensified curiosity about them, but forced individuals to judge unknowns mainly on the basis of what could be seen. Gazing became a complex urban art, requiring as much skill in deflecting attention from the self as in surreptitiously examining others. Crowd situations, like those created at the fair, were ideal places for an intrusive eye, but even here some eyes were more privileged than others. No activity in the late nineteenth century escaped the parameters of race, class, and gender, and gazing was easiest for white, middle-class males.

Though manufacturers wished otherwise, the most fascinating targets of vision were people, not goods. This was well understood by some pedlars of popular entertainment who turned human beings, often non-white, often female, into commercial attractions to be gazed at with impunity by paying customers. But it was also grasped by marketers of consumer goods, who recognized that no matter how elaborate or imaginative a fair display, goods could not speak entirely for themselves. Gender, class, and race characteristics of human bodies were essential in controlling and channelling the meaning of consumption.

This chapter tries to explain why exhibitions were useful for those trying to display commodities, to outline some of the main techniques used to show goods at the Industrial, to describe the parameters of gazing at strangers – a favourite activity of visitors – and to suggest how and why the meaning of goods was inextricably bound to the meaning of bodies.

~~~~~~~~~~~~~~~~

A primary purpose of the Toronto Exhibition, like all exhibitions, was to make the fruits of human endeavour available for public view. The 'big show,' as it was often called, was no misnomer. Everything of significance seemed to be laid out for inspection all at once.[3] Small fees were required to penetrate the arcane mysteries of sideshow tents, but here, too, customers were assured that once inside, nothing would be held back.

People came to see, and when the possibilities of looking were obstructed, they complained. Hindrances to the examination of horses entered for show, for example, created perennial dissatisfaction. Indiscriminate mixing of breeds in the stables, poor signage and general disorganization inspired much of the grumbling, but most galling to serious students of horse flesh was finding prize animals locked up in closed stalls or removed prematurely from the grounds.[4] The association tried to encourage access by building larger pens that facilitated viewing and by requiring deposits on animals taken home overnight,[5] but many owners remained skittish. After the judging in 1903, one stable could not produce a single horse it had entered in competition; its valuable animals had been replaced with hacks. 'The idea that the public who pay their money to see the Exhibition have any right to see the horses, never seems to enter the heads of either grooms or owners,' an exasperated reporter had declared years before. Not much had changed in a decade.[6]

Industry, on the other hand, needed no prodding to make exhibits accessible. Businesses came to the fair to show their goods. Display was fundamental to their participation. This is obvious, and yet it is not entirely obvious why the exhibition format was used so extensively as a venue for gaining public notice. After all, goods were regularly displayed in shops, which often seemed to do a better job. In 1880 the *Globe* admitted that many stores contained four times the number of dry goods shown at the fair. A year later it acknowledged that the cottons display was insignificant compared with what could be found on the floor of a wholesale outlet, while the *Mail* suggested that grocery and provisions exhibits could be matched any day of the week in ordinary shop windows. Reporters insisted that the exhibition was worth seeing because it featured more competitors than most stores, because its displays were 'representative,' and because viewers would experience a 'sense of gratification' not experienced in looking over the stock in a warehouse, yet the differences between the fair and regular stores were not always clear.[7]

The Crystal Palace was full of temporary branches of local retail businesses. Perhaps there was some rationale for the Golden Lion, a leading local dealer in ready-made clothes, to show off new lines, but the presence of Todhunter, Mitchell, grocers on Adelaide Street, or optician Charles Potter, who rented a stand in 1887 to supplement his King Street premises, seemed more distant from the ideals of an exposition.[8] Despite frequent complaints that the real purpose of the exhibition had been compromised and the character of the Main Building destroyed by allowing it to become an ordinary salesroom, the palace inevitably took on the appearance of 'a vast store.'[9] By the end of the century, the extensive presence of Toronto's leading department stores, Eaton's and Simpson's, made the illusion even stronger. Department store buildings tended to draw on architectural and decorative devices developed for exhibition halls, and in Toronto the circle of influence became complete when Eaton's began donating its ample resources to decorate the entire Main Building.[10]

For retailers, the financial return was sufficient to warrant the cost of participation, even though similar goods were available in their regular locations. The example of the department stores is instructive. For many years, they resisted renting space at the fair, encouraging visitors instead to go downtown. Bragging of its five acres of selling space, which took longer to see than the Crystal Palace, one Eaton's ad insisted it was 'an exhibition in itself.' If there was anything in the city that reminded both citizens and visitors of the Main Building of the Industrial fair, the text continued, it was their department store.[11]

A scant three years after publishing this confident puffery, management had changed its mind about direct involvement. Prospective visitors to the Main Building were now told they would think they had been magically transported to the great store on Yonge Street. Simpson's followed suit, also using advertisements that suggested an equation between the grounds and its downtown location.[12] Eaton's and Simpson's were well-known fixtures on the retail landscape. Their decisions to create a formal presence on the grounds suggest

Reception Day in Millinery Department

New Fall Hats and Bonnets will have their first showing to-day. Paris, London, and New York will be represented—and you'll be interested in seeing what's to be the correct styles in Millinery for the coming season.

This 1899 Simpson's ad hinted that ladies should visit a special event at the department store downtown before going to the fairgrounds, but it also revealed the competition between the two attractions.

that a significant proportion of visitors were not making the trip downtown or that they were freer with their money in the Crystal Palace. For centuries, people had come to fairs to buy and sell goods. It was naive to think that ingrained cultural habits would erode simply because the event was called an exhibition.

Local retailers probably were careful about the selection of merchandise for fair booths. Todhunter, Mitchell, the grocers, made a speciality of coffee, chocolate, cocoa, and spices[13] – relatively lightweight luxury goods that may have been scarce or stale in outlying general stores. Perhaps not everything sold well at the exhibition, but some things did, and retailers took maximum advantage. A *World* reporter noted in 1884 that, as a general rule, retail trades had their booths ready by opening day, while manufacturers seemed in no hurry to get things in order until the second week.[14]

Many manufacturers, in fact, claimed that their displays were not intended to make money. Octavius Newcombe of the Newcombe Piano Company acknowledged that the average industrial exhibitor was looking for business, to be sure, but insisted that very few 'count on doing business or receiving benefits from the advertisement anything like proportionate to the cost of the display.' This profession of civic altruism may have sounded good to the public and made the association more beholden, but it is hard to take seriously. Piano and sewing-machine makers were notorious for hiring 'cappers' to eavesdrop on spectators and point out potential customers to booth attendants. 'If you speak favorably,' warned an irritated victim, 'the capper gives them the wink and you are worried half to death with their clack.'[15] As much as retailers, manufacturers came with the expectation of financial returns, from orders if not immediate sales. The chance to reach an exceptionally large market with a constant flow of new traffic, without having to maintain year-round facilities, was too good to pass up.

Retailers and manufacturers made money at fairs, but this does not explain everything about the attraction of exhibitions for businesses. After all, the decline in importance of fairs suggests there are, and were, alternative spaces for the exchange of commodities. So why did businesses bother with exhibitions?

The explanation relates to the changing circumstances of production and consumption. In the second half of the nineteenth century, as things like the American system of manufactures, continuous process technology, and scientific management revolutionized industrial efficiency, business was compelled to market more aggressively.[16] The only way to pay for expensive equipment and middle managers was to sell the expanded production they made possible. Generating consumption created novel imperatives for business. Perhaps the most basic was the need to clear away old inhibitions about spending and, the other side of the coin, to create and legitimize new desires. The task of the market was no longer simply to satisfy stable needs but to invent new ones, not merely to cater to existing tastes but to form those tastes. Traditional reverence for thrift, pride in self-sufficiency, and equation of luxury with moral corruption all had to be undermined. Goods had to be presented in ways that made them seem irresistible, indispensable, and available in such abundance that anyone could legitimately aspire to obtain at least some of them.[17]

Increasingly, business tried to persuade individuals that personal identity depended not on geography, family background, religious values, occupation, or similar things, but on choices made among consumer goods found in the market-place. The message struck a responsive chord. As anthropologists Mary Douglas and Baron Isherwood have pointed out, in any society, material goods make visible and stable the categories of culture, but in nineteenth-century North America and elsewhere, as local and particular identity became unglued, there was an extraordinary inclination to rely on goods as social anchors. Substantial, tangible, and real, goods provided a counterweight to vague but pervasive anxieties that traditional webs of existence were unravelling, leaving individuals to float without attachment to anything solidly grounded.[18] Goods were something to grip on to, something to give weight and identity to the self and others. Goods became devices through which people tried to resolve ambivalent feelings and social tensions, to project images of themselves, and to interpret the meaning of strangers. People responded to the lure of commodities because their own lives, not just the situation of industry, had become destablized by the proliferation of material things. The problem was embraced as the solution. If business wanted the public to be enraptured by goods, the public wanted to know exactly what things now existed in the social field and what their significance was.

For both producers and consumers, the meaning of goods became a central concern, but a problematic one. Business needed to stimulate desire in a society still suspicious of desire. It wanted to enhance the symbolic potential of commodities in a society where the unfixed, multivalent quality of symbols was likely to generate acute anxiety. Not surprisingly, as Jackson Lears has argued, producers struggled to control the flood of meaning let loose by the appearance of consumer goods.[19] In the face of a deep-seated understanding that objective surfaces could just as easily conceal as reveal, they had to persuade buyers that ornamental detail on a piece of furniture or a glittering wrapper was not camouflage for shoddy merchandise. In the face of a tradition of self-reliance, they had to convince customers that factory-made things were practical necessities that made life easier, not self-indulgent luxuries that eroded moral fibre. Marketers understood that channelling the flood of meaning required the careful presentation of goods in spaces where clear directions about the reading of meaning could be impressed. The project of control proceeded on many fronts, including labels, print advertisements, and billboards, but it also focused much more attention on environments where goods were actually exchanged.

Companies sought to present their products in controlled contexts where magical environments could be created to manipulate consumer psychology. The impulse was apparent in regular stores, especially department stores, but also in mundane establishments like corner groceries, where serious attention began to be given to counter, floor, and window display.[20] However, the potential to suggest the transformative qualities of goods by linking consumption to spectacle quickly became obvious, and fairs became a prime site for establishing the connection. They were environments that already carried expectations of spectacle. Indeed, as James Gardner and Caroline Heller have pointed out, awareness is so intensified by the occasion and the environment of an exhibition that even ordinary objects, widely available, are 'seen for the first time.'[21] The cavernous nature of exhibition facilities made it easy to mount unusual presentations. Moreover, fairs stimulated consumer longing because the balance between display and purchase was weighted more heavily towards the former than in regular stores. As Thomas Richards has suggested, they established kinetic environments for inert objects where commodities were elevated above the mundane act of exchange.[22]

For many producers, a more concrete strategy for aggressive marketing was to intervene in the relationship between retailers and consumers. Again, the exhibition was a useful device to accomplish this goal. Many merchants disliked dealing with new products. New stock could create organizational and administrative problems, might prove to be unsaleable and, if already packaged, could erode skills, authority, and profits.[23] On the other side, as consumer enticement became more fully linked to spectacle, manufacturers were willing to invest in elaborate presentations that fostered public interest, while many grocers were not interested or were beholden to other suppliers. Exhibition displays, like print advertisements, were a means of bypassing a conservative or uncooperative merchant to create popular awareness of products and to bring consumer pressure to bear.

When companies had produced mostly bulk goods in anonymous form, they did not worry that messages about commodities were matters left to retailers and their customers. The human voice, applied in personalized encounters, seemed entirely adequate. When those companies had to address the consequences of vastly expanded production, that situation became intolerable. Now manufacturers wanted to be heard. Since companies could not hope to communicate verbally on a one-to-one basis the way merchants did, they tried to develop techniques that allowed commodities to speak for themselves. Trademarks, brand names, slogans, and standard packaging all formed part of this effort. Driven, in effect, to create new languages to reach consumers, they needed new spaces to get their messages across. Peter Stallybrass and Allon White have suggested that 'the formation of new kinds of speech can be traced through the emergence of new public sites of discourse and the transformation of old ones.'[24] Just as the proliferation and increasing sophistication of print advertising stemmed directly from the requirements of the new language of consumption, so too did business support of exhibitions. They were useful precisely because they were not under the thumb of regular retailers.

The relationship between manufacturers and retailers was not always competitive. Realizing that the producers' agenda could increase sales, and hence profits, many merchants happily accepted store display advice and paraphernalia offered by companies, which in turn were eager to gain access to critical sites where desire was translated into fiscal transactions. This sort of cooperation extended to fairgrounds. For smaller producers especially, it was often advantageous to graft messages to a local establishment's reputation, and cheaper to use its staff. For merchants, companies could provide display materials beyond a store's normal resources. At the 1903 Toronto show, for example, Eby, Blain, wholesale grocers, made an impressive showing by borrowing a gigantic percolator from the makers of Kin Hee coffee.[25] However, when producer and distributor pooled resources, there is no doubt that the former usurped a significant proportion of the latter's voice.

There was one more important reason why large exhibitions attracted business interest. The whole point of display was to generate confidence, and, as was suggested earlier, exhibitions were extremely successful engines of confidence. They not only reflected progress but actually seemed to foster it. At a time when many companies were relatively new and unfamiliar to consumers, appearing at the exhibition conferred an aura of respectability, prestige, and quality. As Robert Rydell has pointed out, by the mid-twentieth century fairs derived legitimacy by enlisting the support of private companies, but in the nineteenth century the reverse was true. Appearing at the fair seemed to align a company with all that was modern and noteworthy. A fine display in an exposition hall was somehow akin to a museum exhibit – highlighting what was most noble, creative, and desirable in the culture.[26]

If specific companies were unfamiliar to consumers, so in many cases was the new social ritual of buying. Many nineteenth-century people were reluctant to enter a store unless they were committed to making a purchase. Progressive businessmen, who understood how the allure of goods could break down customer resistance, made special efforts to persuade the public that it was welcome to enter premises with no obligation to buy. At the Mammoth House in 1886, out-of-town visitors were assured they could call in many times a day without ever being importuned by sales clerks. In 1891, when Eaton's remained open in the evening for a grand promenade concert, more than seven hundred employees were at their posts and all machinery was in motion, but nothing could be purchased. 'Don't be afraid to come into our store and ask questions about clothing,' urged an Oak Hall Clothiers ad in 1894. 'Ask all you want as to quality and price. Try on some coats and see how they fit. You can do this without being under any compliment to buy.'[27]

For some, old habits of circumspection were hard to discard. They felt constrained about taking up the time of a clerk unnecessarily, worried about being embarrassed if prices, often unmarked, proved too high, and distrusted assurances that no pressure would be applied. At the fair, however, it was understood that people might be just looking. It was, after all, an exhibition – a demonstration of accomplishments rather than a market-place. It was legitimate to ask questions and to inspect closely, without feeling beholden. As a half-way step towards new buying practices, confidence gained here could be carried back to regular commercial establishments. For merchants, similarities between the two environments were an advantage.

Exhibitions were important spaces for the display of consumer goods, then, not just because purse strings tended to be looser there, or because they were the only places where businesses could bring products to the attention of buyers. They were useful because they offered exceptional possibilities for suggestive presentations, for direct access to consumers, and for legitimizing new industrial products and processes.

Exhibitors of new industrial products came to the fair to redefine the meaning of commodities. Establishing meaning inevitably involves processes of contestation, and, even within the fairgrounds, modern businesses ran up against older forms of merchandising that were inimical to their designs. The debate at the Toronto fair was often cast in terms of the legitimacy of selling versus showing, although this description did not quite capture the character of opposing factions. Manufacturers were not really concerned about the selling of ready-made clothes by the Golden Lion or Oak Hall. They did not care whether Todhunter, Mitchell sold spices, or bee-keepers marketed jars of honey. What they did object to, along with the respectable retailers, were the patent-medicine fakirs and the hawkers of 'cheap john' jewellery.

These latter 'traditionalists,' for want of a better term, never articulated their position in words, at least not publicly. They did not have to. Their reappearance year after year, and the vehemence of their detractors, indicated clearly the viability of their interpretations of the meaning of goods and their methods of distribution. The 'moderns,' unable to expel these opponents on their own, frequently complained to the fair's management and the press.

Taking the high ground, they griped that the Industrial's real purposes were being undermined by too much direct selling. One exhibitor at the 1889 fair complained to a trade paper that the Main Building, instead of being a show-place for manufacturers, had become 'one vast salesroom for all sorts of wares.' A *Globe* editorial several years later expressed concern that the Crystal Palace was being turned into a bazaar, and urged a policy of selling from samples only.[28]

When critics tried to be more specific about what was wrong with selling, they focused on three problems, all connected primarily to the presence of older-style merchandising. They complained about the shoddiness of the goods being flogged. The proximity of cheap jewellery, useless gadgets, and suspect medicines undermined the integrity of all manufactured goods. They complained about the noise generated where selling was the only consideration. The oratorical powers of snake-oil fakirs, which 'awe the average hay seed,' produced a din that discouraged prolonged viewing. Finally, respectable exhibitors insisted that the choicest booth locations were occupied by the most doubtful enterprises. Meritorious displays were crowded into back corners and out-of-the-way places, or simply excluded. Too often, it was alleged, manufacturers who had gone to great trouble to prepare special exhibits could not secure adequate space to erect them, squeezed out by the excess of fakirs and vendors of petty inventions. Too often, access to legitimate displays in back corners was blocked by impermeable jams of people listening to sales pitches.[29]

As the crescendo of charges began to rise in the 1890s, the association felt compelled to respond, though nothing it did seemed enough for the big exhibitors. In 1899, after sales concessions in the Main Building had been reduced by 80 per cent from four years earlier, the *Canadian Grocer* whined: 'There is too much space given up to people whose purpose is not to exhibit, but to sell, and sell goods which are commonly designated "Cheap John" goods.' Despite more cuts the following year, there were still complaints.[30]

The intolerance was indicative of divergences that went well beyond those openly declared. 'Cheap Johns' challenged many of the strategies devised by new companies to stimulate consumption of their products. While modern marketing tried to make goods speak for themselves through visual devices, traditional selling depended on speech.[31] Its power to distract interfered with efforts to train people to look for meaning in new ways. While modern companies tried to interest consumers in things that were familiar and close at hand, traditionalists often used exotic foreign imagery for package designs and stressed the use of rare ingredients or materials from remote, unlikely sources.[32] While corporations pushed the consistency and wide accessibility of brand names, and the thoroughly conventional character of their employees, fakirs often presented themselves as exceptional individuals whose goods were the result of extraordinary experiences, insights, or luck, and unavailable in any other place. While companies appealed on the basis of quality, dependability, and value for money, traditionalists tried to entice with mysterious potencies and unbelievable bargains. While corporations wanted consumers to accept modest satisfactions, small luxuries, and marginal improvements in comfort, the claims of fakirs intimated the possibility of sudden, utopian transformations to perfect health and beauty, fabulous wealth, or intense pleasure. The ongoing presence of traditional marketers did create noise and blocked aisles but, more importantly, it made efforts to establish new kinds and sources of meaning much more difficult. In considering the project of modern manufacturers to recast the dynamics of consumption, it is important to remember that older forms of merchandising also remained compelling.

Largely unrestricted personal interaction with merchandise, including visual interaction, is a relatively recent thing. Although some shopkeepers, as early as the eighteenth century, were conscious of visual appeal, their techniques were limited mainly to trade cards, handbills, newspaper notices, and sometimes beautifully decorated signs. Late into the nineteenth century, windows were viewed primarily as sources of light; merchants who did think to fill them with stock, battling flies in summer and condensation in winter, tended to use makeshift fixtures salvaged from old packaging materials. On sales floors, most stores displayed only a few goods, in order to protect stock. When customers requested to see particular articles, they were brought out and handled by staff. Even in early department stores, if goods were not hidden away on shelves, they were jumbled in haphazard confusion on counters.[33]

Display techniques were not highly developed in other public realms, including ones like art galleries, where visitors were meant to study exhibits. The Toronto situation probably was typical of many provincial cities. At the turn of the century Arthur Hemming, a local artist, was appalled by the condition of the museum in the Provincial Normal School, the closest thing Toronto had in the nineteenth century to a permanent gallery. The identification of exhibits was extraordinarily uneven. There was no signage in the Classical Department, while in the Assyrian Room the labelling that had been done was in 'glaring white, three times too large,' and set into awkwardly placed oak frames that attracted more attention than the objects themselves. Engravings and etchings were arranged on no intelligible plan, a collection of stuffed birds looked 'as if much had yet to be done,' and the cabinet of shells had been thrown together 'higgledy-piggledy.' Display cases were covered with thick layers of dust, and unprotected items were filthy. Neglect was so general that visitors had no compunction about handling objects, to the point of chipping pieces off sculptures.[34] Hemming's complaints may suggest why merchants guarded stock, but also indicate, by contrast, the advanced nature of exhibition display standards.

The specialized art of commodity display struck observers as something quite new and modern, an outgrowth of the exhibition phenomenon. A 1903 *News* editorial pin-pointed the 1851 Crystal Palace show as the seed bed, suggesting that the rapid succession of international shows had advanced the art quickly as businesses began to realize there was utility in beauty. Toronto, it submitted, had finally caught on, perhaps inspired by the Pan-American show in Buffalo two years earlier. In the past, with one or two exceptions, local exhibits had been 'of the primitive, inexpensive and unattractive type.' Now, the show featured 'a collection of displays worthy of an international show, and an all-summer program. The whole thing is a product of the highest development of the art of exhibiting, and it will be a surprise to many that that art is so well developed among us.'[35]

The assessment was no doubt gratifying to both exhibitors and citizens, but it was also familiar. Similar pronouncements had been voiced since the fair began. In 1879 the *Mail* had praised 'the beauty and the apparently permanent appearance' of display structures. Instead of bundling goods together with hardly a dividing line between one firm and another, as was customary at other shows, exhibitors were displaying their wares 'in something like proper style.' It attributed the appearance of colourful canopies, handsome showcases, and expensive carpets to the influence of the 1876 Philadelphia Exhibition. In 1885 the *Mail* considered the 'increased taste and ingenuity shown in the mode of displaying goods' a noticeable feature of the show. The *Globe* expressed virtually the same opinion almost a decade later. Whether the improvement was the result of natural progression or the influence of the Columbian Exposition a year before was not clear, but exhibits in the Main Building, it enthused, 'are more tastefully arranged, the tawdry adornment of former days are giving place to neater and more elegant fittings.' The sophistication of displays seemed to reach new heights at each successive fair. Every year, as the *Mail* once put it, spectators had to admire the ingenuity of exhibitors before judging the merits of manufacturers.[36]

Charting the evolution of exhibition display is not easy. As David

Dean has pointed out, 'exhibition stands are ephemeral, the information about them fugitive.'[37] Even where descriptions or illustrations
exist, there is often little indication of what they looked like in relation to what was adjacent or how they worked. It is particularly hard
to get a sense of how new technologies of glass, colour, and light actually were employed. However, despite the relative paucity of information and evolving standards, the strategies devised by business to
attract attention and manipulate meaning were relatively constant.
They ranged from the most basic technique of focusing on the inherent design of an isolated product to employing extraneous elements
as offsetting devices, offering insights into the creation of goods,
demonstrating their use, altering normal scales of perception, and
playing up structural possibilities. Naturally, approaches varied
with the type of merchandise being shown, since some techniques
were not viable for all kinds of goods. Most displays used a number of
strategies simultaneously.

Large and bulky objects were often placed on floors or platforms by
themselves, partly because they were too cumbersome to manipulate
into grander arrangements and partly because they had sufficient
visual presence on their own. The Victorian fetish for exuberant decoration stood them in good stead. Stoves were 'of such elaborate
workmanship, beauty of design, and so highly finished and polished,
that at first sight they might be looked upon as elegant parlour orna-
ments.' Cash registers were 'ornamented elaborately in nickel work,
in scrolls and leaves.' A coffin was transformed into a 'brilliant spar-
kling object ... fitted in lovely subdued colors and mounted with
exquisite taste in metallic adornment that it seems rather to allure
than repel.' Not long since, reflected a Whitby editor, a rough coat of
red paint and a few black or blue lines were considered sufficient for
farm machinery, but no longer. 'Wood painting is now one of the fine
arts and the rivalry between different firms – each of which has its
own predominant color – is not merely in excellence of machinery but
in wealth of transfer and other embellishments.' It is reasonable to
suppose competition for attention at fairs had something to do with
the change. Speaking at a directors' luncheon in 1904, the premier of
Ontario, George Ross, ventured to suggest that any manufactured
article that did not attract the eye, no matter what its other virtues,
'lacked marketable qualities.' Many interpreted this sort of decorative extravagance as a sign of increasing national sophistication,
showing that Canadians were not given over totally to the practical.

Perhaps, though it more clearly demonstrated the derivation of North American popular tastes from aristocratic European models.[38]

No matter how highly embellished, goods left by themselves could produce an impression of severity, and most displays employed a variety of extraneous devices to give contrast to stark lines and to suggest positive contexts beyond the exhibition floor. Plants were ubiquitous. A simple potted palm, plunked beside a piano, showed up the beauty of wood grain, created an oasis of freshness in a packed, fetid hall, and helped visitors to imagine the instrument in their own parlours. Lacy ferns interspersed among piles of canned goods, like those in a Libby, McNeill display of tinned meat, offset the uniformity of standard packaging, and hinted at the natural origins and healthful properties of the processed product.[39]

Patriotic banners and flags were equally common. They were cheap, colourful, and useful in hiding unsightly elements of display apparatus, and they were also symbolically powerful. One of the biggest lessons advertisers had learned from the 1851 London Exhibition, according to Thomas Richards, was that 'the best way to sell people commodities was to sell them the ideology of England.'[40] Patriotic imagery was more consistent in London than in Toronto, where the Stars and Stripes was not uncommon in displays mounted by American companies, but in this bastion of imperial enthusiasm Union Jacks were endemic. Flags, shields, and bunting proclaimed the good citizenship of a company, intimated an association between national strength and corporate success, and implied an equivalence between the virtue of the nation or empire and the quality of the product.

Plants and flags were by no means the only extraneous paraphernalia employed. Canvas signs, draperies, mirrors, posters, and photographs were all regularly incorporated into displays. By the end of the century, so were electric lights, still a source of wonder as well as illumination. The Bow Park Company studded bulbs into cans of its cream cheese, giving its booth 'a soft creamy appearance.' All these devices gave displays complex visual textures and variety, usually at very modest cost.[41]

Another common display strategy was to offer insights into the origins of finished items. A simple but popular practice was to show samples of raw materials. The Gutta Percha and Rubber Manufacturing Company invariably had a potted rubber tree on hand beside its tables of boots and hoses. E.B. Shuttleworth brought some of the mineral salts and vegetable substances used to colour his inks.

Surmounted by royal coats of arms and Union Jacks, the Lever Brothers' booth at the 1903 fair proclaimed the essential Britishness of Sunlight Soap.

James Russel showed both the raw and the manufactured article in cocoas, chocolates, spices, and coffees. Often, raw materials were presented, not because they were unusual, but to provide assurances about the quality of ingredients. Breakfast cereal makers often decorated their booths with sheaves of grain to underline the natural origins of their products.[42]

Food processors, as a rule, shied away from references to intermediary stages of production between raw materials and finished product, but makers of durables had no such reservations. Specimens of every stage of silk production at the Corticelli Silk Company booth offered, according to one reporter, a whole lesson in natural history which could be gleaned from ten minutes of study. Moyer and Company illustrated the button-making process, and Slater Shoe, the shoe-making process. It was impractical for National Cash Register to transport machines in various stages of assembly, but visitors could take a simulated trip through their factory by examining photos incorporated into the display. Companies that made less cumbersome products sometimes did set up complete production facilities. A jewellery firm at the 1884 show brought a press that turned metal disks into souvenir medals. 'The machine,' said a *Globe* reporter, 'is always surrounded by a wondering crowd, as it may well be, considering the strange work it does.'[43]

Instead of documenting the manufacturing process, some companies tried to simulate the context in which goods would actually be used. Probably the most impressive use of this technique was by furniture dealers. At the 1886 show a model suite, composed of drawing-room and bedroom, was arranged jointly by Charles Rogers and Sons of Yonge Street and W.E. Marrett, painter and paper hanger, of King Street. The parlour, with armchairs, divan, china cabinet, and Brussels carpets, seemed especially realistic because it included an imitation log gas fireplace. Though located on the second floor, it became the stellar attraction of the Main Building, drawing thousands of visitors, including the lieutenant governor, the prime minister, and General Middleton, commander of troops in the recent North-West Rebellion.[44] Recognizing a winning strategy, Rogers duplicated the effort at subsequent shows and was quickly aped by other firms. The technique remained immensely popular. When Eaton's and Simpson's began to rent space at the end of the century, their displays were organized around suites of model rooms, which continued to 'rivet the attention of all spectators.'[45]

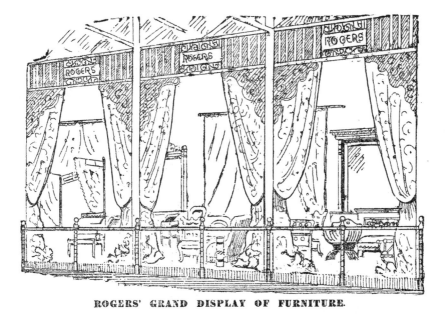

ROGERS' GRAND DISPLAY OF FURNITURE.

The model suite created by Rogers for the 1887 show was considered front-page material by the Toronto *News*.

The realism of model suites struck visitors as something quite unusual, but the essential technique was not peculiar to furniture companies. Piano makers and sewing-machine manufacturers often tried to create parlour settings with carpets, pictures, and curtains, while farm machinery, bicycles, and road-building equipment could all be seen in operation in various sheds or outside around the grounds.[46]

If realism was sometimes a surprising attraction, so were distortions of reality, as the popularity of displays involving alterations of ordinary scale attests. Miniaturization was not limited to 'Little World' sideshows. Many companies exploited the same fascination to draw attention to their productive accomplishments. Ship models, probably prepared originally for naval architects, were often recycled as exhibits. In 1888 the Polson Iron Works featured a model of a Canadian Pacific steamboat under construction in its Owen Sound yard. Two years later, Canadian Pacific itself had a model of the *Empress of India* on hand, and in 1903 the Allan Line showed its new royal mail steamship, the *Victorian*.[47] A number of firms tried to combine the appeal of miniaturization with insight into manufacturing processes. S. Schneider and Company constructed a tiny broom factory driven by a tiny water motor. A.J. Lord and Sons of Saint John, New Brunswick, produced small replicas of their rocking chairs, which were sold as souvenirs.[48]

Miniaturization was slightly problematic as an exhibition display technique because only a few people could get close at any one time. Altering scale in the other direction was more logical. Like most shows, the Industrial abounded with bloated re-creations of normally unremarkable artifacts. The Toronto Bag Works constructed its display room inside a twenty-foot-high bag made from a hundred yards of material. Dunlop made a huge tire to fit a bicycle wheel of corresponding size. The Canadian Rubber Company regularly displayed a nine-foot-long rubber boot. McLaren's Imperial Cheese built a tower using 'three heroic white opal jars' of diminishing volume to remind viewers that the product was available in different sizes. In the next booth, Carlings had a giant beer bottle sprouting flags. These 'polyisomorphs,' the term coined by Miles Orvell, helped visitors to locate individual displays, but, more important, the equation of bigness and goodness suggested the technical sophistication of a company, and the abundant availability, flavour, strength, quality, or value of its products.[49]

Blowing up or reducing everyday articles is common to festivals in many cultures, so it is not surprising that it was done by businesses at festivals of consumption. Dramatic alterations in scale that encouraged viewers to rethink the parameters of ordinary existence perhaps shattered the grip of conservative habits and persuaded them to try new sorts of goods. Regardless of whether intentions were so direct, there was something inherently playful about such manipulations, which disposed viewers to see industrial enterprises not as huge, soulless corporations intent only on extracting profits, but as protean creators, injecting fun into mundane existence. That playfulness was embodied by the 1889 Lever Brothers' display, which featured a forty-foot reproduction of the Eiffel Tower, centrepiece of the current Paris exposition. From one perspective, a miniaturization, from another, a giant object that loomed above visitors, it played with conventional expectations of size from both sides.[50]

The most common display strategies for manufactured consumer goods were rooted in their structural possibilities and associations. There were three main approaches here, though they were not mutu-

MacLaren's towering jars of cheese at the 1903 fair, and, behind them, Carling's giant beer bottle sitting atop a pyramid of kegs and cases. The interior gloom produced by such constructions was reduced by the skylights of the new Manufacturers' Building.

Taylor & Company's 'Pompeian Court' at the 1894 exhibition may have seemed more British than Italian in inspiration, but it took full advantage of the sculptural qualities of soap.

ally exclusive. Some of the most successful and elaborate displays were erected by firms whose products, like soap, embodied inherent structural properties. The Morse 'soap house' created in 1879 was the first of several striking presentations designed by Mrs Taylor, wife of the company president. Using more than twenty-eight tons of material, she carved a merchant's office with a desk and shelves, on which stood a basket of fruit, a clock, account ledgers, newspapers, and busts of the vice-regal couple, all made from different kinds of variously coloured soap. Her 1883 effort included soap urns full of soap flowers in their natural colours, and in 1887 she produced an entire wedding breakfast. The company's 1894 display representing a Pompeian court, carved by Mr Peterkin of Queen Street, featured soap pillars, mottled to look like marble, surrounding a life-size lion.[51]

Taylor's was not the only soap firm that created these sorts of displays, nor was soap the only substance used in this fashion. At the 1884 show, petroleum wax was sculpted into a variety of shapes, including a log house. In 1888 W.J. Stevens, candy makers, produced a model ship from sugar compounds. In 1903 the Canada Metal Company erected a tin man.[52]

A second technique, enamoured by companies that made standardized packages, was to use such goods as building blocks or bricks. The Crystal Palace abounded with towers and terraces of bottles, boxes, and cans. The most popular design was the pyramid. Small triangles of packages graced the counters and shelves of many displays, but, in the first decades of the fair especially, excessive reliance on much grander structures got to be irritating. 'The big pyramids of all kinds of things that now rear their stately heads are truly surprising,' admitted a *World* reporter in 1886. 'Table salt, axel grease, biscuits and patent medicines are piled ceiling high. In consequence, views from the gallery are so obscured as to be scarcely worth taking.' Several years later, another reporter complained that 'owing to the pyramidal exhibits that start up nearly to the ceiling,' a good deal of sunlight was excluded, making the interior 'comparatively obscure.'[53]

There were obvious reasons for the predominance of this particular form. On floor spaces that were congested visually as well as physically, tall displays could be seen easily and from wide distances. Pyramids provided the most height in relation to the amount of goods used, and their diagonal sight lines attracted and channelled vision. However, they were not the only shape employed. George Dawson and Company, wine merchants, stacked liquor bottles into two pyramids, but erected an arch between them. The Bow Park Cream Cheese display, designed by a specialist from New York, also took the form of an elaborate arch. Christie, Brown and Company made a terrace from all their varieties of biscuits. The 1879 display consisted of 296 cases reaching from floor to ceiling, each one containing a different product. As new product lines were added year by year, the display got larger and larger.[54]

Whether pyramid or block, piled to the ceiling or modestly arranged on shelves or counter, stacks of wares in some arrangement were used by almost all makers of packaged goods. This was necessary to compensate for the diminutive size of individual items, but other messages were intended as well. The multiplication of individual goods, each exactly alike, familiarized consumers with the

The 1887 Moxie Nerve Food pyramid (left), easy to construct and highly visible, indicates why this shape was used so extensively. The stand's sparseness, compared with displays erected after the turn of the century, points to a rapid growth of sophistication in booth design. However, compared with the Art Gallery (above) at the same show, the simplicity was strikingly effective.

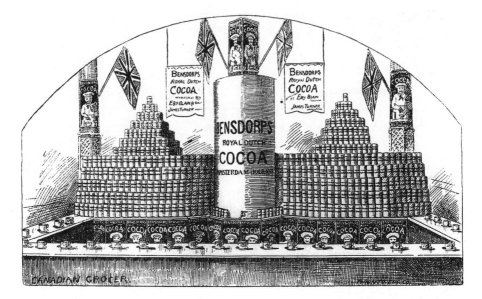

The 1891 Bensdorp's Cocoa exhibit, where visitors were dispensed small portions of the desirable fluid in front of a typical triptych structure.

appearance of products, allowing for quicker recognition on shop counters or shelves, and made the goods seem more normal, more an established part of regular life. It suggested there was a high demand for these items, so that, by implication, they were popular and dependable. It hinted at the size and wealth of the companies that produced them, companies so established and successful that they would not care to tarnish reputations or need to cheat consumers. Such piles suggested the consistency of industrially produced items, their unvarying quality, and their absolute interchangeability. They created an instant impression of an abundance that was minutely divisible, so that anyone with even modest financial resources could obtain a share. Perhaps there was also an intimation of a social philosophy in these arrangements. Just as each package was integral to the stability of the whole display, they seemed to suggest, so the use of the product by individual consumers would produce stability, abundance, and beauty in the whole social fabric.

While stacks of goods underlined the normative quality of industrially produced packages, they also created an impression that con-

sumer products were quite exceptional. Thomas Richards has noted
that almost no household products were displayed at the 1851 Crystal Palace Exhibition; those that were attracted few visitors and pro-
voked disparaging comments. Reactions seem to have been similar
during the early years of the Toronto Industrial Exhibition. 'There is
not much in a mere display of provisions to attract a well nourished
crowd of visitors,' commented a bored *Globe* reporter in 1881.[55]
Imposing towers of goods were designed to lend import to things that
at first glance seemed trivial. Perhaps it is not coincidence that many
displays had an almost spiritual cast. Narrowing pinnacles of tall
pyramids produced a gothic effect, like church spires. Arrangements
on counters and tables often resembled altars, as in a Bensdorp's
Cocoa exhibit that had a traditional triptych design. Such allusions
may have provided subtle reassurance that consumption would not
lead to worldly excess and that material goods were somehow aligned
with religious ends, but they inevitably connected displays with some
of the most impressive, resonant structures in Western culture. Even
if a spiritual link was not consciously grasped, there was something
immediately compelling and positive about many arrangements of
packages.

A third way of insinuating the structural properties of goods was to
frame them within external structures. Instead of simply piling commodities, companies constructed booths within which their wares
were displayed. Although difficult to document with any degree of
precision, there is evidence to suggest that by the end of the century
this framing approach dominated displays of small goods. The
Christie, Brown exhibit is a case in point. In 1894 its traditional wall
of stacked biscuit boxes was replaced with a finished case incorporating 420 triangular plate-glass sections, each containing a distinct
variety identified in elegant gold lettering. By 1903 they were using
an enclosed booth with 520 varieties in glass-faced boxes. From the
extensive photographic coverage in the *Canadian Grocer* of grocery
and related displays at the 1903 show, it seems that this approach
had been adopted by most companies.[56]

One reason for the change, no doubt, was a growing interest in
making displays portable and collapsible. Companies producing
national and continental brands showed their products at a never-
ending succession of fairs and trade shows. They preferred to recycle
exhibits, not simply to save on design, material, and construction
costs but also to reinforce the idea that their products represented

Two exhibits of packaged starch from the 1903 fair indicate the diversity of display techniques. One approach highlights abundance; the other, the preciousness of the product.

The Metallic Roofing Company booth at the 1903 show was more elaborate than most, but this firm was not alone in investing in an impressive, reusable display stand.

universal culture.[57] Christie, Brown, for example, bragged that its 1894 display had been created originally for the Columbian Exposition in Chicago.[58] Companies had to be sure that these structures would be effective, regardless of such things as ceiling heights or light conditions, so there was a tendency to rely less on imposing stacks of packages and more on elaborate decorative effects created with new technologies of light and colour.

A framed booth presented a sophisticated, finished image. Though in fact more portable, it looked more permanent, giving an impression of corporate dependability and stability. Miles Orvell has noted that a dominant mode in the popular culture of the late nineteenth century was 'the tendency to enclose reality in manageable forms, to contain it within a theatrical space, an enclosed exposition or recreational space, or within the space of a picture frame. If the world outside the frame was beyond control, the world inside of it could at least offer the illusion of mastery and comprehension.'[59] Containing the display in a framed booth not only reduced interference from competing attractions by centring an individual's vision more fully but also gave the impression that what was inside had special value.

If the grocery exhibits at the 1903 show were typical, booth designs drew from an eclectic variety of sources. The Crown Manufacturing Company devised something resembling a conventional wareroom to show its extracts, confectionery, and boiled goods, though its 'impressive business-like character' was offset by a ceiling of blue and yellow draperies to give a more festive impression. The Edwardsburg Starch Company booth seemed inspired by grocery store stock cabinets, while the octagonal glass booth of St Lawrence Starch resembled an inflated transparent kiosk.

At one time, domestic motifs had been common. In the first decade of the fair, Gurd and Company erected a little house from breakfast cereal packages, the St Leon Water Company made one from bottles, and the firm that produced Vegitine and Familine had a 'perambulating house that travelled around the exhibition's roadways.'[60] By the end of the century, however, booth designs drew much more heavily from classical architectural forms. Lever Brothers concocted something resembling the porticoed verandah of a stately home or fancy hotel, tying the virtues of cleanliness to aristocratic elegance. Tillson's built a small classical temple, perhaps to suggest the simplicity, integrity, and republican virtue of their pan-dried oats. These booths were fancier than many, but even square posts supporting a plain pediment gave an impression of stability and weight. All the techniques involving structure seemed to point to the possibility of grounding modern existence on the abundance of industrial production and the coherence of human creativity.

By the end of the century, popular expectations about the presentation of many things at the fair had become more demanding. Was it any wonder that Agricultural Hall failed to attract visitors, asked a *News* reporter, when vegetables were dumped in little heaps and fruits spread over a board 'as flat and uninteresting as a buttered pancake?' He advocated prizes for the best arrangements as well as the best qualities of natural products. Paintings jammed on the Art Gallery walls might represent a display of excellent art, commented *Saturday Night*, but 'it cannot be said to be an artistic display ... Four square walls of one room, on which are huddled almost 370 pictures, do not admit of much effective or congenial grouping.'[61]

More developed standards of display were not germinated solely by marketers of industrial products. Mary Douglas and Baron Isherwood have argued that the most effective rituals use material things to fix meaning, and the more elaborate the trappings, the stronger the intention to fix meaning. The growing sophistication of exhibition displays is just one example of a diffuse anxiety about meaning that showed up in the late nineteenth century in everything from theatre to fraternal ritual to state ceremony,[62] and the similarity of solutions to seemingly distinct display challenges is sometimes striking. The shafts, obelisks, and mausoleums that sprouted in garden cemeteries with the romanticization of death, for example, were not dissimilar from pyramids and temples erected in exhibition halls. After all, affluent middle-class families commemorating the departed faced the same task as business people selling wares: both wanted to convey the unique preciousness of their objects of attention in spaces that tended to be confined, crowded, and full of competing attractions.[63]

Although there was something final about funereal monuments, exhibition displays were inherently unstable. It was not simply that they were collapsible forms that everyone knew would be carted away at the end of a show but that what they said, or tried to say, was never entirely self-evident. Some messages were relatively clear. These grand corporate presentations indicated that productive capacity had replaced material need as the driving force of industry, that abundance was a fact of existence. Citizens, they suggested, were now expected to consume everything that technology made available in the market-place, and desire for those things was entirely acceptable. Displays intimated that social bonds increasingly derived not from religion or ideology, but from sharing the same goods. They accustomed people to think of advertising as a creative endeavour that was not out of place in the public spaces of a modern city.[64]

However, while the legitimacy of goods was established by displays, their precise meaning was not. What did a giant coffee pot or an arch of cream cheese packages studded with light bulbs really mean? As a viewer's attention shifted from pyramids of cans, to Greek temples devoted to soap or pan-fried oats, to giant pickles and beer bottles, meaning became elusive. According to Jackson Lears, when industry tried to control the flood of meaning unleashed by consumer goods, it sought a balance between artifice and authenticity.[65] With the purely visual elements of fair displays, that balance was possible only by rocking wildly back and forth between extremes of representation – a condition that did not make for stable understanding. Without a human presence, meaning was hard to fix.

The most unusual person to attend the fair in the nineteenth century must have been Li Hung Chang, the Chinese viceroy in charge of foreign relations who visited in 1896 on his way home from the czar's coronation. Reputedly the most powerful person in China after the emperor, his presence was considered truly amazing. The three greatest living men were said to be Bismarck, Gladstone, and Chang, enthused the *Christian Guardian*; the least likely and most distant of the three had actually appeared in Toronto.[66] Association officials were not slow to exploit a remarkable opportunity to boost the reputation of the show and attract the curious.

Chang was met at the exhibition station by a deputation of dignitaries, the Queen's Own Regimental Band, and thousands of spectators, many perched on fences, roofs, and tree branches. He was carried into the grounds in a sedan chair hoisted by four brawny policemen, where an estimated 100,000 people 'jostled and tumbled over each other' trying to catch a glimpse of his famous yellow jacket. After touring several of the larger buildings, he was conducted to the grandstand platform, where another throng watched more distinguished guests being introduced.[67] Horses and pigs, pianos and tractors took a back seat that day.

Eager to exploit the circus potential of his 1896 visit, fair officials exhibited Chinese viceroy Li Hung Chang on the grandstand stage. Seated in the shade of protective umbrellas, he is barely visible in the photograph, as he must have been to many spectators. Behind is the scenery for the evening extravaganza, *The Fall of the Bastille*.

Chang was not the only celebrity cultivated by the association as a feature attraction. The surest occasion to glimpse someone well known was the formal opening, when some notable delivered a platitudinous speech. For most ordinary folk, it really did not matter what was said, since they were too far away to hear anything. Still, they flocked to the ceremonies.[68] In an era before television, newsreels, or even the widespread use of halftones, and one taken with the science of physiognomy, just glimpsing someone famous seemed worth the bother. The association did its best to oblige the curious. The governor general, Lord Lansdowne, was considered 'a pretty good card' for the 1887 show, 'as it is not everyday that the rustics have an opportunity of seeing a live lord.' The *Telegram* reporter who made this comment hoped that Prime Minister Macdonald would put in an appearance as well: country people who had never seen him would consider it a treat if 'he would allow himself to be gazed at.'[69] Many elected officials sought publicity by attending – and they generally got noticed – but public interest in human exhibits was not limited to the famous and powerful.

'Will it be thought strange and somewhat indicative of stupidity if I say I was more taken up with the people who were examining the show than with the show itself?' asked the correspondent of a Port Hope paper. His reaction was entirely typical. Virtually everyone agreed that the kaleidoscopic crowds were 'a sight of deep interest,' 'the finest and most varied exhibit,' 'the best of all the sights at the fair.' Marketers had to accept that most visitors found their fellow creatures 'far more interesting than pyramids of canned lobsters or the metallic whirr of sewing machines.'[70] Oft-heard suggestions that most people really went to the fair to see the crowd[71] seemed borne out by attendance patterns. Every year, city residents were urged to come before the onslaught of rural visitors, when it was easier to get around and see things in comfort, and, every year, most Torontonians waited until the grounds were thronged.[72] For those at the fair, human bodies, famous or otherwise, were as much objects of display as any formal exhibit.

It wasn't simply that other bodies were endlessly fascinating. They were that, of course, but other pressures also impinged. In the modern city, it was impossible to know everyone by sight or even reputation. Mingling and dealing with strangers was inevitable. To operate successfully in the urban environment, it was vital to study others to try to ascertain where danger lay or where pleasurable sociability might be had. Seeing who existed in the social field was a survival tool as well as an instinctive pleasure. However, the eye was, and is, an aggressive instrument. Getting caught staring at others was not only embarrassing but potentially dangerous. Women who used their eyes too boldly risked unwanted attentions and loss of reputations; men risked provoking violence. In the city, it was necessary to observe others without seeming to be an observer; to practise, as John Kasson has put it, the dual skills of detection and concealment.[73]

One of the most obvious strategies for the successful accomplishment of the urban gaze was looking down on others from above. Hotel mezzanines, department store arcades, theatre balconies and boxes all allowed a viewer to scrutinize those below, whose eyes were less likely to wander upward. These architectural features were designed in the first instance to solve other problems, such as lighting and class relations, but they were popular in part because they were useful vantage points for spying.[74] Another strategy was to inspect others in crowd situations, where the sheer quantity of surrounding distractions meant less likelihood of discovery, and where flows were so constant that new faces appeared every instant. Both possibilities were maximized at the exhibition.

At no other regular time or place in the city were crowds as thick or as diverse. At no other time were there so many diversions to preoccupy those being watched. Lingering on the exterior balconies of the Main Building, hanging over interior railings on its upper floors, navigating the congestion in different halls, relaxing on lawns, strolling along walkways, joining the throng before an amusement attraction, or sitting in the grandstand – it hardly mattered. Everywhere, opportunities abounded to observe others with relative impunity.

There was a price. It was possible to remain undetected while watching others, but it was not possible to escape being the target of someone else's gaze. There was a certain amount of pleasurable excitement in this, but the prospect of being studied intently by strangers could be very disconcerting. Mack, a *Saturday Night* columnist, speculated on the reaction of two hypothetical rural citizens who brushed together in a crowd. As he imagined it, each would glare at the other, then scurry away in indignation, thankful for a narrow escape from a nefarious pickpocket.[75]

The Ladies' Department Committee ran up against this sense of vulnerability for real in 1884. Convinced that 'the type of beauty, which is the special characteristic of our Canadian ladies, is not surpassed by any country in the world,' it organized a beauty contest to be judged from portrait photographs. Contestants were promised the utmost secrecy: pictures would be identified by number, with only the names of the two winners released. The victor was to receive a fifty-dollar gold watch, and the runner-up, jewellery worth half that amount. Despite substantial prizes and lack of entry fees, there were no submissions.[76] The idea of the beauty contest ran counter to conventions of modesty, but its complete failure suggests that people, especially women, were reluctant to court public view deliberately, even at a remove.

Knowing it was impossible not to be the target of someone else's gaze, fairgoers prepared themselves for the encounters. One indication is dress. Genteel respectability was the norm. At a fair picnic hosted by the *Evening News* in 1893 for its street vendors, Davy O'Brien, 'king of the newsboys,' showed up in a 'swagger suit' of clothes consisting of sharply creased trousers, pink-barred shirt, white collar, immaculate tie, and stiff hat. He was not the only guest who 'made some small addition to their toilet in honour of the occasion,' and his impulse was typical. Kit Coleman remarked on an 1894 visit, 'everyone is dressed – more or less – in their Sunday best.'[77]

Photographic evidence suggests that women wore skirts, blouses, and fancy hats, while men, like Davy O'Brien, wore jackets, collars, ties, and hats. Clothing was generally so subdued that when a substantial number of men showed up in uniform on Fraternal Societies Day in 1887, the *Globe* reporter felt compelled to mention that 'the crowd looked more like one assembled for a holiday than is usual with sombre-costumed Canadians.'[78] Obviously, there were occasions when people did deliberately invite the scrutiny of others, but usually they did it as part of a group, often in uniforms that deflected attention away from their faces.

To some extent, gazing was an acquired skill. The lack of proficiency of rural folk, for example, could be striking. Country people from more intimate communities sometimes had no conception of the urban preference for anonymous seclusion in public spaces. Accustomed to forthright interaction with strangers, they assumed that city dwellers behaved in similar fashion. Another *Saturday Night* columnist described an encounter with an elderly rural couple who deigned to address, not just stare at, fellow passengers on a crowded streetcar. The woman was particularly chatty. She pushed aside a businessman's newspaper to engage him in loud conversation, leaned

ON THE STREETS

C.W. Jefferys's 1903 drawing for the Toronto *Star* of 'gawkers' newly arrived in the city.

forward to chat with someone at the far end of the car, revealed intimate details of her personal life, and insisted on saying goodbye in a general way to all on board when she got off. Though she had 'violated every rule that governs conduct in a street car,' none of the other passengers laughed. The reporter attributed this generous treatment to her age and gender, as well as nostalgia for older traditions of socializing, but many witnesses may simply have been floored by her audacity or too embarrassed to pay open attention.[79] Her garrulousness was unusual. Probably the more normal reaction of rural visitors newly arrived in the city was gawking – the involuntary focusing of vision and curtailing of speech produced by a combination of awe and intimidation. Such lack of control over the eye was considered a sure sign of country origins.

Ineptitude at gazing could be overcome, but degrees of opportunity for looking were never equal. Some people were clearly more privileged in seeing than others.[80] Inequalities of gender, race, and class were just as obvious in this as in other aspects of life. The availability, decoration, and posing of bodies was related directly to established social hierarchies. The white, middle-class, male gaze was paramount. It was not simply that it was more dangerous for others to use the eye as blatantly, but that white male preferences for viewing were most consistently normalized into the whole cultural fabric. The inequities of gazing were no more apparent than when the activity was transposed into commercial ventures. At the fair, this was most obvious in sideshows, where the appeal of many attractions derived from the extraordinary access they provided to the bodies of 'low others' – in this case mainly freaks, exotically presented non-whites, and scantily clad females.

A striking instance of the operation of the privileged gaze took place during the 1893 show. The acclaim and financial success of the Columbian Exposition midway induced Toronto officials to contract with Chicago impresario Sol Bloom to transport some of its attractions to the Industrial. He brought the Algerian Palace, with a range of performers from its 'Congress of Nations' – 'from Nautch girls with languorous eyes and henna dyed fingers, to the stolid Esquimaux who sit and say nothing but saw wood.' Such congresses had long been staples of circuses and fairs, and this one, apparently, was not very good. An *Empire* reporter called it the most miserable sideshow ever to get space on the grounds. Still, the opportunity to stare at bodies of supposedly primitive peoples, under the guise of anthropological concern, was hard for many whites to resist, especially white males whose understanding of Nautch girls and similar attractions was deeply embedded in fantasies about Oriental sexual licence.[81]

Perhaps the blandness of the show suggested that an essential component of the original was missing, for some patrons soon indicated an interest in seeing the famous *danse au ventre* that had earned notoriety in Chicago. Bloom was happy to make arrangements. To deflect official attention and take full advantage of prurient curiosities, he let it be known by word of mouth only that a special performance would be given at 9:30 on a Monday night. At the duly appointed time, a hundred and fifty gentlemen were on hand, all willing to pay substantially more than the regular twenty-five cent admission charge. There was some reticence to enter the tent when the morality squad showed up accompanied by a crown attorney, but they gave assurances that the show would be allowed to proceed, which it did. 'After the first maiden went through her ordinary slow marching step and a fencing bout was finished, the Arabian girl, whom the gilded youth are pleased to call "deucedly pretty," made the hit of the night. Her general physical manoeuvres brought down the house. It was according to the correct Chicago Midway, Parisian Moulin Rouge elephantine style.' It was predictably tame stuff: although decrying the performance, police conceded there were no grounds to shut it down. Though its sexual suggestiveness was somewhat exceptional for the Toronto fair, it was not at all unusual as an affirmation of the cultural hierarchies of gazing. This was a white audience ogling women of colour, a totally male audience, and an affluent one. The *World* reporter declined to mention names, but revealed that this was 'a well known lot,' with the legal and medical professions well represented and a titled gentleman or two besides.[82]

The fact that white males' perspectives were catered to most consistently did not mean that others did not want to see. Many regular sideshows that pandered extensively to male prurience attracted lots of females. As Stallybrass and White have argued, things excluded as 'low' and 'other' by dominant groups in their projects of self-definition exercise a powerful fascination and tend to become the primary eroticized constituents of their fantasy life.[83] To the extent that middle-class women identified with white male hierarchies, they undoubtedly shared the same fixations. They were probably more inclined than men to repress desires to explore the forbidden, but that is not to say longings were absent. The midway was a seductive place for both genders because everyone was encouraged to look at normally prohibited attractions. In other places where notions of respectability made it difficult for women to gaze as openly as men, women likely became adept at seeing what they wanted by using furtive glances, vacant stares, reflections in mirrors and windows, and similar strategies, including the protective distractions of crowd situations. Gazing was privileged, but it was by no means exclusive, especially at the fair.

Since staring at others was problematic, marketers may have hoped there would be a compensating inclination to stare at goods. No doubt this did happen to some extent, but it was hard to avoid acknowledging that active humans were almost invariably more fascinating than inanimate mass-produced commodities. More to the point, humans seemed indispensable to attempts to pin down the meaning of industrial products. As a result, the examination of goods in exhibition displays tended to become a justification for staring at bodies rather than an alternative to it.

All displays had human attendants. They were needed in the first instance as guards. Most exhibits were protected at least by railings or cords, but no barrier was foolproof. Attendants had to keep arrangements of goods in neat order and secure them from crashing down on hapless bystanders. They had to keep the overly inquisitive from sticking fingers into moving parts, and the unwatchful from catching clothing in belts and shafting. They had to ensure that display items were not stolen, scratched, dented, or otherwise mutilated. Display staff were also needed for the business chores connected to the sales process. Discussing terms with customers, writing up orders, taking payments, wrapping packages or making delivery arrangements, handling problems encountered by previous customers – all these tasks required a human presence. However, that presence was not something merely appended to display apparatus; it was integral to the whole display strategy.

The human voice was essential to the clarity of corporate messages. There was no guarantee that purely visual display components would be interpreted in intended ways, especially by people still becoming familiar with devices of visual communication. An indication of marketers' anxiety was the prominence in many exhibits of written signs. 'Gillett's Goods Are Standard,' proclaimed a poster at the centre of the company's booth. '"Gold Medal" Coffee and "Kalona" Tea Are Luxuries' read one attached to Eby, Blain's stand.[84] In retrospect, these messages often seem surprisingly trite, but their conventional language implied a human presence that was familiar and reassuring.

Actual voices used by real people were even more precise, emphatic, and flexible, capable of articulating messages that were complex and yet clear. The spiel delivered by the Tobler's Chocolate representative at the 1903 show – 'Made in Switzerland, with pure, rich cream, not only a delicate sweetmeat, but positively a nutritious food'[85] – was a classic example of the effort to balance appeals to luxury and utility. This kind of patter was carefully crafted by companies and rehearsed by employees, but, obviously, it was easy to tailor voice messages to individual circumstances. Aural communications could be much more convincing than inanimate objects, no matter how beautiful or impressive. For wary consumers, insincerity or illogic in a voice seemed easier to detect than poor workmanship or inferior components.

If voices had a symbolic function, so did bodies. The most consistent messages they articulated derived from conventional assumptions about gender. There are no accurate figures for such things, but given the amount of machinery on exhibit, it seems likely that more males than females were employed as attendants. Men were by no means absent from domestic commodities departments, either. These exhibits were almost invariably managed by male supervisors, and often staffed by male travellers who were valuable because they knew the products, could recognize merchants from outlying towns, and were already on salary. Some companies used skilled male workers to demonstrate and tend moving equipment, but for most male staff, voice and carriage probably were more important than hands. They wore regular business dress intended to create impressions of probity, respectability, and integrity. Their manner symbolized competence and efficiency. Their bodies became synecdochal abbreviations for the identities of entire corporations.

Female bodies, on the other hand, were used much more consistently to put products into a context of use. Women prepared and served free samples, demonstrated the operation of appliances, embodied the geniality that supposedly flowed from the use of manufactured products. Their visual image was also crucial. They had to be just as presentable, efficient, and respectable, but without challenging male dominance. Companies had no desire to associate their goods with disturbing changes to traditional gender roles. Men had to be seen to be in charge.

The strategy adopted by many exhibitors to control the image of female bodies was to put them in uniforms. 'Lady assistants,' as they were often called, were often outfitted in costumes that highlighted the authority of a male supervisor in business dress. Some outfits were quite fanciful. Dingman's Soap in 1886, picking up on the popularity of *The Mikado*, dressed women in kimonos and had them blow bubbles beside a massive soap fountain. The 'lady attendants' at the Baker Cocoa display in 1903 were costumed to represent 'La Belle Choclatière,' the company trade mark. The seven young women who worked in the Blue Ribbon Tea booth that year had outfits made in the firm's colours. Many exhibitors, however, like the Pure Gold Manufacturing Company and McLaren's Cheese, simply adapted conventional domestic servants' garb for their employees.[86]

At the 1903 Blue Ribbon Tea booth, as at many others, a male manager in a business suit presided over a bevy of females dressed for domestic service.

For the many women engaged to hand out samples and tidy up the mess, domestic uniforms were practical, but their use had symbolic import as well. Neat, clean uniforms of any sort dovetailed with messages about order, consistency, and purity that non-human display arrangements usually emphasized. They suggested not simply that the goods being proffered were luxury items that the affluent would readily serve, but that recipients were worthy of respectful treatment. They flattered social pretensions, aspirations, or, if domestic help was a remote possibility, fantasies. Uniforms also suggested that factory manufactured goods that made household chores less demanding would not upset entrenched gender roles or class relationships. These products would not liberate women to pursue activities outside the private sphere, but rather would establish new standards of domestic elegance, comfort, and enjoyment.

These sorts of messages, tying the meaning of goods to domestic contexts through the female body, did not always require the use of uniforms. Sewing-machine manufacturers were not about to give an impression that women making clothes in their own homes were on a par with servants. Their demonstrators wore ordinary dress. Nor were these messages necessarily limited to household products. The Massey self-binder display in 1886 featured a tableau incorporating life-sized mechanized figures of a farmer and his wife at the height of harvest operations. While the farmer drove the equipment, the woman turned a revolving panorama that contrasted a voracious harvest crew devouring a substantial spread in a 'before' scene with an 'after' scenario showing the happy couple doing the same work without hired help.[87] The appeal was as much to the farmer's pocketbook as to his wife's comfort and domestic tranquillity, but, either way, the female body was deeply suggestive of the machine's broader social implications.

In the Massey display, mechanical animation compensated for the fact that the bodies were not real, and, besides, plenty of live attendants hovered nearby. If exhibitions were intended to help companies give themselves human faces and establish personal bonds with consumers, actual people in their displays were practically indispensable. However, there was a marked tendency in exhibits for the availability of mass-produced commodities and the availability of bodies to be confused. Visitors often seemed far more interested in those representing goods than in the goods themselves. The hard work of women serving samples of tea, coffee, and cocoa impressed a

The males in this photo perhaps worked for the Appleton Tea Company, but many others who did not positioned themselves in similar ways to gaze at female workers.

Mail and Empire reporter, but he seemed far more taken with their 'immaculate blouses' and 'hair so beautifully arranged.' The *Catholic Register* representative had more to say about the 'bevy of beautiful girls' at the Reindeer Brand booth than the condensed milk they were pushing. Though they had no intention of using the products, young males perennially flocked to sewing-machine exhibits. This department was one of the most attractive at the show, suggested a *Globe* reporter in 1879, 'not solely on account of the machines.' A *Mail* journalist a year later was more explicit about his interests: 'From the liquid eyed damsel who runs a plaiter to the little chubby maid who treads the pedal of an A-1 family sewer, they are all as bright, lively, gossiping and entertaining as could be wished for.' Wherever 'handsome young ladies' presided over exhibits, not just the sewing department, young men could be found, 'ostensibly intent on discussing the merits of goods.'[88]

There was greater frankness about male interest in female attendants, but women visitors could be just as absorbed by men. One observer in the piano department in 1886, struck by the number of young ladies clustered around male demonstrators, was convinced that complimentary remarks about the music were directed more at the players. Several years later, large numbers of women were found at all hours watching with keen interest the operations of two good-looking Cubans making cigars.[89]

The consistency of their choices suggest that those responsible for display staffing thoroughly grasped the connection between goods and bodies. The best-looking women on the grounds were the lady assistants, according to a *News* reporter in 1900. 'For the individual who enjoys looking upon rich edibles and pretty women, and who does not favour such a combination,' he observed, the Crystal Palace was the place to go.[90] Companies deliberately sought to make these workers targets of sustained gazing. Of course, groups most vulnerable to intrusive examination were the same ones most likely to seek employment for exhibition jobs, so not much skill was required to engineer a suitable situation. It was not really necessary to dress female fair employees as domestic servants to signal their visual availability, thought undoubtedly it made some visitors more comfortable about looking.

No less than sideshow operators, businesses used conventional social hierarchies of gender, race, and class to encourage gazing. At times, the line between sideshows and displays got rather fuzzy. Massey Manufacturing, for example, hired an Egyptian dragoman in exotic Eastern clothing for its 1890 exhibit, though what he had to do with farm equipment was not obvious.[91] For the most part, appropriate personnel and costume were easily acquired in the immediate, familiar environment. Local attractions were entirely sufficient for a *News* reporter at the tea and chocolate displays of 1897:

> There are dainty Hebes, with smiling faces to press pleasant beverages upon you. Another symptom of good taste is the manner in which these girls are dressed. Now, it is possible that these maidens may at heart

love garish display, but these tendencies they are not allowed to indulge. They are dressed with neatness and plainness, yet they are wholly charming. The exhibitors seem to have come to the conclusion that pretty girls grace a display, for some of these Hebes are exquisite specimens of Canadian womanhood.[92]

This male observer had no reticence about scrutinizing the physical attributes of working-class, immigrant women. For him, and many others of both sexes, it was reassuring to see that exotic races, despite garish predilections, could be controlled by tying them carefully to industrial capitalist projects.

〜〜〜〜〜〜〜〜

Beside generating immediate sales, displays of industrial products at the fair were intended to encourage people to pay attention to goods within a new ethic of enthusiastic consumption and to help pin down their meaning within a vastly different context of merchandising. Marketers wanted to kindle desire for commodities without generating utopian expectations or fears of excess, and they wanted goods to speak for themselves. Their strategy was to invert the panopticon principle that underlay many disciplinary projects that proliferated in the nineteenth century and after. Instead of a viewing situation that permitted large numbers of bodies below to be observed by a few individuals above who could not be seen, fair displays encouraged those at the bottom to stare at what had been elevated to prominence, things incapable of looking back.[93] However, the artifices used to make people more attentive tended to destabilize meanings. Visually arresting devices often had unmanageable symbolic breadth, while the close juxtaposition of so many disparate display techniques interfered with the logic of any particular exhibit.

Since goods could not speak with clarity by themselves, marketers turned to bodies for help. The meaning of commodities became much more coherent when tied to established social hierarchies of gender, race, and class. Moreover, consumption was stimulated as desires for bodies and desires for goods became conflated. Using bodies as symbolic vehicles was not foolproof. Bodies were hard to control. Immaculate blouses became creased and stained. Voices got irritable. Manners became abrupt or rude when exhaustion set in. Bodies were indispensable, but they worked best when contextualized by materials impervious to fatigue, produced by reputable corporate organizations. Just as the vitality of bodies compensated for the inertness of goods, so the constant uniformity of goods compensated for human failings. The processes of meaning, then, worked both ways. The significance of each was apparent only in relation to the other.

For the public, as well as business, the quest for meaning made gazing at goods and gazing at people activities that were mutually dependent. As the identification of strangers, a key to urban survival, began to depend more and more on being able to ascertain the quality of their accoutrements without appearing to be intrusive, there was an incentive to study commodities carefully. As the projection of respectability, a key to urban success, began to occur more frequently in panoramic public environments where the self was defenceless against undetected surveillance by others, the impulse to consume discerningly became stronger.[94] Increasingly, the meaning of people rested on the material culture that enveloped and extended their bodies. On the other hand, the meaning of products was inextricably linked to who used them and in what contexts. Goods and people had to be judged in relation to each other, and the fair was a prime site for seeing both.

4

Identity

'Do you not find it difficult in such busy times to keep track of your guests and guard against dead beatism?' inquired a *Globe* reporter of the night manager at a large hotel. 'Not very,' was the response: appearance, manner of approaching the desk, and calligraphy generally provided a sound basis for detecting the sorts who needed to be watched. A brusque gentleman who dug holes in the register while scrawling his signature undoubtedly was good for fifty thousand dollars at the National Bank in Buffalo. A swell with elegant looks and exquisite penmanship was likely impoverished. The 'Old Country Traveller' automatically got assigned a room with a bath and took it as a matter of course when the item appeared on his account. The English visitor who claimed blood relationship to the aristocracy probably had a trunk full of lumber. A particular dread was the gentleman of literary or intellectual appearance, 'especially if the individual wears long hair and a dress coat.' As a rule, this sort depleted his meagre resources in a few days and then disappeared. Why did the impecunious not learn to better disguise their situation? That class, the reporter was told, seldom read the *Globe*.[1]

Whatever their accuracy, these assessments were merely an example of the Victorian predilection for identifying social types. Rapid population growth, high rates of transience, and the erosion of class distinctions created, as Elizabeth Wilson put it, 'disorienting confusion as to who was who,'[2] so the urge to stave off social chaos by sorting bewildering numbers of people into meaningful categories was intense. Typing was not the only technique for coping with identity on a mass scale. Michel Foucault wrote at length about the use of hierarchical observation, systems of punishment, and examinations to turn individuals into 'cases' who could be monitored separately yet evaluated according to normalized judgments.[3] This degree of classi- fication was expensive and time-consuming, impossible to implement in the hurly-burly of everyday activity, and unnecessary for many kinds of social interactions. Dividing people according to type was often more feasible. Such distinctions were geared less explicitly to influencing behaviour than Foucault's training methods, though not necessarily less formal in intent. Locating individuals who embodied broader categories was often the basis of rigorous scientific endeav- our, in everything from anthropology to criminal physiognomy and phrenology.[4]

When done rigorously, typing also required patience and careful evaluation, but it was not always done rigorously. In fact, inventing general types within improbable classes became a staple amusement of the late nineteenth century. A *News* reporter who enumerated different kinds of 'mashers' on downtown streets was typically droll. 'Cholly Slim,' the dude, 'living evidence that a human being can survive without brains,' invariably carried a cane and an eyeglass, smoked cigarettes incessantly, and wore a collar so high he had to climb into it with a step ladder. The 'sporting gent' flirted only after completing more arduous duties, mainly attending ball games and horse races. Never without a cigar, he found a suitable pole to lean against and hoped for responses to some conversational ploy. 'The transient visitor from the back townships' could be recognized by his weather-beaten umbrella, faded homespun suit, and cowhide boots, 'the tops of which do not connect with his trousers by about three inches.' He was most active after dusk, and more likely to achieve success through a cash transaction.[5] There were others the reporter admitted, but it was impossible to cover them all in an ordinary column.

As this example suggests, typing was mainly an urban pastime, not just because high volumes of people offered more possibilities for exaggeration. A talent for making clever distinctions was a mark of urban sophistication, a device for demonstrating one was no longer a newcomer to the city. This helps account for the condescending tone of so much popular stereotyping. Typing was easier for males than females, at least in the first instance. Men had more freedom to study those who occupied public space, and women's evaluations were constrained by higher standards of decorum. Still, women did indulge. Madge Merton, on the lookout for stock characters at the

1900 show, found the 'little Dresden China lady,' the 'masterful young woman,' the 'clinging little female,' and the 'country boy.'[6]

This kind of parody of scientific exactitude expressed exuberant delight in human diversity. It was meant to be perversely inexact. As one observer at the 1882 fair acknowledged, each individual 'may be ranked under general classes, though of course, as in the Exhibition, there are 'extras' which can not well be included in any class.'[7] The fun was in discovering possible patterns where others had not thought to look, in hypothesizing discrete components within categories assumed to be monolithic. However, deeply serious impulses were at work here. The night manager did need to evaluate his clientele. Women were interested in who lurked in the streets. For anyone trying to make sense of the city, typing was practically inevitable. In realms too big to be held in the imagination all at once, reducing some people to the level of cartoons was the only way to cope.[8]

Despite its seeming frivolity, playful stereotyping indicates the depth of concern about identity as urbanization and industrialization took hold. That concern was one reason why the fair was considered valuable. People believed it brought together a spectrum of their entire community, allowing comprehension of the whole and opportunities to judge each in relation to the others. 'Every type to be found in Canada may be seen in the Queen City while the big Fair is in full swing,' insisted the *Mail and Empire*. There were representatives from beyond as well. Though no Carnival of Nations attraction had been booked, reported the *Star* in 1896, a good show could be put together from the Spaniards, Mohawks, Chinese, Blacks, French, Italians and Arabs scattered about the grounds. Nothing else in the yearly round afforded the same opportunity to study 'the outside aspect of all manner of men and women.'[9]

This is not to say that all groups were accorded the same respect. Inevitably, Blacks got the worst treatment. Many came to work. Some did menial tasks, such as the men in rainbow-coloured suits who distributed advertising materials at the 1892 show, or the perennial legions of waiters. Others entertained at amusement venues, performing mostly minstrelsy and 'burlesque specialties,' such as the huge cake walk done by twenty 'coloured folk' in the 1900 grandstand show.[10] In both cases, whites expected confirmation of their racist assumptions. Blacks were marginalized, though certainly not submerged. Even as ordinary visitors, they were watched carefully for criminal or comic behaviour. A Black jockey was hooted in

1888 when his horse refused to start. A Black youth got a month in jail in 1890 for stealing an umbrella. A 'suspicious looking darkey' was arrested in 1894 when he could not give a satisfactory account of himself.[11]

minority rep. in fair

Native peoples did not fare much better. Like Blacks, their greatest prominence was in entertainments tailored to white expectations. 'All the scenes in Indian life' promised in Pawnee Bill's Wild West Show at the grandstand in 1892 turned out to be enactments of robbing the stage, attacking the settlers' cabin, the Indian massacre, and the cowboys' revenge on Indian horse thieves. The Indian village on the 1903 midway had no cowboys, but its depiction of Native life was little different. Men in war paint performed dances 'which were the fear of settlers in early days,' demonstrated the 'dreaded war whoop,' and plied war clubs 'with vigor.' Afterwards, they sold souvenirs.[12]

More accurate displays of Native culture were inanimate. Indian artifacts were regularly displayed by territorial and provincial governments, the Canadian Pacific Railway, scientific organizations, and private individuals. Most objects were of ancient rather than contemporary origin and were considered interesting for their relationship to the prehistory of white settlement, or as relics of a dying civilization. Ten cases of artifacts brought by the Canadian Institute in 1886 were intended to show 'future generations the handiwork of a race which at no very distant day will have become extinct.' CPR 'trophies' shown in 1901 formed 'a marked contrast to the rapid history which is being made, especially in the newer parts of the Dominion.'[13]

Without doubt, race was a central device in differentiating people at the fair. Robert Rydell has emphasized the importance of large American expositions in fixing popular notions of racial hierarchies and in generating enthusiasm for imperialist activities. Ethnological exhibits and midway attractions confirmed for many whites the accuracy of Darwinian theories of racial development and the inevitability of American progress. Similar displays and messages with a Canadian or a British bent were common at the Toronto fair.[14] However, race was only one criterion of identity among many, including age, gender, class, place of residence, and behaviour. In late nineteenth-century Toronto, these, too, had great significance, which meant that those from nearby were just as prone to being stereotyped as those from far away.

Since it is impossible to talk about every human category given prominence through the fair experience, this chapter will concentrate on two of the most important: women and country people. For all groups, identity was elusive and unstable, though not necessarily in the same ways. As the example of women shows, an identity that seemed sharply defined could become somewhat fuzzy at the fair. On the other hand, as the treatment of rural people demonstrates, an identity that was diffuse could be dramatically sharpened and distorted. Either way, the fair shaped identity as much as reflected it.

On paper, women presided over the Industrial Exhibition. The most common motif on the illustrated covers of official programs was a regal female, benevolently surveying the fairgrounds from an imaginary vantage point. She symbolized the blessings of fertility and the arts of peace, the harmony of natural and human realms, the necessary link between public exertion and private happiness. She was the patron of creative endeavour and the beneficiary of productive effort. Safely distant from the actual site, she was an inspiration rather than an active guiding force. Her prominence was a reassuring indication that the fair was not a crass exercise in commercialism or a misguided festival of material excess, but a celebration of human skill, ingenuity, and enterprise.[15]

A truer indication of female power was revealed by another annual symbolic gesture – Ladies' Day. On the day officially dedicated to 'housewives and other busy women of the city,'[16] the directors invited a few worthy ladies to lunch, and exhibitions of female arts like cooking and ironing were highlighted. Nothing untoward was encouraged. The offer of American women's rights activist Mary Walker to lecture on 'Women's Franchise,' 'Women's Dress,' or 'Prevention of Diphtheria and Pneumonia,' for example, was politely declined.[17] Not much happened on Ladies' Day that did not occur on any other day. The special designation underscored what a sketch in the *News* made visually explicit: the important visitors were assumed to be mostly male.

What women were formally allowed to claim at the fair as their social contribution was completely circumscribed by conventional gender assumptions. Superficially, women seemed safely contained within the cult of domesticity. But the fair was subversive. It gave middle-class women an opportunity to escape the restrictive family hearth and to practise social interactions in public space. One indica-

Inspiration, protectress, and welcoming hostess, this presiding female figure
hovers over the fairground in a celestial bubble.

tion of its importance to many women as a device to legitimize their public presence was the effort to secure larger, more prestigious, and more versatile accommodation for the Ladies' Department. More subtly, the fair's emphasis on consumption rather than production suggested that female influence was much greater than was generally acknowledged, while the appearance of women performers in sideshows and grandstand acts challenged prevailing assessments of women's capabilities and, for some perhaps, provided inklings of alternative roles.

The authority of women in the Ladies' and Children's Department was uncontested. There was no question about its inclusion in the line-up of attractions, not simply because displays of domestic crafts had a long tradition at agricultural fairs but also because the 1876 Philadelphia show, a benchmark for Toronto, had given over a whole building to women.[18] In 1879 the association was not prepared to go that far, but it did appoint female overseers to supervise exhibits of 'fancy work,' ranging 'from babies' bootees to kaleidoscopic [sic] crazy quilts, from rough knitted farmers' mitts to delicate hand-painted china.'[19]

Newspaper coverage abounded with platitudinous comments about the importance of the department and the skills displayed therein. 'People who seek the ideal and beautiful in their surroundings,' intoned the reporter assigned by the *Mail* in 1893, 'fulfil a duty which they are said to owe their fellow beings.' Readers were regularly assured that these exhibits were a prime attraction. 'Everyday and all day long,' claimed the *Empire* scribe in 1891, fair faces peered eagerly 'within the cases that hold such marvels of dainty needlework.'[20]

Perhaps they did, but this formulaic enthusiasm ran in thin veins that usually petered out quickly into prosaic lists of submissions. A more telling indication of the department's appeal was its location – the top gallery of the Crystal Palace. The 'sky parlour,' accessible only by pushing through the congested main floor and climbing two flights of dirty stairs, had inadequate lighting, a leaky roof, and space limitations that caused 'overlapping, general jamming and confusion' in the displays. According to a *Saturday Night* columnist, 'the committee of arrangement require the qualities of Job and Jacob combined to get them in, and the judges the eye of an X ray to locate them.' For ordinary visitors, figuring out who had created what was virtually impossible.[21] More debilitating was the stifling heat that

To-day Toronto in her fairest dress wel-comes the visitors to the Great Exhibi-tion.

In this 1890 Toronto *News* cartoon, the overwhelmingly male crowd was just as allegorical as the female figure. Compare this image with the photo of the grounds on page 244.

collected under the roof. The health of attendants working for long periods in poorly ventilated conditions was a real concern, but browsers were inconvenienced as well. A *Globe* reporter cautioned against trying to squeeze close to display cases on a warm day when the temperature on the upper floor was unbearable. She herself had given up trying to take in everything.[22]

The biggest disincentive to make the ascent, however, was not the location but the quality of the exhibits. Some charged with describing the department were noticeably circumspect. The woman from the *Mail* used carefully neutral language in suggesting that the 1890 display 'indicates what the ladies of this country can do in all that pertains to making their homes both charming and cheering.' A year earlier, Faith Fenton in the *Empire* had declined to comment altogether. To do it justice would require an entire issue of the paper, she dissembled, 'and I am afraid our husbands and brothers would hardly be willing to yield up the sporting columns even for one day.' Critical evaluations emerged most commonly after the fact. In 1882, when the *Mail* reporter decided that the 'new art dispensation [had] ushered in a reign of charming novelty,' she admitted that the department used to be 'a dull, dreary show of patchwork, cushions covered with specimens of deformed dogs and impossible flowers, antimacassars of pre-historic date, bed-spreads, *et hoc genus omne!*' Those with keen memories may have recalled that her previous assessments were much the same, and so they continued to be. A few brave souls, however, or ones with higher standards, did not hesitate to call a spade a spade. 'There is nothing much over which to enthuse,' was Katherine Leslie's blunt appraisal of the 1900 display. 'Year in and year out this department shows little progress, and this year there is the same scant evidence of development.'[23] The thrust of her complaints was equally predictable.

For two and a half decades, reviewers remarked on the same two basic weaknesses – resubmission of old exhibits and poor design. The *Mail* assessor was particularly exercised about the return of 'old stagers' that made visitors feel 'they had seen each article ever since they were born, and indeed as if the whole exhibit formed part of the family heritage.' Ever the optimist, she detected fewer and fewer with each successive show, but others were not persuaded. Leslie dismissed the decorated china category in 1900 as 'so familiar that it need not be reviewed.'[24] Department organizers tried to minimize the problem. The rules stipulated that award-winning items from earlier shows could not be entered in competition, and that judges would give preference to things exhibited for the first time.[25] No doubt some women who wanted the prestige of having handiwork on display recycled old creations if new ones were unavailable, but it also seems likely that impressions of innumerable tray cloths, doilies, cushions, tea cosies, socks, and mittens began to blur from one year to the next. The reappearance of old items was especially bothersome when they were not impressive to begin with, and there was wide agreement among press critics that local design was seriously deficient. Any hint of improving standards was applauded with a typical backhand slap at earlier faults. 'The reign of the incongruous and absurd is almost over,' claimed a Whitby editor in 1883; 'blue boars and green lions are no longer possible in needlework and art generally.' The *Globe* reviewer of the same show was also relieved:

> The perennial appearance of a host of barbaric natural history rag-mats, with blue, yellow, and altogether impossible cats, dogs, squirrels, cows, etc. on a dull grey ground; of log-cabin quilts, whose only claim to notice was the astoundingly large number of pieces they contained; and of numerous other atrocities in the shape of bead-work, shell-work, seed-work, etc., became so utterly monotonous that the yearly task of saying anything favourable of them was a formidable one.

She was confident things had changed, but two decades later Katherine Leslie was still deriding poor use of colour and lack of basic drawing skills. Few items demonstrated any artistic feeling. 'They are more an evidence of industry than of a striving after something beautiful. There is plenty of patient, painstaking work, but that is all.'[26]

Leslie waxed enthusiastically about women she had seen in London's great museums, 'poring over the gorgeous tapestries, hangings, vestments, and small embroideries which have been collected from all ages and countries – they study the designs and colours, make sketches, never employing bought ones, and from these gain a wonderful field of suggestion for their own work.' Where she expected Ontario women to find similar resources is unclear.

However, unsophisticated designs may have indicated something more than lack of research or artistic creativity. 'When you look over a dozen entries by the same lady,' wrote the *Mail* critic, 'the thought forces itself on the mind that time and attention have not been sufficiently concentrated upon one or two kinds of work.'[27] The observation suggests that many exhibitors had different notions of proficiency. Performing technically competent work in a broad range of activities may have struck them as more difficult, useful, and admirable than producing one or two artistic pieces in a narrow specialty. Patient, painstaking work may have embodied the values and aspirations of women harassed by scores of domestic responsibilities; evidence of time and energy wrested from minute-to-minute pressures of daily life for technical excellence may have seemed much more significant than pretty colours and original designs.[28] Aptitude in skills handed down from generation to generation may have been more meaningful than knowledge of current fads and fashions.

If exhibitors were not merely unimaginative dolts, neither were critics simply haughty élitists. Underlying much of their perspective was an awareness that industrial production had dramatically changed the context of women's traditional crafts. Women had spun and woven since the dim ages, explained the *Mail* correspondent, 'till steam and the power loom and machine embroidery wrested from them their "women's work," and gave it to the strong man, that thenceforth all textile innovations should be manufactured by thousands of yards, to be paid for cheaply and sold only a little less cheaply.' Could women's work still be ornamental, useful, and remunerative? For her, as well as Katherine Leslie and others following Arts and Crafts ideology emanating from New York, London, and elsewhere, the solution was to turn these activities into genuine art that would be valued above machine production. They expected ladies' departments at fairs to be 'schools of art and taste' that would present inspiring examples of new design ideals.[29]

There is some evidence to suggest that many women exhibitors had not made the same leap towards anti-modern aesthetics. In a culture that admired machine production, they responded to the challenge of industry by trying to match it. 'Sama,' the *Globe* columnist, was greatly taken with a pair of knitted cotton stockings at the 1893 show, 'so fine I could not believe they had not been done by machinery.' Admiring a display of work done by women over seventy, Katherine Leslie wondered 'how do they ever accomplish these things with their old eyes and shaking hands that compare so favorably with the garments turned out by the ingenious swift-running machines of these modern days?'[30]

It is hard to say whether one approach produced more satisfaction than the other, but it is clear that both accepted that women's distinctive work involved pre-modern cottage skills. In a period of increasing industrial production, at an event that existed largely to celebrate and promote machine-made goods, formal definition of female identity was pinned to activities that were small scale, time consuming, home centred, and heavily decorative. 'Women's work' – unique hand production – stood in marked contrast to the vast majority of other goods shown at the fair. The Ladies' Department powerfully reinforced the impression that female production, and by extension females, could aspire only to supplementary economic status.

The sharpness with which the Ladies' Department defined gender identity was underlined by the almost complete indifference to it of male visitors. A *Mail and Empire* reporter in 1902 estimated that perhaps one man a day was really interested in examining the displays, and his reactions revealed abysmal ignorance. Some men dutifully escorted womenfolk or friends and struggled to maintain an appearance of dignified interest. 'H.M.Q.' was amused watching the bored-to-death expressions on men's faces, and their efforts to show signs of intelligence when called on for comment. Most men were not prepared to make the sacrifice. 'The Family Man,' a type noticed by a *Globe* reporter at the 1882 show, meekly trailed behind his wife and children through the entire building until they reached the Ladies' Department, and then he scurried off to a refreshment stand. One of the ways to spot hen-pecked husbands, on the other hand, was to see who had not been able to escape the pilgrimage to the third floor.[31]

By the closing years of the century, attempts were being made to expand from the narrow emphasis on 'fancy work.' In 1897 a medal was established for the best new invention by a woman for household or decoration purposes, not connected with clothing. There was only one entry that year, a pair of white crochet curtain bands that could be washed and boiled. It is not clear whether the prize was given, but the award was thereafter downgraded from silver to bronze. The concept was probably more interesting than most of the submissions were. The 1899 entries, for example – an umbrella and cane holder for stores, a boot rack for closets, an adjustable mirror that showed the back of the head, and a spring-handled churn – did not attract much attention. New prizes were introduced in 1900 for Venetian or bent-iron work, and in 1902 for marquetry, basket making, and book binding. In 1902, as well, a new class with nine categories was established for home-made foods. None of these innovations deflected the emphasis on pre-industrial skills. The food class was particularly revealing. Prizes were offered for plum cake, bread, pickles, catsup, preserved fruits and vegetables, marmalade and jelly – exactly the sorts of products women were increasingly likely to buy than make.[32]

The narrow focus and traditional cast of the department had begun to bore many women as well as men. Jean Grant's response in *Saturday Night* to the 1898 exhibit indicated the growing discontent. Women, she insisted, were not worthily represented at the fair. Fancy work and crafts in the ladies' section were 'a very meagre and altogether insufficient index of what industries our women are engaged in.' What with bee-keeping, dairying, raising fowl, growing fruit, cooking, teaching children, and designing such industrial products as carpets and wallpaper, there was enough to mount a fine exhibition on their own. However, she had no wish to promote competition between 'two such dissimilarly constituted entities' as men and women; she was not one of the 'shrieking sisterhood.' What women required was not a separate fair, but a separate building where the full range of their interests could be accommodated.[33]

The proposal was not new. Its direct inspiration was the Women's Building at the 1893 Columbian Exposition in Chicago. The art, crafts, inventions, scientific advances, and lectures presented in its spacious quarters understandably impressed many visitors, and agitation quickly began for a similar facility at the Industrial. Part of the appeal of the Chicago example was the fact that women had been in charge of their space, and this too became integral to the Toronto version. After visiting the 1894 show, Faith Fenton told *Empire* readers it was 'foolish' and 'hardly in keeping with modern progress' that 'in an exhibition by the people and for the people, there should be no advisory board of women to aid the directorate.' Such a board would relieve male directors of matters pertaining to exhibits by women and children, arrange for 'the special comfort and convenience of their sex,' and supervise the women's building, preferably 'a pretty building' with attractive art and needlework, special exhibits, and perhaps even a nook for making butter and selling fresh buttermilk, as at the World's Fair.[34]

One of the most persistent advocates was Mrs Willoughby Cummings, more familiar to *Globe* readers as Sama. She had been special correspondent for the paper in Chicago during the World's Fair. Taking advantage of an invitation to speak at an 1894 directors' luncheon, she put the proposal straight to those who made decisions:

there should be female directors on the board to look after the Women's Department, as in Chicago. President Withrow said he thought the idea a good one, and promised to see what could be done, which apparently was nothing. Undeterred, she kept up her annual lunch-time agitation for a separate building under female supervision, stressing that it would be 'an educational exhibit of everything that pertains to the home life.' The association continued to concede that the Ladies' Department needed more room, but insisted there was no money to erect a separate facility.[35]

At the turn of the century, when it became obvious that larger quarters were required for industrial exhibitors, activists set their sights on the building occupied by piano manufacturers. What was needed, according to Mrs J.E. Elliott, one of Cummings's associates interviewed by the *Star*, was 'a well lighted building about the size of the piano building.' It is not clear whether the directors willingly embraced the project or whether they moved to placate an important constituency at a point when their leadership was coming under serious question, but when the new Manufacturers' Building was finished in 1903, the old music annex was converted to the Ladies' Department. The new quarters were 'somewhat out of the beaten path,' admitted the *World*, but well suited for their purpose and fitted up with a homelike, comfortable atmosphere.[36]

Overseers were not slow to capitalize on their space. They arranged cooking demonstrations for adults and children, manual training sessions, kindergarten classes, displays of chair caning and home spinning, musical performances, and lectures on everything from food chemistry to flower arranging. The program was a resounding success. Even traditional fancy work displays were so popular that nine glass cases were broken by the pressure of crowds trying to get close. Addressing those previously marked by a 'general indisposition to climb stairs,' the *Mail and Empire* pronounced there was much more to the department than 'impossible crazy quilts and overfed pin cushions': the practical utility and artistic beauty of the handiwork was a revelation. Women still had to prove they deserved a permanent separate structure, the editor thought, but an important step had been taken. Half a decade later, when a much more impressive Women's Building was erected, there was no longer any question of its legitimacy.[37]

The establishment of the facility was a notable achievement, notwithstanding its derivative inspiration. The social ideology it embodied was inherently conservative; the building was a hive of middle-class maternal feminism. Perhaps nothing symbolized its character more clearly than the 'little mothers,' dressed in 'pinafores, sleevelets and tiny white lace caps,' who were taught to make and serve dainty tea biscuits and pots of cocoa. Women carved out a larger niche in public space by characterizing it as an extension of the family realm. They had never advertised it as anything else. The structure should be 'designed by women, and managed by women for women,' Mrs Elliott told the *Star* in 1900, but should be devoted entirely to household arts and industries.[38] Had more controversial feminist purposes been envisioned, much stronger resistance to the expansion would have been encountered.

By 1903, then, the formal status of the Ladies' Department had increased in real, visible terms, but its characterization of female identity had not fundamentally changed. Organizers were willing to acknowledge the importance of women's social contributions, but not to threaten the cult of domesticity. According to the official program, traditional gender distinctions remained safely intact.

Women's curiosity at the Industrial ranged far beyond 'women's exhibits.' Unlike men, they had no hesitation about trespassing on domains nominally ascribed to the opposite sex. There is abundant evidence to refute assertions that they had 'little interest in mowing machines, big turnips, steam engines, patent safes, and the like.' At virtually the same time this 1883 comment was written, the *Globe* noticed that many ladies 'lingered long' among the machines in the Agricultural Implement Building. A year later, the *Mail* called for improved walkways through the stables so the many female visitors would not be encumbered by excreta and muck. Fanny Chadwick, at the 1894 show with her mother and several other ladies, chose to look at the honey, cabbage, machinery, and natural history displays.[39]

Farm women had a particular interest in agricultural exhibits. For one thing, many sections featured their work. In the rural economy, females were often responsible for the production of butter, cheese, fowl, wool, and vegetables, to mention just a few things. Naturally, they wanted to compare their efforts with those submitted for prizes. Many actually competed, often under a husband's or a family name. Rural women who managed household accounts may have wanted to take a close look at implement displays, trying to gauge comparative costs, features, and quality if a major farm expenditure was in the offing.[40] Besides, large, complicated pieces of technology were fascinating to many people, not just those intent on buying and not just men.

A similar blurring of gender lines occurred in many other parts of the exhibition. Scores of products far removed from the Ladies' Department were aimed much more directly at women than at men, and not merely corsets, muffs, furs, and millinery. Stoves were inspected most closely by those who had to labour over them day in and day out. According to Kit Coleman, the Stove Building was 'a favorite resort of house-keeperly girls' who loved to explore ovens, turn knobs and investigate little nooks for warming and browning. She herself always found it 'a comfortable place.'[41]

Musical instruments were another example. As Craig Roell has noted, there was a close association between Victorian women and music, especially the piano. Musical proficiency was not only a legitimate female skill but an important element in the moral power of women to curb aggressive male tendencies. Most men, he suggests, were 'either ignorant of or even prejudiced against musical study for themselves.'[42] The extensive piano and organ displays were never explicitly identified as female exhibits, but they were much more part of women's realm than men's.

Obviously, the same was true of sewing machines, another of the most important industrial products shown at the fair. All the major manufacturers, including Singer, Wanzer, Williams, Wheeler and Wilson, and Empress, had large displays, each with a number of machines in operation.[43] So logical was the identification of this device with women that at the first show in 1879, manufacturers were assigned booths in the west half of the top gallery, adjacent to the Ladies' Department in the east. Space constraints, not to mention pressure from exhibitors, subsequently led to relocation in more central areas, but companies had no doubts about the gender of their customers. Male visitors may have come to eye the demonstrators, but women came to test and buy.[44]

And so it was with washing machines, smoothing irons, jewellery, groceries, yard goods, furniture, and innumerable other things. The plain fact was that much of what industrial exhibitors presented was directed primarily at females. At fairs no less than department stores, as Paul Greenhalgh has observed, women were the principal target.[45]

The similarities of fairs and department stores as sites of gender subversiveness went beyond consumer feminism. Just as middle-class women were drawn to big downtown stores because they offered relatively protected environments with greater possibilities of freedom than normally existed on the street, so they were attracted to the fair.[46] With minor exceptions, women had unfettered access to every corner, without requiring male chaperonage.[47] It is hard to measure relative degrees of independence, but one indication of the assumed mobility of women within the grounds was the reliance of the daily press on female reporters for colour commentary. The breezy, informal, gossipy style of writers like Sama and Madge Merton in the *Globe*, Kit Coleman in the *Mail*, Faith Fenton in the *Empire*, and Katherine Leslie in the *World* was perfect for communicating transitory excitement and endless diversity.[48] Although their reports were often published on woman's pages, they were not intended solely for female readers.

These women could be trusted to provide an overall perspective because they had access to everything. Kit Coleman investigated the 1890 show with a female friend. 'We toddled about from one place to another as only two middle-aged bodies could,' she wrote, 'and we really had a peep at nearly everything.' They took a close look at the agricultural implements, the Wild West Show, the midway, and the dog show. They 'panted and perspired' through the displays, got 'bumped and crushed, knocked down and kicked up again' at the evening theatricals. Seasoned traveller and later war correspondent, Kit was more adventurous than many women of her time, but her wanderings at the fair were never depicted as extraordinary. At a time when some proper women felt uncomfortable about lingering in front of shop-window displays, and certainly about sweating in public, the exhibition provided a space where conventional gender expectations could be, sometimes had to be, ignored.[49]

As well as providing a space where women could spectate more freely than normal, the fair also provided opportunities to do things in public that challenged gender conventions, as female equestrian demonstrations indicated. When the ladies' riding competition got under way at the 1880 show, the grandstand crowd became much greater 'and all appeared highly interested.' Miss Schaefer, the winner, 'flew round the ring during the trials and afterwards at the very topmost speed of which her animal was capable, eliciting thundering applause from the delighted spectators.' In 1883 the participation of a number of young ladies in a hurdle-jumping exhibition by the Hunt

Club 'added immensely to the attractions of the field.' The lady riders 'in particular,' reported the *Globe*, 'were loudly admired.'[50] Few visitors had never seen a woman on a horse, but such responses suggest that public presentations of these skills and competitions based on them were rare.

Most locals did not dare depart too fundamentally from prevailing gender expectations, but that was not true of professional performers who earned a living by transgressing normal sex roles. Many female performers demonstrated competencies expected only of men, and a few competed directly with men. At the 1887 show, Loretta Masterman rode an unsaddled gelding a full mile in less than two minutes, a remarkable feat considering 'the well known fractious character of the horse.' More dramatically, she took on Will Furey in a Roman Standing Race in which riders straddled two-horse teams, one foot on the back of each animal. At the 1892 show a woman plucked her sister from mid-air while hanging by her toes from a trapeze bar, and Yucca, the strong woman, hoisted a horse and lifted a group of men standing on a table. At other shows, Cora Beckwith demonstrated unusual endurance in the swimming pool, Queen Sarbro walked barefoot up a ladder of razor-edged swords, and Madame Carlotta took on the winds in her balloon.[51]

The talents of these women, and scores of others, were deeply appreciated by visitors, who sometimes were genuinely surprised at what females could achieve. Alice Raymond had captured the city with her cornet solos, reported the *Mail* in 1893. 'It is rare and therefore more wonderful to see such strength of tone and power in a woman.' Probably the flattery was purchased, but the assessment reflected popular sentiments; a man blowing a horn was not news.[52]

Audiences had to be impressed by the abilities of female performers, but not everyone was comfortable with them. 'S.A.C.' – probably well-known author Sarah Curzon – found the Viennese lady fencers talented and interesting, 'if one can divest one's mind of every idea but the skill displayed'; she wondered whether the art was useful and, 'above all,' whether it was 'necessary, or beneficial, or proper for *women.*' The bicycle race between two ladies was even more upsetting. 'The ugly, unwomanly cut of the clothing, the long legs dangling on either side of the saddle, the ungraceful leaning forward, almost upon the chest, when at work, and the evident strain, forms a *tout ensemble* almost as revolting as that of two women stripped for a fight.' At the 1892 show the editor of *Saturday Night* was convinced that most spectators, 'in the honest bottoms of their hearts,' were disturbed by female acrobats, 'defying Providence and repudiating the assistance of man':

> They were out of their sphere, and, worse still, they were out of their clothes. But standing on the slippery edge of death they could not refrain from posing and strutting and flirting, and those feminine graces employed in such a garb and in such a place produced an effect that to me at least was repulsive and ghastly ... Muscle is a male attribute and a muscular female is so masculine that it looks silly for her to ogle and flirt and trip about in a feminine way, for the interest taken in her is similar to the interest taken in a musical cat or a performing donkey.

[handwritten marginal note: female stereotype]

He hoped some decent man would call them down, dress them in proper clothes, marry them, and take them to respectable homes where the highest wire was a clothes-line. A *Grip* cartoon was more light-hearted, but just as conscious that traditional gender roles were being challenged.[53]

The depth of anxiety about female performers was clearly evident from attempts to ground them securely in the conventional world. The fourteen-year-old cornet player, Daisy Ogden, was described as 'a modest and natural little lady' who travelled under her mother's care. 'Petite, attractive' Annie Ryan, a balloonist, was reassuringly 'pale and trembling' after a difficult landing. Lion tamer Madame Maurel's hands and arms were scarred with 'purple and vicious' lacerations, but Kit Coleman insisted she was 'petite, and very quiet and reticent and honest-eyed,' that she spoke to her animals 'as she might speak *en salon* to those of her own sex.' Faith Fenton may have interviewed the same woman several years earlier. When performing, Madame seemed 'hard-faced' and 'strong-nerved,' but away from the stage she was 'only a slender, homely little creature, with [a] lined, nervous face' and a family of six to support. After all, concluded Fenton, she was 'only a mother working for her children.'[54] As much as possible, the public wanted to be reassured that gender anomaly dissolved as soon as female artists left the stage.

However much these performers were tied to the domestic sphere, they clearly challenged prevailing stereotypes of middle-class womanhood. Living on the road, earning their own livings, demonstrating, with confidence and bravado, abilities that seemed inherently

AT THE INDUSTRIAL EXHIBITION.

HE.—" I suppose you would like first of all to go and see the ladies' work ? "
SHE.—" O yes, let us make a bee-line for the horse ring ; I do so want to see that bicycle race ! "

This 1888 *Grip* cartoon commented on the growing middle-class interest in commercial entertainments, as well as on increasing athletic opportunities for women.

masculine, they may have struck some visitors as little less freakish than midway dwarfs and giants. The *Saturday Night* editor compared the trapeze artists to performing donkeys and musical cats. Even as freaks, though, they blurred gender lines, suggesting that divisions between masculinity and femininity were not as sharply hewed as they seemed.[55]

Lots of spectators, however, viewed female performers in more positive terms. Few women contemplated becoming balloonists or trapeze artists themselves, although some may have been inspired to emulate what they had seen. For most in the audience, the achievements of these skilled women had a more diffuse impact, helping to shape new appreciations of female capabilities. Judith Fryer has pointed to the long-standing tradition that defines private space as female and the realm of the imagination, in contrast to male space, which is public and the realm of behaviour.[56] Giving even a few exceptional women a chance to behave in the public eye could lead many more people to question those underlying assumptions.

Sarah Curzon was perhaps a case in point. In 1888 she was deeply disturbed by lady fencers and bicycle racers; by 1892 her reaction to Yucca, the strong woman, was remarkably calmer:

> The perfect proportion of her figure is well displayed, and the beautiful white arms prove their strength very gracefully as they toy with fifty-six pound iron balls, and lift a man seated on a chair to the chest and carry him forward ... there is more than amusement in witnessing what may be done by the human body under a certain course and amount of training, just as we know what is in the horse when we see him in the Derby ... We then know what stress may honestly be put upon man and beast, and how far we are justified in 'pushing' him, under pressure.[57]

There was nothing in this response that questioned the utility or appropriateness of Yucca's skills. Far from querying the legitimacy of the performance, Curzon put it into a universal context. The strong lady was not a gender aberration, but a living demonstration of training principles that applied to all human bodies, male and female. It is simplistic to think the fair was the only site that offered glimpses of alternative behaviours. By the late nineteenth century, traditional feminine stereotypes were being challenged in many places, including beaches, tennis courts, and bicycle paths. The fair was not unique as a theatre of gender capabilities, but it was impor-

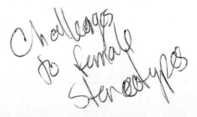

Challenges to female stereotypes

tant because audiences for the performances were unusually large and diverse and because skill levels were so exceptional that spectators had to take notice.

Paul Greenhalgh has argued that the single real benefit the exhibition tradition bestowed on women was visibility. Their presence was so pervasive they could not be ignored.[58] At the Industrial, women certainly were evident. At many times, especially during the regular business day, the number of women visitors probably exceeded the number of men. However, the importance of the Toronto fair for women went beyond their mere appearance there. It was significant for women because it challenged conventional assumptions about female roles, behaviour and abilities.

This is not to say that the exhibition destroyed prevailing gender distinctions. Far from it. As an instrument of hegemonic forces in the culture, the fair's intent was to affirm the rightness of dominant understandings, and from one perspective it was entirely successful. According to the official program, the main contribution of females was the Ladies' Department, which defined women in the most traditional, pre-industrial terms. Aside from this, and perhaps volunteer work in the WCTU refreshment tent, women were conceived as an admiring audience for male productivity. It was a very restrictive view, and yet, without it, the fair might never have existed. Gender was one of the fundamental constructs imposed on the new urban-industrial environment to make it comprehensible. The ability to maintain gender distinctions helped to generate the confidence that large numbers of very disparate individuals could be effectively managed. Moreover, the strict division of gender in public space was a mark of respectability. Had it not seemed to exist at the fairground, middle-class patronage would have been much diminished.[59] The subversive potential of the fair was possible because of the symbolic strength of the Ladies' Department.

Beneath the veneer of official ordering, the line between male and female identity got noticeably warped. First, the emphasis on consumption implicitly accepted that women had significant amounts of economic and cultural power. For many businesses, they were the more important sex. Second, the enclosed nature of the fairground allowed women unusual degrees of mobility in public space. They could envision themselves as *flâneurs*, following interests regardless of where they ended up.[60] To the extent that the grounds were imagined as an ideal city, the situation hinted at women's right to move as freely as men in the urban environment at large. Finally, the transgression of normal gender expectations by female performers suggested that many distinctions between male and female abilities were social constructs, not biological inevitabilities.

On the surface, the relegation of the Ladies' Department to what was probably the most unpleasant exhibition space at the Industrial reaffirmed the separate, unequal character of gender spheres. Below the surface, the fair increased the access of middle-class women to the public arena, the power they wielded there, and the range of physical activities they could practise. Unlike so many efforts that brought women into public purview, such as reform and suffrage projects, the exhibition did so without entrenching essentialist defi-nitions of women or casting gender relations into dualist and opposi-tional terms.[61] On the top gallery of the Crystal Palace, female possibilities seemed tightly circumscribed. On the main floor they were less restrictive, and on the grandstand they became remarkably protean.

~~~~~~~~~~~~~~~~

Some women may have been offended by a few entertainments offered on the grandstand or midway, but for most the fair was a positive experience that confirmed a sense of public freedom and importance. Its impact on the identities of people who lived in the hinterland out-side Toronto was much more complex. Because gender was such a powerful social construct, lots of strictures governed its public presen-tation. With only two, mutually exclusive categories, and a physio-logical foundation for deciding which was appropriate, slotting was not difficult. Geographic identity was much more amorphous. A broad spectrum existed between those whose origins were purely rural and those whose origins were purely urban – a spectrum so broad it was often hard to place individuals along it. Nevertheless, terms like 'city' and 'country' had long been understood as prime categories of what Richard Bushman has called 'a simple but useful vernacular sociology' in which the former stood for fashion, refinement, and excitement, and the latter for simplicity, rudeness, and torpor. Rather than an accu-rate representation of reality, he suggests, 'city and country were a cultural and social polarity in a mental geography.'[62]

However inaccurate, this deeply embedded shorthand was a fundamental tool in organizing the social world. The juxtaposition at the fair of those from within and without the city inevitably raised questions about differences between them. For country dwellers, adrift from the secure moorings of community and daily routine, and trying to make sense of themselves in the swirl of dense anonymity, deciding how and to what extent they were different from regular Torontonians could be difficult. When they got back home, with time to abstract the experience, it was easier to solidify versions of the self and stereotypes of urban 'others,' but while in the city their identities were continually buffeted. It might not have been lasting, but the experience of the fair probably had an unsettling impact on country people's sense of self. Urban residents, on the other side, tried to understand themselves by contemplating the otherness of people unfamiliar with city culture. Close to home and the reassurances of everyday life, with less inclination to question their own norms, they tended to magnify discrepancies in values, appearances, and behaviour into simplistic characterizations. Although there were many exceptions on both sides, evidence seems to suggest that country dwellers at the fair became more conscious of the fragility of their identities, while urban residents' depictions of rural identity became more rigid and exaggerated.

Large numbers of people came to the Industrial Exhibition from outlying areas. Many places were noticeably depleted during the second week of the show. 'Our village is well nigh deserted this week,' reported a Markham editor in 1886. 'Our village is quiet this week, owing in some measure no doubt to the attraction in Toronto,' echoed the Goldstone correspondent of the *Elora Express* in 1892. The proportion of farm to town folk is impossible to determine, but there is no doubt that the former were well represented, despite unrelenting chores. 'I suppose, as usual, nearly every person in the Northern and Western portions of Ontario who can spare the time and money will repeat former experiences and join in the annual crush,' lamented a reader of the *Orillia Packet* in 1890, worried about neglect of the local fair. He estimated that for every farmer who patronized the East Simcoe show, at least five, and more likely ten, would go to the Industrial.[63]

What those from the hinterland truly thought of the fair is impossible to determine, not just because it is problematic to generalize the experiences of so many people over an extended period but also because they left few records of their impressions. Opinions must have been expressed over kitchen tables and store counters, but country people were no more inclined than city residents to preserve emotional responses on paper. Personal documents, especially diaries, almost invariably contain brief recitations of what was done at the fair rather than what was felt. Nor are small-town newspapers revealing. Few covered the fair on a consistent basis from year to year, and many of their reports were taken from Toronto dailies or submitted by special correspondents who lived in Toronto. In the absence of hard evidence, the question of what happened to the identities of country people has to be approached obliquely and speculatively. However, it seems likely that visitors experienced the confusion inherent in any form of tourism. They felt simultaneously an intensification, dissolution, and reshaping of identity. Ratios among these processes varied from individual to individual, depending on personality, comfort with the urban environment, and exigencies of the moment, but few thoughtful travellers could escape their interplay.

The inevitable awareness of difference attendant on leaving home pushed identity in on itself. Comparisons with what was left behind made for clearer recognition of distinctive customs and conditions, for constant self-reminding of who one was and where one lived. A common manifestation of this heightened consciousness was an intensification of local allegiance, as frequent comparisons of the Industrial with fairs closer to home indicate. 'The minerals, coins and paintings are the only things that I think are any better than Londons [sic] as for all the rest it is not any better than London,' wrote John Fallows to his mother in 1881. As the Industrial got larger, people in or near smaller towns found it harder to make this particular claim, but often remained just as critical, particularly with respect to the quality of amusements or inattention to the needs of agricultural exhibitors. A Guelph editor reported with smug disgruntlement on the failings of the 1887 show:

> Great expectations had been aroused because of the balloon ascension and the Roman chariot races with lady drivers which had been announced. However, there was a complete disappointment in the first and a partial disappointment in the other. The accommodation for live stock at the Exhibition grounds is proving more inadequate than ever, and the directors were at their wits' end to meet the increased demand ... On Monday, though there was no judging going on, there was such a

crowd of spectators present that neither cattle nor horses could have been taken out of their stalls for ordinary exercise with any degree of safety.[64]

The account must have made his readers feel better about their own smaller fair.

Local allegiance had more positive aspects. A good showing at the Industrial by neighbourhood enterprises could be a source of great pride. According to the *Peterborough Examiner*, after viewing exhibits mounted by several of the city's industries, and the fine thoroughbred stock of Mr Jos. Redmond, many citizens came home from the 1885 fair 'feeling themselves townspeople of no mean town.' A year later, Orillians gloated in the success of one of their own who 'carried all before him in the Poultry department,' taking eight of nine available prizes. 'Strong efforts were made to keep all the Northern Poultry yards from obtaining a standing at the Exhibition, but they can't keep Orillia and Mr. Goffat from getting ahead.' The Chatham Band was the equal, if not superior, of any on the grounds, bragged the organization's secretary to a journalist back home. 'I mingled freely with the crowd and heard remarks past [*sic*] which bore out my opinion.'[65] The exhibition was just as likely to confirm local proficiency as subservience to the larger centre.

Paying close attention to exhibits produced near home was one way of countering the dissolution of identity experienced by tourists. In the rush and bustle of crowds who cared not a jot for the feelings of strangers, it was easy to lose a sense of self. 'When you walk down Yonge Street and realize how insignificant you are,' two young men from Port Hope were warned, 'you will doubtless wonder how you ever felt so big in Port Hope. Don't be alarmed by this feeling.' Anonymity was desirable to the extent of avoiding unfavourable notice, but could be very disconcerting for people accustomed to environments where identity was assured.[66]

Some groups were well aware of the vulnerability of country visitors and tried to assuage it. Notable efforts were mounted by fraternal orders. These organizations had been a presence at the fair since its inception. The association quickly instituted a 'Societies' Day,' hoping large turn-outs of uniformed members would brighten proceedings and boost attendance figures. Local chapters often felt some obligation to welcome out-of-town members. In 1881, for example, visiting Orangemen were reminded they could find at least one city

branch in session on every night of the week, while the Masons operated a registry and information office out of their Temple during the
show. A decade later, ladies of the Rose of Sharon Lodge, Loyal True
Blues, put on a soirée for visiting sisters.[67]

While the association tried to take advantage of the orders, they,
in turn, piggy-backed on the popularity of the show. By 1890 some
organizations had fallen into the habit of arranging conventions in
the city while it was in progress. In 1894 a formal link was established when some societies moved onto the actual fairgrounds, filling
a sizeable portion of lawn south of the Main Building with gaily
coloured hospitality tents. Patrons of Industry, Knights of Pythias,
Maccabees, members of the Home Circle, and a variety of Foresters,
among others, were invited to 'Society Row' to meet executives of
their orders and pass a few pleasant moments 'in a fraternal way.'[68]

The innovation was very successful. The Canadian Order of Home
Circles, for one, reported an average of five hundred visitors daily.
Accordingly, the row was reconstituted the next year on a grander
scale. Fifteen organizations erected tents covered with flags, bunting, and streamers in a semi-circle near the lake, and the *Mail and
Empire* described it as one of the most popular resorts on the
grounds. The orders were clearly pleased with the response and tried
to negotiate for permanent amenities, including elaborate gardens, a
fountain, proper lighting, conveniences, and signs. The association
was unable to oblige, and the row continued to move as pressures for
space mounted. Nevertheless, its transformation from a feature of
the fair to a fixture, as the *Star* put it, was symbolized in 1903 by the
appearance of a 'log cabin' erected by the Woodsmen of the World.
The light frame building covered with bark garnered so much attention that other societies petitioned to build similar rigid structures to
be stored off-site when the fair was not in progress.[69]

Organizations paid careful attention to their facilities. The 1897
tent of the Independent Order of Foresters, considered one of the pret-
tiest that year, was offset with flower beds designed as emblems of liberty, benevolence, concord, and the order's crest. Palms and ferns
were placed in profusion around it, and on top flew the Canadian
Ensign, the Union Jack, and, to indicate a large American membership, the Stars and Stripes. Inside, rich hangings, beautiful carpets,
and bunting provided backdrops for comfortable chairs, couches, and
settees. At one end, a rest room was partitioned off for lady visitors.
Regalia, badges, and souvenirs were displayed in glass cases, and, as

Tents on Society Row, circa 1902. The Independent Order of Foresters and the Ancient Order of United Workmen were both highly successful fraternal insurance societies.

if presiding over the whole arrangement, large portraits of the queen and of Dr Oronhyatekha, founder of the order, hung on the walls. 'The comfort of visitors has been anticipated in every conceivable way,' concluded the *Mail and Empire*.[70]

Maintaining the tent was often just one part of the Foresters' presence on the grounds. Oronhyatekha, a person of note ever since his introduction to the Prince of Wales in 1860, put in regular appearances that were flamboyantly orchestrated. In 1897, for example, 'arrayed in the full uniform of the encampment,' he entered the grounds escorted by a drill corps of some forty Royal Foresters in brilliant uniforms. They marched to the tent, where the supreme chief heard addresses of welcome and responded in kind, before receiving visiting brethren and their lady friends. Their most striking contribution to the grounds was a grand electric arch, originally constructed adjacent to their downtown headquarters on Bay Street to welcome the Duke and Duchess of York, and donated to the association in 1902. Ornate and impressive, it was the sort of useless symbolic architecture that visitors loved to inspect. Carting it to the lakefront instead of demolishing it was an inspired stroke.[71]

Society Row, as a *Star* reporter put it, was 'a sort of rooftree for wanderers from outside points ... a place where they can be sure of a welcome and an easy chair, a refuge from the surging, eager crowds,' but there was more to it than gracious hospitality and public spirit-edness. The orders were businesses as much as fraternal societies. Many, like the Independent Foresters, operated large and successful mutual benefit and insurance schemes. According to Mary Ann Clawson, by the late nineteenth century they had become fully entrepreneurial organizations, operated to maximize growth and revenue. They prospered only if membership levels remained healthy. Appearing at the fair was a useful way of solidifying existing membership and attracting newcomers, thus ensuring a steady flow of monthly premiums. The Catholic Order of Foresters was gratified by the response to its promotional literature at the 1895 show, 'numerous inquiries about the formation of new courts having been received.'[72] This was exactly what it intended.

For head office, a tent on Society Row helped demonstrate the resources and beneficence of an organization at a moment when clients and potential clients were psychologically vulnerable. Visitors were offered not just a spot for physical recuperation, but reassurances about their identities. Brothers and sisters, united by common interests, common experiences, common standards of accomplishment, were not strangers. Membership was an acknowledgment of worth, measured not in terms of crude wealth or superficial sophistication, but in solid contributions to organizations and communities, wherever they might be. In the tents, webs of association stretched from the city back to familiar relationships and responsibilities at home, and forward across the province, nation, continent, and sometimes beyond, suggesting that members were not backward hicks from podunk villages but intelligent, progressive actors, well integrated into vibrant, flourishing, modern institutions.

It was not necessary to belong to a fraternal society to fight off the dissolution of identity in the city. Probably the easiest and most effective way was to travel with family or friends. Understandably, excursions from country areas were very popular. A cheap train ticket was attractive, but so was the chance to be with people who could provide reassurances about individual standing. Writing home, reading local papers, hunting down former neighbours, or staying with relatives could all staunch a wavering sense of self, as could, no doubt, finding someone on an adjacent bar stool who was willing to hear the latest from East Gwillimbury or Chingacousy Township.

Perhaps the most elusive aspect of the psychological experience of tourism at the fair was the reshaping of identity that occurred in light of new experiences and broader horizons. A short excursion offered limited potential for radical transformations, but even small shifts in awareness and behaviour could have profound implications. This was certainly the view of many country merchants, coping with the seductive attraction of city shopping. 'A great many small parcels have been purchased in Toronto that might otherwise have been bought at home,' worried a Bowmanville paper during the very first show, and things did not change over the next quarter century.[73] For some, those small parcels threatened the whole fabric of community life.

A measure of the concern was the extent to which local merchants and editors tried to encourage home buying. 'Y Go to Toronto for Carpets and Home Furnishing?' asked Burrows Brothers in Guelph. 'We Guarantee to give you as good a quality, and as close a price as can be had there or any other city in the Dominion.' 'If there are citizens who can afford to pay the higher prices that Toronto merchants must, in the very nature of the case charge, why let them do it,' advised another Guelph storekeeper. Gough Brothers, footwear dealers in Peterborough, told of the man who discovered he had paid twice as much in Toronto for the same quality boot available in their store.[74] Country businesses stressed quality and dependability as well as price. Consumers were cautioned continually about the tricks of Toronto money-grubbers. A Halton paper suggested that city department stores counted on exhibition time to get rid of 'old fossils and back dates' at inflated prices. The Orillia *Times* professed amusement at how people were 'gulled' by the loss leadering of a few cheap items. T.N. Rickard, Bowmanville jeweller, offered 'A Timely Warning' to avoid city dealers offering '"a special watch," which is really very ordinary works with no manufacturer's name upon it. They rely on their name to sell it and thus they obtain from you three times as much money as they should.' This was only one resort among many, he warned. Lots of clever people had been taken in. 'Buy at home and run no risks,' counselled another jeweller in Cannington, reminding customers that he was always available to fix the watches he sold.[75]

Underlying these assertions of business competitiveness were deeper claims about the relationship of consumption to responsible social values and community well-being. G.B. Ryan and Company of Guelph began a large advertisement directed at 'Toronto Shoppers' by insisting, 'We do not wish you to think we are asking you to do your trading with us, but simply that you do it in Guelph.' Admitting for arguments' sake that things were a little cheaper in Toronto, they asked, would it pay in the long run to buy there? If everyone patronized the stores and services in Toronto, local businesses would be forced to move. If half the downtown enterprises disappeared, commercial property would be worth half as much and other property values would shrink in proportion. Was it honourable to make a living in Guelph, and have the value of your property kept up by people who shopped at home, when you went off to buy in Toronto? The editor of the *Daily Mercury and Advertiser* thought not, calling it a matter of 'moral obligation' to trade locally.[76]

The editor of the Milton *Reformer* was just as adamant that consumption had ethical dimensions:

> To deal with those who deal with you is a method of getting along which can't be beat. Besides it is a duty we owe to one another. People living in the same community are bound together in bonds both significant and enduring. The neighborly help which fellow-citizens can afford by buying and selling among themselves, in preference to going far afield to transact their necessary business, can scarcely be overestimated. It should be a noticeable feature in Milton life that a decided and a well considered preference be given to local manufacturers and merchants ... [W]hen a feeling of local enterprise exists and manifests itself in the way alluded to, our effect is to retain the circulating medium, called money, within ourselves, instead of exporting it elsewhere for the use of others. This may sound a little selfish to some, yet when it is recollected how many home interests are involved it may be called an enlightened selfishness at the worst. During the coming months expenditures are usually larger than at other seasons of the year. What is more proper than that they should be made amongst those who share with one another the duties and responsibilities of the same life?

Such sentiments were echoed by business leaders in many outlying

districts. The *Northern Advance* in Barrie went so far as to suggest
that residents report the names of 'enemies of the town' seen making
purchases in Toronto, 'not that we want to make use of them at
present, but they may come in handy sometime.' Much of this anxiety was inspired by the success of department stores, which struck
just as much terror in the hearts of small merchants in Toronto, who
could not claim to be defending local interests.[77] Regardless of
whether similar concerns were shared by city people, small-town
business interests were right to suggest that shopping was fundamentally linked to perceptions of identity.

Country people were frequently told at fairtime to choose between
seeing themselves as mutually supporting members of discrete communities or as isolated individuals, stripped of protection in an open
economic system governed by selfishness. They were told that the
town economy was a moral contract, and asked to consider the cumulative impact of many small mundane decisions on its integrity. The
effectiveness of such self-interested arguments is impossible to measure, but simply putting the issue in these terms generated some
feelings of self-righteousness in restraint and guilt at risking a
neighbour's livelihood for the sake of a few pennies.

Even when done without any consciousness of the implications,
shopping in the city changed perspectives. In a culture of consumption, how people positioned themselves in relation to suppliers of
commodities went to the heart of their sense of self. Becoming an
anonymous cash buyer in a vast, palatial department store produced
a very different feeling about one's place in the world from negotiating for credit in a narrow, dim establishment owned by a family that
worshipped in the next pew. Becoming familiar with new products,
greater ranges of goods, fashion changes, better prices, or more
appealing shopping environments expanded an individual's sense of
personal possibilities, and, perhaps, like Dreiser's Sister Carrie,
stimulated submerged psychic desires. Mary Ann Cook of Forestville,
charged with shoplifting at Eaton's, protested that she had intended
to pay for the necktie stuffed into her purse as soon as the clerk
became disengaged. It may have been true, and inquiries in her village produced unblemished character assessments. If not, she was
just one of many previously respectable citizens jolted into behaviour
aberration by new merchandising techniques.[78] Either way, she went
home a different person with a different reputation.

Shopping is just one activity that reshaped identity. There were many others, as a *Telegram* reporter hinted in 1881 in summarizing the effect of the fair. The farmer and his family, he wrote, 'have had some of their conservatism brushed off; they have exchanged ideas, tasted city lager and ginger pop, seen how the bank clerk and the city miss dress, have seen live newspaper reporters, heard the N.P. [National Policy] and politics discussed, have found out other people can grow monster potatoes, raise prize stock and vegetables as well as themselves, have in general acquired new ideas which in time will bear fruit.'[79] Not all experiences were positive. The proverbial attraction of bright lights and glitter may have persuaded many country people that they would be happier in an urban situation, but a run-in with a pickpocket, an argument with a hotel keeper, or a whiff of air near a factory may have confirmed impressions that the city was no fit place to live. Obviously, individuals' reactions varied enormously, and most people probably were pulled simultaneously in a variety of directions that were not always easy to sort out.

Any breaking of routine creates heightened opportunities to evaluate an existing version of the self. For hinterland dwellers, the exceptionally liminal environment of the fair created even sharper awareness of peculiarities, limitations, and desires. The point is that the identities of country folk at the exhibition were more unsettled than normal, but that is not how urbanites tended to see it. At fairtime, city people got an extended chance to study their country cousins at first hand. No other event in Toronto's yearly round brought so many rural people into the city or focused as much attention on them. Residents of the Queen City were fascinated by these outsiders. No other category of people in attendance was singled out more consistently or scrutinized more closely, though by no means did such observation promote an accurate understanding of rural character and conduct.

〜〜〜〜〜〜〜

Archibald Gillies, a schoolteacher and farmer from Minesing, a small village outside Barrie, had a busy two days in Toronto during the 1895 show. He had already been to the fair and gone home, but he came back to attend to other matters. He withdrew some money from his account at the Central Canada Loan and Savings Company, dropped in on a number of friends at their places of business, bought clothes and cartridges at various stores, went to the Parliament

Building to see a cabinet minister who was not in, called on the Canada Permanent Company about insurance, consulted a specialist about his ear drums, went to the Central Canada Employment Agency to see if they could find him a job, made a couple of business calls on his own to check out work prospects, and in the midst of all this, sampled the fare in various eateries.[80]

Here was a country person who was quite familiar with city people, city places, city ways. There were countless others like him. A *Mail* reporter found it a singular thing in 1891 that 'no one could detect any difference in dress, manners, or speech' between visitors from outposts of civilization and the smart citizens of the Queen City. There was hardly a country where 'certain sharp peculiarities do not cut off the rural from the city,' he reflected, but this did not seem to be the case in Upper Canada.[81]

Not everyone agreed. Only a couple of days later, a snobbish twenty-two year old confided to her diary that the city was full of 'queer looking specimens from the country.' Like most Torontonians, she was deeply impressed by differences between city and country folk. Weather-beaten features, sturdy bearings, and well-scrubbed, out-of-fashion clothes with awkward, homemade alterations made rural residents quite visible, as did telltale behaviour patterns. 'When you see a man carrying a carpet bag walking along the street looking at the tops of building[s],' suggested a *Telegram* reporter in 1892, 'it is quite safe to ask him "How are the turnips out in the country?"' City people no doubt realized that many from outlying areas passed quite unnoticed through the streets, but these visitors possessed little interest. Those unfamiliar with the metropolis, especially farmers, were so absorbing that they obscured the presence of the others. The extent to which the complexities of rural identity were ignored by urban observers is striking. Country people, so unlike themselves, were thought to be remarkably similar to each other. Their features were never produced from the same mould, wrote a *Mail and Empire* columnist, 'and yet they have a family likeness by which they are easily identified.' This assumption, which underlay the outlook of many urbanites, helped to produce some simplistic but powerful stereotypes.[82]

Torontonians felt a strong urge to pin down the identities of rural folk, yet their impulse was affected by contradictory attitudes towards rural life. As problems associated with industrialization and urbanization mounted, the supposed healthiness and independence

of farm life was increasingly idealized. Farmers worked, not at someone else's direction in stifling factories or enervating offices, but at
their own paces in pure, fresh air, close to God and the wonders of
creation. Agriculture was the cornerstone of the economy and the
foundation of national greatness. No country could succeed, it was
widely believed, without assured supplies of food or a fit population.
Rural prosperity was essential to the full development of Canada's
potential, and no patriot, urban or rural, could entertain the thought
that deficiencies among the agricultural population would hold the
country back. Indeed, they wanted to believe that Canadian farmers
were much better off than those elsewhere. There was none of 'the
squalor, dejection, heaviness and poverty to be seen here, that is so
prominent in European countries,' enthused a *Telegram* reporter in
1881. 'The Canadian peasant when he leaves home, leaves contented
with his lot and future prospects ... he knows he is the equal of any
man, and knowing it, acquires a manly independence which those
only who enjoy the profit of their own labour can acquire.'[83] From
this perspective, farm people were the backbone of the nation and
deserved a great deal of respect.

However much city people idealized a life close to nature, few had
any wish to live it. Farms required unremitting, exhausting toil,
often in primitive conditions, with little chance of amassing any
degree of wealth. 'There is no doubt that work on the farm is harder,'
editorialized the *Mail* in 1893. 'There eight hours a day never has
been, and never can be, the rule.' Worse, the isolation of farm life and
the repetitive nature of farm tasks made for monotony and stagna-
tion. Farm folk, according to the *Telegram* in 1886, 'run on in pretty
much the same ruts as their fathers ran.' Commentators spoke of
'quiet, uneventful lives,' of an existence that was 'peaceful though
somewhat tedious.' Even when couched in polite phrases, these
assessments constantly affirmed that rural life was marked by
bouredom and cultural deprivation, and that, compared with city
dwellers, farm people were backward and ignorant.[84]

Discrepancies between these views in popular urban discourse
were rarely reconciled. Rather, contradictions were side-stepped by
drawing on a set of rural stereotypes that correlated respect and ridicule with assumptions about age and gender. Characterizations of
the country girl, farm wife, country boy, and farmer were remarkably
common and consistent.

The country girl, combining youth and dignity, was depicted in the most consistently positive terms. City people generally were delighted with the 'rosy-cheeked maiden, with sunshine in her hair and laughter in her eyes,' to use the description of an *Empire* reporter covering the 1893 show. E.E. Sheppard had seen nothing so pretty in a year as the country girls at the 1888 fair, though he could not resist a few condescending digs:

> They are so sweet and unaffected, and their womanly wiles so transparent that one could hardly call them artificial. They would not be less beautiful if they reserved the eating of pie and the squeezing of their sweetheart's hand for places less public than King street. But their enjoyment is so thorough that notwithstanding the fact that their clothes lack the height of style and the expansion of bustle, which mark the attire of the city woman, I like them better. And do not forget that, as a rule, they show good taste in dress and manage to make themselves look pretty.

As these remarks make clear, much of the attraction of this lass for males was her physical appearance, but she had other virtues. The Canadian country girl, wrote a *Telegram* reporter in 1881, 'walks round so evidently able to take care of herself, and so entirely obvious [*sic*] of those little actions which her city sister has acquired, as to make it quite refreshing to look at her. In the majority of cases she appears to be the director of affairs, and not the young man who plays the part of chaperone. To her credit it can be said, that when a gentleman gives her his seat in a street or a railway car she has the manners to thank him, and in this she sets an example that some of the pert city misses might follow.' Unaffected, self-confident, independent, she was a walking embodiment of the best influences of the rural environment. More importantly, unlike single working girls in the metropolis, who were seen as victims and as the cause of so much urban disorder, she would go home.[85]

The farm wife was respected, but, without the bloom of youth, seemed pathetic. Her life was imagined as a never-ending succession of tasks. A *World* reporter in 1888 bid welcome to 'the patient mother who rises at four o'clock, gets breakfast, dresses the baby, and licks the rest of the children, milks nine cows and cares for the milk, feeds the pigs, and teaches the calves to drink milk from a pail, chases the hens from the vegetables and washes the buggy, churns the butter and gathers the eggs, besides the thousand and one things that make up her day's work before she sits down at 9 o'clock at night to do the mending.' All this took its toll, but without diminishing the spirit of self-sacrifice. 'Her shoulders were bent, and her hands were very hard and brown,' apostrophized Madge Merton in 1901, 'but when sickness came into her home or into her neighbours' homes, those hands were very tender, her voice was very gentle, and her footstep soft. Looking into her face one could see past sorrow and present care, and the growing weakness of age.' To a *Mail and Empire* reporter, the 'tired and careworn' farm wife not only looked much older than her husband but seemed to become smaller and slighter each year. 'This is a hard old trip we are making,' mused E.E. Sheppard, 'and the farmer's wife has got the rockiest part of the road.'[86]

The country boy inspired no such compassion. Sometimes he was flattered as an embodiment of the nation's future. 'Young Canada,' as the *World* called him on one occasion, 'may have dandruff on his coat, but there is independence and integrity under it ... He may not ride in elegance to the grounds, but he owes no livery or tailor bills.' However, there was much less inclination to excuse his faults than those of the country girl. Urban inexperience in her was viewed as lack of affectation; in him, it was a sign of ingrown socialization. A *News* reporter with a penchant for lampooning rural males provided a sketch of how this played out in the conduct of 'the farmer's son' at the fair:

> He is a sport by inclination, and wants people to think he is a dead game sport. He keeps a cigar in his mouth the whole time, rolling it around with his tongue, cocks his hat on one side and tries to look as much like a horse dealer as possible ... The farmer's son likes to stop downtown some time and see and be seen. If he meets an acquaintance on King street from his own village the whole street knows it, because questions and answers are put in tones which a commanding officer might use ... At the fairgrounds the rural youth ... takes in the Midway Plaisance and the Midway takes him in, and when it lets him out he has seen all the wonders and spent some money. The hired man takes him down to the trotting horse stables and introduces him to grooms and attendants who stick him for the cigars, while the hired man takes them into a corner and produces a flask. This raises him still further in the youth's estimation, and the latter registers a vow that next year he will carry a flask himself.

Exuberance and lack of refinement in country girls were seen as vitality; in boys, they were braggadocio. Rough edges were aggravated by a proclivity for putting on airs without having any sense of what was appropriate. The 'agricultural dude' described by the *News*, probably the same reporter, wore 'a check suit cut tight, a collar that hung out over his vest, a neck tie that resembled a thunder cloud spreading over the face of creation, pants that refused to have connection with his boots, bow legs and black cotton gloves.' The 'country bachelor' taking his girl for a ride in the city 'believes himself a cosmopolitan, and the rather dowdy young lady at his side a second Langtry. When rude people turn round to stare at the pair, he imagines it is only the ordinary homage paid to beauty in the abodes of civilization.' If this arrogance was sometimes more threatening, the results were no less comic. After a day at the fair, when 'the restraining influence of country bashfulness has departed under the influence of the ardent,' 'Young Hayseed' often tried to demonstrate his pugilistic skills on the bar-room floor. He quickly discovered 'sweeping the pavement isn't nearly so pleasant when one has to play the part of the broom.' If the country girl could teach a few lessons to city sisters, the country boy would be lucky to impress a few cronies back home with stories of 'the "bully" times he had "down to Toronty" in the fall.'[87]

Of all these stereotypes, that of the farmer was the most diverse, not because observers were interested in capturing his complexity but because he straddled the extremes of popular attitudes towards rural life. The figure of the farmer represented the totality of agricultural life in a way the others did not. When considered as the embodiment of the Canadian farming community, he had to be viewed positively; when considered as an outsider venturing into a sophisticated urban milieu, he became a hick.

The dependence of the fair on thousands of paying ruralists inevitably inspired tributes. 'Solid men of the day – level-headed, business-like farmers,' was the description of a *Globe* reporter in 1882, impressed by the expertise apparent in the Agricultural Implement Hall. 'Many a farmer as he discussed the merits of a reaper or seed drill displayed a knowledge of its parts and mechanism which would have done credit to the builder.' They could be seen at their best at the fair. 'Your farmer' wastes no time at the show, insisted the *News* in 1886. 'They salted down more useful information in six hours than a city man would do in two weeks.' Their families were engrossed with amusement features, suggested a *World* reporter more than a decade and a half later, but men of the soil paid no attention to trivialities until real business, connected with the improvement of their farms, was done. 'This is one of the characteristics of the Canadian farmer, the development of which has made him the powerful factor of the country, and made him the dangerous competitor of agriculturists of other parts of the world.' City people who dismissed 'Reuben' as a 'proper hayseed' were admonished by a *Star* correspondent to look past cheap clothing and coarsened features. Reuben was 'the most independent man that walks God's footstool,' and without his labours, Torontonians would soon suffer.[88]

Alas, all too often, cheap clothes and coarse features were the very things that made the farmer visible and a figure of interest. 'Giles Scroggins from the farm,' welcomed to the 1883 exhibition by the poet 'Swiz,' was clearly intended as a representative figure:

> The hayseeds fondly cling to him and cluster in his
> hair,
> And on his homespun trouserloons full many a burr
> is there;
> His hair, well larded, from beneath his ample hat
> brim slips,
> And o'er his shoulders falls and hangs like pounds
> of tallow 'dips.'
> Round-shouldered, too, is Scroggins, his lower
> limbs are bent,
> Full many a weary hour at the plow tail he has
> spent;
> His great flat feet are everywhere in everybody's
> way;
> But welcome, good, kind-hearted Giles; good day to
> you, good day.

Of course, the antics of the farmer trying to cope with the daily intricacies of city life complemented his appearance. Reuben Strawstack from Coboconk, in to visit his daughter 'Sairey Jane' and see the fair, was a *Mail and Empire* caricature drawn in 1899. 'You'll all see him,' readers were told, and, to facilitate recognition, a small illustration of a benignly demonic-looking Reuben accompanied an anecdote about his inability to distinguish between drug stores and candy booths.[89]

The *Mail and Empire*'s 1899 depiction of 'Reuben' from Coboconk, out of place in the city despite his best efforts to appear otherwise.

Illustration was often used to cast the farmer as a hick. Funny hats, scarecrow clothes, scraggly billy-goat beards, unwieldy umbrellas, and cumbersome carpet bags – all standard elements of the caricature – confirmed every inclination towards ridicule, even when used to comment on the foibles of city folk.

The two poles of farmer stereotypes were so entrenched that it was hard to find middle ground. Those striving for rounded portraits tended simply to combine the exaggerations. The *News* reporter who specialized in rural sketches began his coverage of Farmers' Day in 1899 with a description of the boot-polishing 'ceremony' practised, he claimed, by every visiting agriculturist:

> The farmer goes into the bar and procures a cigar with a very bright red and gold label around it, either a Gwillimbury Gwendoline or a Garafraxa Garcia. This he puts in his pocket and strolls out in a nonchalant way to the front of the hotel. The bootblacks are on the watch and make a rush. 'Boots shined, Sir! Shine yer boots, Sir!'
>
> There are two things about this speech which pleases the visitor. The attention of which he is the object and the manner of address, 'Sir.' The bootblack who puts the most reverence and respect into his pronunciation of it gets the contract. The visitor leans against the wall, pulls out his cigar and waits till the boy has turned up the bottoms of his pants, showing the white lining. Then he cuts off the end, as he has seen the landlord do, lights up and dreams of what is before him. The boy finishes, the visitors surveys the work like one who is used to that sort of thing, settles and strolls off for his bosom friend who has just gone through the same performance. The one who has the best shine feels that he has scored over the other and sets up the drinks.

Having established the absurd pretensions of farm visitors, the reporter trotted out some familiar homilies about rural shrewdness and farmers being 'the most intelligent observers along their own lines.'[90]

These stereotypes, of course, were not peculiar to the Queen City or fairtime, and ubiquity made them all the more powerful.[91] They were especially prevalent in Toronto during the exhibition, when city people were anxious to make some sense of the hordes of visitors, without having access to the particulars of individual situations or, indeed, wanting to delve too deeply into the realities of rural life. No one assumed these four types were comprehensive or entirely accu-

AN EXHIBITION SCENE.

FARMER HARDACRE—"Waal, I swan, I've heard o' invenshuns, but ter think o' people bein' loaded on th' car by electricity! It do beat all!"

This 1895 *News* cartoon drew on common presumptions of country people's ignorance about trolleys.

rate, but at a point in the city's yearly round when public spaces were extraordinarily congested with outsiders, they provided a rudimentary scheme for pigeon-holing some of the more noticeable characters who passed in view. It was a classic instance of the impulse towards cartooning in dealing with sensory overload.

This cluster of types was useful because it allowed some acknowledgment of positive rural characteristics, but the truth was, as the last sketch indicated, far more interest was generated by farm people's deficiencies in coping with the city than by their proficiencies at home or abroad. Successful navigation of urban perils drew little comment. Mistakes, on the other hand, were joyfully broadcast. Torontonians never tired of hearing of rural confusions, misunderstandings, inexperience, ineptitude, and other shortcomings. Country visitors' unfamiliarity with trolleys was a continual source of mirth. Faith Fenton saw a woman demand a transfer after another passenger got one. When the conductor asked where she wanted to go, the woman replied, 'I don't want to go anywhere. Land sakes, I am clear beat out as it is. But I might as well have one of them cards since I've paid for it.' Sama encountered two country boys who thought the trailer on a streetcar was for second-class passengers, and on another occasion heard a visitor berate the conductor for not remembering which transfer he needed. 'Don't you know where I went last night?' he asked indignantly. E.E. Sheppard mocked the whole gamut of rural visitors' streetcar manners:

> They get on the car as if it were too much to expect the conductor to wait another half-second for them. They get their fare ready at once and hold it in position until the box comes round. They won't pack themselves in as the neighbours do. They are not as careful to put their feet away where they will not be stepped on, and from the moment they take passage until they get off they are continually alert for the jumping-off place.

'Country cousins' found trolleys so intimidating, he suggested, they inevitably revealed their origins once aboard.[92]

Streetcars were only one source of amusement. There were scores of others. A *News* reporter told of a young bootblack who was asked by a farmer to hold his team during a quick stop in Eaton's. Two hours later the farmer reappeared with a policeman, threatening to have the boy arrested. The visitor had entered the store on Queen Street and exited through another door on Yonge Street. Not seeing his wagon, he assumed it had been stolen and spent the better part of the afternoon hunting for it. Once the matter was sorted out, the farmer paid the lad a mere nickle, oblivious to the inconvenience he had caused.[93]

A *Star* reporter recounted some of the sights witnessed at exhibition luncheons – a sheep breeder who discarded peach pits in the table decoration, a hog grower who poured a whole jug of cream over a slice of apple pie and ate the result with a soup spoon, a granger who fed himself with the flat of a knife. 'It is a startling thing,' this veteran diner confessed, 'to see an honest tiller of the soil pour out a cupful of Worcester sauce, drink it off at a gulp, smack his lips and repeat the dose.'[94]

A *World* reporter inspecting a new electric light stood beside an 'ancient rustic' who exclaimed enthusiastically, 'They moost a tak a sight uf ile, that they must!' A patron in the exhibition dining-hall was heard requesting a bottle of 'corkage' after reading on the wine list, 'corkage a dollar a bottle.' A woman seeking the Visitors' Bureau demanded to know where the 'wardrobe' was. And on it went with everything, from theatre performances to lunch counters to shoe shines.[95] Many of these sketches and anecdotes may have been invented, exaggerated, or recast from other sources to fit Toronto locales. It did not matter; the effect was the same.

Country people naturally resented this mockery. 'It has been the custom of years, when exhibition time came round, for the Toronto papers to work out all sorts of burning sarcasm and offensive jokes upon outsiders who visited the city,' complained the editor of the Whitby *Chronicle*. 'Every ruralist who read the city papers ... had the pleasure of seeing himself pictured out as a hayseed with hog's bristles all along his back.'[96] And yet, while urbanites smirked in superiority, they paid close attention to what was being ridiculed.

When urbanites considered rural people, they were implicitly considering themselves as well, noting unorthodoxies that would diminish their own statures, measuring how far their own urban sophistication had developed, defining themselves by their differences.[97] The degree of scrutiny brought to bear on outsiders suggests that many city people were deeply insecure about their identities. Some stories of country bumptiousness, like the tale of Mrs Noah Jones, recounted by *Saturday Night* columnist Mack, acknowledged this explicitly.

Mrs Jones was called on one afternoon by a Markham farmer who had come to see the fair. He had intended to stay with a former neighbour, who apparently had moved on, and the farmer despaired of finding lodgings. Scrutinizing every face and name for any hint of recognition, he spied a sign for Noah Jones's butcher shop and decided it had to be an old school chum. 'I'd have known you anywhere,' he told the man in a white apron. 'You've grow'd exactly like yer father as he was at your age – jist as like as two peas.' This Noah, alas, had never lived in Markham township, but he knew of another Noah Jones a few blocks away.

The farmer soon descended on the lady of this house, explaining her husband would be overjoyed to see an old school chum who had planned the surprise for years. Afraid to offend, the woman fed him and allowed him to wash up, but otherwise ignored him. A while passed, and she decided to see quietly what he was up to. When she found his dusty coat hanging in the hall and muddy boots in the doorway, her first thought was that he was a thief who had made off with better clothes. Rushing out to see if he was still in sight, she became transfixed with horror.

Half a block away was her husband's school fellow, standing on the sidewalk, talking cheerfully over the fence to two gentlemen, a lawyer and a doctor, the nabobs of the street. As he talked, he frequently jerked his thumb down towards where she stood, and she knew as well as though he had roared it in her ear, that he was telling them he was visiting at Noah Joneses, old friend of Noah's, went to school with Noah and was more like brothers than anything else in them days. But it was not as much what he said as the figure of the speaker. He was bareheaded, uncombed; his coat was off, his vest open, a clay pipe in his lips and last of all, he was in his sock feet. As he explained to the lawyer, the doctor and other neighbours, who had gathered in a friendly way and been embraced at once into the range of his remarks, he 'left his boots down to Noah's and took a little step out to kinder get the kink out of his toes and rest his feet a bit, it's so all-fired tiresome tramping around on these danged pavements.' The mortification was too much for Mrs. Noah. Her husband found her in tears.[98]

'Swoopers' like this farmer, admitted Mack on another occasion, were exceptional, but not so rare that many readers would not have encountered one within recent memory. They were annoying because of inconvenience, but also because of their potential for causing public embarrassment. 'What'll the neighbours think?' despaired lawyer Blackstone to a journalist friend when informed a 'Cousin Elsie' had gone up to his house, children and trunks in tow. Such mortification could be caused by any rural acquaintance, not just the long lost. People worried that country cousins were 'not quite up to their ideals of elegance of manner and correctness of dress,' admitted Madge Merton. What did it matter, she asked? Goodness or badness did not derive from the cut of clothes. 'Lots of us lived in the country ourselves once,' agreed Ben in the *Labour Advocate*, 'and were worse gumps than we think they are.'[99]

It was true, but obviously it did matter. As John Kasson has suggested, pressures for a common code of public conduct grew stronger

Grip's 1880 thumbnail sketch of a family of 'swoopers' about to puncture urban pretensions.

in the nineteenth-century city, just as the culture of consumption was beginning to erode the conditions for a solid, predictable core of self. For those concerned about projecting the right image, which included just about everyone in or aspiring to the middle class, identity was a fragile thing. People close to country origins may have felt especially insecure. 'In the city,' Jonathan Raban has written, 'we are barraged with images of the people we might become.'[100] In the late nineteenth century, those recently arrived in urban places also were inundated with images of people they once were. An inept country cousin could quickly sabotage carefully erected social pretensions.

Precisely because so many city dwellers could imagine themselves in the role, the bumpkin was fascinating. While exceptions to popular stereotypes abounded, acknowledging the diversity of rural identities was difficult. To understand how to be urban, a simplistic image of rural identity was perhaps essential: the sense of urban selfhood became sharper when all country people were defined by the characteristics of those most unfamiliar with urban ways. The seemingly insignificant stories and sketches about visitors' foibles were didactically loaded. Encountered singly in a newspaper, they provided a quick chuckle, a momentary break from more serious matters. Collectively, they created a detailed, extended commentary on how to dress, how to speak, how to act without losing face. No manual of behaviour was as comprehensive in covering all the contingencies of daily life as these short, graphic vignettes.[101] No method of instruction produced as much attention with as little coercion. No incentive to overcome trivial violations of conformity was more compelling than the threat of public ridicule. These were not lessons about the development of proper moral character. They mostly involved habits, styles, accents, mannerisms, gestures – the small things that provided clues about who one was and where one originated. Their effect was to heighten self-consciousness and diminish spontaneity. Better to be anonymous, they taught, than authentic.

Country people, too, were deeply affected by these attitudes. Any who read city papers were aware that rural folk were constantly depicted as bumbling fools, and this stereotyping must have spiralled the processes of identity disruption they felt on trips away from home. When people moved permanently from farm or village, a city perspective seemed to take hold with remarkable quickness. Shortly after starting a job selling machinery, John Fallows came to the Industrial to demonstrate his firm's wares. The letter he wrote to his

mother in Evelyn, Ontario, near London, is a poignant indication of
the confusion involved in the process of transition:

> I often think of you at home in the evening and the morning thinking in
> what a quiet way of life you are in [compared] to what I am in + the
> change in my own life within the last few months. I often think what a
> quiet way the people around home are in + I often fancy I hear them
> enquiring for me or where I am + what I am doing. I could not content
> myself very well at home, now I have just enough stir to suit me now ...
> We had a great many in to see the exhibition today nearly all farmers +
> some of them so ignorant they do not know which end they stand on.[102]

Within a paragraph, Fallows moved from nostalgia for the quiet
ways of a place so small it has disappeared from the official provincial road map to disdain for rural residents. He was well on his way
to being urban.

In current historiography, gender, ethnicity, and class are generally assumed to be the most important constituents of identity. It is
silly to dispute their centrality; the strength of these categories was
abundantly apparent at the Industrial, as was their tendency to fuse
and overlap. For many late Victorian Ontarians, however, the basis
of difference most frequently highlighted by the fair involved the
rural/urban dichotomy. Not that this was the single most important
distinction in nineteenth-century North American culture. In other
places – American cities and regions with large Black populations,
for example – consciousness of race undoubtedly was harder to dis-
place. Even within Toronto, other contrasts predominated at other
times of the year. At fairtime, though, when country folk flooded in,
probings of the self and others were predictably affected, and to a
degree that suggests we have forgotten how great the divide between
farm and city then seemed, and how traumatic transitions from one
to the other could be.

~~~~~~~~~~~~~~~~

In the nineteenth century, as unprecedented numbers of people from
widely distant areas got pushed together, social identities began to
get unsettled. Assumptions about gender, class, race, occupation, age,
and other criteria traditionally used as anchors seemed to be coming
unstuck. People floated, enticed by new possibilities and simulta-

neously disturbed by the unwillingness of others to stay put in distinct niches. Events like the Industrial were popular, in part, because they promised to help sort out confusions about who was who, and what made them that way. Representatives of many, if not most, of the significant elements in a region and beyond came together, providing opportunities to distinguish each in relation to the others. At the fair, it almost seemed possible to arrange humanity into discrete compartments that made the social landscape intelligible.

Such hopes were chimerical. Complex identities could not be accurately reduced to fit simplistic categories. Criteria used to define individuals in one context were not necessarily applied to them in another, generating continual inconsistencies. Farm women were simultaneously female and rural. As women, prevailing sentiment had it that they should be lauded for preserving pre-modern skills associated with 'women's work.' As farm people, they were mocked if they did not understand modern modes of appearance and conduct.[103]

Although the fair certainly did not resolve identity ambiguity and confusion, it did more than just reflect existing notions of social being. It helped to shape them. Here, too, as the examples discussed in this chapter reveal, its impact was not consistent. Because there was so little question about who was female, because assumptions about women's roles were so rooted, explorations of the extent to which individuals within the category departed from conventional expectations were undertaken with relative confidence. On the other hand, because country people were such an amorphous group, because genteel urbanites were so fixated on subdued conduct as the mark of class distinction, there was a greater inclination to abstract and simplify supposed rural characteristics. Those beyond the city who contested the accuracy of these generalizations nevertheless became far more self-conscious of their images, as did those within who learned how to be different. Either way, perceptions pollinated at and during the Industrial were carried far beyond it.

5

Space

As practical barriers, the plain board fences that surrounded the
exhibition grounds, even on the lake side, and the somewhat more
decorative gates were never entirely effective. Those so inclined
found many ways to avoid paying regular admission, from abusing
the free pass system, through sneaking in with supply wagons, to
simply rushing past ticket collectors into the crowd. The most common way was to go over or through the fence. The annual report of
1891 admitted that the structure was so dilapidated that it was
impossible to prevent pickets being torn off to create large holes. This
was not the first time its poor condition had been noted, but even
when it was in better shape it was, with a little dexterity, quickly
negotiated. Getting caught usually meant a dollar fine or a period in
the cells, or, for small children, a prompt escort back outside. However, with thinly spread resources and constant distractions, the
police could never maintain a perfect watch on almost a mile of
perimeter – and more as the grounds expanded.[1]

Neither beautiful nor inviolable, the pickets were still symbolically
potent. If liminality is fostered by an awareness of crossing thresh-
olds, the fences and gates were more than sufficient to indicate a significant boundary. But boundary of what? Deciding exactly what this
space represented was a puzzle. As Stallybrass and White have
pointed out, fairgrounds have always been conceptually confusing,
and the Toronto version was no exception. It was located at the
periphery of the city, yet became for a short interval the centre of
civic activity; it was private yet simultaneously public; it was full of
the unconventional, yet at the same time the familiar and predictable; it was dedicated to the serious, yet was brimming with the

frivolous, a place of work as well as pleasure, a reflection of local identity, yet a nexus where that identity was continually undermined by cosmopolitan influences from elsewhere.[2] There was no doubt that the fences established a discrete zone, but how was the fair to be conceived and categorized?

At one level, the answer was obvious. The fairground was a fairground, a place where the fruits of field and factory were exhibited and traded, where all sorts of unusual diversions were gathered for amusement and edification. This tautological simplicity was maintained by close attention to other well known fair sites. As such, initial understandings of the space, were anchored by the Crystal Palace, the overgrown conservatory peculiar to fairgrounds at the imaginative centre of the enclosure. Yet, while the palace was a compelling emblem of the show, it did not encompass the full complexity of what existed there. More importantly, until the fair site was connected to other kinds of social locations, its meaning was impossible to define. Those who tried to pin the fairgrounds into a broader web of cultural spaces were especially struck by its resemblance to three other social constructs: the park, the city, and the pleasure garden – or, as it eventually became, the amusement park. Chapter 6, on entertainment, will discuss this last identification, dealing, among other things, with the spatial solutions devised for concerns about commercial leisure. This chapter will describe how the fair was conditioned by ideas about the park and the city. These models determined much about how the grounds were perceived, constructed, and arranged.

ᕽᔭᕽᔭᕽᔭᕽᔭᕽᔭᕽᔭᕽ

Throughout the Victorian era, the Crystal Palace dominated the exhibition grounds, physically and imaginatively. Situated on a rise in the southwest quadrant, in front of the only waterfront access on the original site, its relative vastness was offset by a wide expanse of lawn sloping down to the shore. Even without dramatic landscaping, the contrasts, tensions, and visual associations of the exterior were considered beautiful. For all its bulk, it was merely a thin shell, its lightness 'as near grace' as architecture might hope to come, as one admirer put it.[3] Its slender cupola was positively ethereal, hinting that there was no room for crass materialism in the spacious wings beneath. Scores of windows recessed into metal frames created an

This illustration from an 1885 edition of the *Farmer's Advocate* contained two views of the Crystal Palace: one from the lake, highlighting its size; the other from a southeast vantage, with radiant sunlight indicating its symbolic pre-eminence.

intricate textured appearance, the complexity of which was balanced by the symmetrical regularity of uniform components. The simplicity of frame construction spoke of engineering efficiency rather than expensive architectural pretension, yet the combination of sturdy metal ribs and fragile panes seemed tangible proof of a harmony between industry and art. From the lake, the building must have seemed at times like a numinous jewel box, the entire top of which might be hinged back to reveal the treasures of modern life.

Reflecting at the dawn of the new century on the significance of this 'house of wonders to two generations,' a *News* reporter called it the 'heart' of the Industrial Exhibition. 'Everyone bends his footsteps thither as soon as he passes through the gates. Unless the Crystal Palace has been visited, the Exhibition has not been seen, for nearly all that is worth seeing is enclosed within its walls.'[4] The palace certainly did not contain all that was worth seeing, but as a key to the

average visitor's mental map, the comment was not complete hyperbole. The building prompted such assessments for two main reasons.
First, it connected the Toronto show to the wider panoply of fairs and
exhibitions, past and present, and thereby defined Exhibition Park
indisputably and instantaneously as a fairground. Second, it was a
keystone in the system of hierarchies that established meaning
within the grounds.

After the resounding success of London's 1851 Exhibition, a glass
and iron building resembling the original Crystal Palace seemed to
be a requirement for any self-respecting fair in Europe and North
America.[5] In Ontario, all the host cities of the Provincial Exhibition
in the late nineteenth century had one. Toronto constructed its first
version for the 1858 show, and some of its components were eventually recycled into the more substantial Palace of Industry, which the
Industrial Exhibition inherited from the Provincial Fair of 1878.[6] It
was considerably larger than those in Guelph, Kingston, London,
and Ottawa, not because there was necessarily more to display in the
capital, but because Toronto wanted concrete affirmation of the pre-
eminence of its show. The best fairs had a crystal palace, ran the
logic; the bigger the palace, the better the fair; the better the fair, the
more important the city. The deliberately ambitious building did not
succeed in persuading the powers that be to make Toronto the permanent site of the Provincial Fair, as promoters had hoped, but it
became a credential of its leading status.

As a building type, the crystal palace was oddly distinctive. Practical features like ease of construction, economy of maintenance, and
maximum access for natural light made it eminently suitable for
exhibition purposes, but it also had a hybrid character that was
appropriate to such liminal space. It was not domestic, though its
similarity to conservatories and estate greenhouses conjured domestic associations.[7] Too fragile for industrial purposes, its cavernous
quality nevertheless bore some resemblance to factory and warehouse. Though unencumbered with weighty architectural flourishes
and decorative detailing that often distinguished prominent public
buildings, it did have an undeniable hegemonic grandeur. Expansive
glass panels echoed the most modern shop windows and arcades,[8]
but did not resemble any familiar store, at least in Toronto. Despite a
steeple-like cupola, the structure did not resemble the massive styles
favoured for large churches. All in all, a crystal palace made the most
sense on a fairground. By the same token, a fairground was more
comprehensible, more recognizable, if it had a crystal palace.

When Torontonians constructed their exhibition site, therefore, it was natural to erect such a building. It connected their endeavour to the grand, ongoing exposition tradition; it helped to establish their position in the hierarchy of competing fairs; and it anchored the meaning of a somewhat puzzling space at the margin of the city with an badge of civic refinement.

If the Crystal Palace facilitated understandings of the Industrial in relation to phenomena elsewhere, it also helped to structure significations within the fair. In the economies of high and low that determine meaning, the Crystal Palace was indisputably high. Other elements became comprehensible in large measure from their relation to it.

Not that other facilities on the grounds were a source of embarrassment. By the end of the 1870s most large exhibitions no longer tried to cram everything into one or two gargantuan edifices.[9] Like the 1876 Philadelphia show, Toronto had a collection of buildings nominally dedicated to specific categories of things. Machinery Hall, the Agricultural Implement Hall, Carriage Building, Stoves Building, and Horticultural Hall were considered remarkable in relation to what existed at other fairs. 'Many of the buildings on these grounds are unsurpassed for their several purposes by any we have seen, being neat, handsome and convenient,' declared the editor of the *Farmer's Advocate* in 1885. Several years later, an 'observant citizen' was struck by their solidity and finish. There was no 'pine board business' about them, he thought, and, indeed, considerable effort was made to give them an agreeable appearance. The cruciform Agricultural Implement Hall, for example, had gabled entrances decorated with flags and wooden carvings, chiefly depicting sheaves of corn. Machinery Hall was much the same. Both had central towers, not nearly as high as the one on the Crystal Palace, but impressive enough to attach their status close to the top of the continuum culminating with the palace.[10]

Still, despite architectural excrescences, it was hard escaping the fact that these were large wooden sheds, with far less cultural authority than a glass and iron one. Where a particular kind of commodity was placed did not necessarily indicate monetary value, but it did broadly reflect degrees of cultural refinement associated with use. Goods in the Crystal Palace shared in its prestige, and those who wanted to augment the stature of things placed elsewhere often tried to establish a closer visual or mental connection to it. A *Mail* reporter reviewing Horticultural Hall in 1882, for example, deplored its 'ponderous rafters, uniformity of line, and general rigidity of appearance.' He called for a new building 'more in the nature of a glass pavilion, irregular in shape, expansive in size, fragile and attractive in appearance.'[11] A year later, the Dominion Piano and Organ Company urged visitors to inspect its new pavilion, 'a neat little Crystal Palace' with glass on more than half the exterior. Except in its aspiration to appropriate the same cultural authority, it did not much resemble the real palace, and once its success was evident the company began calling it the 'Temple of Music,' drawing on a different set of architectural associations with greater resonance to popular assumptions about music. Actually, it was a cottage that eventually acquired a small band-shell on top. Its external connotations pointed more in the direction of domesticity and recreation than luxury or awe, but it drew well enough for the owners to expand it twice within half a decade, demonstrating that prestige was not tied to a single architectural style.[12]

Nor was prestige tied only to architecture. The temple employed fine paintings, statuary, busts of old masters, silk curtains, carpets, and other interior furnishings, and later electric light, to establish its tone.[13] Nevertheless, among the intersecting hierarchies that created meaning on the fairground, and elsewhere, the exterior appearance of buildings was a key element. At the Industrial Exhibition, nothing rivalled the pre-eminence of the Crystal Palace.

The symbolic importance of the palace was continually reaffirmed by its use as an icon for the entire fair. On postcards, programs, certificates of merit, prize medals – wherever a positive abbreviation was required – a view of the palace concisely encapsulated the magnificence of the whole show. The perspective almost invariably was from ground level, the entire width of the visual frame taken up by the intricate body of the building, while the eye naturally moved upward, to spiritual space, where the cupola stood out in contrast against the empty sky. No other parts of the fair were visible; no other parts were necessary to indicate its magnitude and high purpose.

The effectiveness of the Crystal Palace as a shorthand symbol varied inversely with distance: the farther away from the actual fairground, the better it served as an emblem of the whole. For those actually there, whose view of the building was often blocked, who could see there was much more to the show than a single structure, whose sense of scale could not be manipulated with the ease of two-

The Agricultural Implement Hall (above) and the Machinery Hall (right) in 1879, from the *Canadian Illustrated News*. Towers, gables, decorative woodwork, and flags gave these oversized sheds a festive dignity, at least on the outside.

An 1884 souvenir postcard used the Crystal Palace as an icon for the entire fair.

dimensional perspective, the deficiencies of the Main Building as an interpretive device for the entire space were all too apparent. Seeking wider coherence, they looked outside the grounds for comparisons and often discerned striking resemblances to two familiar cultural constructs, the park and the city. These perceptions of similarity conditioned understandings of what was appropriate to the site and how it should be developed.

As cities began to swell in the late nineteenth century, so did concerns about the possibilities of urban existence. Although few who lived in them saw the changes as an unmitigated evil, anxiety was fed by two related developments: the arrival of vast numbers of newcomers, and the realignment of spaces and services to support an expanding industrial economy.[14]

Most cities had to contend with haphazard growth. The public implications of countless private decisions about the location and conduct of enterprise often caused enormous frustrations, as did the stresses and strains that came with a rapid expansion of population. Toronto was relatively lucky in avoiding the severe degradation that affected some cities, but it could not escape the host of contentious problems demanding immediate responses that got dumped in the laps of municipal governments everywhere.[15] Provision of adequate housing, public health services, utility and transportation networks, pure water supplies, sewage systems, and recreational space was invariably expensive.

For the affluent, especially, not all aspects of the change were regrettable. Handsome residential districts, well segregated from less appealing areas, seemed entirely beneficial, especially since the ideology of domesticity they embodied provided a bulwark against gender disorder. However, even for these classes, unpleasant fumes, unhealthy congestion, new streets laid out in endless sterile grids, and disturbing slums indicated an environment that was damaged. Urban growth was destroying the beneficial qualities of nature.[16]

Along with physical conditions, social relations seemed to be deteriorating as well. A civic unity, stability, and moral consensus that was thought to have prevailed in the old walking city seemed to be fracturing. Increasing distances between work places and residences, between middle classes and working classes, made it more difficult for people to recognize that they were all members of a single community. At times, they were not even visible to each other. The new city was uncomfortably mysterious, full of dark, unpleasant, hidden spaces, humanly contrived spaces, spaces spawned by greed that in turn bred ill health and immorality. Middle-class anxieties settled especially on the recently arrived poor – those not only most unfamiliar with 'respectable' standards of social existence but also subject to the worst forms of exploitation, most inconvenienced by dislocations, and most susceptible to 'degeneration.' Who knew what resentments they harboured, what fantasies of retribution they nurtured? As Paul Boyer has suggested, middle classes began to feel a heightened sense of urban menace, expressed at its most extreme in visions of revolutionary chaos and carnage.[17]

Among those with the wherewithal, few seemed to think the proper way to deal with these problems was through direct economic aid. Instead, they preferred two distinct but overlapping responses. One involved the suppression of vice and the imposition of higher moral standards. The most sustained targets of this approach were the saloon and the brothel, though many other kinds of commercial leisure were monitored as well. The second response – reshaping the city's physical environment with structures that promised an elevated moral tone and a heightened awareness of community – was softer, though no less determined. As part of this strategy, the park became a normative feature of North American cities.[18]

The Park Movement emerged in the 1840s, stimulated by a growing appreciation of the civilizing features of public spaces in European cities and by the example of the garden cemetery, where the quiet contemplation of nature was thought to sooth the sting of death and other vicissitudes of life.[19] While considerable disagreement often existed about what activities were appropriate in parks, there was a broad consensus that they were desirable. Working and middle classes both appreciated the recreational space, but the latter were especially alert to curative and manipulative possibilities.[20] Parks would help prevent epidemics and disease, promote psychic relaxation and physical regeneration, foster an appreciation of beauty and order, and encourage people to be virtuous and self-reliant. They would bring people to spaces filled with light and provide outlets for energies that might be destructive if applied elsewhere. For the affluent, the park promised to check the contaminating influence of the city and to reunite its disintegrating elements.[21]

Aesthetically, the park was middle ground. It was a far cry from the fields of agricultural. However much some city folk idealized the benefits of farm life, few wanted sustained contact with a landscape associated with rigorous toil.[22] Nor was the park wilderness. Wilderness was impossible to recreate in an urban context anyway, but its disorderly tangle did not embody the kind of message that was desired. A harmonious, serene landscape shaped by human sensibility, rather than dependent on what nature provided, was the ideal.[23]

The park was middle ground in social terms as well, providing an intermediary zone between commercial and residential areas, and between residential districts occupied by different classes. Neither work nor home, it allowed release from the pressures of both and some perspective on their new relationship. It allowed classes to mix democratically on common ground, without disturbing prevailing social hierarchies. Implicit in this view was a coercive agenda. If, for middle classes, the park provided an additional environment, an extension of lawn and garden, for lower classes it was meant as an alternative environment. The park was a means of undermining the street culture and saloon culture of working people. It was intended to erode centres of community relatively immune to respectable influence and replace them with ones where middle-class values were deeply embedded and enforced. Parks were not inspired simply by aesthetics;

as park designers like Frederick Law Olmsted continually preached, their purpose was fundamentally moral and, like any moral instrument, they needed to be carefully shaped and administered.[24]

In the first instance, it was the municipal government that decided the exhibition grounds would be shaped into a park. It defined the land in those terms when it took possession of the initial portion of the Garrison Common in 1878. The city's Exhibition Committee, in establishing the position of caretaker, stipulated that all the grounds were to be maintained 'as a park.' Naturally, it had an eye to how the open areas would be used when the fair was not in operation, and it may have been persuaded that more park areas were needed.[25] However, the decision was no less tailored to the needs of the show. As Paul Greenhalgh has pointed out, most exposition managers in the latter part of the century thoroughly understood that the appearance of a site was one of the most important attractions, and complex landscaping became common. In Toronto, exhibition authorities immediately set about to turn the space into something more than an open field. The obvious first step was to add trees,[26] and in the spring of 1879 more than five hundred saplings of eighteen different varieties were planted. Lawns, flowers, fountains, band-shells, drives, and other refining touches common to urban parks soon followed.[27]

Within half a decade, the results were impressive. As the new trees lost their 'gawky juvenility' and the cumulative efforts of the groundskeepers were felt, the site became a 'labyrinth of green leaves, green grass and beautiful flowers,' resembling more the well-tended Horticultural Gardens or, as a *Mail* reporter in 1883 insisted, a private estate. He waxed enthusiastically about ribbon borders of foliage plants along central roadways and 'charming beds of luxuriant flowers' that presented themselves at every turn. The scarlet geraniums, the finest collection in the city, were particularly impressive, 'and as there are countless beds of them, arranged with a view to effect, the lawns and boulevards present an appearance highly creditable to the designer.'[28] Here and there, formality was relieved by simulations of natural beauty spots. Two 'magnificent rookeries' were constructed on the lawn south of the Main Building, for example, and another, incorporating a horseshoe waterfall decorated with ferns and mosses, was put up near the Machinery Hall.[29]

Any piece of ground could be manicured into an attractive arrangement. The appropriateness of this particular spot for a park was underscored by two additional considerations: the natural beauty of the site and its historic associations. A lovelier location for a fair could scarcely be found anywhere, declared a *Globe* reporter shortly after its establishment, and fifteen years later the paper was still rhapsodizing about its virtues:

> Custom does not stale the pleasurable impression produced by the extreme beauty of the spot ... The visitor, whether he enters the grounds for the first or the hundredth time, is likely to remark upon the fact. The lawns slope to the water's edge, and present in their vivid green a splendid contrast in the daytime to the sparkling blue of Lake Ontario and the great arch of the fainter but scintillating sky.[30]

Without doubt, the proximity of Lake Ontario made the grounds special. By the 1870s Toronto's waterfront had been overwhelmed by railway lines. From the mouth of the Don River at the east to the edge of the Garrison Common at the west, the entire frontage was cut off by tracks and largely obstructed by concomitant industrial and commercial activities.[31] Exhibition Park provided the closest mainland public access to open waterfront on the west side, and visitors clearly valued it.

In good weather, a refreshing breeze, 'charged with ozone,' was wonderfully invigorating, and the visual prospect of open water, relieved by fluttering white sails on pleasure boats, was equally soothing. 'There is something peacefully restful in getting out of the crush and looking out to the horizon line of our great inland sea,' editorialized the *Mail*. In stormy weather, the lake provided a different sort of attraction. To the editor of the *Farmer's Advocate*, the sight of waves, 'mountains high,' lashing the shore was 'a thing long to be remembered by those who reside inland.' Prettily picturesque or awesomely sublime: either way, the lake provided landscape perspectives that had long been central to the aesthetics of romanticism. Rich and poor alike might find in them release from mundane cares.[32]

If nature provided fodder for contemplation on the exhibition grounds, so did the past. According to local lore, the first European outpost in the area, Fort Rouillé, occupied by the French between 1749 and 1759, had been built on this stretch of the shore. The city's most prominent antiquarian, Dr Henry Scadding, was ecstatic when a landscaping crew in 1888 uncovered a graveyard with six bodies.

Declaring that these were people who had died at the fort, he insisted that naysayers could have no further doubts about its actual location.[33] He himself had reached this conclusion long before. When preparations for the 1878 Provincial Fair had required the obliteration of what were understood to be traces of the old structure, Scadding had badgered the city to erect a memorial. Within five years this hastily constructed pile of stones had shifted, distorting its shape and considerably reducing its height, while the accompanying inscription had been defaced.

Scadding began to lobby for a sturdier monument, one worthy of both the city and the object of commemoration. He suggested an obelisk, similar in size to the Egyptian relics recently erected in London and New York, but without decoration. Massiveness and severity would be enough to make the structure impressive. He took pains to point out that while the obelisk was now commonly associated with graveyards, the ancient objects were broadly commemorative rather than funereal, and their design was distinctively different. Most people cared less about fine distinctions between ancient and modern obelisks. If this type of thing was acceptable in New York and London, it would do for Toronto. Whatever its form, Scadding thought the setting entirely appropriate. It was a 'most fortunate circumstance,' he concluded in a letter to the mayor, 'that the most interesting spot, historically, within the bounds of the city ... should have been included in the grounds of the Industrial Exhibition; a place already become a favourite resort of citizens and strangers, and destined to become more and more so hereafter. A conspicuous obelisk of the character sketched out will add to the charm and dignity of the spot.' The case was not hard to make. Toronto had only two other monuments at the time, both in Queen's Park.[34]

The city readily allocated sufficient money to pay architects Langley and Burke for a design and to erect a foundation, but not enough for the actual cairn. Two years later, Scadding started prodding once more. In the spring of 1887 the Exhibition Association, city, province, and local historical society, the York Pioneers, agreed to put up funds to complete the monument for an unveiling by the governor general at the official opening of the fair in September.[35]

The thirty-two foot column of dressed limestone was austere. Had it recalled the British rather than the French colonial past, Orange Toronto might have insisted on more elaborate iconography. Still, this 'cradle spot ... of all the subsequent trade and commerce of

The severe Fort Rouillé monument was commemorative rather than cele-brative of the city's French past, even to the extent that the site was called 'Fort Toronto.' The latter half of the 1880s, when the cairn was produced, was a period of heightened anti-French feeling in Ontario.

Toronto,' to quote Scadding's 1886 plea to the mayor, was perfect for contemplating the drama of progress and the fruits of community endeavour. In less than a century and a half, proclaimed the monument, Toronto had grown from wilderness outpost to bustling city. Although perhaps ironic to put a memorial commemorating the eradication of nature in a park, the deeper civic message, articulated by Sarah Curzon in a commemorative poem written for the unveiling, fit precisely with the park movement's broad ideological goal:

> These were the men, and those the daring times
> That, by potentiality of things
> They saw but faintly, built our fortunes up
> And poured into our coffers untold wealth –
> Wealth not all sordid, wealth of virtue's strain
> That finds its best return in widening
> The avenues of Nature; looks far on
> And sees humanity a unit, one –
> Spending itself to prove the brotherhood.

These pioneers, suggested Curzon, had worked on a common project, for the common good. Their city, though just an embryo, was a cohesive entity, committed to progress; hers would do well to be the same. Like most monuments, this one projected a future as much as it recalled a past.[36]

Civic authorities in Toronto generally frowned on strenuous activities in their parks,[37] and this was certainly true of the exhibition grounds while the fair was in progress. It was meant for sedate forms of relaxation in the fresh air. The most common pastime, aside from picnicking, was strolling along the paths and across the lawns, especially in the early evening before the fireworks. Instead of the usual pre-dinner promenade along King Street, citizens and visitors of all classes turned out to inspect the flowers, admire the sun setting into the lake, watch the shadows forming, and see each other.[38] Mackenzie King was not the first or the last to enjoy a 'pleasing walk and talk' with a comely companion. When conditions were right, as in 1889 when an *Empire* reporter jotted his impressions, the atmosphere was positively enchanting:

The lawns display their beds of flowers and rich foliage plants with a gorgeousness ... softened by gaslight [that] appeals more strongly to the

imagination than under the strong light of day. The avenues of trees
that half obscure the buildings, add to the effect of the graceful architecture and the long lines of Chinese lanterns that sway gently with every
motion of the air. Fountains are playing their spray resplendent in ever
changing colors, the music of brass instruments, organs, and pianos
floats on the air, and blending with it the hum of the multitude, the
units of which emerging into the light or fading away into the shadows
give a kaleidoscopic rapidity of change and variety of motion that adds
to the pleasing effects of the scene. The harder side of life is absent, in
the bit of fairyland that seems transferred to the border of Lake Ontario
every night during fair time.[39]

If parks were intended to soften the hard edges of urban life, relieve
petty cares and frustrations, momentarily obscure sterner inevitabilities, and inspire a sense of the harmonious coexistence of all citizens, Frederick Law Olmsted himself could hardly have wished for a
better response.

From one perspective, the exhibition halls were elements in a larger
park; from another, the park was an adjunct to the buildings. Perceptions of the grounds as a pastoral middle landscape blended into ones
of a garden city. For some, the fairground seemed to be a totally self-
contained urban space. It 'reminds one of a small town,' wrote the
Mail in 1885. 'It has its roads and sidewalks, its hotel, post office,
telephone office, telegraph office, police station and fire hall.' In a
similar vein several years later, a *Globe* reporter added to the list a
barber shop, hospital, and press bureau, restaurants, and places of
amusement. 'Its buildings look as if they were erected to last,'
declared another observer, 'the drives resemble city streets, the
refreshment booths have the appearance of stores.'[40]

Perhaps the most vivid indications of this conception were cover
illustrations on many of the official programs. The back of the 1888
version (see pages 234–5) featured a bird's-eye panorama of Toronto
proper viewed from the lakefront. Stretching from one edge of the
frame to the other, merging imperceptibly with the horizon, the
drawing conveyed a dramatic sense of the extent and density of the
city. Beyond the waterfront strip, meaningful landmarks were hard
to distinguish. It was impossible to divide the space into identifiable

districts or neighbourhoods. How easy to get lost here, suggested the image; how easy to hide. On the front cover, a bird's-eye rendition of the fairgrounds from a similar vantage point implied an analogous urban status. Here, however, an unmistakable perimeter bound the space. Every building was distinct; every roadway clearly visible. The Crystal Palace dominating the visual forefront left no question about where the centre of authority lay. In this image, the real city beyond the grounds was excised, leaving a stronger impression that what existed within was unconnected to anything beyond.

If middle-class people looked to the park as a mechanism to redeem the city, they also dreamed of the city entirely redeemed. In the fairground, that possibility seemed much closer to fulfilment. The city by the lake was finite and manageable. There was something miniature about it. If the real city threatened to overwhelm human comprehension, the diminutive city allowed an understanding of all its discrete parts and their relationship to each other. If the real city was a kind of grotesque body whose growth could not be controlled, the miniature one was classical – well distanced from other social systems, its components free standing and symmetrical, its orifices few and well regulated. If the real city was diseased, dissolute, and dark, the tiny one was salubrious, orderly, and light.

One of the attractive features of the fairground city was its centralized authority. There was no squabbling and confusion produced by widespread ownership of property. Every decision was subject to the control of managers, who could insist on rational organization. If one arrangement did not work, it was relatively easy to move structures, reapportion facilities, eliminate obstacles. Rules could be applied consistently and fairly. The boundaries here represented a true border, not simply a change of jurisdiction that allowed all sorts of anomalies and evasions.

Perhaps the perception of the fair as a city appealed as well because it implied the possibility of universal, consensual citizenship. Those who entered the grounds did so of their own free will, happy to abide by its rules and conditions. The disposition towards community was so strong, it was felt by those normally incapable of regular social inclusion. The nearly two hundred patients from the Provincial Asylum who visited in 1892 were 'carefully and neatly dressed and were quite unnoticeable in the crowd unless pointed out.' A year later, boys from the Mimico Reformatory were given perfect freedom on the grounds, yet not a single instance of misconduct

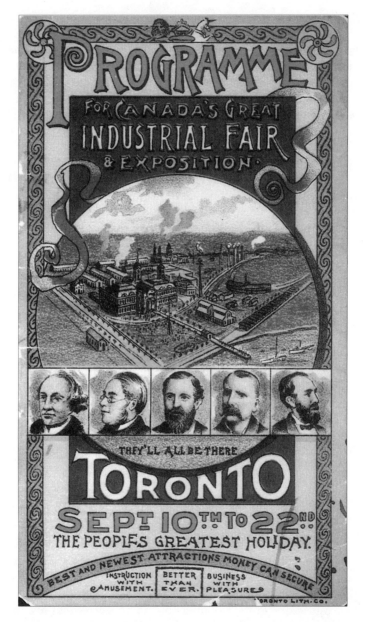

The 1888 program cover, contrasting the garden city by the lake at the exhibition grounds (front cover, above) with the actual city (top panel of back cover, right).

occurred and every boy showed up on time to be taken back. On
another occasion, when organized in pairs, some voluntarily bound
their wrists together to encourage good behaviour.[41] The seeming
desire of all visitors to coexist in concord was reassuring to those who
felt groups in the real city were coming apart. If the Toronto experience is any indication, the inclination to view fairgrounds as model
cities began well before the white City materialized at the 1893
Columbian Exposition in Chicago.

Alas, the city by the lake, as with its real counterpart, was plagued
with problems of rapid growth. Like the situation downtown, the biggest headache was lack of suitable accommodation. The Agricultural
Implement Hall, for example, proved inadequate at the very first
show, so its capacity was doubled for the next by building a platform
completely around it, making it the largest facility of its kind on the
continent, according to the *Globe*. It was still too small. By 1883
there were almost as many exhibitors on the lawns as inside.[42] The
situation was similar in the Carriage Building. In 1885 it was supplemented by a huge tent, half as long and almost as wide as the hall
itself, but even then some heavier items had to be placed outdoors
without cover. Three years later, after the building had been
expanded by a third yet again, the tent was still required.[43]
    As resources got stretched to the limit, many organizations began
to consider independent solutions to space limitations. A few were
granted permission to erect permanent structures. The Dominion
Organ Company and the E.T. Barnum Wire and Iron Works led the
way in 1883. Others followed in 1884 and in the years after, although
by 1886 the association was bemoaning the impossibility of accepting
all applications.[44] Groups that had been turned down, and those that
were unwilling to invest substantial resources for fixed quarters, put
up 'canvas pavilions,' which compensated lower prestige with the
possibility of use at other fairs. Any separate structure, however
flimsy, had advantages. At night, as sleeping quarters, it was not
just cheaper but more pleasant than a hotel room crammed with
strangers. It eliminated the possibility of cut-backs in space allotments. It allowed better control over exhibit set-ups and the atmosphere of displays.[45] It was also more private; with door or flaps shut,
a trusted customer could be offered a hospitable drink or told a ribald
story. The fairground was quite capable of spawning its own version
of dark corners and mysterious places.

Within a few years, the grounds were 'literally dotted with tents,' generating complaints about spoiled views and cramped green areas. 'There is hardly enough room for a man to lie down now and stretch himself,' grumped a *Mail* reporter in 1886. The south lawn in particular had become a 'large village of tents with streets and lanes.' Conditions eased somewhat in 1892, when more of the Garrison common was taken over, but by the end of the century the problem was as bad as ever. Tents and temporary stands were going up in such profusion, noted a *Globe* reporter in 1899, that it seemed as if a vast army was about to settle between the buildings.[46]

Intimations of dissatisfaction crystalized sharply after the Columbian Exposition of 1893 in Chicago. For many North Americans who visited that monumental fair, saw pictures of it, and read about it in magazines and newspapers, its beauty provided an astounding vision of what the modern city might be.[47] As David Schuyler has written, the purity of the White City seemed to promise redemption for urban society:

> Here was a city free of the corruption characteristic of machine rule, a city powered by electricity and thus remarkably untouched by the soot and filth that were the legacy of heavy industry and urban congestion, a city whose transient population virtually excluded Emma Lazarus's 'huddled masses' ... The White City promised to supplant the seeming confusion of the Victorian era with a new and grand urban environment.[48]

Much of this impression derived from the fair's physical appearance. The magnitude of its gleaming buildings, the harmony of their designs, their stately arrangement around broad plazas and lagoons, confirmed the convictions of many urban planners and reformers that important keys to restoring civic cohesion were neoclassical architecture and grand public spaces where throngs could safely assemble. The City Beautiful Movement that sought to restore urban unity through monumental structures and grand thoroughfares was deeply influenced by the Columbian Exposition.[49] From a purely intellectual standpoint, City Beautiful was not consistent with the park movement: the emphasis on natural beauty in the park was at odds with the desire to fill the city with sophisticated cultural monuments.[50] In practice, however, as Chicago proved, park and City Beautiful were easily meshed. Both represented solutions to the same problem of how to recivilize urban space.

Though the impact of Chicago on real cities was somewhat delayed,[51] its effect on other fairgrounds, including Toronto's, was immediate. The gates of the White City had scarcely closed before local deficiencies began to draw comment. 'It must be universally acknowledged,' lamented the *Empire* in 1894, 'that the "City of the Lake" in architecture is not a triumphant success.' Individual buildings now seemed disappointing, not just too small but ugly. Many, insisted the reporter, 'might aptly be described as "Queen Anne in the front and Mary Ann in the back," there being none that are quaint, picturesque and beautiful.' Moreover, there was 'no degree of uniformity or unity which is essential to good architectural effects.' A year later an editorial demanding a 'proper arrangement' of the various buildings into streets or squares sounded a more insistent note.[52] As these criticisms took root, the Crystal Palace, once the fair's leading claim to cultural prestige, began to seem a dowdy liability. According to one trade publication, the Main Building and the others intended for the display of manufactured goods, 'although good enough twenty-two years ago,' were now 'entirely behind the age.' To expect the industrial portion of the fair to progress was like trying 'to compel a full-grown man to try and walk in the shoes that he wore when he was a boy.'[53]

Once again, the cover of an official program captured aspirations about the symbolic meaning of the grounds (see pages 240–1). The single illustration spanning both front and back of the 1895 Prize List depicted not a park city with buildings set among spacious lawns and gardens, but an ordered city. The compelling feature of the scene was a stark regularity that drew attention to the extent and logical arrangement of exhibition facilities. Except for the faint outline of exotic teepees, no canvas or clapboard was evident here. Though it still provided a focal point for grasping overall coherence, the Crystal Palace had receded into the background. Running up to it was a broad, tree-lined boulevard, almost a plaza, on both sides of which were ranged the larger exhibit buildings. Uniform, well-spaced livestock sheds, set down with geometrical precision, looked like a modest residential neighbourhood of tidy workers' quarters, well separated from places of commerce and industry. Spacious sidewalks on either side of an expansive roadway kept pedestrians safely apart from rigs rushing efficiently to and fro. Minuscule railway trains positioned conveniently just outside the boundary in perfectly parallel rows not only made the halls gigantic in comparison but suggested that public spaces could be insulated against soot, noise, and commotion from industrial activity. Aside from the Crystal Palace, the buildings were not ornate, but this depiction of a rationally organized environment was undoubtedly attractive, and a clear indication of desires to stamp the city with a rigorous unity.

It was not until 1902 that these pressures began to produce concrete results. When they did, the influence of Chicago was apparent. Many older buildings, 'which although in a good state of preservation, were not architecturally satisfactory,'[54] were replaced by new ones with neoclassical facades, while the clutter created by many small structures was swept away to create broad, open spaces.

The first expressions of the new architectural ideal were the Art Gallery, opened in 1902, and the Manufacturers' Building, finished a year later. Artists and connoisseurs considered a gallery long overdue. By the end of the century, the unsuitability of the wing of the Crystal Palace where paintings and drawings were displayed was becoming galling. This annex had represented a great advance over existing facilities when constructed, but a growing appreciation of art by the public and the increasing ambitions of the local community of artists combined to create dissatisfaction.[55] Complaints about the 1897 show by a *News* reporter were typical: not only was it impossible to view works properly that hung high on the walls but it was 'rather incongruous to lump in pictures with commercial exhibits.' He urged the addition of a designated gallery within the Main Building. The Ontario Society of Artists had more ambitious plans. It wanted a separate building, and in an 1899 petition to the Exhibition Association, offered two suitable neoclassical designs.[56]

Although these specific suggestions were not adopted, the project was. In the aftermath of the White City, where fine art had been placed in its own 'palace,' the impetus for a special-purpose facility was stronger. As well, with increasing attention to the social role of art as a civilizing force that underscored the importance of élite leadership and taste, there was more inclination to separate it emphatically from practical, mundane objects. If art was to lift people from a narrow preoccupation with their appetites and develop their spiritual natures, it required more protection, more obvious cues to its elevated status.[57]

The new gallery was commonly described as a Greek Temple, though it more resembled a Palladian villa. It hardly mattered to visitors. Either way, its classical inspiration was perfectly suited to the idealization of objects connected to the highest cultural traditions of

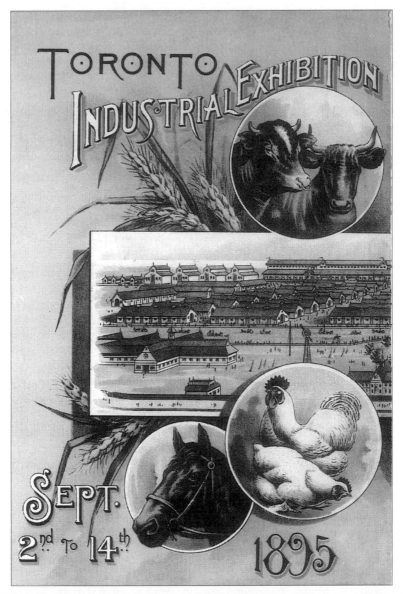

The fairground depicted across the front and back covers (opposite and above, respectively) of the 1895 Prize List featured a highly geometric layout of roads and buildings. Though the image was illusory, it symbolized growing aspirations to impose a rational human order on the landscape of the city by the lake.

Western society. It was not overly large, though it may have seemed commodious in comparison with the smaller buildings of 'an advertising character' formerly on the site.[58] In any case, diminutiveness helped establish that art was rare and precious. The walls were 'the lightest grey, showing clear and pure against the background of grass and sky'; some described them as white. The Ionic capitals and pillars were 'quite fine, simple and yet delicate in detail.' Compare it with what you may, enthused a *Star* reporter in 1902 – with 'the beautiful buildings of the White City a few years ago, or the more gorgeous array of architecture across the lake last summer' – it would hold its own.[59] It was an unmistakable mark of civic sophistication and civic harmony.

It was also built on the cheap. Although original specifications called for stone or brick, the association had decided on wood, which meant that insurance costs remained prohibitively high. Within two years, the directors realized that a fireproof structure was essential, and by 1905 a completely new building, designed by George Gouinlock, had been erected.[60] Though not quite as elegant as the first, it was a little larger and still firmly in the classical mould. It was the most impressive repository for art the city had to that point.[61] Wealthy patrons who loaned canvases for exhibition here could be proud as well as confident of their security.

The Manufacturers' and Liberal Arts Building, with a 'great red dome-shaped roof and walls of white brick,' had a vaguely classical appearance as well. It was not experimental or innovative in design, and no one claimed it was stunningly beautiful. Some effort to compensate for its situation on lower ground was evident in a wide staircase on the southern side that looked out over the lake and the western end of Toronto Island. Touches of Beaux Arts ornamentation at the entrances and corners, and pillared porticos at the ends, provided enough festive exuberance for one tourist to describe it as 'a good deal on the World's Fair Plan.'[62] Its claim to authority derived mainly from size and solidity. It was doubtful, suggested the *Mail and Empire*, whether any other permanent exhibition building on the continent was more suitable for its purpose.[63] Though lacking the baroque splendour of Chicago's halls, it was the first of a whole generation of new buildings on the grounds, all designed by George Gouinlock, which made much more extensive use of domes, columns, statuary, and detailing. Moreover, its 420-foot facade formed a visually solid backdrop for new Beaux Arts landscaping arrangements.

In tandem with the new buildings, the association had launched its own version of a clearance program. Visitors entering from the western gate in 1902 discovered not only that the leaky cupola of the Crystal Palace had been removed, but that the old Natural History and Stoves buildings had been razed, leaving 'a vista of a grassy slope leading up to Machinery Hall, perched on its well-known eminence.' According to the *Star*, 'greatly increased dignity' had been produced, although further modifications were needed. 'Let us have the spaces between the principal buildings as clear as possible of tents and kitchens,' it urged.[64]

More improvements were made the next season. The *Dry Goods Review* reported that the former scheme of scattered buildings in irregular positions had been done away with as much as possible. 'Clusters of small structures that blocked the way, opened in all directions and confused the visitors' had given place to larger buildings arranged more logically. Many walks, it continued, had been widened by tearing down or moving small, unnecessary structures, 'and the open view obtainable from almost any quarter of the grounds is one of the great features and one that prevents much confusion and wasted steps.' Two changes in particular were dramatic.[65] The Carriage Building in the northwest corner was demolished for a 'fine new driveway' extending from the Dufferin Street gates well into the grounds, 'giving a side view of Machinery Hall and far beyond it.' As well, the electric tower to the east of the Crystal Palace had been moved, creating a 'fine open space' between it and the new Manufacturers' Building, with a new bandstand in the centre.[66] This 'grand plaza' did not hold a candle to the Court of Honor at Chicago, but it could certainly accommodate large crowds.

The association had aspirations to do more in this line. Shortly before the acquisition of the remaining portion of the Garrison Common in 1903, two plans of suggested improvements to the grounds were drawn up. Both envisioned a broad boulevard extending from the railway station to the lake, with a graceful fountain mid way, and culminating in a terraced esplanade in front of a lakefront lagoon.[67] Probably the priority of new buildings prevented implementation of the plan, but the features were entirely in keeping with the spirit the City Beautiful Movement.

By the end of the century, notions of what the exhibition should look like had changed significantly. Chicago in 1893 had displaced London in 1851 as the immediate reference point for fairground

The 'grand plaza' at the centre of the redesigned fairgrounds in 1903, with
the new Manufacturers' Building on the right and the Art Gallery on the left.

architecture and landscaping. There was more to this than simply
the substitution of one model for another. What the transition indicated was a growing reliance on spatial rather than appeariential
principles of ordering.[68]

In the pre-industrial city, status was heavily connected to appearance. Because urban centres were small in population and area,
direct recognition of individuals was more common, but social position was obvious from dress and deportment as well. Because the
scale of enterprise was generally limited, there was less inclination,
even by the wealthy, to live great distances from places of work. In
the old walking city, the well-off existed close to the less well-off,
their social position and the social order protected by entrenched
habits of deference.[69] In a sense, the Crystal Palace at the Industrial

fairground Map

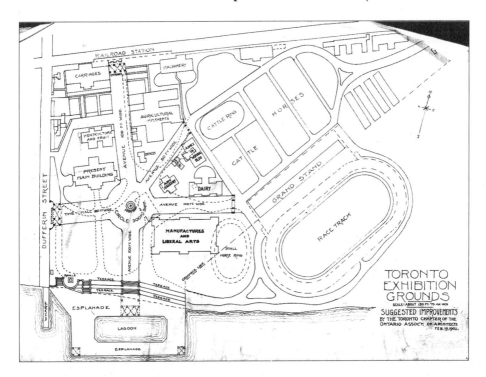

A 1902 plan for suggested improvements to the fairground. Dotted lines indicate existing landscape features. The terraces, esplanade, and lagoon proposed for the southwest corner reflect the continuing influence of the 1893 Columbian Exposition.

exhibition retained echoes of this kind of ordering. It did not really matter how things were arranged around it because its pre-eminence was taken for granted.

With the advent of greater numbers as well as anonymity in the industrial metropolis, broad social intimacy evaporated. Rising property values, mass immigration, the cult of domesticity, and the increasing size of factories all contributed to much more intensive differentiation of space. Middle classes became more inclined to quarantine problematic social groups, isolate unpleasant activities, and insulate their own territories from competing sources of power. They became more emphatic about imposing a disciplinary order on space.[70]

The differences between appeariential and spatial ordering were never absolute. In the pre-industrial city, there were always elements of spatial ordering, and appearances remained fundamental when spatial organization became more dominant.[71] The centrality of neoclassical architecture in the City Beautiful Movement was just one indication. Nor was this transition a sudden innovation. However, as the keys to social identity became rooted in distinctions based on where one lived and worked, specifying the function and hierarchy of spaces became much more imperative.[72] After 1893 that desire showed up more insistently in the physical layout of ideal cities on fairgounds.

For middle-class people, then, the disappearance of the walking city cut in opposite directions. They fretted about the impact on social cohesion and morality, wondering how dangerous elements could be controlled if no one else could see them, but they also wanted the security of distinct zones, which inevitably promoted dispersion and loss of control. Even if landscaping innovations were difficult to transpose to the real city,[73] the exhibition ground was symbolically useful because it seemed to reconcile these contradictions. As a park, it was an antidote to the drifting apart of social classes. It provided a common ground where people of all stations could meet, and generous tracts of open greenery where nature could sooth urban ills. As a city, it demonstrated the efficiency and aesthetic beauty of spatial ordering, and allowed an increasingly rigorous application of it without encountering the obstacles that so often hindered the process when everyday living and work places were involved. At the same time, within the real city, it conformed to the logic of spatial ordering. The area could be designated according to a single specific function, enclosed with fences, and administered throughout with a consistent set of regulations. On the fairground, it seemed that the middle class had created a space that was moral, hierarchical, and yet attractive to other classes. The space provided a text on what the broader urban environment might be, while helping forge the community cohesion prerequisite to changing it.

There was one hitch. To make this space useful as an example, people had to see it; to get them to come, it had to be filled with frivolous commercial entertainments, many of which seemed subversive to the moral purposes of the park and miniature city. However strong the desire to shape the grounds according to what was considered culturally high, it was impossible to exclude the low. It too had a significant impact on how the space was perceived and arranged.

6

Entertainment

Not many people remembered the Provincial Fair of 1851, mused the *Canadian Advance* nearly four decades later, but those who did realized that a revolution had taken place in the character of such events: the horse racing, tight-rope dancing, balloon ascents, optical illusions, and lady fencers, which would have been viewed with 'unreserved horror' in the past, had to a large degree become the main attractions. While the greater earnestness of previous generations was questionable, and while it would be silly to suggest that other displays were not entertaining, it was true that the number and the importance of amusements had increased dramatically. The exhibition was crowded with such features, so crowded, complained the *Mail* as early as 1884, that it was impossible to see the whole show without going every day, and those without that option increasingly seemed to bypass serious presentations.[1]

Peter Stallybrass and Allon White have argued that the bourgeoisie has consistently laboured to reduce the conceptual confusion around fairs by trying to make them purely pleasure grounds or purely trade events.[2] This separation did not happen consistently in Toronto. Although some visitors were disconcerted by the intertwining of light frivolity with education and commerce, most desired both. Conceptual ambiguities between the fair as miniature city and as pleasure ground, between the fair as market and as amusement park, if indeed noticed, were hardly immobilizing. More likely, the leavening of higher purposes with relaxing diversions seemed entirely logical.

The proliferation of 'extra-cost attractions' on the fairground reflected a general expansion of commercial leisure in the late nine-

teenth century. This growth was one of the most distinctive characteristics of the developing urban milieu.[3] Though undoubtedly viewed by
Victorians as peripheral to the central concerns of life, entertainment
was for them no insignificant matter. New possibilities for socializing
were pleasurable but also unsettling. Unsupervised gender mixing
and consequent sexual dangers at parks, rinks, theatres, soda shops,
and the like were disturbing, as were resilient links between many
forms of entertainment and male vice. Marking boundaries between
reputable and disreputable distractions was not always easy.

Much of the significance of fairground commercial amusements
derived from their contrast with what existed beyond. What made
the show distinctive was not so much the types of features offered as
their greater distance from male sporting culture. Because the exhibition was a quasi-public institution, aimed at the whole community
and managed by directors concerned about their reputations, care
was taken in deciding what would appear. Safely grounded in conventional middle-class standards, the Industrial Exhibition was an
example of rational leisure lauded by respectable social elements.[4]
Yet even the diversions it sanctioned did not always escape controversy. Leisure was central to the practices and structures through
which groups defined their existence, constructed interpretations of
the 'proper,' and tried to impose more widely their own particular
values. Entertainment embodied power and therefore produced contestation. The fair's was no exception.

In what follows, a brief survey of some of the main amusement possibilities in Toronto during the exhibition will highlight the suspicions that hovered around much of the commercial leisure sphere.
Second, a description of entertainment changes at the Industrial will
demonstrate that its offerings differed more in tone than in kind
from what was available outside. The third section explores briefly
what audiences may have looked for in these presentations. The last
section examines the most persistent controversies about entertainment at the fair, involving their morality, quantity, and quality, all
of which point up the challenges posed by leisure to those contesting
for social power. Standards disseminated from larger metropolitan
centres could be adjusted to local tastes, but the popular appetite for
light diversions had to be gratified.

～✄～✄～✄～✄～✄～✄～✄

At no time of the year were amusement possibilities in Toronto more numerous than during the exhibition. People expected to be entertained not just at the grounds, but before they got there and after they left. Not all distractions required cash outlays. Strolling through parks, listening to free band concerts, touring residential neighbourhoods, watching parades, window shopping, and inspecting public buildings were no less pleasurable for being universally affordable. Locals were often exceptionally indulgent of tourist curiosity. On one day in 1882, more than five thousand people were shown through the general hospital, while fire companies repeatedly ran out horses and rigs for the benefit of sightseers.[5]

Though city attractions could be enjoyed on the most restricted of budgets, many in the exhibition crowds were prepared to spend more liberally. Where money flowed, enterprise was on hand to tap it. As the fair began, the city was inundated by legions of travelling shows, ranging from grand circuses with entourages numbering in the hundreds to lonely individuals carting two-headed calves and wheels of fortune. They blew into town, erected tents or rented storefronts, unfurled banners, and, a fortnight later, packed up just as quickly and blew out, often to another fair down the road.

Toronto's own entertainment entrepreneurs were no less intent on exploiting opportunity. The opening of the fall theatrical season, for example, which coincided with the beginning of the Industrial, was about a month early by North American standards. Sometimes performances had to be cut back dramatically as soon as the fair was over. In the week after the 1896 exhibition, the Grand reduced its schedule from six nights a week to three, while the Princess shut down for an indefinite period.[6] In this unpredictable business, full houses at fairtime were probably essential to overall success. All managers, not just Ambrose Small, then at Jacob's and Sparrow's Theatre, 'made it a point to have something good for the second week of the Fair' when crowds were greatest.[7]

If visitors and residents could find plenty of ways to spend a dime or a quarter, the quality of their options varied significantly. In this period, suspicion hovered over an unusually extensive portion of the entertainment spectrum, with good reason. Traditionally, commercial attractions had flourished in and around the strongholds of sporting male culture. From saloons, pool rooms, gyms, dance halls and theatres, an increasing number of clerks, apprentices, and labourers with money to spend forged an aggressive masculine culture organized around gambling, alcohol, and sex. Their gaming obsessions (such as horse racing, animal fighting, and boxing), their celebration of sexuality and promiscuity, and their rejection of constricting domesticity appealed to men of all backgrounds and ages, not just to bachelors.[8] Because they had the wherewithal and desire to be self-indulgent, because being assertive in public was so much a part of their identity, and because they were unusually willing to socialize on the basis of gender alone, forgoing strictures of class, religion, and ethnicity, their connection with commercial leisure was virtually inevitable. They were anxious to patronize, and many businesses were happy to oblige.[9]

In late nineteenth-century Toronto, sporting male culture may have been tame by New York standards, but the 'select ball' in the rear of McQuarry's saloon on York Street in 1879 suggests it was deeply entrenched. A *Mail* reporter, though modestly imprecise about what went on, professed disgust with 'the lewd jokes of the men as they swung their youthful partners and the bold effrontery of the pert little damsels as they responded to their villainous looking fancy men.' He was particularly upset by the conspicuous presence of two Engineers in Her Majesty's uniform, who themselves obviously felt no shame about participating. According to the observer, this little fête was not exceptional. The noise of music and dancing feet proceeding from a number of dives was a normal part of the evening experience on York Street.[10]

Genteel folk, who wanted nothing to do with sleazy holes like McQuarry's, were nevertheless increasingly attracted to other kinds of public socializing where the sporting male influence was, if less virulent, still apparent. This was part of the appeal for some, but not all. More and more entrepreneurs, realizing that sedate presentations acceptable to ladies sold more tickets, were attempting to exclude or discipline older clienteles. Since sporting males did not willingly relinquish their grip, transitions to respectability were often slow and uneven.[11] Commercial entertainments remained suspect. It wasn't that respectable amusements were non-existent. Rather, as the situation with respect to Toronto sports events, theatres, museums, and pleasure gardens indicates, a given entertainment form could not be penetrated very deeply before encountering at least suspicions of disreputable behaviour.[12]

The pastime permeated most thoroughly by the standards of the swagger fraternity was athletics. At some events, like an illegal 1885 boxing match staged at an isolated house on the outskirts of town, reformers' aspiration to use sport to undercut vice was a remote possibility. This affair was publicized by word of mouth only, but promoters were not discreet. Before the end of the second round, to the chagrin of spectators who had paid a substantial five dollars to attend, police burst through makeshift screens of laundry to arrest the fighters. Organizers insisted that the match was purely an exhibition of skill, to be decided on points after ten rounds. However, the use of kid gloves rather than regular boxing gloves, the steep ticket price, and the secrecy all point to the involvement of gamblers who would have insisted on a knock-down fight to the finish to prevent disputes about the outcome.[13] Such contests, with their concomitant betting and drinking, were at the heart of male sporting culture. It was difficult to eliminate these practices, even at events where the presence of women was sanctioned to encourage decorum both on and off the field. The 1899 'Grand Lacrosse Match' at the cricket oval in the posh Rosedale neighbourhood was aimed at a fashionable crowd, but some gents in the twenty-five and forty cent seats likely indulged in small wagers and surreptitious nips. For many men, this was simply part of sport.

While athletics were just beginning to emerge as commercial entertainment, theatre in Toronto was a long-established though still perilous business: the three most prominent houses in operation when the exhibition was founded – the Queen's, the Royal Opera House, and the Grand – had all burned down by 1883, though the latter, destroyed in November 1879, was rebuilt within two months and continued to operate well into the next century. After the Queen's and the Royal both went up in flames in 1883, the number of real theatres was significantly reduced until the end of the decade, when impressive new structures opened, notably the Princess and the Academy of Music. In the interim, places like the Adelaide Street Rink and the Horticultural Gardens pavilion were pressed into service. Most productions were mounted by American touring companies.[14]

The most risqué featured variety acts and burlesque with ample leg displays. Though the manager of the Empire was arraigned in 1899 for conducting an immoral show,[15] these performances rarely ran afoul of the law. Still, concern about their moral tone was common. In 1879, perhaps the same *Mail* reporter who visited McQuarry's launched a vociferous attack on the Queen's, then called the Lyceum, after attending 'one of the vilest performances ever witnessed in this city.' The fare included bad singing, worse dancing, lewd jokes, a mixed-sex boxing match, and a can-can number, all presented to an audience of 'boot-blacks' and 'street Arabs' who smoked, spat, and shouted through the entire evening. This particular show took place after the exhibition, but probably the only difference at fairtime was more rural people in the audience and more disruption outside. Two years later, complaints were voiced about the 'blowers' who clogged sidewalks in front of the Lyceum, importuning passers-by to see 'the delectable female show' given inside. Theatres traditionally had been places of disorder and sexual commerce; the Lyceum conjured up all the excesses that made polite society so suspicious.[16]

Still, more refined establishments, with pieces like *Under the Gaslight*, which purported to expose shams in high society and villainy in low, and *Later On*, which promised fascinating dancers and beautiful girls, seemed just as inclined to cater to prurient tastes. After accompanying Inspector Stephens on an evening tour of the downtown during the 1898 exhibition, Mackenzie King commented that the plays at the Grand, Opera House, and Princess, the pre-eminent stages in the city, were all poor, and those at the first two 'of a common vulgar sort.' Nevertheless, all the theatres were crowded, and not just with men. Fanny Chadwick, too late for the vaudeville performance at Shea's in 1903, ended up at the Grand, where she saw 'a ratty show – *The Show Girl* – beastly vulgar.' As this remark suggests, by the turn of the century proper young ladies like Chadwick had fewer compunctions about attending even 'vulgar' plays, but they were not entirely at ease in the audience.[17]

The city's dime museums were also a mixed bag. The Cyclorama, part of an American chain of panoramas, was the most prestigious. The large circular building next to Union Station drew huge crowds when it opened during the 1887 exhibition with a fifty by four-hundred foot representation of the battle of Sedan. In its third season, if not before, live acts and wax works were added to sustain public interest.[18] These extras remained even after the large scene was changed, first in 1890 to Gettysburg, then to a combination scene of Christ's life and parables, and finally to Jerusalem on the day of the Crucifixion, which remained in place until the theatre shut down in 1897, undone by moving pictures. While it operated, the Cyclorama was highly successful at cultivating a reputable audience. Vivid depictions of war and religion probably induced a fairly serious frame of mind, though riff-raff were discouraged by a hefty fifty-cent adult admission charge.[19]

The Cyclorama was an unusual type of museum because so much of its appeal derived from a single spectacular feature. It was not the only establishment to try this approach. Another American venture, an anatomy museum, opened in 1884 to demonstrate the 'marvellous construction of the human frame,' but quickly shut down after being attacked as a 'disgusting and demoralizing show.'[20] Most museum operators adopted the eclectic formula associated with P.T. Barnum's famous American Museum in New York, which involved a more equal balance of permanent exhibits and live presentations, including, though not necessarily on the same bill, lectures, drama, variety acts, menageries, and freak shows. The fare in these establishments overlapped significantly with that of circuses and regular theatres. In fact, Barnum consciously pitched his appeal to people interested in dramatic presentations, but suspicious of conventional playhouses. While some of his artifacts were of dubious provenance, nothing presented in the American Museum was morally offensive.[21] New York City could sustain his institution. The quick demise in the 1880s of a succession of ventures founded on similar lines indicated that Toronto was a riskier proposition.[22]

The only establishment to last any length of time, the Musée Theatre, opened in 1890 with an art gallery, wax museum, menagerie, aviary, chamber of horrors, lecture hall, and theatre where a program of performing animals, contortionists, singers, dancers, clowns, and other variety acts was continuous from ten in the morning until ten at night.[23] Though intended to have an appeal as broad as the spectrum of departments, it floundered repeatedly, changing hands and names several times during the decade. Every time patronage began to fall off, owners turned to burlesque to boost attendance. With each reincarnation, the Musée was as much concerned with refurbishing its reputation as its permanent collections. In 1896, for example, the new operator, M.S. Robinson, advertised that 'certain features' of last year's management had been entirely eliminated. Now, only first-class novelties and people 'that will tend to elevate instead of degrade' would be presented, and no act would be offensive to ladies or gentlemen. Despite his good intentions, he too was soon forced to book scantily dressed females.[24] In 1903 the building was sold to Michael Shea of Buffalo, who made it profitable by junking the fixed exhibits and starting Toronto's first large, strictly vaudeville theatre.

The difficulties encountered by permanent facilities help explain why so much of the dime museum trade was transient or intermittent: new audiences were easier to find than new attractions. The nature and repute of small travelling sideshows varied greatly. Will J. White, 'humorist, vocalist and eccentric monologuist,' who rented space on Queen Street in 1901; the *Crystal Maze*, a bewildering arrangement of mirrors put into a Yonge Street store in 1895; the remains of a mammoth recently unearthed in Dufferin County displayed in a tent on York Street in 1889: these were innocuous.[25] Others, perhaps a majority, were of more questionable merit.

During the 1890 fair a *World* reporter who toured the 'score odd shows' that had set up shop downtown judged most of them to be '"fakes" of the most pronounced character.' The *World's Museum* consisted of canvas sheets with peep holes, behind which were pasted clippings from the *Illustrated London News*, *The Graphic*, and comic pictorials. Down the block, *Paris by Gaslight and Mountain Pink Beauties Supported by the Great and Only St. Delle Family* promised to reveal the mysteries of the Turkish court. It also had a peep show, with stereopticon views of figures in carnival dress representing residents of Hell, and a 'menagerie' consisting of a sick-looking monkey. On a three-foot platform, the St Delle girls, aged twelve and fourteen, sang 'As Happy as the Bees among the Clover,' followed by their mother, who recited a ballad about low-necked dresses and short skirts. The Dime Museum on the other side of the street offered a fortune-teller, clog dancer, and group of trained goats. Some albino rodents from Madagascar had escaped fifteen minutes before the reporter arrived. At 123 Yonge a collection of stereopticon views from Dante's *Inferno* were featured, while the *Selection from Hamlet* playing on Queen Street consisted of a woman enveloped in muslin holding a lamp and a dagger. From what the reporter could see, all these enterprises, and at least as many more of similar character, were doing a thriving business. A few advised explicitly that females were not admitted, but their signs were part of the come-on to men; ladies did not need warnings to stay out.[26]

At pleasure gardens, women were welcome. Landscaped grounds with menageries, bands, acrobats, freaks, theatrical spectaculars, fireworks, and similar diversions had existed for decades and were in the process of evolving into modern amusement parks.[27] They had preserved many traditional fairground entertainments when fairs themselves had come under pressure, but they too often generated anxiety because shady recesses provided opportunities for indiscriminate mixing and questionable behaviour by patrons.

In the latter part of the nineteenth century, Toronto had several facilities along these lines. The Horticultural Gardens, near fashionable Jarvis Street, had a glass pavilion that was frequently used for concerts, balls, flower shows, and receptions. The combination of greenery, promenades, and festivity, including fireworks on some occasions, gave the park something of a pleasure garden atmosphere.[28] The Zoological Gardens had less shrubbery but more exotic diversions. Begun in the 1870s by Harry Piper, later an alderman, they had expanded by the next decade to a site at the corner of York and Front streets which operated for about five years. Beside a motley collection of animals, it offered a standard assortment of quality dime museum entertainers as well as dog shows, baby contests, athletic competitions, and fireworks, all enlivened by Anderson's Zoological Band.[29] The relative smallness of both these spaces mitigated against serious violations of propriety.

Hanlan's Point, the most successful resort in the city, was another matter. Though amenities for visitors had existed on Toronto Island since the 1830s, only in the 1880s did extensive developments appear, mainly at the western end, where a complex of summer hotels, baths, boathouses, and amusements were constructed. Ned Hanlan's own establishment, built by the celebrated oarsman's father in the 1860s, was expanded and tarted up considerably in the early 1880s, with the addition of a luxury dining-room, band-shell, fountain, and waterfront promenades. An open-air variety theatre opened in 1879 was later augmented by an amusement park with rides, shooting galleries, museum curiosities, variety acts, and, eventually, a baseball park.[30]

Although the island became one of the city's chief summer attractions, it was always a centre of moral concern. It had been and remained a bastion of male culture, partly because the sporting fraternity was drawn to Hanlan's establishment, where it could drink and bet while admiring his trophies, but mainly because an abundance of secluded nooks sheltered prohibited activities. Hanlan himself reputedly organized dog fights in an old rookery near his hotel.[31]

Especially worrisome was the mingling of young folk on hotel dance floors and around the shore. *Saturday Night* complained at the turn of the century about couples lolling about the lagoon at midnight or sitting exceedingly close together on the beach. 'The lateness and loneliness of the hour are unlikely to make them anything but reckless,' it warned. Some years earlier, in a crusade against lakeside boathouses rented as summer quarters by young men about town and used for immoral purposes, the *Empire* had made a similar point, offering the recent experience of Sadie Lavelle as a cautionary tale. The teenager and a friend had gone to the island, where two fellows picked them up, rowed them back across the harbour to one of these shacks, and plied them with whiskey. Not long after her seduction, Sadie succumbed to a fatal sickness. On her deathbed, she 'raved about her visit to the boathouse and its result.' Her ruination, suggested the *Empire*, was not an isolated occurrence. Although many women frequenting boathouses were streetwalkers, most were 'shop girls who go to the island and there they fall into the clutches of the human hounds who are looking for some innocent girl to entrap.'[32]

For ladies, real and aspiring, the island was a danger zone. Not that they stayed away: among the crowd and with the exercise of proper reticence, there was little chance of embarrassment. Still, as at most commercial leisure facilities in the city, caution was necessary. Sporting culture was losing ground, but it was not vanquished. Increasingly comfortable with public socializing, respectable citizens were starting to push it back underground, but the tussle went back and forth. Around the playing field, in the theatre and the dime museum, and at the pleasure garden, no gentle folk felt confident that the fight was won.

With respect to entertainment, the Industrial Exhibition was essentially another pleasure garden with a particularly broad range of diversions, though its more direct models were probably international expositions. The 1867 Paris show was the first to add amusements to the official program, and well before the end of the century, at Paris in 1889 and Chicago in 1893, extensive entertainment facilities had been fully integrated into the fabric of world's fairs.[33] Toronto officials kept a close watch on these developments, and on new amusement parks like Coney Island as well. The editor of the Whitby *Chronicle*, for one, described the grounds as 'a park of the most approved sea-side pattern.' He had a point. All its diversions – games, rides, sideshows, sports, and theatrical productions – were things or variations of things that had been around for years.[34]

Despite their ongoing traditional cast, amusements at the Industrial changed during the late Victorian era in significant ways – and not just because of new technological possibilities. Most obviously, they became more numerous and more elaborate; but the instructive character of diversions also diminished, and spectacular theatricals displaced sports as the entertainment pinnacle. This growth and evolution were possible, to no small degree, because sporting male culture on the grounds was relatively weak.

From the start it was understood that the exhibition had to include diversions, but it did not take long to realize that more were needed. In the mid-1880s entertainments started to mushroom. For the most part, managers simply contracted for more transient attractions, but they did experiment with some permanent facilities, notably Harry Piper's zoo. This did well enough in its downtown location during the warm months, but paying customers were scarce in winter. After a failed attempt to raise money from the sale of shares in a newly formed Zoological and Acclimatization Society of Ontario, the city was approached to take over the zoo as a public amenity. It passed the buck to the exhibition directors, who, probably with the example of St Louis in mind, agreed that the best place for such a facility was the fairgrounds.[35]

The arrangement worked out by the association and the Zoological Society in 1885 provided the zoo with a ten-year lease on two acres at the eastern end of the grounds at a rent of a dollar a year in return for a portion of its revenues. The society would make a renewed effort to raise money from the sale of shares to provide facilities and to buy animals. Its new board, stocked with local academic and business luminaries, was convinced that the venture would return a profit. The move went ahead. Construction had not quite finished by the opening of the 1885 show, but was sufficiently advanced to permit visitors. In 1886 a further ten thousand dollars was invested in additional buildings and animals.[36]

As an exhibition attraction, the zoo was an undoubted success. Twenty thousand people went through during the 1886 show. The following season, when adult admission was fifteen cents, it paid $2171.30 to the association, which means it drew just as many or more. In 1888 the *News* reported that the zoo continued to be the most popular extra-cost feature, and the *Mail* estimated that, on one day alone, ten thousand people had come in.[37]

As a financial solution for high maintenance costs, however, the move was not effective. Though the zoo remained open when the fair was not in progress, few people ventured to the isolated grounds. As early as the spring of 1886, the Zoological Society was back pressuring the city to assume ownership, arguing for its worth as an educational tool and pointing to grants given to similar enterprises by American municipalities. Councillors were not persuaded. In 1888 the strapped society engineered a rate payers' plebiscite on the issue of municipal purchase which lost resoundingly. The next year its space was relinquished and most of the animals were shipped off. By 1890 some bears, a cage of monkeys, and a few small critters were all that remained at the fairground.[38] Despite the loss of a proven revenue generator, fair managers were prepared to let it go. They were happy to offer space, but understandably wary of permanent obligations.

The same logic applied to the provision of rides. If small swings or merry-go-rounds operated during the early years, they were very modest affairs. By the mid-1880s, however, desire for unusual forms of locomotion was clearly evident, inspired mostly by amusement park developments elsewhere, but also perhaps by the Industrial's own electric railway. Only the second of its kind in North America, the 300-yard line was constructed in 1883, but remained mostly stationary that season because of technical problems. The following year, on a redesigned system, customers could ride a strip of track laid out along the northern edge of the grounds; the season after, the line was extended to the streetcar terminus nearest the eastern gate, becoming an integral link in the fair's transit facilities.[39] Intended initially as an industrial display, the electric railway evolved quickly into infrastructure, but during the seven seasons it operated, a period before regular city cars were electrified, it was also a novelty.[40] Perhaps inadvertently, the railway demonstrated that visitors to fairs were no longer content just to inspect machinery; they wanted to experience it.

The first real thrill rides appeared in 1885 with the construction of two permanent facilities, both variations on the same theme. The roller-coaster carried twenty people in a car along 518 feet of trestle work in circular form, boasting a top speed of eighty miles an hour. The Switchback, a 'roller-coaster straightened out' copied from a Coney Island attraction, ran up and down 500 feet of hills in thirteen seconds. One visitor compared it to a 'trip on a toboggan on wheels down a hill, the chief characteristic of which was the exciting jumps over the cahoots.'[41] It is not clear who actually financed and owned the devices; perhaps, as with the zoo, private interests were permitted to build permanent installations for a portion of the revenues.

From this point, the number and diversity of rides increased steadily. Despite the fact that steam rides had appeared in England in the 1860s and at Coney Island in the 1870s, and despite the precedent of the electric railway, the initial rides depended on gravity or muscle power. The Aerial Railway first erected in 1888 consisted of handles attached to wheels that ran down inclined wires. A water novelty introduced the same year used modified bicycle mechanisms for aquatic propulsion. It attracted much attention, but not many customers, since the artificial pond on which it operated was too constricted to allow much movement.[42]

By the mid-1890s mechanically powered rides had arrived, providing more intricate effects and more dramatic twists and turns. The Phantom Car of California, a fun-house that appeared in 1894, incorporated a variety of mysterious sights. According to Kit Coleman, 'the walls slid away in the most astonishing manner – a spotted carpet burst out on the ceiling like a crash. Two little tables stood on their heads – so did we, though we never stirred from our seats; the clock danced a wild can-can ... and the way the pictures turned upside down was indecency itself.' Because they were more expensive to construct and maintain, and, hence, had to generate more revenue, mechanical rides were more gaudy. The Gondola Chutes, a round-about hired in 1897 which 'sailed up and down like a ship,' had crimson cars fronted with golden monsters. Another merry-go-round that appeared at the same time incorporated thirty-two cycloramic views of the world.[43] Mechanical rides were also transient, which suited the Exhibition Association to a tee. It got a maximum of excitement and flash, with no long-term commitments. By the turn of the century, the cacophony of chugging engines, whirring gears, and thumping metal, all camouflaged by wailing calliopes, was an integral part of the fair experience, just one more indication of the growing conspicuousness of entertainment.

Although their number, diversity, and elaborateness increased substantially after the mid-1880s, rides were not nearly as prominent in the Victorian era as they later became. Much more important during the first quarter century were what contemporaries called 'extra-cost attractions' – sideshows and marvels that paralleled dime museum exhibits. The changing character of the fare provided by the

Exhibition Association indicates clearly the growing tolerance of less didactic amusement features.[44]

The earliest ones had a reputable, instructive cast. Many were technological innovations, such as the 'Glass Hen' that amazed visitors at the initial exhibition. Invented by the Axford Brothers of Chicago, this incubator resembled a huge cheesebox with glass sides. With a capacity of about a thousand eggs, it was carefully stocked so births took place every five or ten minutes and all customers could see chicks emerging from the shell. More than six thousand were hatched during the show and sold as souvenirs.[45]

Despite a ten-cent admission charge to the shed where it was housed, the 'Hen' was constantly thronged. A *Telegram* reader complained that the real wonder of the exhibit was 'the admirable way adopted of packing a hundred people in a room that might accommodate twenty.' About three thousand dollars was collected at the door, which means almost one-third of all who attended the show saw the device. An improved version with electrically rotated trays was put in a larger building the following year. It did not generate the same excitement, but still earned the association seven hundred dollars, more than enough to pay for its new quarters.[46] In subsequent years, incubators continued to be shown at the fair, but as practical tools rather than as technological wonders. Their place was taken by a succession of marvels and gizmos, including the phonograph, moving pictures, and wireless.[47]

Not all the early attractions were technological in nature. Of the 1886 line-up – the Japanese Pavilion, zoo, and 'The Little World' – only the last involved mechanical gadgetry. The first housed nine traditional Japanese craft workers who sat along the sides of the building, beneath specimens of their art mounted on the walls. 'Every lady,' recommended the *Globe*, 'should make it a point to spend an hour or two in witnessing operations of which we have hitherto only had a theoretical knowledge.'[48]

As the number of features mounted, fewer merited such intense scrutiny. The very next season, a branch of the downtown Eden Musée opened in a building near the grandstand. Its main exhibits, an elaborate clock with fourteen scenes of the life of Christ and a life-size wax figure of Queen Victoria in her jubilee dress, were very much in keeping with previous ones. Still, the door had opened wider to lighter dime museum fare, and a year later, when Morris's Temple of Mysteries and Illusions set up shop with a marble statue brought to life and a living mermaid, it was clearly ajar. Morris did so well that he returned the next year in a building twice the size, with a Punch and Judy show outside to attract attention. The association never looked back. Especially after the success of the Chicago midway in 1893, it began to increase the number of sideshows, usually hiring a wide variety to satisfy broad ranges of age and interest.[49]

In 1900, for example, a dozen sideshows were engaged, though 'The World's Smallest Railway' was a ride rather than a spectacle. Animals figured in a number of tents. A swordfish, touted as the only one in captivity, disappointed many who paid the nickle for a 'liberal education in zoology.' They found a stuffed fish, its hide torn in several places, propped in a 'tank' made of cotton stretched around pine posts. Ellen Drew described it as 'a curiosity to be sure,' but a *News* reporter dismissed it as a 'fifteen second show.' Fortunately, other creatures were more animated.[50]

A giant oxen and Lundy's ostriches were carry-overs from previous years. 'Bostock's Animal Show' had trained lions, leopards, Siberian wolves, and a dancing bear, all described by a lecturer who introduced the trainers. Kit Coleman was particularly taken with an orang-utang that fouled her blouse when she was allowed to handle it. In another tent, Madame Essaw, a snake charmer, teased a rattler, tossed asps and moccasins in the air, and nearly swallowed something else. A *News* reporter thought it the most revolting show ever seen at the exhibition, though Kit admitted to a perverse fascination with it.[51]

Chiquita, the 'living doll,' also a repeat performer, professed to speak no English, so her appearance was prefaced with a fifteen-minute lecture by an 'eminent young orator' who explained that she made a thousand dollars a week, dabbled in stocks, and dressed as a child when travelling to avoid paying adult fares. The movies at the Cinematograph were 'old to city folks and more than usual shaky,' but they were accompanied by a live performance involving a girl in underwear 'half hid behind a piece of veil as big as a table cloth.'[52]

'Electra,' the 'Flying Lady,' starred 'La Belle Flora, the Parisian Queen of Fire,' whose 'fire dance' consisted of dissolving magic-lantern views projected against her white costume, with flashes of pink tights revealed when the skirt was fluttered. Though Flora never lifted her feet from the floor, her co-star, the 'Queen of the Air,' levitated under hypnotic influence. Actually, she was pulled up by a

rope, invisible in the dark tent. The act would have been more effective, thought one reporter, if the man doing the hoisting had not let
his feet stick out from the bottom of the curtain.[53]

The 'Crystal Maze' was the usual confusing arrangement of mirrors. 'Roltair's Palace of Illusions' had two rooms: in 'Night,' supposedly an exact replica of the Suicide Club in Paris, an audience
member, placed in a coffin, was turned into a skeleton, then revived;
in 'Day,' a statue was brought to life. A similar impression was created by the last of the 1900 sideshows, Astley Cooper's painting of
George du Maurier's heroine Trilby, depicted posing nude in a Paris
studio. 'The treatment is so thoroughly artistic,' assured the operator, 'that maidenly modesty breathes in every curve and especially in
the beautiful upturned face.'[54]

The shows were patronized unevenly. According to the annual
report, Bostock's animals took in $2414.40, about $400 more than
Trilby, the second most successful feature. Chiquita made more than
$1500, and the Cinematograph, more than $1200. The fat ox at $200,
the ostriches at $150, and the swordfish at $100 probably made up
the bottom end, for while these figures sound more like flat charges
for display rights than gate receipts, they likely were based on experienced assessments of drawing power. Of the shows reporting actual
monies collected, the least successful, at $338.40, was the miniature
railway.[55]

It is impossible to account conclusively for the relative success of
attractions, but a comparison of 1900 receipts with those from 1901
and 1902 suggests two sharp tendencies. Menageries usually did
well, and things geared specifically to children, like the railway, did
not. In all three years, an animal show took in the most money. The
Animal Arena in 1902 grossed more than twice as much as the next
most popular attraction. The least popular show that year, a
Children's Theatre, did only 12 per cent of the arena's business. In
1901, of shows reporting actual monies received, a puppet show for
children did most poorly, collecting just over $250, compared with
$588.40 for the next least-popular attraction, an oil painting.[56] The
comparative absence of children at night and their financial depen-
dency may have been key factors here. It is clear that the midway,
though catering to all ages, depended heavily on adult patronage.

The combination of animal acts, freaks, illusions, and exotica was
never exactly the same from year to year, but it was entirely predictable. Some elements continued to be instructive and worthy, but, by

the turn of the century, the day had long since passed when these qualities were prerequisites for an exhibition contract.

The most prestigious diversions took place at the horse ring, and it was there primarily that the third significant change in entertainment occurred. When the fair began, the chief grandstand draw was sports; by the new century, variety and theatrical spectacle had taken over. The transition was gradual and uncontentious, and while sports were certainly never eliminated from the grounds, the change underscores the weakness there of sporting male culture.

The association hosted many different kinds of athletic contests, including Caledonian, military, and firemen's games, football, cricket, lacrosse, and baseball, as well as the first Canadian polo match, staged in 1889 by players from Buffalo. The most common competitions, however, were races. Dog, donkey, bicycle, and human foot racing were all featured at various times, but horse racing was the constant. Sometimes professionals were hired to put on exotic displays, such as an 1891 chariot race that pitted a 'stately Roman matron' against a 'revered Patrician.'[57] The backbone of the racing program, however, involved local horses.

The 'trials of speed,' as they were called to distinguish them from ordinary horse races, were designed to 'afford visitors a better opportunity than is usually offered for inspecting horses brought for exhibition, and to enable those who may be desirous of purchasing to judge of the speed and style of the various animals.' They were also justified as a practical necessity to improve breeding. The entry criteria of most contests reflected these priorities. Of nine events in 1884, two were limited to working farm horses, one to animals regularly used as hacks, another to 'gentlemen's road horses' used exclusively for that purpose for at least two months, two more to pairs of horses judged on style and value as well as speed, and one to stallions that had covered at least ten mares during the 1884 season. Two-thirds of the contests required wagons or harness.[58]

Still, differences between trials of speed and racing were hazy. Some events required riders to appear in jockey costume. After 1883, horses had numbered cards attached to their heads, and a catalogue was available which indicated the pedigree and 'a few other particulars' about the animals. For owners, winning purses often seemed a bigger priority than improving breeds. An old ringer entered under an assumed name in a farmers' race was caught by judges in 1885.

Several years later Dr McDermott of Sunderland tried to enter the same animal in races for horses over and under sixteen hands by changing the thickness of it shoes.[59] Other ruses probably escaped detection.

However rationalized, the speed trials were typical of trotting and pacing races held in rural parts, where emphasis was placed on endurance and strength. According to Alan Metcalfe, these events were every bit as commercialized as thoroughbred racing. The biggest disappointment with exhibition racing was not the kind of horses involved, but the poor quality of the events. If the prize in an 1880 'pace' had been awarded correctly, suggested a *Mail* reporter, it should have gone to the horse that came in last. In a boys' race a year later, all the horses bolted, causing panic as they ran among judges and spectators. Inept starting in an 1894 contest left several of the main contenders at the post while the rest of the field took off. Such deficiencies were all too common. In early years, they were often blamed on the track, which was short, with sharp turns liable to injure horses running at top speed. However, after turns were widened in 1885 and the track bed improved in 1886, there was no remarkable improvement in quality.[60]

Though speed trials continued to be staged throughout the Victorian era, popular interest declined noticeably in the 1890s. The pull of sideshows may have siphoned away spectators, but increasing opportunity to watch better racing elsewhere was probably the key factor. By the 1890s, when thoroughbred racing revived from a post-1870 slump, newly established tracks offering larger purses attracted the best horses. For those who cared about racing as a sport, the exhibition had less and less to offer.[61]

The association attempted to revive flagging interest in 1895 by arranging to host the colt stakes of the Ontario Trotting Horse Breeders Association, but the addition of three races with $500 purses did little to change the situation. General Manager Hill's proposal several years later to allow authorized gambling on thoroughbred racing was a clear admission that existing competitions no longer drew. His idea went nowhere, and enthusiasm continued to shrink.[62]

Declining interest in racing was inversely matched by the growing popularity of theatrics. The variety program started from modest beginnings in 1882 when 'Professor' MacPherson was hired to demonstrate his trained horses between heats. He garnered so much attention that, the following year, two special features were arranged – a balloon ascension and a performance by the Beckwith swimmers, previously engaged at Hanlan's Point. In a glass tank, Willie Beckwith demonstrated eating, drinking, and smoking under water while his sister 'showed some cleverly assumed postures,' including a mermaid impersonation.[63]

Public interest was so great that management decided to charge an extra ten cents to sit in the centre of the grandstand. Some grumbled, but almost ten thousand people paid the dime, convincing proof of the market for variety entertainment. Greater revenue allowed for more extensive fare. In 1884 a considerably expanded program, including trapeze artists, jugglers, balancing acts, and trained animals, was presented twice daily, at the horse ring in the afternoon and in the north wing of the Main Building at night. Within three years, matinée and evening stage productions had become a fixture.[64]

Through the rest of the decade and beyond, the daylight program expanded significantly. When an enlarged grandstand was constructed in 1892,[65] enough performers were hired for two continuous rings of entertainment at the afternoon show. In 1894 three rings were provided, an experiment abandoned when spectators complained about missing too much of the action. Regular variety acts were sometimes supplemented by special troupes. In 1890 cowboys in Captain Harry Horne's Wild West Show demonstrated bronco busting, trick riding, and sharp shooting before re-enacting the rescue of the Deadwood stage. Subsequent years featured a knights' tournament, Paunee Bill's Wild West Show, and Hassan Ben Ali's Arabian Circus.[66]

Inevitably, a few complained about the quality and predictability of acts. A churlish correspondent for the Whitby *Chronicle* in 1892 described the acrobats as fat and clumsy, their stunts old hat, the clowns looking as though they had been assembled that day and put on without rehearsal, and a roller skating act as 'scandalous.' Most of the audience was less discerning, including the often acerbic editor of *Saturday Night*, who thought anyone regretting the twenty-five-cents admission 'must be in a very unhealthy frame of mind.'[67]

The appeal of the afternoon show was routinely eclipsed by the evening program. According to the *World*, this was the Industrial's greatest feature: without it, 'the exhibition would virtually fall to pieces.' An overstatement, perhaps, but it was indicative of audience enthusiasm. In 1887 spectators packed themselves into an area of eight to ten acres 'almost as tightly as they could stand.' In 1898 twenty to thirty thousand people turned out on a single evening.[68] In private diaries as well as press accounts, reactions of delight were obvious. A Richmond Hill reporter described the 1891 performance as 'never to be forgotten.' Larratt Smith judged the 1896 show as 'the only thing really worth seeing.' The 1898 production, thought Edward Ardagh, was 'splendid.' Year after year those in a position to compare insisted that the current production outdid all previous ones.[69]

Like variety entertainments, the spectacle grew from modest beginnings. The earliest evening shows, in 1883 and 1884, were little more than pyrotechnic displays. Both were billed as *The Bombardment of Alexandria*, and consisted of an illuminated outline of a fort over which fireworks were exploded to simulate shelling by the British fleet. The 1884 production, described by a *News* reporter as 'something surpassingly beautiful,' never before seen in Toronto, was typical of night shows long mounted in pleasure gardens and amusement parks in London and elsewhere. Pain and Sons, who arranged it, were well known for such things on both sides of the Atlantic.[70]

After General Manager Hill caught their 1886 Manhattan Beach production of *The Last Days of Pompeii*, full of the latest effects, he booked a version for Toronto. Local theatre artist S.R.G. Penson painted a scene of the ancient city, with Mount Vesuvius rising behind. This mural was erected in an enclosure in the southwest corner of the grounds, probably because the grandstand was too small. In front of that backdrop, with the aid of electric lights, variety entertainments were presented, followed by the historical re-enactment. This formula persisted well into the next century.[71]

Some years, the variety acts were integrated into the narrative of the spectacle, creating some interesting anachronisms. In 1890 bicycle sports were demonstrated in a Roman town square. In 1896 elephants emerged from the gates of the Bastille before its fall. Integrated or not, audiences sometimes complained that the acts were tedious repetitions of afternoon performances which kept them shivering too long in the cold. A *Telegram* reporter once suggested politely that people were getting too much for their money.[72]

The real attractions were the fireworks and the dramatic pageantry, which became increasingly grand. The size of backdrops increased from a modest two hundred feet to seven hundred. With dramatic lighting effects at night, they seemed simultaneously real and magical. Even during the day they were impressive. An 1891 vis-

A 1903 photo of the horse ring, site of afternoon sport and variety entertainments and the evening extravaganzas. On the left, a corner of the grandstand is visible. On the right is the set for *The Carnival of Venice*, complete with artificial lagoon. The scaffolding holding up the two-dimensional Campanile is clearly visible.

itor who set off to picnic on hills made of canvas and pigment was not the only person struck by the artists' skill.[73] Larger sets were necessary to accommodate more extensive casts. As early as the 1890s, productions employed almost three hundred actors; by the end of the decade, they required a hundred more. Bolossy Kiralfy's 1902 production, *The Orient*, boasted more than eight hundred performers, with an orchestra of sixty. Toronto regiments were usually enlisted for battle re-creations, giving the events a tone of civic pageantry.[74]

As experience accumulated and lighting capabilities got better, plot lines and choreography became more complex. The 1888 *Siege of Sebastopol* had involved a straightforward assembling of troops, who immediately began a grand assault. When the fort exploded and the

Union Jack appeared on the battlements, the show was over. Five years later the *Battle of Tel-el-Kebir* was complete melodrama. It began with a parade and dance by Arab defenders of the city. When they departed, leaving only a few sentinels, a solitary British Dragoon appeared, who was killed after a desperate struggle. Three more Dragoons arrived to rescue the body under a hail of bullets. When they were done, the mass of troops came on, led by a Highland brigade with eight pipers, followed by Grenadiers, a naval brigade with field guns, and a cavalry column. This assemblage went through some drill routines, sang a martial air, stacked arms, and pretended to rest. Only after these preliminaries did the assault begin and, when it was over, a victory parade capped the show. It was, wrote the *Mail* reporter, 'a splendid representation of a war scene.'[75]

Most of the spectacles depicted war. Of eighteen shows between 1886 and 1903, thirteen were re-creations of battles, sieges, or bombardments, ranging in time from the Fall of Ninevah to recent British and American engagements in South Africa and the Philippines. Two more depicted natural disasters, and a third was built around an assassination attempt on a Venetian Doge. Audiences were especially appreciative when British triumphs were featured, but imperialist posturing alone was not sufficient to please the crowd. The only critical flop was a slow, tawdry replay of the 1897 Jubilee Procession through London.[76]

Many of these productions were imported after initial successes elsewhere. The *Siege of Paris* in 1891 used scenery from a previous version at Manhattan Beach. Kiralfy's *Orient* had already been a hit in London, Hamburg, Berlin, Brussels, and Paris. Even the shows from 1894 to 1901, designed in Toronto by Penson, were entirely derivative in spirit.[77]

In fact, all the entertainment at the Industrial was derivative, not merely of contemporary exhibitions and amusement parks but of the long tradition of fairground diversions.[78] Nor was it different in kind from what was available elsewhere in the city at the same time. Only the evening spectacles, which could not have been mounted inside a regular theatre, were exceptional. The fair's entertainment was distinctive because of its variety and scale, which in turn were directly contingent upon the willingness of large numbers to attend. That willingness depended on the quality of amusements, but also on the quality of audiences. The unusual extent of offerings rested on presumptions of the relative respectability of both – in particular, presumptions that ladies and children, husbands and fathers, would not be inconvenienced by improprieties and uncouth disruptions.

This is not to suggest that sporting males avoided the exhibition. Far from it. They gambled at the horse track, tested their prowess at ring-the-bells and shooting galleries, ogled other bodies and strutted their own. Now and then, a sideshow crept in that catered to their values,[79] but their practices rooted shallowly in this ground. Many had to be indulged in surreptitiously, and the most pernicious forms were rare. What accounts for this weakness? If sporting culture thrived at sites of commercial leisure, why was there a failure to insinuate itself into this public space?

The efforts of the Exhibition Association were partly responsible. By hiring clean attractions, it created an atmosphere less likely to spawn rowdy licentiousness. The association was careful about what was allowed not only on the grounds but near them. With an eye to the experience of Philadelphia in 1876, where an unregulated amusement strip had materialized just outside the gates, organizers in Toronto made sure they were given authority over the roads leading to the grounds. They were able to keep at a distance many hucksters and bootleggers more hospitable to male excess. It remained a long hike back to the saloons, pool rooms, and brothels where rough masculinity was least inhibited.

Other groups contributed as well. The extensive police presence discouraged untoward behaviour. The success of temperance advocates in having the grounds designated as legally dry obviously had a big effect. More generally, large numbers of women and children made even hardened sports realize that certain activities were inappropriate. The less they pushed themselves forward, the more confidant management felt about allowing amusements to become more numerous, frivolous, and elaborate. The more respectable folk were attracted by these changes, the less inclined sports were to be assertive. By the late 1890s they were not even much interested in the horse races there. In the end, sporting culture was submerged at the exhibition because adherents were unwilling to rigorously contest the ground. They were overwhelmed.

〜〜〜〜〜〜〜

Fairtime entertainment was never simply mindless diversion, though, like all things susceptible to multiple and contradictory interpretations, pinning down its meanings is not easy. The difficulties are compounded by the fact that few people recorded what they took, or thought they took, from amusements. Of necessity, they have to be approached as mass phenomena, but to assume that everyone responded to similar things in similar ways is clearly simplistic, as distinctive male and female reactions to Cooper's Trilby demonstrated. An elderly woman noticed by a *Star* reporter was shocked by the nudity and wanted to leave; her husband insisted he did not like it, but was riveted and had to be dragged away. Kit Coleman sharply resented the males who came to leer. She described one old man who 'put on his spectacles and gloated' over the image. 'We women,' she apostrophized to Trilby, 'could hardly bear to see you in the altogether.'[80] It was not nudity in itself that bothered Coleman, but the way the male gaze fractured the character's aura of innocence. Men and women did not see Trilby the same way. It is logical to assume that other amusements inspired equally diverse responses.

Much of the existing analysis of entertainment at fairs and exhibitions emphasizes its racist and sexist character, which was undeniable. Many males obviously patronized Trilby because of its nudity. Some visitors undoubtedly attended the evening spectacle looking for overt assurances of British imperial might and Anglo-Saxon superiority. And yet, most were probably not seeking narrowly conceived, conscious goals; even those with specific objectives in mind were propelled as well by deeper impulses that remained inchoate and vague, though all the more powerful because of it. At bottom, perhaps, they were looking for what Jackson Lears has called 'lost intensities of feeling'[81] that seemed to have evaporated from mundane existence.

Imaginative intensity took many forms, far too many to discuss here in any satisfactory way. However, some notion of the complexity of meanings in the entertainment realm can be gleaned by looking at two recurring themes that had widespread popular resonance. Audiences were persistently drawn to spectacles involving questions of actuality and control. They loved the artifice of illusion, but also puzzling, unfamiliar elements of reality. They were enthused by demonstrations of human ability to manipulate nature, other people, and themselves, but also fantasies of destruction and flirtations with danger. Some of the most successful entertainments were ones that set up tensions among these qualities, combining their appeals or playing them off against each other.

Imitation and confusion of the real were ubiquitous, in everything from carousels carved like horses, through Cyclorama panoramas, to mock battles at evening spectacles. No less than in product display areas, sideshows and dime museums were full of them. L'Amphitrite, Goddess of the Sea, defied the laws of gravity. Zarro performed a decapitation. Galatea, the marble statue, came to life. There may have been some who believed these were actual revelations of higher mysteries, but most, like Kit Coleman, who was intrigued by Galatea's commonplace speech and Irish-American accent, recognized them as entertaining hoaxes. As Neil Harris has suggested, the chance to debate the issue of falsity, to discover how the deception had been managed, was more exciting than the discovery of fraud itself.[82]

There was just as much fascination with some dimensions of reality, particularly with what was ordinarily hidden or remote, and with unusual phenomena that raised questions about accepted categories of existence. Revelations of the urban underworld, the nature of battle, freaks, and the female form were perennial attractions. Bodies of all sorts, animal and human, were an obsession. They were deliberately contextualized to encourage scientific and erotic speculation. 'Little old Sis,' an orang-utang from Borneo, was dressed in stockings and tights to amplify her Darwinian implications. Foreign peoples on display, manipulated only slightly less blatantly, inspired similar kinds of wonder. The 'dusky, bare-armed Cingalese women' with gold nose rings and 'massive, barbaric-looking' silver bracelets, on view a year later, were 'beautiful looking creatures,' according to a *Star* reporter, despite their fondness for little black cigars.[83]

The real and the not-real were constantly juxtaposed. Living pictures, for example, were a tightly woven interplay of actuality and illusion. Tableaux vivants or art pictures, in which live models adopted the poses of famous paintings and sculptures, had gone through cycles of popularity since the 1830s. Producers continually flirted with sensationalism by staging scenes of nudity or near nudity, using actors in body tights. An 1894 midway attraction, with segments titled *Lorelei, Psyche by the Sea*, and *Eve with the Apple*, was no exception. Though performers 'were draped a great deal more than were the inhabitants of Eden,' many patrons were drawn as much by real body contours as by interpretations of religious and mythical scenes. The groupings appeared as sudden, intense illuminations in a darkened chamber, vanishing quickly and leaving viewers a bit dazed.[84]

Native
ppl at
fair

The discipline required by tableaux actors in holding poses points up the emphasis on control in many fairtime entertainments. Acrobats, contortionists, tower divers, and wire walkers demonstrated a self-control rooted in strength, stamina, agility, and courage. Trained animal acts, including Lockhart's elephants, which danced, bicycled, played harmonicas, and stood on their heads, provided memorable images of human control over nature. Native villages and 'ethnological congresses' seemed to confirm white dominance over the rest of the globe, especially when non-white females were made to perform sinuous dances.[85]

While racist voyeurism expresses as well as anything the arrogance that infused much of the fair's discourse on control, another side questioned the degree to which humans were able to impose their will. Many of the evening spectacles, for example, seemed to suggest the ease with which moral fibre was worn down by luxury and self-indulgence. The bevy of women in the court of Sardanapalus who 'exhibited their shapely limbs in a way that was quite fetching' explained why Nineveh was about to fall. The dancing that took place before the Arab bey in *The Siege of Algiers* and before the King of Oude in *The Relief of Lucknow* justified, as well as accounted for, their defeat by British forces.[86] Of course, while these performances implicitly condemned Orientals for sensuality, they were enjoyed by white Toronto audiences. It was classic displacement. These morality tales about the cumulative impact of abundance and luxury indicated far more about North American anxieties than foreign cultures.

If pageants of conquest revealed concerns about the corrosive effects of materialism, celebrations of technology were counterbalanced by affirmations of nature's immense power and unpredictability. Some of the most vivid demonstrations were balloon ascensions. On the first flight at the fair, in 1883, Mr Williams of Cincinnati ascended until his basket was 'a small mote,' and began to drift, now to the east, now to the west, coming down eventually in a meadow by the Don River. Spectators were impressed by his ability to regulate the height by alternately letting out gas and jettisoning ballast but the limits of manoeuvrability were apparent two days later when he had to be fished out of the lake.[87]

His associate, Annie Ryan, was even more at the mercy of the elements when she went up using hot air. With no valve or ballast, she descended quickly towards the water, once again causing much anxiety. She avoided a dunking, but the balloon was torn from end to end.

Distressed by her vulnerability, the *Globe* published two editorials urging that hot-air balloon flights in Toronto be outlawed because of the proximity of the lake. Williams and Ryan, however, had gone up only on good days. A flight scheduled for the last day of the fair was cancelled because of high winds.[88]

Balloon ascensions continued to lure huge crowds. 'Tens of thousands' congregated on the lawn near the Main Building to witness preparations in 1888. Twenty thousand watched 'Professor' Stewart go up in 1903. People were fascinated by the apparatus and the technical processes that allowed humans to challenge gravity, but they were also aware that courage and will might not always prevail over natural capriciousness. In 1891 the directors hired balloonists, but did not advertise them in the program, so no one could complain if the weather was bad.[89]

Spectators delighted in the possibility of danger – though not danger to themselves. Few 1883 visitors paid a dollar to ascend four hundred feet in Williams's securely tied gasbag. Cost was a deterrent, but so was concern about what would happen 'should the balloon get away from its captives.'[90] When the electric railway operated as a novelty ride in 1884, many prospective riders were put off by the streak of blue fire that shot out behind in wet weather. In 1895 the Ferris wheel had to be advertised as perfectly safe and under the watchful eye of 'reasonable men,' while, several years later, the Gondola Chutes promised patrons 'complete immunity from danger.'[91] Danger to performers was another matter.

Visitors demanded 'something better or more daring' each season, lamented one director in 1900, the year they were offered 'Marvellous' Marsh who raced a bike along an elevated wooden track, launched into the air, and somersaulted into a pool of water. 'From start to finish, it is a feat that makes every spectator hold his breath,' enthused a *World* reporter. Daredevils like Marsh occupied remote spaces where unusual degrees of control were in continuous tension with heightened consequences of its loss. The possibility of death, as Charles Rearick has argued in the case of late nineteenth-century France, exhilarated audiences looking for release from the familiar and routine. The same was true in Toronto. The editor of *Saturday Night*, for one, had no qualms about including dangerous acts in the program. They demonstrated that some people still valued other things more dearly than life, and the consequences of losing one's life, he pontificated, were not nearly as serious as losing one's soul.[92]

The problem for performers was that margins of safety continually shrank because audiences were quickly bored. Balloon flights, for example, became increasingly dramatic. Five years after the first ones, Williams of Cincinnati jumped out of his balloon with a parachute. It was dangerous, he acknowledged, but necessary to get work. 'The days of mere balloon ascent are over, and you have got to drop in a parachute or you are no good.' A decade later, Ida LeRoy shot herself out of a cannon suspended beneath her basket, and several years after that, Leo Stevens, who had done straight parachute descents at previous exhibitions, exploded out of an aluminium capsule packed with cotton. The speed with which the novel became familiar suggests why crowds craved intensity; the escalation of risk, why people looked increasingly to the realm of entertainment to find it vicariously.

〜〜〜〜〜〜〜〜

The failure of male sporting culture to make serious intrusions at the fair created a vacuum that channelled complaints about amusements towards the association rather than obnoxious patrons. Many visitors responded to disagreeable features silently, by turning their heads at uncomfortable moments or by avoiding disturbing attractions. However, because the show was perceived as a quasi-public institution where high standards of decency were meant to prevail, the disgruntled thought they had a right, an obligation, to point out the exhibition's failings. Some individuals and groups felt they stood to lose by not speaking out.

The biggest controversies over entertainments concerned their morality and their prominence. In themselves, they were teapot tempests, but they had implications that extended far beyond the fairground. Debates about decency, while framed in terms of acceptable bounds of female stage performances, were more fundamentally contestations about middle-class identity. Debates about quantity and quality were really struggles for influence by agricultural and corporate interests. Both disputes were skirmishes in more extensive battles that marked the transition from a producer to a consumer society.

During the first decade, there were remarkably few complaints about the moral tone of exhibition entertainments. A *Globe* reporter once objected to a clown who called too much attention to 'certain parts of his anatomy not generally named to ears polite,' and comments surfaced occasionally about female performers in tights, but there was no significant controversy. In 1886 the *Dominion Churchman* pronounced the fair entirely worthy of patronage, and the *Farmer's Advocate* agreed that 'obscene and demoralizing exhibits were not allowed.' An *Empire* editorial two years later reported approvingly that there was nothing to offend the most fastidious.[93]

The calm was dispelled the very next season after a 'Hungarian Ballet' appeared on the grandstand. The dancers – 'eight washed-out, dizzy-looking beauties, who are under the direction of a big, fat woman with a foreign cast of countenance' – were American, supplied by the Eden Musée of New York. During the first performance, they kicked up their heels, displaying 'nether raiment in a manner that is alleged to have shocked ladies in the stand,' some of whom apparently walked out. As the *Globe* put it, the dancers did not understand Canadian tastes and had furnished an exhibition 'too strong for the public palate in this country.' The troupe quickly altered its routine and donned longer skirts.[94]

The matter might have subsided had not two clerics in the audience, Messrs Stone and Benson, reported their experience the next day to a meeting of the Western District Methodist Conference. That body promptly passed a resolution of disapproval and appointed a delegation, including the two instigators, to convey it to the fair's managers. The deputation met with exhibition officials, who assured them the unfortunate features had been eliminated and requested them to see the modified show. Dr Stone thought one dance still savoured too much of a variety theatre can-can, though without the vulgar music and shouting, but he and Benson remained for almost the whole program, a sign generally interpreted as a lukewarm endorsement of its propriety.[95]

The ministers were not the only males offended. Even association directors were divided on the issue. Some felt it was just the 'regulation ballet' performed regularly at respectable theatres; others thought it should not be tolerated at the Industrial, regardless of where else it was done. No doubt emboldened by the public discussion, some in the audience on Citizens' Day hissed the act. The protest was deserved on grounds of quality if nothing else; the dance was conceded to be 'so bad it could not be worse.' Madame director admitted the real company had gone elsewhere for a higher offer, and she had thrown together a new one at the frantic behest of man-

ager Hill. However, patrons reacted to more than lack of talent.
Shouts of 'rats' greeted the dancers' arrival on stage, before they had
a chance to demonstrate ineptitude.[96]

On the other hand, some thought the fuss was entirely overblown.
A correspondent for the Pickering *News* joshed that it was hard to
see the ballet for all the churchmen in attendance. The *Globe* suggested that if ministers needed two visits to decide the dance was a
can-can, no demoralization would come to those who saw it only once.
The concern of *Saturday Night*'s editor was censorship, not immorality. Who, he wondered, gave these clergy the right to dictate standards? His worries about creeping theocracy were unwarranted. The
show was thronged. No part of the exhibition was better patronized,
claimed the *World*. 'The People evidently want to see it judging by
the thousands that pack the Grand Stand every day.' In subsequent
years, 'graceful posturing and high kicking' remained a standard
part of shows, though performers probably were instructed to tone
things down for conservative Toronto audiences.[97]

The association had to walk a fine line. If some took offence at displays of the female form, others clearly wanted them. Trying to balance the demands led to some erratic shifts of strategy. On occasion,
controversy as a stimulant to public interest was welcomed, yet at
other times there was great sensitivity to charges of immorality.

Hubbub during the 1894 show seemed deliberately engineered.
When local Baptist minister O.C.S. Wallace returned some complimentary passes, president Withrow made public the accompanying
letter and suggested that the motivation was opposition to the 'Living Pictures' sideshow. In response, Wallace pointed out that his letter, sent privately, contained no explanation of why the tickets were
refused; if Withrow thought the 'Living Pictures' were the cause, it
was the prompting of his own conscience. Though Wallace was careful not to make any specific judgment about the *Pictures*, perhaps to
avoid increasing their notoriety, Withrow had successfully primed
the publicity pump.[98]

The *News* was particularly zealous in taking up the cause. In an
article boldly headlined 'Nude Women,' it charged that special
attractions had grown annually more indecent since the Hungarian
Ballet episode, but that the climax had now been reached with 'the
most indecent exhibition of the female figure ever given in this city.'
When such things were shown at an exhibition where boys and girls
were allowed the utmost liberty, it was a thousand times worse than

when they appeared at a theatre. 'Adolescens' took up the same theme in a letter to the *Empire*. He had been horrified on Children's Day to find the audience comprised of twenty-five to thirty boys ranging from ten to sixteen years of age:

> As the exhibition proceeded, and picture after picture of scantily dressed women was presented to our gaze, it was only necessary to notice the whispered conversations of the youngsters and to overhear an occasional word to realize the evil effect it was having on their youthful minds ... I decided there and then that my younger brothers should not enter the door of an exhibition the sole cause for the existence of which is the baser passions of man's nature. If I had a sister I would not take her there; nor would I permit to enter any woman whose innocence and purity I held sacred if I could prevent.

Like other critics, he was outraged that the 'Pictures' were justified as 'art.' 'Naked marble and naked women are two totally different things,' wrote L. Byron to the *News*, 'and no man with a spark of purity in his soul would see anything but vulgarity and uncleanness in the latter, while the former is altogether a different thing.'[99]

Others, including many women, saw nothing objectionable in the show. 'Lady Gay' in *Saturday Night* wondered why anyone took offence to the 'Pictures.' Sama, in the *Globe*, found them quite beautiful; she had gone twice and wanted to see them again. The editor of the *Mail* congratulated management for the entire class of performers that had been secured, while the *World* suggested that Rev. Wallace was hopelessly old fashioned. Meanwhile, crowds flocked to the attraction and, when the fair ended, the show moved immediately into the Academy of Music downtown.[100]

If management was looking for a fight in 1894, it seemed genuinely surprised by the fuss over the *Festival of Nations* grandstand show two years later. The pattern of response was predictable. Many people were charmed. The *News* reporter thought it an exceedingly bright and pretty feature. Kit Coleman described all the entertainment that year as 'clean, wholesome, refining.'[101]

Others, however, were put off by a 'ballet' troupe of sixty-four women in short skirts and flesh-coloured tights. Rev. J.C. Speer of the Broadway Tabernacle asked his congregation how Christ would have felt watching the 'low, obscene, vulgar production of the ballet.' The editor of the *Christian Guardian* could not imagine what induced a pure woman to appear publicly in ballet costume. Speaking from profound sorrow and regret, as a public teacher in a most responsible position, touching twice as many families as there were individuals in the grandstand, he called for a close watch on future productions. If the course of competition with the lowest theatre performances was continued, it would be the plain duty of Christians to desert the grandstand. 'Mack,' in *Saturday Night*, complained that the ballet was not just immoral but inartistic. Without suitable music, scenery, or costumes to soften the presentation, without a plot to justify its presence, attention inevitably centred on the fact that women were dressed in garb that would probably cause their arrest on the street. It was not sufficient to say that those who did not like the show need not witness it. 'Our exhibition is not for a class, but for the nation.'[102]

The directors were taken aback by the degree of protest. The annual report later admitted that some features would not have been missed if left out. In arranging a program like this, they apologized, it was hard to know what to include; they would do better next time. Indeed, the 1897 Jubilee tableau went so far in the other direction that it raised even greater complaints. *Saturday Night* addressed the directors' dilemma. 'There must be a large area of sensible middle-ground between those things that are lewd and those that are virtuous but stupid, and if the general influence of the exhibition tends for good, some few concessions must be made in order to attract the masses of people who are not interested in the ordinary features of a fall fair.' In 1898 short skirts and flesh-colored tights returned with little comment.[103]

But the controversy was far from over. By the end of the century, objections were directed mostly at sideshows. Some of the acts performed outside to lure customers were 'sufficiently suggestive to satisfy the wildest devotee of the Bowery,' asserted the *World* in 1902. The midway was threatening to become nothing but 'a dazzling array of female artists in tights in front of each tent,' agreed the *Star*. These charges were investigated immediately, but management claimed it could find no one who had seen anything indecent.[104]

The lack of consistency among complainants is striking. In 1894 the *News* led the charge against the 'Living Pictures'; two years later it had no difficulty with the Festival of Nations ballet. The reverse was true for *Saturday Night* and for Rev. Speer. His exhibition sermon in 1894 extolled the fair; in 1896 it decried the immorality on public view there. These flip-flops suggest more was going on here than simply efforts to generate sensational publicity. The fundamental issue in these controversies was not the acceptable height of a can-can kick, but what it meant to be middle-class women and men, matters very much in flux and therefore subject to inconsistency.

Those who criticized the immorality of exhibition entertainments defended a traditional understanding of middle-class identity based on character and gentility. Social responsibility, high-mindedness, self-restraint – these were its primary qualities. Chorus lines of scantily dressed young women flaunting their charms may have been tolerable in 'low' theatres frequented by rowdies, but they did not merit the attention of ladies and gentlemen, and did not deserve to be part of civic celebrations intended to show off the community's highest achievements.

Others were moving away from this view. For 'Mack,' the *Saturday Night* columnist, refinement was based more on the capacity to make discerning cultural judgments, a skill presumably honed by patronizing the arts and reading publications like his own. His standards affirmed the importance of self-development, but self-development aimed at improving sophistication of taste rather than moral character. His priorities pointed clearly in the direction of a more informal class culture, rooted not in duty, restraint, and thrift, but in pleasure, expression, and consumption.

Those heading along this route found it much easier than the Victorian rearguard to articulate values with actions rather than words. They did not need to protest declining standards, only to enjoy new opportunities. Perhaps M.O. Hammond, *Globe* reporter, home owner, and devoted family man, typified the new middling sort. He and his wife signalled their class affiliation at the 1903 fair by making a bee-line for the art gallery, because 'she was anxious to have some real paintings in our house.' Then, at the *Carnival of Venice* in the evening, he and a friend teased their wives 'by manifesting great anxiety to view the abbreviated dresses through opera glasses,' and, on the way out, everyone 'feasted on "Coney Island hot" sausages and rolls, in great disregard for conventionality.'[105] Cultural refinement was not the only alternative basis of class identity, nor was wearing revealing clothing the only issue around which it crystallized, as Hammond's reference to hot dogs indicates. Entertainment figured prominently in the shift, since the leisure sphere was associated so closely with permissive values, but all aspects of life were affected.[106]

Quite Obvious.

Rev. Dr. Saintly : " It's scandalous ! If I had my way I'd have all such people arrested as vagrants."

Flipjack : "It wouldn't be any use doctor. They evidently can show visible means of support."

This cartoon, from a Toronto review published in 1902, reflects the growing middle-class comfort with commercial entertainment.

While it is important to remember that few people had consistent responses to these changes, the prominent role of clergy in the exhibition protests is not surprising. Their own social status was at stake. As experts on and exemplars of character, they saw their field of authority shrinking. Their relative incomes were shrinking as well, causing much despair about the effect of penury on the profession's sense of self-worth and its ability to attract talented recruits.[107] Increasing material abundance in industrial society aggravated their declining influence rather than compensated for it. Some clergy were among the most perceptive critics of modern urban society precisely because they stood to lose so much. What they had to say sometimes resonated profoundly with listeners, but sometimes they mostly sounded puritanical, hypocritical, and foolish. Such was the case when they objected to entertainments at the fair. Complaints about moral laxity at the exhibition ground never gathered much force because the association kept a close eye on the parameters of acceptability. When defenders of traditional standards tried to rally opinion, they swelled audiences more than their own influence.

If some were disturbed by the quality of entertainment, many more were concerned about the quantity. Revelry seemed to be swamping more serious pursuits. This was by far the biggest issue relating to diversions at the fair. What was the purpose of exhibitions – to educate or to amuse? The question occurred to almost everyone who considered the role of the fair, but it was posed most vociferously by two groups that feared their specific needs were getting sidetracked. A portion of the farming community and manufacturers protested the prominence of entertainments, but they did so at different times and with different effectiveness. Agricultural interests, though ostensibly representing a large constituency, had little power to change exhibition priorities; businessmen were much more influential, though they too had to acknowledge the power of amusements.[108]

Complaints about the number of entertainments surfaced early on. The editor of the Galt *Reformer*, glancing at the 1881 program, worried that there were 'so many other features of such a novel and promiscuous character that the merely agricultural and industrial is apt to be lost sight of.' The correspondent of the Newmarket *Era* reported the same year that displays in the Main Building and the Machinery Hall suffered because of excessive attention to what directors thought would amuse. Comments like these became sharper and more common as time went by. Their frequency in small-town and rural papers may have been inspired by jealousy of the city fair, but the farm constituency was not alone in making such suggestions. The *World* was soon lamenting management's tendency to turn the fair into a 'jim-crack show,' the *Telegram* urging that the 'circus business' be done away with and the money added to the prize list, and the *Labour Advocate* warning that what was intended as an instructive show was turning into 'a mere gallery of mountebanks and hawkers.'[109]

All groups with more serious purposes fretted, but the general feeling, especially during the first decade and a half, was that agriculture suffered most deleteriously because it depended most on the fair as a mechanism of advance. The farmer 'who wishes to give himself an honest chance,' editorialized *Saturday Night* in 1892, 'must visit the Fair and study the progress of a year and then go home and move himself forward a peg or two.' This required disciplined attention to the regular exhibits. To mark, learn, and digest every department took at least four days, suggested one authority. Time wasted on amusements meant less income in the long run.[110]

This was the theory. Judged against common practice, it often rang very hollow. The educational effect of the fair, 'so paper-puffed and praised,' as the *Empire* put it in 1894, was 'absolutely nil.' A Bobcaygeon editor made the point after conversing with a local farmer whose strongest recollection was 'the circus':

> Tim Melaney, on being questioned, admitted that he did not see any live stock, nor any grain, nor any vegetables, and that he spent most of the two days he was there about the horse ring, and seeing the Circus business. He acknowledged having seen a new kind of mowing machine, but he mentioned the fact only incidentally, and gave our agricultural editor a very long and deeply interesting account of a lady in flesh tights who did a most attractive performance on a trapeze ... by all means let the show go on ... but don't give us too much bosh about its being an Agricultural educator.

Four-fifths of the visitors would not miss the livestock and agricultural implements if they were absent, asserted the editor of the Whitby *Chronicle*.[111]

For many, it was a worrisome trend. The editor of the *Farmer's Advocate* was unusually apocalyptic in warning that the 'Hippodrome has been the great educator of those nations whose walls and people are now no more,' but he was not alone in lamenting its influence.[112] Typically, his discontent was inspired not so much by distaste for trivial amusements, per se, as by what their prevalence suggested about rural influence in an increasingly urban world – and perhaps, more specifically, about the growing dominance of Toronto over surrounding communities. The 'real, plain, practical farmers and their products are only of second or third rate consideration' to the Exhibition Association, he huffed.[113]

Counter arguments were equally emphatic. Once the drawing power

MODERN AGRICULTURAL EXHIBITION.

This *Farmer's Advocate* cartoon was not subtle in suggesting that the Industrial Exhibition had become excessively given over to inconsequential diversions. In the bottom left corner, Ontario premier Oliver Mowat and General Frederick Middleton, leader of the forces that put down the second Riel Rebellion, are depicted inspecting some of the main attractions at the 1885 show. With one exception, all the stage performers, including the band, appear to be female.

of amusements became obvious, city papers became much more supportive of them. In an editorial that asked, 'What's the Good of It?' the *Globe* pointed out that entertainment generated revenue that could be used to create better displays in other departments, brought those with lighter things on their minds into proximity with more serious matter, and was itself educational: the person who learned nothing from a balloon ascension or demonstration of athletic feats was a hopeless dullard. Besides, it insisted on another occasion, after the exhausting work of touring the displays, the desire to rest in the grandstand for an hour or so was natural.[114]

For many defenders of the varieties, it was not rest from the exhibition that was essential, but rest from the labour of farming itself. A total change of scene was healthy for anyone, but it was most valuable for people tied to the land. They had come to look on the fair as 'the occasion for their holiday outing,' as the association report put it in 1891, and they demanded entertainment. A little more holidaying of this kind would do much to keep the boys on the farm, thought the *Empire*.[115]

The most persuasive argument in favour of amusements, however, was the behaviour of rural visitors. The *Canadian Manufacturer* estimated that three-quarters of country people came to see 'attractions peculiar to the city,' and only a very small proportion to look at improved farm stock. The *World* and the *Globe* put the figure closer to 90 per cent. The editor of the Whitby *Chronicle* guessed that four-fifths of visitors went directly to the grandstand and stayed there all day, 'the only idea they ever gain of the exhibition being the paid-for puffs printed in the daily papers.' It was strange, he noted on another occasion, that farmers so readily left the stock and crop exhibits to go wild over a horse race, cheering for a nag worth about as much as the purse it trotted for, when ninety-nine out of a hundred got a living from everything but race horses.[116]

Still, critics could do little except to urge rural visitors to spend more time in animal barns and at crop displays. Since the financial well-being of most farm families did not depend directly on anything that transpired at the fair, these injunctions were not overly compelling. With so many farm people patronizing the attractions, the association shrugged off complaints, suggesting it was meeting the real priorities of rural visitors.

It had a harder time with businessmen. Their numbers were relatively small, but their objectives were more coherent and their voices more easily harmonized. When they began to be concerned that entertainment features were becoming too prominent, they not only protested but put forward strategies to pull people away. The association listened carefully.

During the first two decades of the fair, business had few complaints about amusements. When H.A. Massey, president of the large farm equipment manufacturing company, suggested at a directors' luncheon in 1892 that sideshows detracted a good deal from the benefit manufacturers were supposed to derive from the exhibition, F.T. Frost of Smiths Falls, another implement maker, responded that he saw nothing objectionable in the shows; indeed, he considered the fair a great benefit to his company and felt that the quality of displays had never been better. Five other businessmen echoed Frost's sentiments. At the end of the century, the directors were hearing a different tune.[117]

Grumbling proliferated through the latter half of the 1890s as extra-cost attractions became more numerous and more raucous. Carnival barkers seemed to monopolize the grounds, carped the *News* in 1897. The proliferation of sideshows was matched only by the meagreness of their fare, railed *Saturday Night* two years later. A *Canadian Grocer* editorial in 1900, in endorsing a petition for federal aid for the exhibition, made back-handed complaints about the declining quality of manufacturing exhibits, lack of attention to manufacturers' concerns, and, above all, the tendency to make the fair a circus 'where sideshows abounded which were either suggestively immoral or deceiving and fraudulent.'[118]

Discontent crystallized in the fall of that year when the Toronto *Star* spent a solid week probing the exhibition's shortcomings. Visitors who went through with honestly inquiring minds were greatly repaid, it decided, but most did not do the show systematically. The majority

> drift in with the tide of people, and the tide carries them towards the steam organ, towards the place whence comes the voice of the showman, and where the gilt and tinsel of the sideshow glitters in the sun. The great circus fills the public eye and decoys the people away from the sober halls of the mechanics, arts and sciences. The inventor, alone with his invention, glares at the crowd flowing past to where a colored man with a ring in his nose perspires under furs and barks as wild men are wont to do.

'Solid, instructive exhibits' were being ignored, echoed the *News*, while the show was 'sinking into the slough of fakirism.'[119]

In speaking to dozens of exhibitors, the *Star* documented a litany of complaints. While manufacturers received little encouragement, fun makers got every assistance and had thereby become too prominent. By locating sideshows along the main roadways, people were drawn away from substantial features, especially those in Machinery

Hall and the Agricultural Implement Hall, which were now off the beaten track. The grandstand show was so long that people had little time to see anything else, especially if they were drawn into the side-shows. These were mostly fakes of poor value, inferior to variety entertainments downtown and far more expensive. The public had a right to be protected from such shams. Business, on the other hand, had a right to more input into decision making. Men who had been exhibiting at the fair for years might have ideas that never would occur to the general manager; soliciting their suggestions was 'the only way to ensure constant development.'[120]

Management defended its practices. The new president, Andrew Smith, insisting he had heard no complaints, reiterated the organizers' firm belief that sideshows drew visitors. Business critics found it just as hard as farm critics to refute the assertion. Most businessmen interviewed by the *Star* acknowledged that the fair had to be more than a series of commercial exhibits.[121] So, while the association was softened up to respond to manufacturers' complaints, business recognized it had to live with the amusements, and in the pages of the *Star* a strategy congealed to shore up the industrial section.

The first step was to isolate sideshows in a less prominent corner of the park. They should be given a part of the grounds entirely to themselves, away from the main roads, suggested John Kay of the carpet-ware rooms on King Street, voicing sentiments expressed by many others. 'The people would know where to find them and could enjoy them without hindrance. As it is,' he rationalized, 'the shows are a nuisance to a great many people, who do not go there for that sort of thing, but who have to force their way through the crowds that block the principal thoroughfares.'[122]

Concentrating extra-cost attractions was not a new concept. Since the success of the midway at the 1893 Chicago fair, the legitimacy of a separate amusement area had been solidly established in North America. In fact, the featured sideshow in Toronto that year was a *Streets of Cairo* supplied by Sol Bloom, secretary of the White City's midway. Because of the nature of the attraction, a Midway Plaisance was created extending from the railway track to the Main Building, though other amusements were scattered in the usual spots along the road between the Main Building and the horse ring. In 1899 the olio for another *Streets of Cairo* was set up on the lawn in front of the lake. What business now proposed was to consolidate all sideshows permanently in a completely peripheral location.[123]

The second step was to refurbish the physical plant. According to the *Star*, the fair had reached the point where it 'must remodel its premises, shift its scenery, and put on a fresh front so that persons who have not entered the grounds for ten years cannot, as now, sit on their doorsteps at home and with their mind's eye see the general outlines of the whole thing.' New buildings were essential. There could be 'no really important developments along the lines of industrial display without new buildings,' not just because the old ones were in disrepair, but because the monumental beaux arts style had become the new standard for exhibition facilities.[124]

New buildings, in themselves, would not sustain popular attention. The third step was to put something interesting inside, and the onus here was on individual companies, not the association. Businessmen were convinced they knew how to compete successfully with sideshows. John Catto, a dry goods merchant who had recently returned from the Paris Exhibition, said he was not bothered by the fake shows there because his attention was absorbed by manufacturing processes in miniature going on all around him; that was the kind of exhibition he proposed for Toronto. At a directors' luncheon, A.F. McLaren, butter and cheese maker, called for a new facility in a conspicuous spot where the public could see every step in the making of these products, and all the latest machinery and methods. His remarks drew 'the heartfelt applause of the day from the assembled exhibitors, showing that the speaker had struck a popular chord and that others in different lines desired the same state of affairs for their own particular exhibits.'[125] The *Star* quickly grasped the baton: 'If the Fair is to fill its mission, the talent of the showman must be placed enthusiastically at the disposal of the manufacturer. If suitable buildings are provided, these two working together can provide attractions along the line suggested by Mr. McLaren that will rival in interest anything that can be found on the Fair grounds.' If manufacturers were being ignored for leisure attractions, they would fight back by turning manufacturing processes into leisure spectacles in imposing settings. By doing so, the public would come to appreciate the debt owed to business for developing the intricate technology and coordinated effort that made mass consumption possible.[126]

Within three years, all three suggestions had taken concrete form.[127] Over concessionaires' protests, the midway was moved in 1902 from the thoroughfares between the Crystal Palace and the

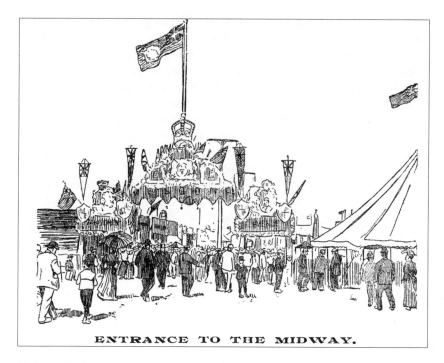

ENTRANCE TO THE MIDWAY.

This 1903 illustration from the Toronto *World* depicts the new decorative arch at the entrance of the midway. The concentration of amusement features coincided with a dramatic increase in their number.

grandstand to the less congested eastern end of the horse ring, where it was run 'like its own separate fair with an individual entrance.' The site was confirmed the following year when tons of tan bark were laid down to improve the walks and an elaborate entry arch, costing $150, was constructed.[128] Minor beautification was small compensation for displacement from the centre of the grounds. The midway in 1903 brought in almost exactly the same amount of money as it had in 1900, when general admissions were half as great. Operators could do little but fume and fight back with their most effective weapons – colour, noise, and transgression.[129]

If sidetracking the midway helped to focus more attention on serious elements of the show, so did the construction of new buildings. The Art Gallery, which opened in 1902, was crowded to the doors during the entire show, while the 600-seat lecture theatre in the Dairy Building could not accommodate everyone who turned up for talks and demonstrations. A year later, the new Manufacturers' and Liberal Arts Building and the Process of Manufacture Building were equally strong magnets.[130]

Having secured improved facilities, many businesses did fill the space with process displays. For all the hoop-la about them, they were nothing new. At the very first fair, a printing company churned out souvenir lithographs of farm scenes that sold for five cents, and, over the years, the manufacture of everything from lumber to pearl buttons had been demonstrated.[131] The wheel may have been reinvented in 1903, but it was an impressive wheel. The new Process Building housed thirty such displays, producing carpet, canvas, cork, wire nails, bicycle parts, and rubber overshoes, to mention just a few. After only a week, a *Mail and Empire* reporter claimed that the facility had already justified its existence. 'As an educator, the Process Building leads the procession.'[132]

It was the right moment for process displays, when the limitations of handcrafting were familiar and the toll of automation not fully apparent. Separated from the real contexts of production, polished and dramatically presented, machines took on a romantic aura that seemed to promise liberation from physical labour and abundance for all. They were hypnotic, almost human, as a *Globe* editor had realized only a few years earlier at a similar exhibit:

> There is something companionable in an intricate piece of machinery, in spite of its inconsiderate haste. It has a satisfactory air, and attends to its own affairs in a methodical way that precludes interfering or meddling. It is pleasant to stand and watch an agreeable piece of machinery whirling on without apparent effort, each part doing its duty at the proper time, and all harmoniously controlled by a single impulse.[133]

The mesmerizing regularity of mechanical action remained a standard display tactic at exhibitions, but as demonstrations of technological coordination became less novel, their impact faded. For many, industrial machinery increasingly pointed to monotony, not liberation. As imaginative manufacturers sought to downplay connection between factories and products, they covered up the gears and belts, and presented instead futuristic visions of the good life just around the corner.[134]

The manufacturers' clamour for new spaces to demonstrate their technology was not just about more effective display. It was about power. The buildings and their contents were meant to inspire instinctive associations of prestige and consequence. If hegemony depends on the spontaneous consent of the ruled, on creating an impression that the leadership of dominant groups is just common sense, the cavernous Manufacturers' Hall, crowned with a great rotunda and humming with machinery, went a long way towards that goal. 'Here is a spectacle,' lectured G.C. Porter in the *World*, 'that teaches a valuable lesson to that element in the Dominion who do not regard seriously the claims of the big manufacturers to the best considerations of the government.'[135]

Yet, although business had successfully flexed its muscle, it had not swept away the competition. Even in 1902 and 1903, when new buildings with more enticing exhibits generated unusual excitement about the industrial portion of the show, the midway remained the epicentre of wonder. In some ways, isolation was an advantage. With diminished concerns about distracting attention from adjacent features, not to mention more room, the number of acts was allowed to mushroom, from twelve in 1900 to thirty in 1903.[136] The pleasure zone had more to offer in a more distinctive environment dedicated exclusively to fun.

Visitors intent on inspecting the Art Gallery and the Process Building had less time for sideshows in 1902 and 1903, but that is not to say they avoided the olio. Free performances outside the flaps were understood to be as good as or better than the ones inside. The show just beside the entrance arch in 1903 offered 'two barkers, two tiny tots who try to sing, a negro instrumental trio, and a young woman whose costume is abbreviated.' It was much the same all the way down the avenue. Many people, including children, came mostly to listen and stare.[137]

Shouting through megaphones, spielers tried to push every button imaginable, as Katherine Leslie had noted in 1899. Here, one advised that all intelligent people came to see the fat boy. There, another explained in earnest tones that the 'Streets of Cairo' had been brought to Toronto solely for the edification of viewers and would make no profit. Further along, someone insisted that his ghost show had attracted the peers of England, and further still, a young man proclaimed an inspection of his ostriches was essential to understanding the South African situation. When voices gave out, brass instruments and banjos, steam whistles, revolvers, and gongs were used to sustain the commotion.[138]

With shows packed cheek to jowl, all competing for the attention of the same pool of customers, the din was awesome. Spectators came just to track down the source of commotion, but they were also lured by the erotic, exotic, and absurd – by young women fluttering diaphanous petticoats over strawberry tights, by Native peoples in feathered head-dresses shouting war-whoops, by men with blackened faces wearing animal hides and bones in their hair. They were drawn by the barkers themselves: sunburned, sweating, hoarse yet eloquent, inventive, spontaneous, audacious.[139] These were all marginal people – wanderers and mountebanks whose normal stock in trade was deformity, perversion, and sexual titillation. However impressive the business community's demonstration of hegemonic influence, its attractions were matched by the transgressive pull of freaks, frauds, and floozies.

In a real sense, the new spatial arrangements indicated capitulation rather than victory. The industrial portion of the show had scored a short-term coup,[140] but only by implicitly acknowledging the appeal of the amusement portion. Business exhibitors had been forced to accept that to compete successfully with leisure features, their presentations had to be framed as entertainment and put into spectacle contexts. They too had to supply not simply products, but intensities of feeling.

For all the antagonism between these high and low forms of cultural authority, perhaps they needed each other more than they realized. Without the marginal, the atmosphere created by the mainstream might have seemed stiflingly conventional, too closely connected to work. Without the mainstream, the bizarreness of the marginal might have become oppressive. Within the fair's alternating current of order and transgression, establishing the meaning of one almost necessarily required the presence of the other.[141]

7

Carnival

An impressive four-colour poster advertising the 1895 show called it 'the People's Great Annual Carnival of Instruction, Business and Enjoyment.' The Industrial Exhibition was not a carnival in the technical sense – the ancient celebration preceding Lent. In terms of the traditional calendar, it was more akin to a harvest festival, though this association was not stressed, perhaps because the model of the international exposition was too powerful. Still, in nineteenth-century Toronto, fairtime was the closest thing to carnival that occurred.[1]

In the medieval and early modern periods, carnival, like fair and feast days at other times of the year, was an occasion for overindulgence and disruption. While variations among regions, between city and countryside, even within the same locality from one year to the next, were significant (much depending on the weather, the economy, and the political situation), general features were similar throughout Western Europe. These were times of gorging, excessive drinking, and increased sexual promiscuity. The riotous expenditure of resources carefully husbanded during the rest of the year lured outside traders to markets usually held in conjunction with the festivities, and with them came show people, including actors, exotic animal handlers, giants, dwarfs, and other grotesque figures who supposedly offered insights into weird and wonderful marvels that lay beyond familiar boundaries. Much of the entertainment, however, was generated by locals, who simultaneously became performers and spectators. Carefully staged events, such as processions with elaborate floats, athletic competitions, bonfires, and fireworks, were complemented by uninhibited, impromptu merrymaking, facilitated by widespread masking and costuming. Impersonations of animals, demons, clerics, notables of all kinds, and members of the opposite sex were customary, in part because they figured prominently in the production of mock rituals that seemed to be a standard feature of these occasions. Irreverent parodies of weddings, trials, coronations, and similar ceremonies turned the world upside down, allowing common folk to ridicule authority figures who normally dictated to them, though reversals covered the whole gamut of community interactions, including ones closer to the base of the social pyramid. Masters were depicted waiting on servants, wives bullying husbands, and children instructing adults.

Throughout the carnival, aggression was endemic. Much of it was verbal. Adulterers, cuckolds, spouse beaters, and other transgressors of community norms were berated for misdeeds, but insults were hurled about generally. So were more tangible substances like fruit, flour, and water. These were fairly harmless, but festive crowds did not necessarily restrict themselves to good-natured fun. Animals and outsiders, like Jews, were especially vulnerable. Since rites of misrule provided a convenient cover to work out personal animosities, activities sometimes escalated into more extensive and serious forms of violence, giving authorities excuses to suppress proceedings that they tended to view suspiciously at the best of times.[2]

This sort of disorder has a deep fascination for many investigators, perhaps because it seems so far removed from public behaviour in contemporary industrial society. Historians and other scholars have been preoccupied especially by two questions: what carnivalesque occasions meant to performers, and what impact they had on social life.

With respect to the first, no one has been more thought-provoking than the Russian literary theorist Mikhail Bakhtin, who saw carnival as a triumphant plebeian deflation of all forms of authority and privilege. In a seminal study of Rabelais, he claimed that the protocols and customs of carnival embodied 'a completely different, nonofficial, extraecclesiastical and extrapolitical aspect of the world, of man, and of human relations.' Carnival created a 'second world and a second life outside officialdom,' where orthodoxy was completely absent. It suspended prevailing truths, prohibitions, and hierarchies, allowing common people to enter a realm where perfect community, freedom, equality, and abundance were potentially possible. It was not directed against specific institutions, but, as Renate Lachmann put it, 'against the loss of utopian potential brought about by dogma and authority.'[3]

During carnival, every device of status was undermined. Because equality reigned, complete familiarity and frankness in speech was permitted across the social spectrum. Because being was considered entirely in human terms, no subject was taboo. Language and gesture tore away any attempt to put distance between one body and another. Every pretense of immutability was punctured. Closed, completed forms were rejected, including the classical body, which was displaced by the grotesque. Attention shifted from head to belly, genitals, and buttocks, loci of appetites, of regeneration, of sounds, smells, and shapes that insistently proclaimed human failings. Parodies, travesties, and reversals promised the possibility of escaping rigid confines. These were celebrations of change and renewal, of becoming rather than being. These were not spectacles to be passively observed, but lived experiences that embraced everyone. 'While carnival lasts,' Bakhtin wrote, 'there is no other life outside it.'[4]

The power behind carnival was laughter, the people's joyous laughter that deflated grand theory and ideals, that rejuvenated the spirit. In the seventeenth century, that power began to be stifled as the state encroached on festive life, restricting its privileges and pushing it back into the private sphere. Increasingly, it was confined to literature, and, even there, interest in the grotesque, which carried its message, declined in the nineteenth century. However, the carnivalesque spirit was indestructible, he felt, surviving under the most oppressive of political regimes.[5]

Bakhtin's analysis has not gone unchallenged. Peter Stallybrass and Allon White have suggested that carnival is only one instance of the wider phenomenon of transgression, and that carnivalesque events, including fairs and markets, were never pure folk expressions, nor entirely outside ordinary life. Teofilo Ruiz has argued there was no sharp separation between popular and élite festive forms. Others have disputed Bakhtin's nostalgic, overly benign characterization of such festivities. Nevertheless, his basic conception of the carnivalesque as an expression of popular yearnings, as a mode of understanding and shaping existence, has become widely influential.[6] It is important less as an accurate historical depiction of every carnival than as a sightline for approaching popular culture, a benchmark for assessing popular resistance.

The second issue that has preoccupied historians involves the impact of carnival on social life – in particular, on regular relations of power. Most investigators now acknowledge the extent to which these events highlighted fundamental social tensions, but some insist that periods of misrule acted as safety valves, allowing disaffected groups to blow off steam without jeopardizing existing structures and hierarchies. Gerard Nijsten has argued that the reversal rituals he studied 'ultimately resulted in a confirmation of order,' while Ruiz has described resistance from below as 'just noise in the machine, almost always deflected by the ways in which those above continuously appropriate and transform popular unrest and culture for their own benefit.'[7] Other scholars, however, have been impressed by the extent to which carnival inspired concerted efforts at change. One of the most dramatic instances occurred in the French town of Romans during its carnival of 1580, when long-standing resentments erupted in a plot to murder wealthy landowners and merchants. The scheme was anticipated by the intended victims, who proceeded to massacre their rivals, mainly urban craftsmen and labourers. According to Emmanuel Le Roy Ladurie, both groups had symbolically acted out this violence during the preceding carnival and had used its traditions to conceal tactics and identities. While this was an extreme case, the adaptation of carnivalesque practices to achieve more limited goals was not unusual. Natalie Davis, for example, suggests that rural rites of misrule got carried into towns and used in class protest. Reid Mitchell has shown that Mardi Gras in New Orleans was, and continues to be, a vehicle for pressing class, race, and gender causes.[8]

What relevance do these discussions of pre-industrial folk culture have for the investigation of a modern, élite-dominated institution? This is precisely what this chapter will explore. What did carnival in Toronto, a fairly typical North American City, entail in the late nineteenth century? More specifically, what were the elements of festive life and to what extent did they embody a topsy-turvy carnivalesque spirit? What impact did the occasion have on ordinary life? Answers to these questions will be sought by looking at some of the most important fairtime practices in Toronto, as well as the actual experiences of being in the city and going to the show.

Certainly, there were continuities in festive motifs. The most obvious were in the entertainment realm. What more evidence is needed to demonstrate that sideshows and spectacles in and around the Industrial remained repositories of the grotesque and utopian than the appearances of some of the most famous show freaks of the time, including the giant Chang and the midget Admiral Dot?[9] However, traditional elements carried into the industrial age did not necessarily retain the same spirit. Similarities with early modern antecedents were more apparent in some practices than others, but, on the whole, Victorian carnival was quite different in tone, as a consideration of three of the most prominent activities indicates. While shopping, parading, and illuminating public space were not peculiar to the exhibition period, their prevalence helped to make this phase of the yearly round distinct. A couple of things in Toronto were unique to fairtime – the stress on city facilities and the show itself, which usually required significant exertion by those who attended. Both suggest that something more than 'the people's joyous laughter' lay at the heart of this celebration – namely, fatigue. Many were undoubtedly relieved when life settled back to routine, yet sometimes they had gained insights into possibilities, both positive and negative, of urban life, and were inspired to think of alternative arrangements.

Most festive practices that predominated at fairtime, including the three discussed here, were long standing. For out-of-town people especially, shopping was a priority, so, for obvious reasons, merchants did their best to make stores visions of abundance and excitement. Parades had no regular pattern, but the presence of a large audience encouraged a variety of processions, including some of the largest held in the city to that point. With the spread of commercial electricity at the end of the century, illuminations became increasingly common, but spectacles of light continued to be unfailing delights. Although none of these things was limited to the exhibition period, all of them tended to be more extensive and impressive while the show was in process.

Whether or not shopkeepers realized that markets were a traditional part of carnival, they were not about to ignore a dramatic increase in consumer traffic. Grand emporiums could draw visitors with the everyday magnificence of their premises. The Golden Lion, for one, urged newcomers to inspect the reproduction of a Roman mosaic at its front door, as well as elevators, the pneumatic cash system, and the central dome, 'the largest connected with any private building in the Dominion.'[10] However, taking full advantage of the crowds required more active strategies, and one of the most noticeable features of the city during the fair was the attempt by merchants to lure customers with well-stocked shelves, low prices, and unusual enticements.

Fall merchandise was arriving in any event, but it had to be readied in time for the influx. The John Eaton Company, concerned that its new department store might not seem chock full in time for the 1895 show, emphasized that staff were working flat out to get set. 'Hourly case after case is being opened up; tons upon tons of the grandest goods that the world produces are here and coming.' Most shops, not just new ones, promised generous reductions. Canada's great show of 1883 was 'doubly attractive by reason of Russell's Special Sale during September.' The Adams Furniture Company in 1896 presented the 'Great Exhibition Sale of Furniture and Carpets.'[11]

Sales generally featured older stock; new merchandise was promoted with special attractions. Fashion shows, staged mainly but not exclusively by department stores to draw attention to fall clothing lines, were always popular. James Rogers got such a throng at an 1884 fur exhibition that he repeated it the next night. Many establishment mounted striking window displays. In 1896 H.A. Lozier separated all 1497 parts of a Cleveland bicycle to show how they fit together. In 1888 the Atradome put scenes in two of its King Street windows, one representing a widow and her daughter mourning over a 'most realistic grave,' the other a wedding ceremony with a bride, groom, and clergyman. The figures, made by a New York firm that produced the best mannequins on the continent, were said to be 'most extreme in their cost.' Interiors often received the same lavish attention. With more time to get ready in 1896, the John Eaton Company filled its store with mechanical figures imported from France. Even H.W. Petrie, a dealer in industrial machinery, put up flags and bunting to glamorize his engines and drills.[12]

Business in some establishments was remarkably brisk. In 1888 customers were lined up outside a Church Street gun and jewellery store at 7 a.m. and kept coming until the 10 p.m. closing time. An *Empire* reporter calculated that if only one in five people made a purchase, the store did more than a thousand transactions that one day. W.R. Brock, wholesale merchant, did more selling in the two weeks of the 1897 show than in any similar period of his twenty-seven-year career.[13] Perhaps the best evidence of increased mercantile prosperity during the show, however, was the annual arrival of a legion of vendors with far more questionable merchandise.

'To a certain extent,' observed a *Saturday Night* columnist, these fakirs were always around, 'but during exhibition the itinerant men of business or "honest tradesmen" who yearly wander over nearly the whole civilized part of the continent gravitate to Toronto and the streets fairly blossom with them.' People flogging toy balloons, beaded moccasins, fancy pocketbooks, false moustaches, bird whistles, stain removers, and countless other sundries clogged the commercial districts, filling the air with competing cries for attention. Their ploys were ages old. In 1890 a seller of novelty bottles loosened pocketbooks by feigning blindness. Hank, a patent-medicine concocter who showed up every season, drew crowds that year by producing eggs from an empty carpet bag. Local merchants frequently complained that these birds of passage were spoiling legitimate commerce. In 1891, Yonge Street shopkeepers petitioned the mayor to remove 'the fakirs, fruit vendors, organ grinders and religious mountebanks' who disgraced the street with their antics and interfered with traffic. Police were instructed to clear the area in question, but eliminating them was quite impossible, that or any other year.[14]

These slippery operators, full of colour and energy, spouting a continuous, aggressive patter, not only changed the atmosphere of downtown shopping areas during the fair but injected into them something approaching an authentic carnivalesque spirit. Insinuating themselves into public space, they certainly transgressed respectable retail practices and often seemed indifferent to accepted moral codes as well. They were classic tricksters whose appearances and claims were always ambiguous. The 'magic bottle' seller was blind only 'of one eye, the other strictly attending to business.' Hank was just as likely to show up resplendent in a black velveteen coat accompanying a 'man-eating cannibal girl' as with a few eggs and a moth-eaten carpet bag. Of course, the carnivalesque spirit was equally apparent in some customers. As a *Globe* reporter once observed, the exhibition visitor 'often puts on liberality with his good clothes, and throws away his money with a recklessness in marked contrast to the petty economies of the rest of the year.'[15] Aside from some kinds of entertainment, the hustle of commerce was probably the aspect of the late Victorian fair that most resembled what transpired at traditional carnivals. Continuity lay not just in the exchange of commodities, but in the fostering of desire, which intensified sensation and destabilized emotional control.

For merchants, incessant streams of potential buyers in front of sales counters were the most important processions, but the public paid more attention to formally structured events. According to Peter Goheen, in Victorian Toronto parading was 'the most frequent and popular street performance,' with a broad repertoire of forms.[16] While not all public spaces were employed during the exhibition period, the extent to which they were appropriated by marchers of various sorts is striking. Most processions in the city during fairtime were linked directly or indirectly to the show, although they did not necessarily take place on the actual grounds. Some were very modest affairs, such as a fraternal society's outing in 1887 involving fewer than two hundred members. Others were grand excursions with thousands of participants and tens of thousands of spectators. In 1897 an estimated hundred-thousand people lined the streets as four-thousand workers trooped past. More than a decade before, another labour parade mobilized upwards of six-thousand marchers in what the *Labour Reformer* speculated was the largest demonstration ever seen in Toronto. Even apart from the fair, these parades would have generated an impressive festive atmosphere.[17]

The parade repertoire at exhibition time involved four main types. The most common civic and state processions were militia street marches. Officers used the fair to promote both public relations and morale. For rank and file of the Royal Grenadiers and the Queen's Own Rifles, duty was sweetened by an opportunity to show off in front of adulatory tourists. During the first week of the 1883 show, the Rifles turned out over four hundred strong for an evening march through the business district; attendance at other times of the year was generally much smaller. A week later, followed by an immense crowd, they set out for the exhibition grounds, where they joined the Grenadiers for a march past in front of the grandstand.[18]

Much more august state performances were also mounted, none more lavish than the 1879 escort of Princess Louise and Lord Lorne from the train station to the Horticultural Gardens. The lieutenant governor, mayor and council, sheriff, city clerk, department heads, members of the legislature, school trustees, police, soldiers, and firemen, as well as private citizens in carriages, all arranged according to proper protocol, set off over a scarlet carpet, giving masses of spectators a vivid indication of local hierarchy. Generous access to public resources for music and decorations was part of the drawing power of this and similar events, but they were memorable in the first instance because of both the participants and the strict formality.[19]

Commercial parades were the least structured. In many cases, they were extensions of regular theatrical performances. The Barnum show put on a traditional circus parade in 1885. Paunee Bill's Wild West company in 1892, and the Gentry Dog and Pony Show in 1900, toured the downtown area drumming up interest in the grandstand extravaganza. The main features of these enticements were usually animals, which needed to be exercised in any event. Local businesses also occasionally used processions as publicity devices. Before treating its newsboys to a picnic at the fairgrounds in 1893, the *News* led them through the city core in a dozen vans covered with booster slogans. In 1902 Simpson's department store tried to impress visitors with a grand promenade of all its delivery wagons. Messages intended by these mobile advertisements were not hard to grasp.[20]

Many parades mounted by voluntary associations such as bicycle clubs, bands companies, and lodge brotherhoods were probably so small that only those who participated paid much attention, but a few were exceptionally large. The grand march of the International Order of Oddfellows in 1880 required a printed order of procession. A fireman's demonstration in 1884 needed four separate staging areas to organize ten marching bands and more than thirty brigades from southern Ontario and nearby American states. With their well-groomed horses, elaborate equipment, and colourful uniforms, fire companies were always a popular sight, and local outfits were usually ready to oblige.[21]

Somewhere between commercial and voluntary parades were trade processions. The first to be held in conjunction with the exhibition, though not the first in the city, was the mammoth 1886 march to the fairgrounds at the time of the founding of the Canadian Labor Congress. The next was mounted in 1892 when the congress returned to Toronto. By 1895, after the establishment of Labour Day as an official holiday, the Labour Parade became an annual occurrence, though its destination was not always the fairgrounds. Some of its most memorable features were 'allegories' constructed by various associations depicting their trades. Plasterers had a 'neat little cottage with a tidy job of plastering in process.' Longshoremen pulled a fully rigged ship on wheels. Bakers, white capped and aproned, made little cakes in an oven and tossed them to the crowd.[22] With so many local people participating, it is not surprising that workers drew huge crowds.

Distinctions among these four types of parades were by no means rigid. The newsboys' were led off in 1893 with music provided by the Royal Grenadiers. Toronto regiments also appeared in labour processions, as did the mayor, aldermen, fire companies, and some employers who sponsored company bands and floats, publicizing their products while demonstrating goodwill towards working people.[23] Meshing elements was easy because all the varieties sat firmly on the orderly side of the parade spectrum. The Oddfellows consulted closely with the police on the logistics of their 1880 extravaganza, and sent detailed instructions to participating lodges emphasizing that marchers should walk four abreast, preferably in uniform clothing, with no carriages other than those provided by the organizing committee. Labour groups, which in other circumstances exhibited strong oppositional sentiments, used parades to project an image of respectable citizenship. Dress was a prime signal. Except for marshals in uniform and a few people in costume on floats, unionists walked in their Sunday best, not working garb. A *World* reporter thought participants in 1892 could have been taken for cabinet ministers or bank managers as soon as wage earners. The 1897 procession, according to a *Globe* reporter, was calculated to show that the Canadian workingman was 'a well-educated, well-dressed, sound-bodied and contented citizen.'[24]

While all these parades revealed much about the culture of nineteenth-century Toronto, it is difficult to see them as vibrant manifestations of the carnivalesque. There were hints here and there. Music, exotic animals, trade allegories, and bright clothing were traditional elements of carnival, to be sure. The long line of Simpson's delivery wagons and the distribution of cakes from the bakers' float alluded to abundance and self-indulgence.[25] Disruption of normal street activity carried faint intimations of inversion. A stronger argument can be made that labour processions embodied a utopian sense of community and equality, but they certainly did not challenge prevailing hierarchies. Indeed, they entrenched some. As overwhelmingly male affairs, which suggested that public space belonged to men, and ones that excluded 'foreign-born aliens,' these parades were assertions of the legitimacy of gender and race privilege as much as expressions of common humanity. Perhaps the closest a Toronto Exhibition parade came to Bakhtin's spirit of carnival was the 1893

Two trade 'allegories' from the 1892 Labour Parade: the ironmongers' working forge (above) and the longshoremen's fully rigged ship (right). The orderly, well-dressed crowd was also a source of civic pride.

newsboys picnic, when a majority of celebrants showed up with horns, which were blown 'with a vigor that will never be equalled until A. Gabriel gets his line of work in.' Alas, before the journey was half over, many of the instruments had been lost or smashed.[26]

While parades generated enthusiasm, illuminations produced wonder. Lighting up the night was an ages-old festive practice,[27] but in the late nineteenth century new technology created unparalleled opportunities for brilliant demonstrations. Just a few months before the founding of the fair, Thomas Edison had developed the first commercially viable incandescent electric light bulb and, by 1881, the first Toronto experiment in centralized generating had been successfully conducted.[28] Like people elsewhere throughout North America and Europe, Torontonians were eager to examine the qualities of the new light, and expectations of increased revenues at exhibition time often justified expenditures on expensive new equipment. However, while electric light spread through the city and the fairgrounds, it was not the only source of illumination during the show, especially as the gas company tried to ward off competition.

Electricity made even ordinary street lighting exciting. In 1883, when Consumers' Gas competed with the Electric Light Company to illuminate different portions of the downtown area, thousands of residents from all parts of the city, as well as visitors, came to compare.[29] They also came to inspect decorative effects created by private businesses. McConkey's ice cream parlour created a sensation in 1882 by running two electric lights inside and one outside from a generator in the basement.[30] As familiarity grew, it took more effort to inspire comment, but popular delight with imaginative illumination of any kind remained high. In 1889 hordes of strollers came to see the Arlington Hotel, marked off at each storey with strings of Chinese lanterns and highlighted along the wings and centre portico with blazing gas jets. In 1902 the Order of Foresters created an effect 'more gorgeous than any individual display at the big fair' by outlining their towering headquarters on Bay Street with more than fourteen thousand coloured lights. Governor General Lord Dundonald spoke for many in describing it as one of the finest sights he had ever witnessed. A half-dozen policemen had to be detailed in front to keep the crowd moving. Most decorative uses of light involved outdoor effects, but occasionally inside novelties were attempted, notably in theatres. The Toronto Opera House packed an 1899 production by putting tiny electric lamps on a troupe of female dancers, concealing

The illumination of the Temple Building in 1902 was sufficiently intense to allow this nightime photograph. Presumably, the publicity value to the Order of Foresters was worth the cost of the fourteen thousand lights.

the wires with flowers. There was said to be a certain amount of danger, but no accidents occurred.[31]

Most years, such uses of light were advertising ploys made independently by individual businesses. Because relatively few buildings were decorated extravagantly at any one time, the ones that were got lots of notice. On a few occasions, however, more coordinated efforts were made. One of the most elaborate and successful was arranged in 1879, well before the widespread availability of electricity, as part of the welcome for Lord Lorne and Princess Louise. On two evenings during their visit, more than eighty establishments lit up their facades with lanterns, globes, gas jets, and transparencies, presenting 'a scene of fairy brilliancy such as must live in the memory of those who saw it for all their lives.' As darkness descended, illuminations began to appear, one after another, until every major thoroughfare appeared to be 'a perfect avenue of fire.' The entire population of the city seemed to be on hand, turning the streets into 'great sluggish rivers' of people. The corner of King and Yonge became so congested that a storekeeper had to open his premises to accommodate several ladies who had fainted in the press. 'The bewildered spectator,' wrote the *Globe* reporter, no doubt describing his own experience, 'is roughly aroused from his contemplation of the fiery scene, and finds himself being slowly carried along by the surging mass withersoever it pleases.'[32]

Not every ambitious project was successful. In 1887 the Exhibition Association persuaded downtown merchants to pay for festive lighting along Yonge and King streets. Pain and Company was hired to string up thousands of Chinese lanterns, supposedly duplicating an effect they had created for the recent Jubilee Review of the British Navy at Spithead. Unfortunately, much of the apparatus was held up at customs, so instead of oil lamps, candles had to be used. To make matters worse, the ropes holding them quickly slackened and had to be propped with wooden poles. About 9 p.m. on the first of what was intended to be six successive nights of illumination, a team of men began the slow chore of lighting the wicks. Those that did not sputter out almost immediately could barely be seen; one resident described them as 'ghastly sick room night lights.' When spectators started to pull on the ropes and knock out their supports, many of the glass cups were grabbed as souvenirs. Within an hour, a few forlorn tapers glowing dimly here and there were all that remained. Before merchants could protest, the contract was cancelled and refunds to contributors were promised. The idea of festooning lights across downtown streets was floated again less than a decade later, though no action was taken.[33]

The association was far more successful lighting its own turf. As was the case elsewhere in this period, while the fair was in progress the exhibition grounds were the brightest spot in the city. Suggestions that electric light be installed were made as early as 1880,[34] but it was not until 1882 that the Ball Electric Company of London was hired to put in the first fixtures. Unable to get all the necessary equipment, it shared the work with the Fuller Electric Lighting Company of New York, which had already put in similar displays at a number of other shows. Together, they ran five miles of wire and mounted sixty-one lights. One was a 6000-candle-power bulb placed in the cupola of the Main Building; the rest, all 2500-candle power, were scattered through various buildings and outside around the grounds.[35]

Technical difficulties marred the inauguration of the lights on the evening of the second day of the fair. The Ball Company could not get the globes for its bulbs from the express office, while Fuller had trouble with slipping belts. On Friday, two nights later, the power was turned on again, with no hitches and an added attraction – 'electro-hydraulic fireworks,' produced by manipulating coloured glass shades in front of a lamp directed at the spray of a fountain. Although only two evening openings had been contemplated, once the directors realized that gate receipts at night equalled those taken in during the day, they announced that the illumination would continue for the duration.[36]

Although this was not the first use of electric light in Toronto, it was, by far, the most extensive to date, and it became the universal subject of conversation not just on the grounds, but in the city, where outlines of roofs, spires, and chimneys on the western horizon were clearly visible. Outside illumination levels were about equal to that of the full moon, but observers found something almost magical in the glow. Couples posed themselves, as if expecting the light to produce a photographic effect. Interiors, particularly the Crystal Palace, which had the most fixtures, were stunning. 'The general effect,' according to a *Globe* reporter, 'was finer than by daylight, for all the gorgeous colouring was preserved unchanged, while the countless points of steel, glass and silver in every part of the hall glistened with an intensity which no diffused sunlight could ever impart in the interior of a building. The main building was simply dazzling.' Inside or out, when the current was turned on, a dreamy, ethereal wonderland seemed to materialize.[37]

The association was not about to disappoint a public fascinated with electricity. In 1883 three firms were hired to supply a total of eighty-nine lights, making more buildings accessible at night, including the Art Gallery and the Apiary.[38] Probably the only group displeased with the installations was the gas company, which, with an eye to protecting its lucrative street-lighting franchises, decided to meet the challenge head on with its own demonstrations on the grounds. Besides mounting an extensive display of gas appliances, it erected a variety of improved gas lamps in various spots, trying to keep them far enough from the electric bulbs to prevent interference, yet close enough to allow comparisons. Beneath a new Seimens regenerative burner, which provided the centre of the Crystal Palace with three times the light of an ordinary gas lamp, the president of Consumers' Gas tried to persuade a reporter that while the electric glow was brilliant in the immediate vicinity of the bulb, it became dark and shadowy a short distance away; gas beams, he maintained, radiated much further, blending imperceptibly into the darkness. As he spoke, one of the electrical systems in the building failed, but not even this inadvertent demonstrations of unreliability dampened enthusiasm for the competition. 'It would be unreasonable to expect everything to go smoothly where so much has yet to be learned in the business of electrical lighting,' rationalized a *Mail* reporter.[39]

As a sop, the gas company was asked to illuminate the approach to the eastern gate, since carriages trying to pass in the dark were having accidents, but the triumph of electricity was symbolized by the erection in 1884 of an iron tower from which six powerful lights were aimed over the entire grounds. Year by year, more fixtures were installed, until, by 1899, five hundred arc and a thousand incandescent lamps were being run off a power plant suitable for a medium-sized city.[40]

While adequate lighting was soon taken for granted, the festive power of illumination was undiminished. Spectacular effects continued to be an important part of the fair's attractions. In 1888 prismatic lamps of various hues were hung across the full length of the grandstand to form a sign that read, 'Welcome to Toronto's Great Fair,' and hundreds more were distributed about the grounds, creating 'a fairyland appearance.' In 1892 walkways were lit with double rows of

Although the uniform glow emanating from every window of the Crystal Palace was artistic licence, the 1885 Prize List cover accurately reflected the popular appeal of festive electric lighting.

Chinese lanterns and arches of gas at 50-foot intervals. Garlands of coloured lamps were suspended high in the air in front of the Main Building, giving the whole grounds 'a fairy-like appearance.' In 1897 illuminated arches were erected over the roadway from the palace to the grandstand, while the tower was set ablaze with strings of small lights, some of which were stretched to the corners of other buildings. In 1903, with more electric light in use than ever before, the name of every building was spelled out in cream-coloured bulbs.[41]

None of these arrangements was original to the Industrial. With electrical journals full of suggestions about how to achieve various effects, it was easy to pick up ideas, and no one cared if techniques were derivative. In the late twentieth century it is hard to appreciate the impact of powerful artificial illumination. Though gas lighting was well established in North American urban areas by the time electricity was introduced, most cities remained murky, gloomy places at night. In 1882, only a few days before the first experiment on the exhibition grounds, the *World* had rhapsodized on its front page about an evening of exceptional moonlight when 'signs over-hanging the street were as legible as in the day, and men stood on the side-walks and read the posters on the dead walls.' The concentrations of brilliant, steady light at exhibition park and in pockets of the downtown core were marvels, both for those watching the glow from afar as well as those nearby.[42]

Besides shopping and entertainment, illumination was the most consistent festive element at fairtime, and it did embody some carnivalesque aspects. The quantity and intensity of light, much of it aimed profligately at the vast night sky, suggested utopian abundance and unlimited resources. It was used in playful, unusual ways, hinting at the possibility of protean creativity. It did invert the natural order, turning night into day, as observers continually remarked with an earnestness rooted in true amazement.[43]

However, while carnivalesque features were evident, they were hardly popular in origin. Light was a complex technological product, bestowed on the public by benevolent experts and conditional on accepting their ascendancy. Night could be inverted, but not the power of those who authorized and operated the apparatus. As with parades and shopping, most folk were expected to be passive admirers and consumers of spectacles premised on the necessity of order and control. They were not equal participants. When they intervened more actively, as in the downtown fiasco of 1887, there was little to admire, and the spirit of mischief sputtered as quickly as the candles.

The passive quality of nineteenth-century Toronto's version of carnival was underlined by traditional characteristics that were almost completely absent. There was almost none of the deliberately targeted aggression associated with early carnival. Aside from ones dealt with by the law, violators of community standards were not picked out or punished. Masking and costuming, if practised at all, were confined to private functions and the theatre. Social inversions, the core element of carnivalesque behaviour according to several commentators,[44] were sometimes carried out within the liminal safety of the fairgrounds, but usually they affirmed prevailing hierarchies more than they challenged them. In the streets, there were no mock rituals to turn the world upside down and to comment on the essential artificiality of human structures, no parodies to ridicule authority figures. To some extent, these things could be found in commercial entertainments, and therefore experienced vicariously, but opportunities for direct cathartic release were rare.

Parades, imaginative merchandising, and illuminations could be experienced at virtually any time in late nineteenth-century Toronto. City life was attractive, in part, because such festive elements seemed to be woven into ordinary routine. These practices were distinctive at fairtime because they were grander and more intense than at other times. However, two things that happened during the exhibition period were unique in the city's yearly round: the city became inundated with far more visitors than at any other time; and there was the fair itself. The first meant that while regular authorities and structures were not directly challenged, normal conditions could not always be maintained. The second demonstrated that actually trying to enjoy the grand celebration of a large city involved considerable stress and strain.

〜〜〜〜〜〜〜〜〜

'The feature of the week just drawing to a close,' mused the *World* at the end of the 1898 show, 'has been the crowd of visitors, not less than the exhibition.' The editor was convinced that the number of people in the city was unprecedented, and while he may have been right, his impression was nothing new. 'Streets are full of people,' jotted Henry Scadding in his diary in 1880. 'The general commotion is not pleasant.' 'Bustle and rush, bustle and rush,' was how the special correspondent to a Peterborough paper described the great thorough-fares a year later, so congested, it was 'hard work pushing along them.' Though civic facilities expanded as the Victorian era came to a close, the annual influx seemed to outpace them. By the beginning of the new century the crush was starting even before the show got under way. The plain fact was that at fairtime, Toronto became, as a *Globe* reporter put it, 'the abode of a population large enough for another city.'[45] It simply did not happen at other times of the year.

Certain spots became particularly jammed. The intersection of King and Yonge got 'literally packed,' to the extent that 'the crowds of holiday makers were a show of themselves.' The Esplanade, a thoroughfare parallel to the waterfront lined with railway tracks, sixteen pairs abreast in some places, was always a concern because thousands of people crossed it going to and from the docks. Union Station was sometimes unbearable. On a memorable morning in 1893, fifteen trains arrived within the same hour, creating chaos, but it did not take nearly so much traffic to choke the concourse. Percy Beale arrived home from a trip abroad in 1886 when the show was barely under way and special excursions were not yet running, yet still he found it almost impossible to collect his trunks. Depar-tures were no better. There never seemed to be enough officials to direct people to proper platforms, so travellers pressed about in con-fusion, oblivious to the danger of moving cars, and sometimes so anxious to secure seats for the journey home that they boarded the wrong trains.[46] Some had trouble just getting into the building. In addition to travellers, the station was full of the idle and curious watching others being busy, as well as conscientious hosts looking for friends and seeing visitors off, social duties akin to torture, according to an irate *Star* editor. Better, he thought, to go home and let visitors find their own way. They would probably get there sooner.[47]

Exhibition crowds not only made movement difficult but they also severely overloaded city facilities or pointed up their absence. Public toilets were sorely lacking. More than once during the early years of the show, the chief constable reported to City Council that many cases of indecent exposure were ignored because 'police cannot see their way clear towards interfering.' Streetcars generated perennial complaints. Packed sometimes with more than double their intended capacity, they were excruciating when they worked and annoying

THIS WAY OUT.

PRO BONO PUBLICO—"Oh no, this ain't no Bulgarian atrocity, it's just the crowd getting away from the train at the Union Station, Toronto, Canada."

Union Station was one of the most congested spots in the city at fairtime, as this 1903 cartoon from the Toronto *Telegram* suggests.

when they broke down, which happened frequently. Distressed by
the 'want of system and inadequate means of security against disorder and over crowding,' the *Mail* in 1881 called for police supervision
to ensure 'both comfort *en route* and rigid punctuality in starting.'
The force could not have done much, even had it wished.[48]

Some residents were more concerned about horses than passengers. 'Humanity' blasted the traction company in 1886 for making
animals drag fifty people in coaches made for twenty. Three years
later, Kate Watts called for extra cars or extra horses at exceptional
inclines. The enjoyment of anyone with a spark of humanity, she
insisted, was ruined by scenes of ill treatment. Her plea had little
impact. A week later, the *Mail* was moved to complain about the
'shocking cruelty' to an animal unmercifully beaten at every stop
because it did not have the strength to get an overloaded car moving
again. When concerns about horses faded after electric trolleys were
introduced in 1892, vehicles remained just as crammed, and critics
began to emphasize the danger of being pushed under the wheels
while trying to board.[49]

The most serious deficiency in city services was accommodation.
The luckiest visitors could rely on friends and relatives, though
strains in private homes at exhibition time were a constant source of
comment. Light-hearted ditties on the tribulations of hosting, such
as 'Why Ma Is Going Batty' and 'The Advantages of Country
Cousins,' filled the press:

> They came from prairies and from thickets,
> They swooped on me from near and far;
> I bought them ice cream, bought them tickets,
> And paid their fares on boat and car.

> I gave them all my house afforded,
> I even gave them up my bed,
> The little stores that I had hoarded
> Were yielded that they might be fed.

Images of houses exploding with people, and weary homeowners
stretched out on sofas or kitchen tables, were standard cartoon
fare.[50]

How many residents actually were affected and to what degree is
impossible to say, but contemporary observers, including furniture
suppliers, were convinced that putting up company at fairtime was a

"All the Comforts of Home"; A Snapshot of a Toronto Residence at Fair Time.

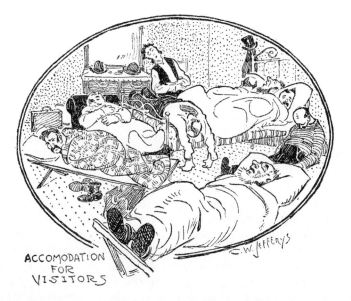

Saturday Night's 1902 depiction of the effects of fairtime on homeowners (top) was exaggerated, but the cartoon probably struck a sensitive nerve with many hosts. C.W. Jefferys's drawing for the *Star* a year later indicated that overcrowding was just as common in hotel rooms.

widespread obligation. In 1881 Patterson and Son advertised iron-framed, canvas-bottom cots that needed no mattresses – 'just the bed for exhibition times.' More than a decade later, Charles Rodgers promised prompt fulfilment of all bedroom furniture orders. Well past the turn of the century, the *News* presumed that over the two weeks of the show, almost every house in the city would have one or two guests.[51]

Many, like Stephen Radcliff from a village near Strathroy who imposed on a cousin, were received warmly. Families owing return favours for farm vacations probably were especially conscious of obligations. Needless to say, not all hosts were enthusiastic. 'Paterfamilias' complained to the *Telegram* in 1879 of being eaten out of house and home by 'a horde of devouring fiends.' Rail fares should be doubled, he thought, not reduced. Others were irritated by inconsiderate behaviour and annoying habits, including the things enumerated in the *Dominion Churchman*'s 'Hints to Visitors' – getting up too early, staying up too late, not being on time, refusing to participate in planned events, complaining about the cooking, and using poor table manners. Some folks just wore out their welcome, no one more than a Mrs Rees who asked her friend Mrs McKeown for a bed during the show. After ten weeks, McKeown decided Rees was a boarder, charged her rent, and confiscated her trunks when payment was not forthcoming. The case ended up in court, where a judge decided Rees did not have to pay because McKeown was not a legal boarding-house keeper. Clearly, this was an extreme case. One of the advantages of offering to take in friends during the fair was the fact that it did have a limited duration.[52]

While arrangements were uncomfortable at times, most who bunked in with kith and kin had some idea of what to expect. That was not always true for those dependent on public accommodation. A broad range of establishments offered beds, including dozens of hotels. In the 1890s the principal ones were listed in the exhibition program. At the bottom end, places like the Black Bull and the Bay Horse, each with fifty rooms, probably catered mostly to farmers who paid a dollar a night; at the top, the Queen's Hotel, reputedly Toronto's most elegant, with 350 rooms, charged 'tourists' three or four times as much. Lots of smaller or less reputable establishments did not get official acknowledgment. Regular boarding houses with empty rooms also took in guests, as did many ordinary householders with spare bedrooms or a willingness to double up their own families to earn extra cash. Some institutions with sleeping facilities were inspired with similar thoughts. The Electro-Medical Institute on Jarvis Street advertised board and lodging without treatment during the 1881 show. Two decades later, alumni were invited to put up at the Victoria Industrial School for Boys.[53]

On paper, some of these places sounded very appealing. The Arlington Hotel on King Street boasted of elegantly furnished parlours and reception rooms, 'excellence of table,' 'completeness of ventilation,' and spacious bedrooms both detached and *en suite*. In normal times, the description may have been accurate, but during the exhibition, when the city's hostelries did more business than in the rest of the summer combined, conditions were not normal.[54]

Hotels were swamped. By early evening during peak periods, which lasted longer and longer,[55] it was impossible to get a regular room. With one eye on profit and the other on the plight of the desperate, proprietors filled offices, bars, billiard rooms, sitting rooms, and any other rooms available (except dining-rooms) that could be fitted with cots and camp beds. Parlours were said to resemble hospital wards.[56] When none of this space was left, corridors were used. By late evening, after these pallets too were gone, cushions were sometimes laid out on the floor and chairs rented out for fifty cents.[57] And still desk clerks were besieged by those who had lingered too long at the fair, gotten in on late trains, or been turned away after long waits elsewhere. It was not uncommon at 11 p.m. to see lobbies thronged with people, lined up three and four deep in front of desks, imploring harassed staff for a spot to lay their heads. With no where else to turn, some of the frustrated roamed the halls, hoping to snag spots vacated by travellers leaving on late trains.[58]

Managing to secure a regular room was no guarantee of comfort. Bed linen seemed 'resurrected from the slimy past, bearing the dirty impress of contact with other sight-seers at past exhibitions.' Corridors echoed with creaks, luggage thumps, and drifting conversations of latecomers stumbling about in the dark. Nor did a regular room guarantee privacy. These, too, were fixed up with temporary beds and packed as full as possible.[59] Some veteran fairgoers claimed that the only way to get a decent night's sleep at reasonable cost was to stay at hotels in the suburbs and the outlying villages, but by the 1890s places on the fringe were routinely turning away applicants.[60]

Hotel keepers insisted there was no undue exploitation of the situation. They claimed that prices were not raised beyond normal levels

AT THE FAIR.

Visitor. " What's my bill ?"
Clerk.   " Let me see—your room was—"
Visitor.   "I didn't have any room. I slept on the billiard-table."
Clerk.   " Ah, me ; I'll just charge you fifty cents an hour for the use of the table.
That's what we generally get."

The Toronto *News* saw some humour in Toronto's inadequate accommodation facilities, as this 1885 cartoon indicates, but many of those inconvenienced no doubt felt somewhat differently.

and that visitors were not inconveniently crowded.[61] Guests had rather different stories to tell. 'A Traveller,' already upset with a tiny back room he was assigned in one of the city's leading establishments a few days before the big rush in 1884, became indignant two days later when informed he would have to pay 50 per cent more – and share the room to boot. A.R. Frey, a New York merchant, paid two dollars in advance for a room in a prestigious house during the 1903 show, assured by the clerk he would be the sole occupant. On returning to the hotel at 11 p.m. after a full day, he was told his room had been changed to one on a higher floor. He took this in stride, but had scarcely made the climb when the proprietor appeared with a stranger who was to occupy an adjacent bed. Protest was of no avail; he was told he could leave and apply for a refund if dissatisfied – not a practical option for a tired person at midnight at the best of times. To cap it off, the merchant discovered that his roommate was paying half as much. When Frey raised the inequity the next morning, the owner dismissed him out of hand, saying he had no time to discuss the matter. Pressed by the *Globe*, to whom Frey had sent his complaint, municipal authorities admitted that the case was not an isolated occurrence.[62]

From one perspective, Frey was lucky to have a real mattress, secured without undue effort. Less fortunate tourists 'paraded street after street in search of a place to lay their heads for the night.' Many were unsuccessful. Disconsolate visitors wandering from one hotel to the next, exhausted families looking perplexedly up and down the streets, knots of people fanning out through the city hoping to spot boarding-house window cards, bodies slumped in parks and on doorsteps, parties of young men tramping aimlessly all night long – all these were standard sights at exhibition time in Toronto.[63]

'While carnival lasts,' wrote Bakhtin, 'there is no other life outside it.'[64] In Victorian Toronto, this was a fairly accurate observation. People could not stay on the sidelines, totally unaffected; everyone was involved. Even for curmudgeonly citizens who tried to remain aloof, it was difficult to avoid congested streets, overloaded services, and perhaps an extra mouth or two at the dinner table. Sheer numbers made Toronto a different place at exhibition time, and no one in the city could ignore them, especially at night. For people assured of comfortable beds, there may have been something festive about homes full of friends, and animation in public spaces that persisted long after things normally quietened down. For those coping with too many bodies in too few rooms, or those without any accommodation, the enhancement of communal life was a more ironic experience.

〜〜〜〜〜〜〜〜

There were never enough seats on the grounds. Management tried to provide adequate resting facilities, sometimes even boasting about their arrangements, such as the rustic benches scattered over the grass at the very first show. These were 'never unoccupied,' so more were added next season and most subsequent ones. Every year, though, damage done by people perching on 'flower decked rookeries and other spots sacred to the gardener' gave force to new complaints about the lack of 'flop-down' room. Whether attending the carnival in Toronto rejuvenated the spirit or not, it certainly took its toll on the body. The price of pleasure in this case was not danger as much as discomfort and fatigue.[65]

'First and chiefest,' advised the experienced Faith Fenton, 'don't tire yourself out before arriving on the grounds.' For those like the woman in 1880 who stood all the way during a sixty- mile journey, or the one a decade later who came a hundred miles scrunched against the stove in the corner of a packed coach, this was easier said than done.[66] No one emerging from a crowded excursion train was entirely fresh.

Getting from the city to the gates, a couple of miles from downtown, could also take a toll. In good weather, steamboats were pleasant, though wharfs got uncomfortably, sometimes dangerously, congested; on windy days, schedules were quickly disrupted and rides less relaxing.[67] Trains leaving from Union Station were supposed to be quick, but often got shunted aside for priority traffic. After waiting an hour and a half, some passengers on a delayed run in 1882 got off and walked. On busy days, rail cars as well were 'crowded to suffocation,' to use Henry Scadding's description of an 1884 trip.[68] Trolleys had similar problems. Before electric traction was introduced, nimble males who could not force their way on board sometimes climbed onto the roof. Overloads of this nature caused frequent breakdowns, forcing visitors to twiddle their thumbs while the line was cleared. On top of these drawbacks, for many years tracks did not go all the way to the grounds. The *Canadian Manufacturer* complained of the 'mean deception' of cars with signs reading 'To the Exhibition' that stopped half a mile away. A motley collection of taxis shuttled back and forth between the end of the line, but they were not always inviting. 'To those who have not yet tasted of the pleasures which this journey affords,' cautioned a *Globe* reporter, 'we would humbly vouchsafe one word of advice – "don't."'[69]

If reaching the gates required energy, so sometimes did getting through them. As early as the mid-1880s, excessive jams were occurring at peak periods – and they got worse as attendance grew in subsequent years. Some gave up if the line-up was unreasonable, as Henry Ardagh did in 1898, but once absorbed in a crush it was just as hard to get out. On one afternoon in 1903, the mass at the Dufferin Gates extended well into the field on the other side of the road. As streetcars deposited people faster than they could be admitted, exits from that side of the grounds were barred and every possible entrance was opened, with a number of city aldermen stepping in to take tickets. Hats, parcels, satchels, and umbrellas were battered or lost. Frantic parents lifted children over the fence to avoid injury, while police turned a blind eye. One woman suffered a broken leg. This was a particularly bad day, but not unique.[70]

Once inside, more aggravations had to be faced. Almost every kind of weather created some degree of discomfort. On hot days, quantities of dust kicked up at the racetrack and along the paths were the source of many complaints.[71] Wet weather was worse. Blown-out umbrellas, hats lost in the wind, soaked clothing and footwear, and hems and pantcuffs splattered with mud inevitably put a damper on a festive mood. 'It is often pathetic,' mused Madge Merton, 'to see pleasure seeking humanity trailing through mud and over damp sod, struggling so hard to make itself believe that it is having a good time.'[72]

Noise was another constant irritant. In some parts of the grounds, specific sources of racket were ear-piercing, such as canine howls at the dog show, the incessant clack in Machinery Hall, and the din of barkers trying to outdo one another on the midway – the last causing a *News* reporter to conclude that Dante's *Inferno* had been written three hundred years too soon. In other places such as the Crystal Palace, where sound reverberated easily off iron and glass surfaces, noises got overlaid into 'a *tout ensemble* that baffles description.' At times it became oppressive. 'Oh! noise and confusion worse confounded,' exclaimed a *Star* columnist in 1899:

The phonograph with the largest possible magnifier attachment shouting out a song ... The roar of the big sewing machines, as the needles

tear their way through the heavy cloth and the thick leather! The cease-
less rattle and clatter of cups and saucers at the various advertising
stands! The continuous scruff of feet on the ground floor, the sharp tap
of heels overhead, the tramp, tramp around the galleries! The never-
ending chit-chit-chatter of human voices! And these are but the kernel
in the great shell of the noises of the out-of-doors.

For some, these concatenations seemed oddly melodic; many simply
felt assaulted and wondered why so many buzzers, bells, and steam
whistles were necessary.[73]

Taking care of bodily needs on the grounds involved more tribula-
tion. Toilet facilities rarely got proper attention. In response to complaints about the lack of conveniences at the 1878 Provincial
Exhibition, several 'commodious urinals' had been installed for the
first fair, and a few more were added the following season. Within
two years, it was clear that these were insufficient, but nothing was
done, despite a rising chorus of discontent. Men could relieve themselves discretely in dark corners of the animal sheds, an option more
difficult for women. In 1887 another ladies' washroom was constructed near the Dufferin Gate, and some were included in the new
grandstand opened in 1892. Notwithstanding a doubling of attendance, these seem to have been the last major additions provided by
the association for the next decade, though some exhibitors, including Eaton's, installed women's toilets within their display spaces.[74]
These may well have been greater attractions than the goods for sale.

The inadequacy of facilities was compounded by lack of signage. The
Farmer's Sun in 1896 protested that many strangers suffered severely
because they could not find washrooms. Those who did may have considered it a mixed blessing. The stench was fierce and the condition,
according to Dr T.C. Mewburn, who was moved to write to the Globe
in 1883, indescribable. 'Common decency forbids it, and my stock of
profanity is utterly unable to do justice to such a state of affairs,' he
fumed, calling for regular applications of dry earth and daily disinfect-
ing of seats and floors. The medical officer of health made a few suggestions the following year, but improvements were marginal or short
lived. Almost a decade later, Saturday Night described sanitary
arrangements, in both quality and quantity, as 'a shame and a dis-
grace to any place laying claim to common decency and should not be
tolerated for another season.'[75] The situation did not change until the
new Manufacturers' Building was completed in 1903.

Bladders were given short shrift; not so stomachs. The whole fair, as a *News* reporter put it, was 'a wide eating emporium.' Fast food, including fruit, nuts, popcorn, ginger bread, doughnuts, candy, and sandwiches, was the most dependable fare. The only real innovation in snacks was the introduction in 1896 of the Coney Island sandwich, guaranteed to 'create hunger within a radius of fifty feet.' Many of these treats were sticky or greasy, none more so than honey, sold in vast quantities at the Apiary. 'Every other person seems to have a cabbage leaf or something else with a large piece of honey on it, which he or she is devouring with what speed and want of cleanli- ness they may,' observed a *Globe* reporter in 1886. 'The consequence is that the whole place has a stickiness about it which is calculated to repel visitors rather than attract them.' After the syrup was gone, wax combs were often littered on the ground, creating more gooey blobs to snare cuffs and hems.[76]

Those desiring substantial repasts were more likely to experience aggravation. The safest, thriftiest course was to bring food and to pic-nic on the lawn in front of the lake. The disadvantage was having to lug baskets and bundles for prolonged periods, often through packed spaces.[77] Many people, therefore, patronized dining-halls, where vast quantities of food were consumed. From a distance, the traditional feast of carnival seemed well and truly celebrated. On busy days at the 1902 show, Mrs Meyer's restaurant went through a thousand to fifteen hundred pounds of beef, twelve to twenty lambs, hundreds of chickens, and large quantities of pork, sausages, and fish. The same was true at the other ten or so establishments operating that year. One to two hundred gallons of ice cream were consumed every day, and two or three thousand loaves of bread, not to mention rolls, bis-cuits, and cakes.[78] Of course, when this quantity was translated into individual portions, opportunities for gluttony were diminished. So were inclinations. The complaint in 1879 of 'One That Was Victim-ized,' that his twenty-five-cent meal was 'insufficient and distaste-ful,' echoed down the years. 'Iron-bound steak' was how one reporter described his meal; a 'choice cuttin' off the hoof' was the verdict of another.[79]

If cuisine was poor, service was worse. When mobs gravitated en masse at the sound of lunch and dinner bells, restaurants could not cope. Would-be guests sometimes stood for an hour outside a dining-tent, and then just as long inside waiting for a table, which, once obtained, did not guarantee prompt attention. A *Telegram* reporter in 1888 saw many who had paid in advance get up and leave without seeing a morsel. 'They got so used to hunger that they seemed to like it and went away fodderless.' He stayed until 'the waiters got tired hiding behind the screens' and was rewarded with 'what would have been a good dinner if the portions had not been broiled quite so hard.'[80] Relative to the scene described by the *Mail* several days earlier, he was lucky:

> It would be impossible to describe the state of affairs around the dining hall, or to give any kind of idea of the bedlam which prevailed within up to eight o'clock. Thousands lined the approaches to the main dining hall, scrambling for admittance. Ladies were crushed, and some of them were carried in a fainting condition from the scene of the awful confusion which prevailed. Caterers realized in very little time how tremendous was the crowd of yesterday, for they had to admit that they had nothing left in less than two hours to satiate the hunger of those who filed, at great risk to their lives, limbs, and headgear, into their halls. 'No milk, meat, or bread left' was the languid answer of the tired out waiters to the calls of men, women, and children for something to eat, and yet throngs were still entering places of entertainment on the same fruitless mission.

It was not the first time people waited for prolonged periods, only to be informed supplies had run out. Caterers were often blamed for inefficiency, but that was not the whole story. It simply was not profitable to recruit additional staff or to provide extra equipment for rush periods of short duration, nor was it worth the risk of being stuck with quantities of unsold perishables.[81]

Mobs that interfered with the pleasures of dining also made sightseeing a tortuous experience. On Citizens' Day in 1885, people could barely move about the grounds. Roads were so congested that occasional cyclists who tried to weave through 'had to give it up as a bad job.' Sideshows were virtually inaccessible. Over time, pressures became more intense. 'To squeeze Hamilton and London into an eighty acre field and expect the people to move about in comfort is taking altogether too much for granted,' complained the editor of the *World* in 1898.[82]

Two spots were consistently jammed. The Crystal Palace was an annual trial. 'Lady Victim,' jostled through in 1879 without seeing anything, 'was glad to make my exit as quickly as possible, owing to

This 1903 photo of a performance by the Coldstream Guards Band gives some idea of the crowd congestion that could occur on the grounds. The building behind the band-shell is the new Art Gallery.

the frightful crush.' After the first year, visitors knew better what to expect, though that did not make inspections any easier. Going through with any degree of comfort or in any reasonable time was impossible, according to a *Globe* reporter several years later, 'and a person to retain his equanimity would require the patience of Job.' 'Too much in too little' was Madge Merton's comment a decade later; most people, she guessed, breathed thankfully when they got out-side.[83]

The grandstand, during both afternoon and evening shows, was equally demanding. Just getting a ticket could be an ordeal. On one afternoon in 1890 vendors were 'in a state of siege' from one o'clock until three, when sales were cut off for lack of room. Despite police assistance, they had trouble controlling the crowd clamouring to get in. Three years later, there was just as much turmoil in a line that stretched the length of a new, much larger facility. 'There the rich man shoved the poor and the poor man shoved the great. Silk ties were ruffled and polished shoes bedaubed. Buttons were lost and hairpins fell like dew.' Even when line-ups were relatively sedate, people sometimes queued for more than an hour before getting to a wicket. On busy days, thousands were denied admission, despite the fact that space was generously oversold. Once turnstiles opened, races for good seats could be fierce, as in 1895 when, according to the *Star*, 'the rush in was too vicious for some, and women fainted by the score.' Needless to say, those who did manage to squeeze through were 'packed like sardines in a box' and sometimes had trouble seeing the stage. Management eventually responded to complaints – predictably, by offering cushioned, reserve seats at four times the regular price.[84]

Getting home usually entailed another struggle if public transit was required. After evening extravaganzas, surges for streetcars were 'wild and dangerous.' The risk of being trampled or pressed under trolley wheels was real enough, although the experience of Fanny Chadwick in 1895 was more common. The three people in her party were all pushed into a different car, despite their best efforts to stay together. Those too late for the first batch of vehicles endured long waits for more to arrive. According to a *Mail* reporter in 1890, the only way to manage a ride between 10 and 11 p.m. was to get well away from the grounds, then board a car going back to the fair. Many preferred to walk rather than be packed 'like herring in a box' for the slow journey back to town, in a gridlock of carriages and hacks.[85]

Those heading for more distant parts faced similar discomforts for longer periods. A return to Newmarket in 1886 was particularly gruelling. The 'tremendous crowd' waited in rain at Parkdale Station for a train that was an hour and a half late. When it finally got under way shortly before midnight, a few 'unruly and decidedly refractory boys' started playing with the brakes:

Until Richmond Hill was passed the crew and passengers were tormented almost beyond endurance. The whole of that distance they tried to stop the train, succeeding once or twice, while the jerking by the engine was something fearful. It was nearly 2 am when the train got to Newmarket and those who rode in a boxcar without light had a 'sweet time.'

Under the best of circumstances, most travellers were anxious to reach home and bed. The condition of Elora folk who got back 'about the time chanticleer is straightening himself for his first crow' was far from unique. 'A more tired lot of excursionists are seldom to be seen,' reported the local editor.[86]

City people were also beat. J.J. Kelso, inveterate diary keeper, scribbled three short sentences when he got home at 11:40 after a day at the 1885 show. He had enjoyed it, but was 'very, very tired.' Schoolboy Ned Ardaugh had a 'dandy' time in 1894, but was unable to get up for breakfast. Twenty-one-year-old Mackenzie King put in a ten-hour stint at the 1895 event, went to bed about midnight 'feeling very tired,' and did not get up until noon the next day, which was taken slowly. 'Tired after exhibition' was his summary of its highlights.[87]

Of course, fatigue set in long before people crawled between the sheets. They did the fair on adrenalin and sheer endurance, propping themselves on railings and counters, or plopping down on lawns and benches when they could. No wonder the grandstand was so popular. Sometimes, exhaustion got the better of visitors. Kit Coleman described a confrontation between her son and a 'fat woman' who 'flopped' onto his seat at a fireworks display, refusing to budge. He and his sister stood in front, blocking the view, until she conceded defeat. Kit was not sympathetic, but the desperation caused by sore feet is understandable. Excitement and activity helped to distract attention from bodily aches, but few were immune from them. As Frances Burton Clare put it in 1889, 'the grounds were over run by a crowd of people, who were standing and walking around firmly impressed with the idea that they were enjoying themselves, when in reality they were tired beyond endurance.'[88]

The editor of the *Empire* was only being realistic in suggesting that the fair was a 'tax on the nervous system.'[89] It did entail significant degrees of weariness and frustration. These could be reduced by going on quieter days, though the majority did not take that course, and those who did could not entirely eliminate strains. If anything came close to a universal fair experience, it was fatigue. Was there occasion for 'festive laughter' in any of this? Undoubtedly.[90] Yet it is hard not to conclude that psychic renewal was bought with physical and emotional depletion. Going to the Industrial Exhibition required effort, and not everyone was able or willing to put it out every year.

Charles Rearick has claimed that French amusements in this period were 'feints at an enveloping somberness ... [F]estive moments were but instants of a delicious liberation, instants stolen from a heavy fate.' Ontarians probably had a less gloomy outlook on life, and were not disappointed when festivities came to a close. Country folk were glad to get animals back safely into regular pastures and coops, and to unwind in the comfort of their own homes. Torontonians thankfully reclaimed their city. 'With the close of the exhibition,' remarked the *Markham Sun* in 1900, 'it is possible once again to navigate Toronto streets with a certain degree of comfort and the average citizen heaves a sigh of relief that the agony is again a thing of the past.'[91] Some must have been grateful just to arrive at work after a decent night's sleep in a real bed.

Does this mean that the exhibition was a safety valve that conditioned people to accept regular structures of authority? For some individuals, it must have been. Without sounding too conspiratorial, it is reasonable to suggest that a celebration which directed excess energies into safe channels, and made people appreciate the resumption of ordinary routine, met the requirements of industrial capitalism rather neatly.

This is not to say that the fair stifled all impulses for change. It may have reconciled people to the rhythms of life in industrial society, but not to precise conditions. For many interests, the whole point of the show was to stimulate desire and the will to change. Nor did inspiration derive solely from planned displays; any impression, intentional or not, could inspire notions of different possibilities and produce concrete changes in ordinary life. In 1888, for example, a nearby resident complained that the electric light erected at the corner of King and Tecumseh streets for the two weeks of the exhibition had been removed. It was not right, the correspondent thought, that municipal services should benefit only outsiders who paid no taxes.[92] 'Grumbler' had been vouchsafed a small vision of alternative arrangements and was inspired to push gently for change. Some inklings of other possibilities were much grander, among them the dream of a luxury hotel.

Despite the construction and enlargement of hotels throughout the latter part of the century, additions were never sufficient to keep pace with ever-increasing fair crowds.[93] When Torontonians thought of accommodation deficiencies, however, they did not usually consider the thousands of ordinary tourists looking for reasonably priced places to stay. Rather, they were preoccupied by the lack of a deluxe palace for the rich. What was needed, according to a *Globe* editorial reviewing the 1887 fair season, was not just a building to house exhibition visitors, but one that would be an attraction in itself – a hotel whose 'beauty of situation, architectural grandeur, splendid furniture and excellent management' would serve to make Toronto a stopping place. It was not the first or last time that the conclusion of the Industrial stimulated such a call.[94]

Some of the city's most prominent capitalists were intrigued. They cared not a hoot about investing in establishments to serve modest clienteles, but for more than a decade they flirted with proposals for sumptuous hostelries. In 1892 Sir Frank Smith, one of the nation's largest grocery and liquor wholesalers, recently retired, and the former owner of the Toronto Street Railway Company, asked City Council for its cooperation in the erection of a 'superior hotel,' for which he submitted a draft scheme. Two years later, one rumour had it that an unknown group of businessmen intended putting up a palatial structure on the site formerly occupied by Upper Canada College, and another that Smith, along with Sir John Carling, senator and brewer, William Mackenzie, railway magnate, and David Walker, proprietor of the Walker House, had prepared plans for a seven-storey building at Front and York to cost a million dollars. In December 1895 Robert Jaffray, J.W. Langmuir, and Fred Rodgers, all prominent local businessmen, organized an informal meeting of those interested in erecting a million-dollar, first-class hotel on the old UCC grounds. A year later there was talk of two different projects near Queen's Park.[95]

In the most determined of these mid-decade efforts, a group that included foundry owner Edward Gurney, biscuit manufacturer William Christie, miller and produce merchant W.D. Matthews, bank manager and eventually bank president B.E. Walker, and grocery wholesalers Joseph Eby and Hugh Blain tried to raise half a million dollars for a structure also proposed for the UCC grounds. They managed to get an endorsement for a free site from the University of Toronto, which controlled the land in conjunction with the province, but they encountered objections not only to the gift of public property, but to a request for government bond guarantees. More important, perhaps, they encountered indifference from New York investors who

Artist's rendering of the proposed new King Edward Hotel, with a disproportionate street scale to increase the impression of grandeur.

were supposed to put up most of the funds. Still, they persisted, having joined forces, it seems, with the Jaffray, Langmuir interests. By
1897 the government had agreed to provide a site, and plans were
unveiled for an eight-storey building to cost over half a million dollars. The project now became contingent on a ten-year exemption
from city taxes and a reduced water rate. The city probably gave the
requests serious consideration, for in October 1898 it received a
letter from some of the most prominent hotel owners objecting to
special deals. Faced with opposition from a significant constituency
waving a populist flag, the city backed away.[96]

As that scheme floundered, another that eventually involved at
least some of the same individuals was taking shape around a site
on King Street, just east of Yonge. An early report indicated that
plans had been drawn up by an American architect for a 'mammoth
hotel' costing three-quarters of a million dollars, to be advanced by

an English syndicate. Three months later, word was that banker Aemilius Jarvis had persuaded New York capitalists to put up two million dollars for a much grander structure with seven storeys and a roof garden. While the details proved to be inaccurate, promoters went ahead with an application for incorporation early in 1899, appointed an executive committee (which included Gurney, Jaffray, and distiller George Gooderham), hired architects, and continued to hunt for investors. In December 1900 they showed the city's Board of Control a plan for a building with five hundred rooms. In the spring, they began levelling the site and, at the end of the year, they got a building permit for a million-dollar, six-storey structure. The plans were quickly amended to include two more storeys and additional ornamentation to the rotunda, at a cost of $200,000 more. Toronto was getting its palace hotel.[97]

Visitors to the 1902 exhibition got some intimation of what it would look like from a model suite on the second floor of the Main Building. The dining-room was set up with Wedgewood china, gleaming silver, and glittering glassware, all bearing the crest of the new King Edward Hotel. The bedroom, with Marie Antoinette curtains overhung with flowered chintz, brass bed, beautiful dresser with oval mirror, chintz-covered easy chairs, and inviting escritoire, gave an 'exact idea of the comfort and elegance' soon to be available to the weary traveller. Crowds flocked to the exhibit. A year later, when the building opened just in time for the next fair, many probably went to see the real thing.[98]

Visions of a posh hotel derived from more than the requirements of exhibition time, yet these desires seemed to be felt most keenly during that period, as if the magnificence of the show was somehow diminished by the absence of an equally splendid place to stay. Certainly, there was something appropriately carnivalesque about an institution designed to foster conspicuous consumption, and yet the existence of the King Edward symbolized how much carnival had changed over the centuries. At one time, the whole community was invited to the feast; now, most people could only imagine the experience of extravagance from the lobby.[99]

⌇⌇⌇⌇⌇⌇⌇⌇

During Mardi Gras in New Orleans and Mobile, according to Samuel Kinser, carnival happens twice, once in white businessman's land

and again in blacktown, where a 'disorderly embroidery' on the official image is celebrated. Does carnival everywhere and always have this dual character, he wonders.[100] In nineteenth-century Toronto, it did not. No alternative public festivity supplemented or commented on the dominant proceedings.

What the carnival in Toronto did offer was a dichotomous view of the possibilities of modern urban life. Parades, illuminations, and store and exhibition displays provided tangible demonstrations of civic dynamism, community cooperation, social harmony, technological proficiency, and material abundance. Formal presentations, both on and off the grounds, embodied a version of the carnival's traditional representation of conspicuous consumption and utopian fulfilment. At the same time, however, perceptions of excess also included the thousands of visitors who overwhelmed civic facilities. Fairtime meant line-ups, oppressive crowding, struggles to get from one place to another. It meant disruptions of routine, shortages, exhaustion. It meant people wandering streets at night with nowhere to sleep, and streetcar horses worked to the breaking point. This was a city coming apart at the seams, going out of gear, coming off the rails – sometimes literally. While carnival may not always happen twice, as Kinser hypothesizes, it may always be double sided, creating dystopian situations while simultaneously giving expression to utopian longings.

Carnival in Victorian Toronto was not the same as carnival in early modern Europe. While it was time apart from regular existence, with many of the same festive elements in evidence, the spirit and the intent were significantly different. The traditional fête, at least in some places, was driven by people at the bottom who overrode normal authority. The nineteenth-century one pointed up the necessity of technical experts and organizational efficiency. Like carnivals in other North American cities in the same period, it was dominated by a middle-class agenda.[101] The traditional fête accepted and compensated for the loss of utopian potential in real life. The Victorian one was meant to show that the material limitations of ordinary life could be pushed back. Of course, the more thoroughly people tried to take in marvels laid before them, the more tired they got. The Industrial Exhibition, like carnivals of old, did underscore a fundamental human equality that no amount of social pretension could erase, but it did so inadvertently, not deliberately. Classes, races, genders did get levelled, but mostly after the gates had closed and visitors sought relief in sleep.

Epilogue: Modernity

Becoming modern; being modern: few people in the late Victorian period thought of their experiences in these terms. They did not see themselves as mere ciphers in a vast, amorphous transformation that could be summarized by neat terms like 'industrial capitalism,' 'the culture of consumption,' or 'modernization.' The meaning of their lives did not derive from abstract measurements of increasing bureaucracy, state regulation, population movement, or manufacturing output. Processes that seem so sharply etched and fundamental in hindsight were gradual and complex for them, part of the broader context for more important matters like finding happiness and making ends meet. Becoming modern, as a deliberate goal, was not something most people considered consciously with any consistency. Yet, in ways that were piecemeal, uneven, and obscurely understood, modern they became – either willingly or in spite of themselves.

While modernity defied, and defies, definition in formulaic terms, in the decades around the turn of the century it was hard to escape indications of profound change, indications that emanated most strongly from cities, but did not stop at urban boundaries. Neighbourhoods were uprooted. Pastures were converted to city blocks. Nets of utility wires were suspended from the sky. Office towers blocked more sunlight. Downtown streets and sidewalks became more congested. Shop counters and windows overflowed with goods. Trolleys picked up speed. Money circulated more quickly. Fashions continually metastasized. Schedules became more intricate and insistant.[1]

The rapid succession of images, spectacles, and social environments that began to characterize day-to-day experience inevitably shaped internal consciousness. As Dana Brand puts it, 'in the modern world, the phenomenological character of experience is less unified, coherent, or continuous than it was in earlier historical periods ... It has become harder to connect the individual components of experience with each other ... It is harder to be oriented, rooted, or convinced of the solidity or permanence of anything one believes or observes.'[2] In the vortex of consumer capitalism, life seemed more a matter of becoming rather than being. Again, it is important to remember that people felt these changes in different ways, to different degrees, but the sense of flux was pervasive.

Coping with this fluidity spawned many different projects, among them rituals like the exhibition in Toronto. If the annual fair of a provincial city lacked the prestige of a world exposition, permanence compensated by enhancing its local importance as the anchor of a large chunk of the yearly round. If displays were not as extensive and elaborate as ones at grander events, they were used just as intently to disseminate and make natural the evolving standards, hierarchies, and loyalties that made a common life possible. Here, too, the exhibitionary impulse was inspired by a desire to coax stability through popular assent rather than coercion. It was driven by a need to make principles of order visible and obvious, by a confidence that individuals so instructed would be more willing and able to regulate themselves.[3] Like much else now styled 'modern,' the assertion of the universal over the particular, the positing of essentialist qualities and categories, was an attempt to subdue a worrisome sense of unfixedness.[4]

As a device to induce order, however, the exhibition was flawed. To some extent this was predictable, though still ironic. The very success of the show attracted the likes of prostitutes, pickpockets, hotel sneaks, and confidence criminals, not to mention ordinary citizens who took advantage of crowd anonymity to be deliberately disorderly. Not even the implementation of more arbitrary policing procedures could neutralize the heightened anxiety they caused. As well, the success of the show attracted so many visitors that ordinary city facilities were overwhelmed. Many residents and tourists were more impressed by systems that did not mesh efficiently than by ones that did.

More fundamentally, however, the fair was flawed as a mechanism of order because its purposes were inherently contradictory. As much as hegemonic elements wanted to use it to impress the desirability of system and harmony, they also wanted to break down established habits, values, and expectations. Industrial capitalism needed people to experiment with new objects, indulge in new forms of behaviour, abandon certain kinds of restraint, and internalize new desires. It required people to become acclimatized to constant, pervasive change. It deliberately engineered liminal sites where conventional forms dissolved and different possibilities became apparent. The tightly circumscribed space and duration of the fair made it attractive for this project, compensating for the festive tolerance of suspect features.

Fairgrounds have usually been conceptually confusing, and the one in late Victorian Toronto was no exception. Its current alternated continuously. The most sophisticated products of human ingenuity were counterposed with dwarves, siamese twins, and other forms of biological accident. Gender stereotypes reinforced in one corner came apart in another. Confidence generated one moment was stalled the next. Intimations of a smoothly running garden city were spoiled by hordes of individuals constantly getting in each other's way. Visions of a cooperative community were dispelled by warnings to be on guard against nefarious villains. Principles of order were made manifest and entrenched, then dissolved, unravelled, undermined. Cultural categories here posited as eternal and universal were there questioned and rearranged. The traditional, the official, the conventional, the classical were affirmed in one instant, while the next endorsed the new, the popular, the unusual, the grotesque. Back and forth the armatures swung, the potency of one pole continually recharging the other.

No wonder the fairground was contested space. Countless groups and individuals manoeuvred to insert their values and ways of being. Sporting males connived against liquor inspectors. Refreshment booth operators disputed with temperance advocates. Criminals parried with police. Farming and manufacturing interests vied for attention with carnival barkers. Patent-medicine fakirs squared off against respectable retailers. Groundskeepers battled exhausted tourists to preserve flower beds. Women pressured male managers for better space and more control over it. Piano salesforces fought with each other to be heard. The contests themselves were not unusual. They were simply part of the give and take of life in a complex, dynamic society. The fairground was distinctive partly because such a profusion and variety of contending interests were compressed into a limited space, but, more important, because so many competitions were focused internally on the middle class, a social constituency whose numbers and authority were expanding.

The fairground was indisputably middle-class territory. Others resisted bourgeois agendas, but never seriously challenged bourgeois control; their important battles occurred in spaces where they had more at stake – like neighbourhoods and workplaces. As much as middle-class people intended the exhibition to inspire other parts of the community, because their control was secure they felt less necessity to close ranks. Greater freedom to take on each other made the fair a useful site for probing their own class identity. There, they had a chance to debate what it meant to be middle class – to consider options, investigate alternatives, and define standards and expectations in terms of concrete particulars of everyday existence. They could peruse the panoply of material goods that grounded social status. They could evaluate the appearance and behaviour of those who fulfilled or fell short of class ideals. They could test their own reactions to the anonymity, discontinuity, and material enticements that characterized so much of modern life in a milieu where these attributes were unusually intense. The fair was a giant forum for appraising matters relating to taste and sensibility.

Some of the debates, like those about the morality of grandstand entertainments and the consumption of alcohol, were public and extended, conducted by individuals already committed to a point of view. Many, however, were small scale and restricted, reflecting individual confusion as much as lack of group consensus. The liminal atmosphere of the fairground, where anything might or even should happen, encouraged postures that were more experiments into what was possible than grand assertions of what should be.

Consider J.J. Kelso, newspaper reporter and eventually founder of the Ontario Children's Aid Society. On the afternoon of 15 September 1888 he ventured down to the exhibition grounds with a friend to take in the show that had opened a few days earlier. They had been in the Crystal Palace only a few minutes when he spied two young ladies – Ella and Mabel, according to a later diary notation – whom he had first noticed a year before at Barnum's Circus. 'At every meeting since then,' he reminded himself, 'our eyes have lit up with recognition, and when we encountered at the Exhibition it was like renewing a familiar acquaintanceship.' Both parties wandered around the building, trying to cross paths as often as possible:

These meetings must have been painful as well as pleasant to the girls. One of them – the one in whom I was most interested – would look at me with a deep smiling gaze and then turn away with a sad, heart wounded look. As for me, my heart was kept in a painful flutter all the time. When I met them my pulse seemed to stop beating and my blood turn hot and cold in turns. I longed to keep my eyes fixed on them and yet every fresh glance was a source of pain. Once I watched them from a distance and found that they were looking for me in every corner of the building. When at last they saw me, and noticed that I had been watching them, they seemed a trifle annoyed. After this had gone on at frequent intervals during the afternoon, I approached them and asked if I might introduce myself to them, as we had met so often and were already so well acquainted. They blushed violently and my especial one said with something of reluctance 'I'd rather not, thank you.' With an apology, I raised my hat and withdrew. They nodded a friendly good-bye.[5]

What was it about the atmosphere of the Crystal Palace that encouraged Kelso to violate social convention? Was the ambiance of respectability so strong that regular prophylactic protocols of the street seemed to be unnecessary? Did he imagine the building was almost a domestic parlour where such intimacy was permitted? Was the stimulation of desire by exhibitors so powerful that he conflated the availability of goods with the availability of bodies? Did Ella's and Mabel's ability to indulge in the predominantly male practice of social gazing legitimize his transgressions? Was his grasp of self so jarred in the crowd that mere visual recognition of other individuals seemed to justify exceptional familiarity? Did a shared urban identity in the presence of many outsiders seem to bridge their social circles? Did the festive mood persuade him that the approach would not be misconstrued? Probably not even he could have said, yet something about this environment made him feel betwixt and between ordinary space and time.

It was hardly a giant step in the forging of modernity. It was not a turning-point in his life or in the lives of the girls. Nevertheless, encounters like this, recorded all too rarely, are worth considering, just because they were so commonplace. They demonstrate that not everyone grasped new possibilities at the same time, in the same way. Even the liminally charged fairground was not a level playing field: becoming modern was affected as much by constraints of

gender, class, race, and age as by personal predilictions. They reveal that adapting to changing circumstances was a slow, tentative,
cumulative process that occurred more at ground level than at
heights of intellectual abstraction. If modernity was flux and discontinuity, becoming modern involved more than grasping grand
theological and scientific schemes or master narratives propagated
by popular media. It meant learning how to control fleeting moments and impressions, how to interpret delicate, shifting gradations
of taste, how to interact with strangers in chance encounters, how
to cope with ambiguity, how to sustain coherence and self-possession
in the face of dizzying sensory overload.

In the nineteenth-century literary adventure of developing urban
existence, the hero was the *flâneur*, the elegant, unhurried, urbane,
'benignly tolerant' connoisseur of street activity whose piquant
observations made city life comprehensible.[6] Many North Americans
at the end of the century, like the Toronto *Mail and Empire* reporter
whose byline was 'The Flaneur,' were just as drawn to this figure as
were mid-nineteenth-century Parisians.[7] The *flâneur*, however, was
mostly a romantic conceit. Few real people had the freedom to spend
their days idly strolling, experiencing life for its own sake. Few possessed such extraordinary powers of perception and interpretation.
Perhaps Kelso flattered himself that in following Ella and Mabel, he
was chasing down urban delights with true *flâneurial* proficiency,
but he had something else on his mind than the detached decipher-
ing of subtle mysteries. He was not a *flâneur*, but neither was he a
badaud, a simple gawker, incapable of discriminating between one
diversion and another, so emotionally void as almost to lose self-
consciousness.[8] How, then, to characterize him, and thousands of
other men and women who edged their way towards modernity, two
steps forward, one step back?

Perhaps they were *gonces*. In the nineteenth-century French
second-hand clothing business, this was the derogatory slang for
passers-by. Philippe Perrot, who lists the term in a short lexicon of
the trade,[9] does not elaborate on its meaning, but it can be imagined.
Gonces were people in motion, with things to do and places to get.
Shopping, travelling to and from work, running endless little errands,
they had moments to linger more than time to waste. Slightly anaes-
thetized to surrounding hubbub by routine and impulses to self-
protection, they passed along the streets, partly cocooned in their own
worries and speculations, partly alert to dangers, familiar faces,

temptations. The shifted from one distraction, one surrounding, one level of consciousness to another without strain. They juggled the fragments of experience more than studied them.

Exhibitions were popular in part because they were said to be places where people could become *flâneurs*, tracking the unusual, pinning down its significance. Perhaps some visitors actually succeeded, for limited periods. Most, however, were more like *gonces*. With its extensive circuits of stalls and concessions, diversity of departments and landscapes, and eclectic variety of attractions, the fair was ideal for *goncing*. There was always something more to see or do – across the aisle, around the corner, across the way. Patrons flitted from one diversion to another and, when exhaustion began to draw them towards the comatose indifference of *badauds*, they rested and watched others being *gonces*.

In the process, they learned to expect discontinuous spectacle as an ordinary occurrence. They learned that their own identities and the foundation of community were bound up with possibilities of leisure and consumption. They learned the vocabulary of signs that defined the hierarchies of social existence. Other lessons, some contradictory, came from other sources. The fair was not the only formative influence in shaping understandings of modernity, in Toronto or anywhere else. Nevertheless, with its exceptional power to fracture normal routines and perspectives, and, in so doing, open spaces for anxiety, desire, and wonder, the fair nudged Kelso, Ella, Mabel, and millions like them towards new meanings, new ways of being.

Notes

Abbreviations

CIHM/ICMH   Canadian Institute for Historical Microreproductions/
             Institut canadien de microreproductions historiques
CNEA   Canadian National Exhibition Archives
CTA   City of Toronto Archives
MTRL   Metropolitan Toronto Reference Library
NA   National Archives of Canada
OA   Ontario Archives

Unless otherwise noted, newspapers referred to were published in Toronto.

Preface

1 In 1904 the name was changed to the Canadian National Exhibition of
  Toronto. Over the next decade or so, the last two words were dropped. See
  V.M. Roberts, *The Trail of the Canadian National Exhibition: An Illus-
  trated Historical Souvenir* (Toronto 1925), 42.
2 In Canada, for example, see Peter DeLottinville, 'Joe Beef of Montreal:
  Working-Class Culture and the Tavern, 1869–1889,' *Labour / Le Tra-
  vailleur* 8/9 (autumn/spring 1981/82), 9–40; Bryan Palmer, *A Culture in
  Conflict: Skilled Workers and Industrial Capitalism in Hamilton,
  Ontario, 1860–1914* (Montreal and Kingston 1979); Yvan Lamonde and
  Raymond Montpetit, *Le Parc Sohmer de Montréal, 1889–1919: Un lieu
  populaire de culture urbaine* (Quebec 1986); Suzanne Morton, *Ideal
  Surroundings: Domestic Life in a Working-Class Suburb in the 1920s*

(Toronto 1995); Keith Walden, *Visions of Order: The Canadian Mounties in Symbol and Myth* (Toronto 1982).

3 On these recent tendencies in anthropology, see S.N. Eisenstadt, 'The Order-Maintaining and Order-Transforming Dimensions of Culture,' in Richard Munch and Neil J. Smelser, eds., *Theory of Culture* (Berkeley 1993), 65; Neil J. Smelser, 'Culture: Coherent or Incoherent,' ibid, 15.

4 George Lipsitz, 'Listening to Learn and Learning to Listen: Popular Culture, Cultural Theory, and American Studies,' *American Quarterly* 42, 4 (Dec. 1990), 618.

5 Catherine Belsey, 'Towards Cultural History – in Theory and Practice,' *Textual Practice* 3, 2 (summer 1989), 163; Roger Chartier, 'Text, Symbols and Frenchness,' *Journal of Modern History* 57, 4 (Dec. 1985), 688. See also Roger Chartier, *Cultural History: Between Practices and Representations* (Cambridge 1988), 13–14; William J. Bowsma, 'Intellectual History in the 1980s: From History of Ideas to History of Meaning,' *Journal of Interdisciplinary History* 12 (autumn 1981), 279–91; Lawrence W. Levine, 'The Folklore of Industrial Society: Popular Culture and Its Audiences,' *American Historical Review* 97, 5 (Dec. 1992), 1384–93; Robert W. Rydell and Nancy Gwinn, 'Introduction,' in Rydell and Gwinn, eds., *Fair Representations: World's Fairs and the Modern World* (Amsterdam 1994), 3–4.

6 Richard Wightman Fox and T.J. Jackson Lears, 'Introduction,' in Fox and Lears, eds., *The Power of Culture: Critical Essays in American History* (Chicago and London 1993), 1. On these tendencies within the study of urban culture specifically, see William R. Taylor, *In Pursuit of Gotham: Culture and Commerce in New York* (New York and Oxford 1992), xix.

7 Lynn Hunt, 'Introduction: History, Culture, and Text,' in Hunt, ed., *The New Cultural History* (Berkeley 1989), 12, 22. Other Canadian historians who have investigated the construction of meaning include Ian McKay, *The Quest of the Folk: Anti-modernism and Cultural Selection in Twentieth-Century Nova Scotia* (Montreal and Kingston 1994); Tina Loo, 'Dan Cranmer's Potlatch: Law as Coercion, Symbol, and Rhetoric in British Columbia, 1884–1951,' *Canadian Historical Review* 73, 2 (June 1992), 125–65; Michele Martin, 'Hello, Central': Gender, Technology and Culture in the Formation of Telephone Systems* (Montreal and Kingston 1991); Mariana Valverde, *The Age of Light, Soap, and Water: Moral Reform in English Canada, 1885–1925* (Toronto 1991).

8 The main treatments of the Toronto Industrial / Canadian National Exhibition are Roberts, *Trail of the Canadian National Exhibition*; Oswald Withrow, *The Romance of the Canadian National Exhibition* (Toronto

1936); James Lorimer, *The Ex: A Picture History of the Canadian National Exhibition* (Toronto 1973); *Once upon a Century: 100 Year History of the Ex* (Toronto 1978).

9 Sally Alexander, *The St. Giles Fair, 1830–1914: Popular Culture and the Industrial Revolution in 19th Century Oxford* (Oxford nd); Anne Lincoln Fitzpatrick, *The Great Russian Fair: Nizhnii Novgorod, 1840–1890* (Oxford 1990). See also Patrick Logan, *Fair Day: The Story of Irish Fairs and Markets* (Belfast 1986).

10 Wayne Caldwell Neely, *The Agricultural Fair* (New York 1935); Ted Ownby, *Subduing Satan: Religion, Recreation and Manhood in the Rural South, 1865–1920* (Chapel Hill and London 1990); Chris Rasmussen, 'State Fair: Culture and Agriculture in Iowa, 1854–1941,' (PhD thesis, Rutgers University, The State University of New Jersey, 1992); Karal Ann Marling, *Blue Ribbon: A Social and Pictorial History of the Minnesota State Fair* (St Paul 1990).

11 David Jones, *Midways, Judges and Sharp-Tongued Fakirs: The Illustrated Story of Country Fairs in the Prairie West* (Saskatoon 1983); Elsbeth Heaman, 'Colonial Leviathan: Central Canadian Exhibitions at Home and Abroad during the Nineteenth Century' (PhD thesis, University of Toronto, 1995); Elwood H. Jones, *Winners: 150 Years of the Peterborough Exhibition* (Peterborough 1995). See also David Breen and Kenneth Coates, *Vancouver's Fair: An Administrative and Political History of the Pacific National Exhibition* (Vancouver 1982); David Breen and Kenneth Coates, *The Pacific National Exhibition: An Illustrated History* (Vancouver 1982); Brian Osborne, 'Trading on a Frontier: The Function of Peddlers, Markets and Fairs in 19th Century Ontario,' *Canadian Papers in Rural History* 2 (1979), 59–81; Hervé Gagnon, 'Des animaux, des hommes et des choses: Les expositions au Bas-Canada dans la première moitié du XIXe siècle,' *Histoire sociale / Social History* 26, 52 (Nov. 1993), 291–327; Yves Bergeron, 'Le XIXe siècle et l'âge d'or des marchés publics au Québec,' *Journal of Canadian Studies* 29, 1 (spring 1994), 11–36.

12 Robert Rydell, 'The Literature of International Expositions,' in *The Books of the Fairs: Materials about World's Fairs, 1834–1916, in the Smithsonian Institution Libraries* (Chicago and London 1992), 1–62. The extensive bibliography found in that volume has been supplemented by Bridget J. Burke, 'World's Fairs and International Expositions: Selected References 1987–1993,' in Rydell and Gwinn, eds., *Fair Representations*, 218–47.

13 Neil Harris, *Cultural Excursions: Marketing Appetites and Cultural Tastes in Modern America* (Chicago and London 1990), 111–13.

14 Thomas J. Schlereth, *Victorian America: Transformations in Everyday*

Life, 1876–1915 (New York 1991); Deborah L. Silverman, 'The 1889 Exhibition: The Crisis of Bourgeois Individualism,' *Oppositions* 8 (spring 1977), 82. Others who have used exhibitions in this way include Merle Curti, 'America at the World's Fairs, 1851–1893,' *American Historical Review* 55 (1950), 833–56; John G. Cawelti, 'America on Display: The World's Fairs of 1876, 1893, 1933,' in Frederic Cople Jaher, ed., *The Age of Industrialism in America* (New York and London 1968), 317–63; Asa Briggs, *Victorian People: A Reassessment of Persons and Themes, 1851–1867* (1955; Chicago 1970), 14–51; Asa Briggs, *Victorian Things* (Chicago and London 1988), 53–102.

15 Reid Badger, *The Great American Fair: The World's Columbian Exposition and American Culture* (Chicago 1979), 7, 116, 128; Robert Muccigrosso, *Celebrating the New World: Chicago's Columbian Exposition of 1893* (Chicago 1993), xii, 193.

16 Alan Trachtenberg, *The Incorporation of America: Culture and Society in the Gilded Age* (New York 1982), 231; Paul Greenhalgh, *Ephemeral Vistas: The Expositions Universelles, Great Exhibitions and World's Fairs, 1851–1939* (Manchester 1988), 27 and passim; Burton Benedict et al., *The Anthropology of World's Fairs: San Francisco's Panama Pacific International Exposition of 1915* (London and Berkeley 1983), 2, 6, 9; Robert Rydell, *All the World's a Fair: Visions of Empire at American International Expositions, 1876–1916* (Chicago and London 1984), 2–3; Robert Rydell, *World of Fairs: The Century-of-Progress Expositions* (Chicago and London 1993), 9–10; Harris, *Cultural Excursions*, 123–7.

17 Trachtenberg, *Incorporation of America*, 211; Harris, *Cultural Excursions*, 25; Benedict, *Anthropology of World's Fairs*, 5; James Gilbert, *Perfect Cities: Chicago's Utopias of 1893* (Chicago and London 1991).

18 Warren Susman, 'Ritual Fairs,' *Chicago History* 12 (1983), 4–7; Benedict, *Anthropology of World's Fairs*, 6; Rydell, *All the World's a Fair*, 3.

19 Robert Darnton, *The Great Cat Massacre and Other Episodes in French Cultural History* (New York 1985).

20 Dominick LaCapra, 'Chartier, Darnton, and the Great Symbol Massacre,' *Journal of Modern History* 60, 1 (March 1988), 103–4; James Fernandez, 'Historians Tell Tales: Of Cartesian Cats and Gallic Cockfights,' *Journal of Modern History* 60, 1 (March 1988), 120; Harold Mah, 'Suppressing the Text: The Metaphysics of Ethnographic History in Darnton's Great Cat Massacre,' *History Workshop* 31 (spring 1991), 7.

21 Mah, *Suppressing the Text*, 8. Mah argues not only that Darnton's selection of significant details is subjective but that he has completely ignored later portions of his source which demonstrate the 'direct opposite' of

what he has argued (11–15). The methodology of 'thick description' advocated by anthropologist Clifford Geertz, from whom Darnton has drawn much of his theoretical understanding, has been criticized on the same grounds of subjectivity. See Aletta Biersack, 'Local Knowledge, Local History: Geertz and Beyond,' in Hunt, *New Cultural History*, 79.

Introduction

1 *Empire*, 3 and 5 Sept. 1892. See also 'Death from the Electric Streetcar,' *Scarborough Historical Notes and Comments* 16, 2 (Dec. 1993), 14–15. On the prevalence of accidents during the introduction of the electric trolley, see R.B. Fleming, 'The Trolley Takes Command, 1892–1894,' *Urban History Review / Revue d'histoire urbaine* 19, 3 (Feb. 1991), 220.

2 Stephen William Foster, 'Symbolism and the Problematics of Postmodern Representation,' in Kathleen M. Ashley, ed., *Victor Turner and the Construction of Cultural Criticism: Between Literature and Anthropology* (Bloomington and Indianapolis 1990), 123.

3 As Clifford Flanigan puts it, all language 'is unavoidably entwined in a system of differences, of oppositions that cannot be overcome, so that every form of meaning can only be deferred and can never reach the unambiguous object which it seems to seek.' These oppositions exist not just among the different parties in a discourse but within each utterance of individual participants: every communication contains traces left by previous speakers, and every representation of reality involves an accommodation between existing structures of meaning imposed on or accepted by the speaker and what it is that she or he ideally tries to say. Language, which encompasses many more sign systems than conventional speaking and writing, incorporates a thoroughly dialectical process in which ultimate synthesis is never achieved. The Flanigan quotation comes from 'Liminality, Carnival, and Social Structure,' in Ashley, *Victor Turner*, 42. A more poetic expression of the relation between language and understandings of reality can be found in Allan Pred, *Lost Words and Lost Worlds: Modernity and the Language of Everyday Life in Late Nineteenth-Century Stockholm* (Cambridge 1990), 1–7.

4 Peter Stallybrass and Allon White, *The Politics and Poetics of Transgression* (Ithaca 1986), 2–3.

5 The spread of bicycles and, later, automobiles also intensified competition for control of street space – and meaning. See Clay McShane, *Down the Asphalt Path: The Automobile and the American City* (New York 1994), 174–202.

6 *Empire*, 6 Sept. 1892.

7 The figures are taken from Randall White, *Ontario, 1610–1985* (Toronto and London 1985), 340.

8 Ian M. Drummond, *Progress without Planning: The Economic History of Ontario from Confederation to the Second World War* (Toronto 1987), 362.

9 Drummond points out that it is impossible to calculate rural living standards in the period before the 1920s with any certainty because necessary data on farm incomes was not collected. From indirect evidence, he suggests that 'Ontario agriculture was sufficiently rewarding an occupation to expand and adapt over more than forty years.' Ibid., 38–9, 43–4, 51. Using the 1871 census, Gordon Darroch and Lee Soltow have concluded that in Ontario, at least until the early 1870s, 'men and women could still secure an "independent" living, mostly on the land, and fulfil their hope of providing minimally secure beginnings for their children.' See *Property and Inequality in Victorian Ontario: Structural Patterns and Cultural Communities in the 1871 Census* (Toronto 1994), 202.

10 On the changing character of Ontario agriculture, see Drummond, *Progress without Planning*, 4–5, 366–8; D.A. Lawr, 'The Development of Ontario Farming, 1870–1919,' *Ontario History* 64, 4 (Dec. 1972), 239–51; Marvin McInnis, 'The Changing Structure of Canadian Agriculture, 1867–1897,' *Journal of Economic History* 42, 1 (March 1982), 191–8; Robert E. Ankli and Wendy Miller, 'Ontario Agriculture in Transition: The Shift from Wheat to Cheese,' *Journal of Economic History* 42, 1 (March 1982), 207–17; Jacob Spelt, *The Urban Development in South-Central Ontario* (Assen 1955), 139–43; Robert Leslie Jones, *History of Agriculture in Ontario, 1613–1880* (1946; Toronto and Buffalo 1977), 250–88, 304–27; Robert Bothwell, *A Short History of Ontario* (Edmonton 1986), 74.

11 Drummond, *Progress without Planning*, 6–7, 11; J.M.S. Careless, *Toronto to 1918: An Illustrated History* (Toronto 1984), 111.

12 Drummond emphasizes the fact that there was no extended economic depression. See *Progress without Planning*, 105, 111. The production statistics come from table 7.9.

13 Ibid., 105.

14 White, *Ontario*, 148. On Ontario emigration in this period, see Randy Widdis, 'With Scarcely a Ripple: English Canadians in Northern New York at the Beginning of the Twentieth Century,' *Journal of Historical Geography* 13, 2 (1987), 169–92.

15 Drummond, *Progress without Planning*, 167; Careless, *Toronto to 1918*, 109. On the early development of Toronto, see also Frederick H. Arm-

strong, *A City in the Making: Progress, People and Perils in Victorian Toronto* (Toronto and Oxford 1988), 34–71; Frederick Henry Armstrong, 'Toronto in Transition: The Emergence of a City, 1828–1838' (PhD thesis, University of Toronto, 1965), 367–495; Eric James Jarvis, 'Mid-Victorian Toronto: Panic, Policy and Public Response, 1857–1873' (PhD thesis, University of Western Ontario, 1978), 274; John McCallum, *Unequal Beginnings: Agriculture and Economic Development in Quebec and Ontario until 1870* (Toronto 1980), 58–61.

16 Dean Beeby, 'Industrial Strategy and Manufacturing Growth in Toronto, 1880–1910,' *Ontario History* 76, 3 (Sept. 1984), 202.

17 Careless, *Toronto to 1918*, 16, 149; Gregory S. Kealey, *Toronto Workers Respond to Industrial Capitalism, 1867–1892* (Toronto 1980), 18–34. On the meat-packing business in Toronto, as well as the development of financial institutions there, see Michael Bliss, *A Canadian Millionaire: The Life and Business Times of Sir Joseph Flavelle, Bart., 1858–1939* (Toronto 1978).

18 Drummond, *Progress without Planning*, 171.

19 On Toronto's railway network, see Careless, *Toronto to 1918*, 78, 118; Drummond, *Progress without Planning*, 250–1; Peter G. Goheen, *Victorian Toronto, 1850–1900: Pattern and Process of Growth* (Chicago 1970), 61–4.

20 Brenda Newell, 'From Cloth to Clothing: The Emergence of Department Stores in Late 19th Century Toronto' (MA thesis, Trent University, 1983), 87. For a case study of one of the largest retail establishments, with extensive mail order and manufacturing components, see Joy L. Santink, *Timothy Eaton and the Rise of His Department Store* (Toronto 1990).

21 Toronto's cultural leadership is especially emphasized in D.C. Masters, *The Rise of Toronto, 1850–1890* (Toronto 1947).

22 The statistics come from Careless, *Toronto to 1918*, 200–1. See also 109.

23 Ibid., 120; Goheen, *Victorian Torotono*, 77.

24 Careless, *Toronto to 1918*, 120, 201–2; James Lemon, 'Toronto among North American Cities,' in Victor L. Russell, ed., *Forging a Consensus: Historical Essays on Toronto* (Toronto 1984), 330. On two of the most important minority groups in the city, see John Zucchi, *Italians in Toronto: Development of a National Identity, 1875–1935* (Montreal and Kingston 1988), and Stephen Speisman, *The Jews of Toronto: A History to 1937* (Toronto 1979).

25 Brian Clarke's recent study argues that Irish Catholics in Toronto were not ghettoized and were socially mobile. See Brian P. Clarke, *Piety and Nationalism: Lay Voluntary Associations and the Creation of an Irish-*

Catholic Community in Toronto, 1850–1895 (Montreal and Kingston 1993), 13–30. For a contrary view, see Murry W. Nicolson, 'The Irish Experience in Ontario: Rural or Urban,' *Urban History Review / Revue d'histoire urbaine* 14, 1 (June 1985), 37–45. On Protestant-Catholic tensions, see Clarke, *Piety and Nationalism*, 158–9, 168–98, 208–10; Kealey, *Toronto Workers*, 115–23.

26 A recent study of late nineteenth-century working-class standards of living in urban Ontario suggests that falling prices and greater availability of employment provided working-class families in the 1880s with very modest improvements in purchasing power, but that in the following decades these gains receded. See David Gagan and Rosemary Gagan, 'Working-Class Standards of Living in Late-Victorian Urban Ontario: A Review of the Miscellaneous Evidence on the Quality of Material Life,' *Journal of the Canadian Historical Association*, new series, 1 (1990), 171–93. For Toronto, Gordon Darroch has suggested that workers experienced modest increases in their economic situations from the 1870s to the end of the century. See his 'Occupational Structure, Assessed Wealth and Homeowning during Toronto's Early Industrialization, 1861–1899,' *Histoire sociale / Social History* 16 (Nov. 1983), 389.

27 See, for example, the page of text accompanying *Toronto Photographs in Black* (New York 1891). Although most Torontonians, including those in the middle class, did not own their own homes, the city took pride in the fact that it had no extensive district of miserable tenements. For those who inhabited substandard shacks and cottages in the Ward, the city's largest slum, the distinction probably seemed a fine one. On home ownership, see Darroch, 'Occupational Structure, Assessed Wealth and Homeowning,' 381–410.

28 G. Mercer Adam, *Toronto, Old and New: A Memorial Volume, Historical, Descriptive and Pictorial, designed to mark the hundredth anniversary of the passing of the Constitutional Act of 1791, which set apart the Province of Upper Canada and gave birth to York (now Toronto), to which is added a narrative of the rise and progress of the professions, and of the growth and development of the city's industries and commerce, with some sketches of the men who have made or are making the Provincial Capital* (1891; Toronto 1972), 42. After a long publishing career in Toronto, Adam moved to Akron, where he edited *Self-Culture* from 1895 to 1902. He died in New York City in 1912. See the entry in *The Canadian Encyclopedia* (Edmonton 1988).

29 The similarity of Toronto to American cities is also suggested in Jarvis, 'Mid-Victorian Toronto,' 327–8.

30 On fairs in the classical period, see, for example, Joan M. Frayn, *Markets and Fairs in Roman Italy: Their Social and Economic Importance from the Second Century BC to the Third Century AD* (Oxford 1993); L. De Ligt, *Fairs and Markets in the Roman Empire: Economic and Social Aspects of Periodic Trade in a Pre-Industrial Society* (Amsterdam 1993). On fairs in the medieval period, and for its extensive bibliography, see S.R. Epstein, 'Regional Fairs, Institutional Innovation, and Economic Growth in Late Medieval Europe,' *Economic History Review* 47, 3 (Aug. 1994), 459–82.

31 Richard D. Altick, *The Shows of London* (Cambridge, Mass., and London 1978), 35; Ian Starsmore, *English Fairs* (London 1975), 16; Robert W. Malcolmson, *Popular Recreations in English Society, 1700–1850* (Cambridge 1973), 53–6, 77–80; Frances Brown, *Fairfield Folk: A History of the British Fairground and It's People* (Upton upon Severn 1988), 57–65; Stalleybrass and White, *Politics and Poetics of Transgression*, 33–4; Samuel McKechnie, *Popular Entertainments through the Ages* (London 1931), 29–47. As late as 1896 the *Globe* commented that 'between the revelries and orgies of Smithfield and the pageantry of Toronto there was and is as wide a divergence as between gold and a very much baser metal,' evidence of Smithfield's lingering reputation and of ongoing suspicions of fairs generally. *Globe*, 22 Aug. 1896.

32 Stalleybrass and White, *Politics and Poetics of Transgression*, 31–5; Wayne Caldwell Neely, *The Agricultural Fair* (New York 1935), 14; Howard Newby, *Country Life: A Social History of Rural England* (Totowa 1987), 93–5.

33 Stalleybrass and White, *Politics and Poetics of Transgression*, 34–5.

34 'After the Fairs,' *Farming* 13, 2 (Oct. 1895), 65; Neely, *Agricultural Fair*, 21–3, 37–40, 46–50; Leslie Prosterman, *Ordinary Life, Festival Days: Aesthetics in the Midwestern County Fair* (Washington, DC, and London 1995), 43–54.

35 John Withrow, 'Born Out of Protest,' *Once upon a Century: 100 Year History of the Ex* (Toronto 1978), 10; *Globe*, 23 Sept. 1878.

36 Withrow, 'Born Out of Protest,' 13–14; James Lorimer, *The Ex: A Picture History of the Canadian National Exhibition* (Toronto 1973), 1; Elsbeth Heaman, 'Commercial Leviathan: Central Canadian Exhibitions at Home and Abroad during the Nineteenth Century' (PhD thesis, University of Toronto, 1995), 49–93. On the founding of American agricultural societies and fairs, see Neely, *Agricultural Fair*, 76–8.

37 Oswald C.J. Withrow, *The Romance of the Canadian National Exhibition* (Toronto 1936), 53–7; V.M. Roberts, *The Trail of the Canadian National*

Exhibition (Toronto 1925), 33–6; John Withrow, 'Born out of Protest,' 17; Lorimer, *The Ex*, 2.

38 Patricia Mainardi, *Art and Politics of the Second Empire: The Universal Expositions of 1855 and 1867* (New Haven and London 1987), 7, 17, 22; Paul Greenhalgh, *Ephemeral Vistas: The Expositions Universelles, Great Exhibitions and World's Fairs, 1851–1939* (Manchester 1988), 6–10; Neely, *Agricultural Fair*, 17; Toshio Kusamitsu, 'Great Exhibitions before 1851,' *History Workshop* 9 (spring 1980), 85 and passim; Kenneth E. Carpenter, 'European Industrial Exhibitions before 1851 and Their Publications,' *Technology and Culture* 13 (July 1972), 465–86; Hervé Gagnon, 'Des animaux, des hommes et des choses: les expositions au Bas-Canada dans la première moitié du XIXe siècle,' *Histoire sociale / Social History* 26 (Nov. 1993), 291–327.

39 Greenhalgh, *Ephemeral Vistas*, 15; Robert Rydell, 'The Literature of International Expositions,' in *The Books of the Fairs: Materials about World's Fairs, 1834–1916, in the Smithsonian Institution Libraries* (Chicago and London 1992), 2–3. For a complete listing of international shows between 1851 and 1988, see John E. Findling and Kimberly D. Pelle, eds., *Historical Dictionary of World's Fairs and Expositions, 1851–1988* (New York 1990).

40 Greenhalgh, *Ephemeral Vistas*, 41. Reid Badger suggests that the allure of purely technological displays began to fade in the 1850s. See *The Great American Fair: The World's Columbian Exposition and American Culture* (Chicago 1979), 8.

41 Greenhalgh, *Ephemeral Vistas*, 193; Mainardi, *Art and Politics*; John G. Cawelti, 'America on Display: The World's Fairs of 1876, 1893, 1933,' in Frederic Cople Jaher, ed., *The Age of Industrialism in America* (New York and London 1968), 322.

42 Altick, *Shows of London*, 483–4; Justus D. Doenecke, 'Myths, Machines and Markets: The Columbian Exposition of 1893,' *Journal of Popular Culture* 6, 3 (spring 1973), 535.

43 Greenhalgh, *Ephemeral Vistas*, 37.

44 See Elaine G. Spencer, 'Policing Popular Amusements,' *Journal of Urban History* 16, 4 (Aug. 1990), 366–85.

45 Neil Harris, *Cultural Excursions: Marketing Appetites and Cultural Tastes in Modern America* (Chicago and London 1990), 25. See also Cawelti, 'America on Display,' 319.

46 *Telegram*, 24 Sept. 1880. For other examples of world's fair ambitions, see *Mail*, 9 Sept. 1881; *Globe*, 8 Sept. 1883; *Globe*, 20 Sept. 1887; *Mail and Empire*, 8 Sept. 1898. Toronto was not successful in having the Industrial

Exhibition designated as a world's fair, but it may have prevented Montreal from hosting one. See Heaman, 'Commercial Leviathan,' 406–8.

47 Cover of 1893 program, CIHM/ICMH Microfiche Series no. 62204; *News*, 28 Aug. 1903.

48 'A Talk about the Fair,' *Globe*, 20 Sept. 1890. American shows, for example, tended to place more emphasis on agriculture than European ones. See Burton Benedict et al., *The Anthropology of World's Fairs: San Francisco's Panama Pacific International Exposition of 1915* (London and Berkeley 1983), 38.

49 Kit Coleman, 'Woman's Kingdom,' *Mail*, 15 Sept. 1894.

50 On Canadian interest and participation in international expositions, see Eva-Marie Kröller, *Canadian Travellers in Europe, 1851–1900* (Vancouver 1987), 149–65; Dianne Newell, 'Canada at World's Fairs,' *Canadian Collector* 2, 4 (July/Aug. 1976); Suzanne Zeller, *Inventing Canada: Early Victorian Science and the Idea of a Transcontinental Nation* (Toronto 1987).

51 NA, Dr Charles Brodie Sewell Travel Diary, 1883, MG 40 F7, microfiche A-1621 (original in Wellcome Institute), 16. The literature on modern spectacle environments is extensive, but see in particular John Kasson, *Amusing the Million: Coney Island at the Turn of the Century* (New York 1978); Robert W. Snyder, *The Voice of the City: Vaudeville and Popular Culture in New York* (New York and Oxford 1989); Harris, *Cultural Excursions*; Susan Strasser, *Satisfaction Guaranteed: The Making of the American Mass Market* (New York 1989); Dane Lankin, *Montreal Movie Palaces: Great Theatres of the Golden Era, 1884–1938* (Waterloo 1993); William Leach, *Land of Desire: Merchants, Power, and the Rise of a New American Culture* (New York 1993); David Nasaw, *Going Out: The Rise and Fall of Public Amusements* (New York 1993).

52 'Toronto Exhibition,' *Orillia Packet*, 26 Sept. 1890; 'The Toronto Industrial Exhibition,' *Farming* 14, 2 (Oct. 1896), 108.

53 *Mail and Empire*, 22 Aug. 1900; *The Week* 6, 41 (13 Sept. 1889), 643.

54 Carl Boggs, *The Two Revolutions: Gramsci and the Dilemmas of Western Marxism* (Boston 1984), 159; Joseph V. Femia, *Gramsci's Political Thought: Hegemony, Consciousness, and the Revolutionary Process* (Oxford 1981), 44; Roger Simon, *Gramsci's Political Thought: An Introduction* (London 1982), 26.

55 The mechanics of hegemony are, of course, complex. A dominant group must be able to claim with some plausibility that its world view embodies the interests of society at large. This may require it to dilute some of its preferences. On the other side, acceptance by subordinate groups tends to

be something less than unreserved endorsement of élite interpretations. Consent can take the form of apathy, fear, resignation, and limited shows of resistance. See T.J. Jackson Lears, 'The Concept of Cultural Hegemony: Problems and Possibilities,' *American Historical Review* 90, 3 (June 1985), 571; Paul Ransome, *Antonio Gramsci: A New Introduction* (New York 1992), 136. On the hegemonic role of world's fairs, see Aram A. Yengoyan, 'Culture, Ideology and World's Fairs: Colonizer and Colonized in Comparative Perspectives,' in Robert W. Rydell and Nancy Gwinn, eds., *Fair Representations: World's Fairs and the Modern World* (Amsterdam 1994), 62–83.

56 CNEA, Toronto Industrial Exhibition Association, Prize List for 1883, 25–7. By 1900, when representation of the Manufacturers' Association was increased from five to twelve seats, the Exhibition Association had 120 members. See MTRL, Baldwin Room, W.A. Craik Papers, 'Notes from Toronto Papers,' vol. 20, 19 Nov. 1900.

57 Oswald Withrow, *Romance*, 60.

58 Robert H. Wiebe, *The Search for Order, 1877–1920* (New York 1967), 44.

59 According to Jacob Spelt, for example, fifty places in southwest Ontario classified as rural villages in 1881 were no longer on the map by 1911. See Spelt, *Urban Development*, 163.

60 Much of this information was gleaned from the city directories for 1878, 1879, and 1880. Additional information about W.H. Howland can be found in Desmond Morton, *Mayor Howland: The Peoples' Candidate* (Toronto 1973), and the *Dictionary of Canadian Biography*, vol. 12 (Toronto 1990). The same volume of the DCB contains information about Wm. Christie, L. O'Brien and J. Withrow. On A. Smith, see the entry in *The Canadian Encyclopedia* (Edmonton 1988). The quote about J. Hallam comes from J. Morgan, *Canadian Men and Women of the Time* (Toronto 1898). On J. Fleming and D.C. Ridout, see *Commemorative Biographical Record of the County of York* (Toronto 1907). *Globe* obituaries contain information about W.F. McMaster (8 Jan. 1907), W. Rennie (25 July 1910), and G. Booth (21 Feb. 1919). On G. Leslie, see G. Mercer Adam, *Toronto Old and New*, 171.

61 Careless, *Toronto to 1918*, 124, 128. On the older Toronto élite, see Barry Drummond Dyster, 'Toronto, 1840–1860: Making It in a British Protestant Town' (PhD thesis, University of Toronto, 1970); David Gagan, *The Denison Family of Toronto, 1792–1925* (Toronto 1973); and John Lownsbrough, *The Privileged Few: The Grange and Its People in Nineteenth Century Toronto* (Toronto 1980).

62 Careless, *Toronto to 1918*, 124.

63 This arm's-length relationship to regular political structures was common in the late nineteenth century. Nicholas Pearson has pointed out that while the cultural sphere was increasingly controlled by the state in this period, the preferred form of administration for cultural institutions was through boards of trustees, an arrangement that allowed effective supervision of policy without having to intervene in day-to-day operations. See *The State and the Visual Arts: A Discussion of State Intervention in the Visual Arts in Britain, 1780–1981* (Milton Keynes 1982), 8–13.

64 Careless, *Toronto to 1918*, 128, 163.

65 Stuart Blumin, *The Emergence of the Middle Class: Social Experience in the American City, 1760–1900* (Cambridge 1989); Mary P. Ryan, *Cradle of the Middle Class: The Family in Oneida County, New York, 1790–1865* (Cambridge 1981); John Gilkeson, *Middle-Class Providence, 1820–1940* (Princeton 1986); Paul E. Johnson, *A Shopkeeper's Millennium: Society and Revivals in Rochester, New York, 1815–1837* (New York 1978). On the importance of evangelical religion to middle-class formation in England, see Lenore Davidoff and Catherine Hall, *Family Fortunes: Men and Women of the English Middle Class, 1780–1850* (London 1987). For a thorough description of the family rituals that defined bourgeois existence in nineteenth-century France, see Anne Martin-Fugier, 'Bourgeois Rituals,' in Michelle Perrot, ed., *A History of Private Life*, vol. 4: *From the Fires of Revolution to the Great War* (Cambridge, Mass., and London 1990), 261–337.

66 Jurgen Kocka, *White Collar Workers in America, 1890–1940: A Social-Political History in International Perspective* (London and Beverly Hills 1980), 85–91; Ileen A. DeVault, *Sons and Daughters of Labor: Class and Clerical Work in Turn-of-the-Century Pittsburgh* (Ithaca and London 1990), 165, 172–3, 177; David G. Burley, *A Particular Condition in Life: Self-Employment and Social Mobility in Mid-Victorian Brantford, Ontario* (Montreal and Kingston 1994), 61, 170–1, 195, 235; Gordon Darroch, 'Class in Nineteenth-Century, Central Ontario: A Reassessment of the Crisis and Demise of Small Producers during Early Industrialization, 1861–1871,' in Gregory S. Kealey, ed., *Class, Gender, and Region: Essays in Canadian Historical Sociology* (St John's 1988), 67–8; Robert H. Wiebe, *Self-Rule: A Cultural History of American Democracy* (Chicago and London 1995), 123.

67 James Gilbert, *Perfect Cities: Chicago's Utopias of 1893* (Chicago and London 1991), 7; Richard Hofstadter, *The Age of Reform: From Bryan to FDR* (New York 1955). For Peter Gay, the diversity of the middle class throughout the Victorian period was in the end perhaps its most consis-

tent quality. There was no typical bourgeois, he contends. 'What nineteenth century bourgeois had in common was the negative quality of being neither aristocrats nor laborers, and of being uneasy in their middle-class skins.' See *The Bourgeois Experience: Victoria to Freud*, vol. 1: *Education of the Senses* (New York and Oxford 1984), 31.

68 Exhibition attendance statistics are taken from Oswald Withrow, *Romance*, 100.

69 *News*, 18 Sept. 1883; *Guelph Daily Mercury and Advertiser*, 9 Sept. 1891.

70 University of Western Ontario, Weldon Library, Regional Room, M 910, Henry Roswell Diary, 17 Sept. 1883.

71 See, for example, OA, MS 297 (2), John H. Ferguson Diary, 9 and 17 Sept. 1880, 15 Sept. 1881; MTRL, Baldwin Room, Abram S. Johnson Papers, Diary 1881–5, 11 and 15 Sept. 1882; OA, MS 185, Archibald Gillies Diary, 18 and 19 Sept. 1889.

72 *Mail*, 10 Sept. 1881.

73 *Globe*, 10 Sept. 1880

74 See CTA, City Council Minutes, 8 Sept. 1884, no. 843; 19 Aug. 1885, nos. 699 and 700; 18 Aug. 1886, nos. 909 and 923; 20 Aug. 1888, nos. 935 and 970; 14 July 1890, no. 929.

75 With the formal establishment of Labour Day in 1894, many employers granted a holiday then rather than on Citizen's Day.

76 'Labour Day,' *Dry Goods Review*, Sept. 1894, 5; *Empire*, 12 Sept. 1892; Greenhalgh, *Ephemeral Vistas*, 29; Robert W. Rydell, *World of Fairs: The Century-of-Progress Expositions* (Chicago and London 1993), 5. A producer ideology, which stressed the mutual interests of capital and labour, remained popular in Ontario until near the end of the century. See Bryan D. Palmer, *A Culture in Conflict: Skilled Workers and Industrial Capitalism in Hamilton, Ontario, 1860–1914* (Montreal and Kingston 1979), 99–122.

77 *Star*, 11 Sept. 1903 and 8 Sept. 1906. Some workers unable to attend the fair by circumstances of employment also expressed unhappiness. Streetcar company employees were particularly resentful because they had to work so much harder during the show. Many had never gone themselves. One exhibition director suggested that the show be opened on a Sunday for their benefit, and for others in similar positions, but the board as a whole was unwilling to violate Toronto's well-known Sabbatarian traditions. See *Globe*, 16 Sept. 1889; *World*, 13 Sept. 1889. On class and gender mixing in nineteenth-century urban culture, see William R. Taylor, *In Pursuit of Gotham: Culture and Commerce in New York* (New York and Oxford 1992), 71–4.

78 Letter of R. Glockling, *News*, 2 Sept. 1898. The association had cancelled the arrangement because receipts for the previous Labour Day had fallen by $1700 from what they had been the year before, on top of which a $1000 commission had to be paid to the TLC. See CNEA, Industrial Exhibition Association, Annual Report for 1897, 12.

79 *Mail and Empire*, 29 Aug. 1901.

80 E.J. Hobsbawm, *The Age of Empire, 1875–1914* (London 1987), 171, 174, 180–1; Nasaw, *Going Out*, 43–4.

81 Wiebe, *Search for Order*, 112–13; Burton Bledstein, *The Culture of Professionalism: The Middle Class and the Development of Higher Education in America* (New York 1976); Olivier Zunz, *Making America Corporate, 1870–1920* (Chicago and London 1990), 9, 39; Samuel Haber, *The Quest for Authority and Honor in the American Professions, 1750–1900* (Chicago and London 1991), 199–205. Haber points out that between 1830 and 1880, the professions in America came under 'withering attack,' almost lapsing into 'indistinction' but rebounding rapidly in the last two decades of the nineteenth century (xii–xiii). More recently, Wiebe has argued that in the late nineteenth century the American middle class was 'sliced in two,' creating a three-class system. One class was geared to national communities, another dominated local affairs, and the third sank beneath these two. See Wiebe, *Self-Rule*, 115, 144, 148. On the role of universities in creating a Canadian middle class, see Paul Axelrod, *Making a Middle Class: Student Life in English Canada during the Thirties* (Montreal and Kingston 1990).

82 Similar arguments are made in Ted Ownby, *Subduing Satan: Religion, Recreation, and Manhood in the Rural South, 1865–1920* (Chapel Hill and London 1990), 191–3, and Whitney Walton, *France at the Crystal Palace: Bourgeois Taste and Artisan Manufacture in the Nineteenth Century* (Berkeley and London 1992), 23–48.

83 Sally F. Moore and Barbara G. Myerhoff, 'Introduction: Secular Ritual: Forms and Meanings,' in Moore and Myerhoff, eds., *Secular Ritual* (Assen/Amsterdam 1977), 17.

84 Victor Turner, *The Ritual Process: Structure and Anti-Structure* (Ithaca 1977), vi, 95; Victor Turner, 'Variations on a Theme of Liminality,' in Moore and Myerhoff, *Secular Ritual*, 37–47. Turner distinguished between 'liminal' experiences, which marked the rites of traditional tribal societies, and 'liminoid' phenomena, which occur especially in the leisure rituals of industrial societies. The latter are produced by a relatively few individuals for consumption by others, rather than being a truly shared experience. See Turner, 'Variations on a Theme,' 42–8; Robert C. Allen,

Horrible Prettiness: Burlesque and American Culture (Chapel Hill and London 1991), 37. Ronald Grimes has pointed out that Turner's theory of ritual differs from his explicit definition of it. See 'Victor Turner's Definition, Theory, and Sense of Ritual,' in Ashley, *Victor Turner*, 143.

85 Stallybrass and White, *Politics and Poetics of Transgression*, 3–5, 39, 44.

86 On the reach of the Toronto daily press into the hinterland, see Thomas L. Walkom, 'The Daily Newspaper Industry in Ontario's Developing Capitalist Economy: Toronto and Ottawa, 1871–1911' (PhD thesis, University of Toronto, 1983), 120–5,150–2.

87 Aside from a few committee meeting minutes, there are almost no administrative records of the fair from this period.

88 Walkom, 'Daily Newspaper Industry,' 135, 231.

89 Ibid., 231–2, 259–60.

90 On the changing character of the press, see Gerald J. Baldasty, *The Commercialization of News in the Nineteenth Century* (Madison and London 1992), 46–7 and passim; Paul Rutherford, *A Victorian Authority: The Daily Press in Late Nineteenth-Century Canada* (Toronto 1982), 115–55; Garth S. Jowett, 'The Emergence of the Mass Society: The Standardization of American Culture, 1830–1920,' *Prospects* 7 (1982), 214–18; Douglas Fetherling, *The Rise of the Canadian Newspaper* (Toronto 1990), 63–106; Taylor, *Pursuit of Gotham*, 82–3.

91 Rutherford, *Victorian Authority*, 157–89.

Chapter 1: Order

1 *Mail*, 6 Sept. 1886.

2 Typical descriptions of opening-day activities can be found in the Newmarket *Era*, 10 Sept. 1880; *Mail*, 6 Sept. 1886; *Globe*, 11 Sept. 1888; *Mail*, 5 Sept. 1893; and *Star*, 26 Aug. 1901.

3 *Globe*, 7 Sept. 1880; Hamilton *Spectator*, 3 Sept. 1879.

4 *Mail*, 8 Sept. 1880; *Globe*, 11 Sept. 1885; *Globe*, 7 Sept. 1880.

5 On preoccupations with order in the nineteenth century, see Robert Wiebe, *The Search for Order, 1877–1920* (New York 1967).

6 Burton Benedict et al., *The Anthropology of World's Fairs: San Francisco's Panama Pacific International Exposition of 1915* (London and Berkeley 1983), 2.

7 *Globe*, 20 Sept. 1890.

8 Discussions of the ordering arrangements of the great expositions can be found in Paul Greenhalgh, *Ephemeral Vistas: The Expositions Universalles, Great Exhibitions and World's Fairs, 1851–1939* (Manchester

1988), 10; John G. Cawelti, 'America on Display: The World's Fairs of 1876, 1893, 1933,' in Frederic Jahr, ed., *The Age of Industrialism in America* (New York and London 1968), 322–3; Suzanne Zeller, *Inventing Canada: Early Victorian Science and the Idea of a Transcontinental Nation* (Toronto 1987), 79–81.

9 John Maass, *The Glorious Enterprise* (Watkins Glen 1973), 66–71.

10 Deborah L. Silverman, 'The 1889 Exhibition: The Crisis of Bourgeois Individualism,' *Oppositions* 8 (spring 1977), 78; Aram A. Yengoyan, 'Culture, Ideology and World's Fairs: Colonizer and Colonized in Comparative Perspectives,' in Robert W. Rydell and Nancy Gwinn, eds., *Fair Representations: World's Fairs and the Modern World* (Amsterdam 1994), 79.

11 *Mail*, 5 Sept. 1879; *Mail*, 12 Sept. 1882; *Globe*, 14 Sept. 1888.

12 *Mail*, 15 Sept. 1892.

13 *Globe* 12 Sept. 1887; *Globe*, 11 Sept. 1888; *Globe*, 25 Aug. 1901.

14 *Mail*, 11, 15, and 17 Sept. 1884; *Globe*, 13 Sept. 1884.

15 *News*, 16 Sept. 1884; *Mail*, 17 Sept. 1885; CNEA, Industrial Exhibition Association, Annual Report for 1885, 8; *Globe*, 9 Sept. 1886; *Globe*, 9 Sept. 1887; *Mail*, 8 Sept. 1887.

16 *Mail*, 15 Sept. 1884; *Globe*, 12 Sept. 1887. On the nature of fascination with miniature toy worlds, see Susan Stewart, *On Longing: Narratives of the Miniature, the Gigantic, the Souvenir, the Collection* (Baltimore and London 1984), 56–60.

17 *News*, 30 Aug. 1899; *World*, 7 Sept. 1901.

18 *Globe*, 11 Sept. 1886; *Globe*, 10 Sept. 1887; Whitby *Chronicle*, 16 Sept. 1887.

19 See, for example, Neil Sutherland, *Children in English Canada: Framing the Consensus* (Toronto and Buffalo 1976), 11.

20 Newmarket *Era*, 12 Sept. 1879.

21 *Telegram*, 11 Sept. 1879; MTRL, Baldwin Room, Henry Scadding diary, 11 Sept. 1879; University of Toronto Archives, B82–0003/003, Robinson Family Papers, G.H. Robinson diary, 10 Sept. 1879; *Mail*, 13 Sept. 1879. George Morse and Company, for example, wrote to the *Telegram* to point out that the royal couple had admired their house made of soap. See *Telegram*, 12 Sept. 1879.

22 *Globe*, 11 Sept. 1889; *Mail and Empire*, 28 Aug. 1901.

23 *Evening News*, 12 Sept. 1888; William Lyon Mackenzie King, *The Mackenzie King Diaries, 1893–1931* (Toronto 1973), 31 Aug. 1897; *Globe*, 9 Sept. 1891; *News*, 1 Sept. 1897.

24 *Mail*, 17 Sept. 1890; Mack [Joseph Thomas Clark], 'Folks at the Fair,' *Saturday Night*, 16 Sept. 1893, 7.

25 See, for example, Kit Coleman, 'Woman's Kingdom,' *Mail*, 8 Sept. 1894; *Globe*, 5 Sept. 1882.

26 *Mail*, 14 Sept. 1882; J. Lawlor Woods, *Toronto Illustrated: Guide Book and Souvenir* (Toronto 1897), 96. A curate at St James complained in 1887 that forty or fifty people were being admitted to the tower simultaneously. 'Grumblers Corner,' *News*, 17 Sept. 1887.

27 On the origins of the panoramic view, see Hans Bergmann, 'Panoramas of New York, 1845–1860,' *Prospects* 10 (1985), 119–37; William R. Taylor, 'Psyching Out the City,' Richard L. Bushman et al., *Uprooted Americans: Essays to Honor Oscar Handlin* (Boston and Toronto 1979), 247–87; William R. Taylor, 'New York and the Origin of the Skyline: The Visual City as Text,' *Prospects* 13 (1988), 225–48; John Urry, *The Tourist Gaze: Leisure and Travel in Contemporary Societies* (London 1990), 136; Sam Bass Warner Jr., 'Slums and Skyscrapers: Urban Images, Symbols, and Ideology,' Lloyd Rodwin and Robert M. Hollister, *Cities of the Mind: Images and Themes of the City in the Social Sciences* (New York and London 1984), 193.

28 Bergmann, 'Panoramas,' 119; John F. Kasson, *Rudeness and Civility: Manners in Nineteenth-Century Urban America* (New York 1990), 72–3.

29 *Mail*, 16 Sept. 1885.

30 See, for example, ibid., 13 Sept. 1880; *Telegram*, 13 Sept. 1881.

31 *Mail*, 20 Sept. 1889.

32 Ibid., 15 Sept. 1884. In some areas and activities, women were able to transgress conventional gender boundaries. See the discussion in chapter 5 on women and the fair.

33 *Globe*, 15 Sept. 1888; *World*, 15 Sept. 1888; *Globe*, 14 Sept. 1889; *Mail*, 13 Sept. 1890; Guelph *Daily Mercury and Advertiser*, 13 Sept. 1890.

34 *Globe*, 9 Sept. 1882; *Globe*, 14 Sept. 1888; *Telegram*, 9 Sept. 1893.

35 Some churches did schedule special events for exhibition crowds off the fairgrounds. In 1893, for example, the Salvation Army held a 'festival' at their downtown auditorium which had 'many features of a mini-exhibition.' See *Mail*, 11 Sept. 1893.

36 Ibid., 4 Sept. 1879; *Globe*, 12 Sept. 1888; *Mail and Empire*, 7 Sept 1895.

37 *Shaftsbury Hall Weekly Bulletin* 5, 40 (27 Sept. 1884); *Globe*, 15 Sept. 1893; *Empire*, 13 Sept. 1894; *Globe*, 1 Sept. 1887.

38 *Globe*, 11 Sept. 1883; *Shaftsbury Hall Exhibition Bulletin*, Sept. 1880.

39 *Shaftsbury Hall Weekly Bulletin* 2, 36 (10 Sept. 1881).

40 *Globe*, 11 Sept. 1883; *Mail*, 16 Sept. 1879; *Shaftsbury Hall Weekly Bulletin* 3, 22 (16 Sept. 1882); *News*, 11 Sept. 1884; *Globe*, 10 Sept. 1881.

41 *Mail*, 15 Sept. 1887; *World*, 12 Sept. 1888; *Globe*, 12 Sept. 1889.

42 OA, MU 8398. 1, WCTU Collection, Report of the Fifth Convention of the

W.C.T.U. held at Ottawa from June 17 to 21, 1892; Ellen C. Rugg, 'Fair Work, 1898,' *Woman's Journal*, July 1898, 5; Ella S. Cosford, 'Ontario Fair Work,' *Woman's Journal*, Sept. 1893, 5; 'Fair Work,' *Woman's Journal*, Oct. 1891, 4. See also 'Fair Work,' *Woman's Journal*, Oct. 1890, 3; 'Department of Exhibitions and Fairs: Suggested Programme for WCTU Meeting,' *Woman's Journal*, Aug. 1900, 7. For an overview of WCTU activities in this period see *"Through Sunshine and Shadow": The Woman's Christian Temperance Union, Evangelicalism, and Reform in Ontario, 1874–1930* (Montreal and Kingston 1995), esp. 48–52.

43 *Empire*, 14 Sept. 1892; OA, WCTU Collection, MU 8398. 3, Report of the Seventh Convention of the Dominion Woman's Christian Temperence Union held at London from June 1st to 4th, 1894, 88; MU 8398. 4, Report of the Eighth Convention of the Dominion Woman's Christian Temperence Union held at Quebec from November 15th to 19th, 1895, 110–11; MU 8407. 5, Report of the Seventeenth Convention of the Ontario Woman's Christian Temperence Union held at Cornwall, Oct. 30 to Nov. 2, 1894; MU 8398. 5, Report of the Ninth Convention of the Dominion Woman's Christian Temperence Union held at Toronto from November 6th to 10th, 1896, 75; MU 8398. 6, Report of the Tenth Convention of the Dominion Woman's Christian Temperence Union held at Toronto from October 20th to 22nd, 1897, 62; MU 8407. 8, Report of the Twelfth Annual Convention of the Ontario Woman's Christian Temperence Union, 1897. In 1898 a soapstone griddle for frying pancakes was put in; in 1900 the building was improved by the amount of $110, and an enlarged bill-of-fare was offered; in 1903 a new kitchen costing $285 was built. See OA, WCTU Collection, MU 8398. 7, Report of the Eleventh Convention of the Dominion Woman's Christian Temperence Union held at Halifax, N. S., from November 10th to 14th, 1899, 89; MU 8407. 11, Report of the Twenty-third Annual Convention of the Ontario Woman's Christian Temperence Union held at Smith's Falls from Oct. 29th to Nov. 2nd, 1900; MU 8398. 9, Report of the Thirteenth Convention of the Dominion Woman's Christian Temperence Union held at Ottawa, Ont., from November 6th to 10th, 1903, 85–6.

44 OA, WCTU Collection, MU 8407. 10, Twenty-second Convention of the Woman's Christian Temperence Union of Ontario held at Guelph from Oct. 31st to Nov. 3rd, 1899; letter of Mrs J.W. Savage, *Woman's Journal*, 1 and 15 Oct. 1900, 10.

45 *Mail*, 13 Sept. 1894. The pre-industrial atmosphere of the tent was probably deliberate. See Rodris Roth, 'The New England, or "Olde Tyme," Kitchen Exhibit at Nineteenth-Century Fairs,' in Alan Axelrod, ed., *The Colonial Revival in America* (New York 1985), 159–83.

46 *Mail*, 30 Aug. 1879; *Globe*, 14 Sept. 1880.

47 *Globe*, 18 Sept. 1888. On the range of police duties in the nineteenth century, see Eric H. Monkkonen, *Police in Urban America, 1860–1920* (Cambridge 1981).

48 *Mail*, 27 Aug. 1879; *Globe*, 27 Aug. 1900; *Mail and Empire*, 27 Aug. 1903.

49 *Globe*, 14 Sept. 1892; *Globe*, 18 Sept. 1888; *Telegram*, 3 Sept. 1881. In 1882 the chief constable reported to City Council that 'some of the serious sickness which attacked the men on duty there [the Exhibition] was due to their having to sleep over the water closets.' *Toronto City Council Minutes, 1882*, Appendix 12, Report of the Chief Constable.

50 David R. Johnson, *Policing the Urban Underworld: The Impact of Crime on the Development of the American Police, 1800–1887* (Philadelphia 1979), 110.

51 *News*, 3 Sept. 1897.

52 *Globe*, 1 Sept. 1903; *Mail*, 16 Sept. 1882.

53 Sporting male culture is discussed more extensively in chapter 7.

54 There is no good study of the culture of alcohol in nineteenth-century Toronto, though it was obviously a significant part of life. See C.S. Clark, *Of Toronto the Good: A Social Study. The Queen City of Canada as It Is* (1898; Toronto 1970), and Desmond Morton, *Mayor Howland: the Citizens' Candidate* (Toronto 1973), 72–4. On the role of alcohol in American communities, see Roy Rosenzweig, *Eight Hours for What We Will: Workers and Leisure in an Industrial City, 1870–1920* (Cambridge and New York 1983); Perry R. Duis, *The Saloon: Public Drinking in Chicago and Boston, 1880–1920* (Urbana and Chicago 1983); Jon Kingsdale, 'The Poor Man's Club: The Social Functions of the Urban Working-Class Saloon,' *American Quarterly* 25 (Oct. 1973), 472–89. On the culture of alcohol in nineteenth-century Halifax, see Judith Fingard, '"A Great Big Rum Shop": The Drink Trade in Victorian Halifax,' in James H. Morrison and James Moreira, eds., *Tempered by Rum: Rum in the History of the Maritime Provinces* (Porter's Lake, NS, 1988), 89–101.

55 *World*, 19 Sept. 1884.

56 'Young Hayseed,' *Saturday Night*, 22 Sept. 1888, 6; *Globe*, 9 Sept. 1881; *Globe*, 11 Sept. 1884; *Telegram*, 18 Sept. 1890; letter of J.C. Speer, *Mail*, 20 Sept. 1888; *News*, 20 Sept. 1888; *News*, 21 Sept. 1889.

57 Port Hope *Weekly Guide and News*, 26 Sept. 1884.

58 'Amateur Street Musicians,' *News*, 14 Sept. 1885.

59 Letter of "G.H.," *Telegram*, 8 Sept. 1882; *Globe*, 13 Sept. 1881; *Empire*, 5 Sept. 1891; *Mail*, 5 Nov. 1879. On prostitution in Toronto in the nineteenth century, see Constance Backhouse, *Petticoats and Prejudice:*

Women and the Law in Nineteenth Century Canada (Toronto 1991), 228–
59; Carolyn Strange, *Toronto's Girl Problem: The Perils and Pleasures of
the City, 1880–1930* (Toronto 1995), 56, 91–2, and passim; Lori Rotenberg, 'The Wayward Worker: Toronto's Prostitute at the Turn of the Century,' in Janice Acton et al., *Women at Work, Ontario, 1850–1930* (Toronto
1974), 33–69; Christina Burr, '"Roping in the Wretched, the Reckless,
and the Wronged": Narratives of the Late Nineteenth-Century Toronto
Police Court,' *Left History* 3, 1 (spring/summer 1995): 94–8. Although
soliciting was done aggressively, it is important to remember that prostitutes were often victimized by clients. See Backhouse, *Petticoats and
Prejudice*, 229; Judith Fingard, *The Dark Side of Life in Victorian Halifax*
(Porters Lake, NS, 1989), 108.

60 *Mail*, 5 Nov. 1879; *Mail*, 4 Sept. 1888; *Mail*, 10 Sept. 1887. Secondary
literature on prostitution in the nineteenth century is extensive. For a
recent analysis of prostitution in New York City, with a good bibliography,
see Timothy J. Gilfoyle, *City of Eros: New York City, Prostitution, and the
Commercialization of Sex, 1790–1920* (New York and London 1992).

61 *Mail*, 30 Aug. 1879; *News*, 12 Sept. 1885; *Mail*, 19 Sept. 1890; *Mail*, 1
Sept. 1881.

62 C. Pelham Mulvaney, *Toronto: Past and Present* (Toronto 1884) 44; *Mail*,
1 Oct. 1879.

63 *Mail*, 1 Oct. 1879; *Empire*, 5 Sept. 1891; letter of 'A Resident,' *Telegram*, 2
Sept. 1887. For other references to the brothels and all-night dives of
York Street, see 'The Social Evil,' *News*, 19 Dec. 1881; *Globe*, 20 Dec.
1881; *Toronto by Gaslight: The Nighthawks of a Great City as Seen by the
Reporters of the Toronto News* (Toronto [1885]), 4. On the criminal tendencies of second-hand dealers, see Johnson, *Policing the Urban Underworld*, 45.

64 *Mail*, 13 Sept. 1883; *Telegram*, 16 Sept. 1886.

65 *Telegram*, 18 Sept. 1885; *Telegram*, 13 Sept. 1886.

66 *World*, 21 Sept. 1883. Respectable Toronto viewed such establishments as
the hangouts of local gangs. Some organized criminal conspiracies did no
doubt exist. A 'villainous Fagin lately unearthed in his York Street den'
in 1881, for example, had trained a group of young theives, paying them
five dollars for every hundred dollars worth of goods brought in. It
was assumed he was not the only operator of the sort. See *Grip*, 17, 18
(17 Sept. 1881). Most gangs, however, were probably loose collections of
young, unskilled working people who drifted between legal and illegal
activities and whose criminal activities and associations were more spontaneous than planned. Very little is known about gangs in nineteenth-

century Toronto. For recent discussions of the phenomena in New York, where some gangs were more organized, see Luc Sante, *Low Life: Lures and Snares of Old New York* (New York 1991), and Dennis J. Kenney and James O. Finckenauer, *Organized Crime in America* (Belmont 1995), 74–8. For brief remarks about juvenile gangs in Toronto, see Burr, 'Roping in the Wretched,' 105–7; Susan Houston, 'The "Waifs and Strays" of a Late Victorian City: Juvenile Delinquents in Toronto,' in Joy Parr, ed., *Childhood and Family in Canadian History* (Toronto 1982), 134–5.

67 *Mail*, 17 Sept. 1892.

68 Ibid., 17 Sept. 1888.

69 *Star*, 13 Sept. 1897; *Telegram*, 9 Sept. 1886.

70 *World*, 7 Sept. 1899; *Telegram*, 18 Sept. 1885.

71 *Mail*, 16 Sept. 1882; *World*, 19 Sept. 1884. For an overview of urban crime in nineteenth-century America, see David R. Johnson, *American Law Enforcement: A History* (St Louis 1981), 35–53.

72 See, for example, *Globe*, 13 Sept. 1880; *Empire*, 16 Sept. 1890.

73 *Star*, 8 Sept. 1897; *Mail and Empire*, 4 Sept. and 8 Sept. 1896.

74 *News*, 13 Sept. 1887; *Mail and Empire*, 11 Sept. 1897; Newmarket *Era*, 17 Sept. 1897; *Empire*, 13 Sept. 1894; *Globe*, 13 Sept. 1887; *Mail*, 18 Sept. 1888.

75 *Star*, 6 Sept. 1899; *Mail*, 17 Sept. 1884; *News*, 17 Sept. 1885; *Mail*, 18 Sept. 1879.

76 See, for example, *News*, 18 and 19 Sept. 1883; *News*, 11 Sept. 1886.

77 *Mail*, 14 Sept. 1888; *Mail*, 16 Sept. 1881; *Mail*, 16 Sept. 1890.

78 *Mail*, 12 Sept. 1882; *Mail*, 7, 9, and 13 Sept. 1882; *Globe*, 20 Sept. 1883.

79 'Woman's Kingdom,' *Mail*, 8 Sept. 1894. Pickpocketing in Toronto, of course, was nothing new. See Eric James Jarvis, 'Mid-Victorian Toronto: Panic, Policy and Public Response, 1857–1873' (PhD thesis, University of Western Ontario, 1978), 116.

80 See, for example, *Telegram*, 14 Sept. 1886; *Mail and Empire*, 9 Sept. 1895; *Mail*, 11 Sept. 1894; *Mail*, 9 Sept. 1893.

81 *Star*, 2 Sept. 1898; *Globe*, 17 Sept. 1883; *News*, 23 Sept. 1885; *Telegram*, 14 Sept. 1886.

82 CTA, *Toronto City Council Minutes for 1894*, Appendix C, no. 2, Report of the Chief Constable, 20; *Mail*, 6 Sept. 1879; *World*, 18 Sept. 1890. There are no reliable statistics on the gender or origins of victims, but press comments confirm the vulnerability of women and rural people. All seven cases reported on 7 September 1894, for example, involved women. Most of the dozen cases that occured on 1 September 1897 involved country visitors. See *Empire*, 8 Sept. 1894, and *Mail and Empire*, 2 Sept. 1897.

83 See, for example, *News*, 12 Sept. 1885; *Mail*, 4 Sept. 1894.

84 *Empire*, 12 Sept. 1894; *Star*, 14 Sept. 1897; *News*, 14 Sept. 1894.

85 *Mail*, 11 Sept. 1894; *Mail*, 17 Sept. 1880; *Mail*, 16 Sept. 1893; *Telegram*, 13 Sept. 1892.

86 *Empire*, 10 and 15 Sept. 1894. On the specialization of pickpocketing in the nineteenth century, see Johnson, *Urban Underworld*, 44–45; Kellow Chesney, *The Victorian Underworld* (New York 1972), 144–60; Edward Crapsey, *The Nether Side of New York or, the Vice, Crime and Poverty of the Great Metropolis* (1872; Montclair 1969), 19–20.

87 CTA, *Toronto City Council Minutes for 1893*, Appendix C, Chief Constable's Report, 22.

88 *Globe*, 7 Sept. 1897; *Star*, 14 Sept. 1897; Metropolitan Toronto Police Archives, Register of Criminals, 1887–95, entries for Charles Thompson, 15 Sept. 1887, and Jessie Thompson, 23 June 1893; *News*, 27 Aug. 1901.

89 *Telegram*, 19 Sept. 1890.

90 *World*, 9 Sept. 1896; *News*, 9 Sept. 1896; *News*, 27 Aug. 1901.

91 *Mail*, 1 Sept. 1879; letter of C.R. Beswetherick, *Mail*, 6 Oct. 1879; *Mail*, 2 Sept. 1879; *Mail*, 30 Aug. 1879.

92 *Mail*, 1 Sept. 1879; *Globe*, 11 Sept. 1879; *Mail*, 24 Sept. 1879; letter of C.R. Beswetherick, *Mail*, 6 Oct. 1879.

93 Letter of 'A.B.,' *Telegram*, 25 Sept. 1879; *Mail*, 2 Sept. 1879; letter of 'Exhibitor,' *Telegram*, 26 Sept. 1879.

94 Beswetherick letter, 6 Oct. 1879. See also *Mail*, 2 Sept. 1879.

95 *Mail*, 9 and 10 Sept. 1880; *Globe*, 18 Sept. 1880; *Telegram*, 9 Sept. 1880; *Globe*, 15 *Sept.* 1880; *Mail*, 17 Sept. 1880; *Globe*, 16 Sept. 1880; *Globe*, 14 and 15 Sept. 1881.

96 CTA, Toronto City Council Minutes for 1881, items 178 and 206, Feb. 7; *Mail*, 1 Sept. 1881; *Globe*, 13 Sept. 1881; *Globe*, 6 Sept. 1881.

97 *Telegram*, 12 Sept. 1881; *Globe*, 6 Sept. 1881; Port Hope *Guide*, 28 Sept. 1881.

98 *World*, 9 Sept. 1882; *Globe*, 9 Sept. 1882; *Telegram*, 11 Sept. 1882; *Globe*, 7 Sept. 1882; *Mail*, 7 Sept. 1882; *News*, 6 Sept. 1882.

99 *Mail*, 9, 12 and 14 Sept. 1882; 'The Exhibitions,' *Farmer's Advocate*, Oct. 1882, 249; *Globe*, 5 Sept. 1883.

100 *Telegram*, 21 Sept. 1883; *Canadian Statesman* [Bowmanville], 28 Sept. 1883; *Mail*, 22 Sept. 1883; *News*, 22 Sept. 1883; *Globe*, 10 Sept. 1884; Markham *Economist*, 11 Sept. 1884.

101 Markham *Economist*, 11 Sept. 1884; *Globe*, 6 Sept. 1884; *News*, 15 Sept. 1884; *World*, 15 Sept. 1884; letter of 'Simcoe,' *News*, 10 Sept. 1884; CTA, RG 2 B2, box 8, Executive Committee/Board of Control Communica-

tions, no. 1269, James Thompson to Mayor Boswell, 27 Nov. 1884, and box 9, no. 235, press clipping of letter of James Thompson, 2 March 1885.

102 *Mail*, 10 Sept. 1885; Orillia *Packet* 25 Sept. 1885; *Globe*, 17 and 18 Sept. 1885. On the history of liquor licensing legislation, see Joseph Schull, *Ontario since 1867* (Toronto 1978), 88–91.

103 *News*, 22 Sept. 1885; *News*, 26 Sept. 1885; *Globe*, 26 Sept. 1885; *Globe*, 29 Sept. 1885; *Globe*, 2 Oct. 1885.

104 *Globe*, reprinted in the Acton *Free Press*, 22 Sept. 1887; *Dumfries Reformer* [Galt], 29 Sept. 1887; *Globe*, 15 Sept. 1887. Beer with a low alcohol content was referred to as 'blue ribbon.'

105 *World*, 14 Sept. 1887; Orillia *Packet*, 25 Sept. 1891; *Globe*, 15 Sept. 1886; *Empire*, 22 Sept. 1888; *Empire*, 14 Sept. 1894; *News*, 18 Sept. 1890; *Grip*, 31, 761 (15 Sept. 1888), 3. Growlers were tin pails used to carry lunches and, frequently, beer. See Duis, *The Saloon*, 102.

106 For examples of charges laid, see *Globe*, 14 Sept. 1886; *Mail*, 18 Sept. 1888; *World*, 17 Sept. 1889; *Empire*, 18 Sept. 1890; *Mail*, 17 Sept. 1891; *World*, 10 Sept. 1903. On fines, see *Empire*, 16 Sept. 1891; *News*, 11 Sept. 1896.

107 *World*, 10 Sept. 1894; *Globe*, 13 Sept. 1886.

108 *Mail*, 13 Sept. 1892.

109 *News*, 31 Aug. 1894.

110 *Mail*, 14 Sept. 1893.

111 The figures are based on a manual count of entries in the Toronto Police Register of Criminals, which lists every charge that came before the police magistrate. For the period under consideration here, records exist only for 1879 and for 1888 to 1903. The thirteen-day control period a month before the fair was chosen arbitrarily. During the 1893 fair, from 4 September to 16 September, there were 207 drunk and disorderly cases, compared with 164 cases in the period from 31 July to 12 August. For the same periods, vagrancy rose to 20 from 11, prostitution to 7 from 0, while larceny remained relatively constant at 27, up from 26. Liquor licensing offences, on the other hand, declined to 13 from 42, and assault to 31 from 33. A similar comparison for 1898 shows increases in drunk and disorderly to 200 from 102, larceny to 62 from 19, vagrancy to 32 from 14, and prostitution to 3 from 1. Liquor licensing offences declined to 1 from 25, and assault to 25 from 27. See CTA, RG 9 A1. 14 – A1. 22, Toronto Police Register of Criminals. The monthly tabulations for Warrants in the First Instance, found in the Annual Reports of the Chief Constable, are less helpful because they cannot be itemized for specific

days and because, in some years, the fair overlapped August and September. Generally, they show high figures for September, but not always the highest for the year.

It should be noted that the categories used by authorities were relatively imprecise: prostitutes were often charged with larceny, disorderliness, and vagrancy as well as soliciting. See Backhouse, *Petticoats and Prejudice*, 229–30; Constance Backhouse, 'Nineteenth-Century Canadian Prostitution Law: Reflection of a Discriminatory Society,' *Histoire sociale / Social History* 36 (Nov. 1985), 396; Michael McCulloch, '"Drunk and Disorderly in D'Artigny Street": Prostitutes and Civil Disorder in Quebec City, 1840–1850,' unpublished paper presented to Canadian Historical Association, Calgary 1994, 14–15.

112 Metro Toronto Police Archives, Annual Reports of the Chief Constable of the City of Toronto, 1890 to 1903.

113 *Empire*, 10 Sept. 1888; *Empire*, 17 Sept. 1888; *Empire*, 5 Sept. 1891.

114 *Empire*, 17 Sept. 1890; *News*, 20 Sept. 1883; *Mail*, 3 Sept. 1888.

115 *Globe*, 7 Sept. 1881; *Mail*, 15 Sept. 1887.

116 *Telegram*, 6 Sept. 1886; *Mail*, 14 Sept. 1888; *Mail*, 17 Sept. 1890; *World*, 9 Sept. 1896; *World*, 5 Sept. 1900; *Globe*, 14 Sept. 1881; *Globe*, 16 Sept. 1884. Throughout this period, not just in Toronto, vagrancy was viewed as a crime of status. General appearance and lifestyle, as much as specific criminal activities, were considered appropriate grounds for arrest. See David Bright, '"Loafers Are Not Going to Subsist upon Public Credulence": Vagrancy and the Law in Calgary, 1900–1914,' paper presented to the Canadian Historical Association, Calgary 1994, 30.

117 *Mail*, 30 Aug. 1888; *Mail*, 13 Sept. 1883.

118 *News*, 10 Sept. 1888; *Star*, 11 Sept. 1896; *Mail*, 7 Sept. 1887; *Mail*, 13, 14, and 22 Sept. 1883.

119 On the efforts of the Toronto police to use the law as an instrument of class control, see Helen Boritch and John Hagan, 'Crime and the Changing Forms of Class Control: Policing Public Order in "Toronto the Good," 1859–1955,' in *Social Forces* 66, 2 (Dec. 1987), 307–35. This analysis questions Monkkonen's arguement that American policing shifted in the 1890s from proactive efforts at class control to reactive efforts at crime control. On the use of vagrancy laws elsewhere, see Sidney L. Harring, *Policing a Class Society: The Experience of American Cities, 1865–1915* (New Brunswick 1983), 243–4; Jim Phillips, 'Poverty, Unemployment, and the Administration of the Criminal Law: Vagrancy Laws in Halifax, 1864–1890,' in Philip Girard and Jim Phillips, eds., *Essays in the History of Canadian Law*, vol. 3: *Nova Scotia* (Toronto 1990), 128–62; John

C. Weaver, *Crimes, Constables, and Courts: Order and Transgression in a Canadian City, 1816–1970* (Montreal and Kingston 1995), 150.

120 *News*, 18 Sept. 1882; *Mail*, 9 Sept. 1891; *Globe*, 10 Sept. 1880; Metropolitan Toronto Police Archives, Board of Police Commissioners Minute Book, 1879–87, 1 Sept. 1880; *Globe*, 7 Sept. 1881; *Telegram*, 8 Sept. 1886; Board of Police Commissioners Minute Book, 1879–87, 2 Sept. 1886; *News*, 12 Sept. 1885; *News*, 12 Sept. 1887; *Empire*, 18 Sept. 1890.

121 *News*, 9 Sept. 1892; *Mail and Empire*, 3 Sept. 1896.

122 Most of this information comes from the Metropolitan Toronto Police Archives, Detective Order Book, 1878–1907. See also *Mail*, 11 Sept. 1882; *Mail*, 9 Sept. 1884; *Telegram*, 7 Sept. 1887; *Empire*, 18 Sept. 1890.

123 *Telegram*, 6 Sept. 1881; *Mail*, 6 Sept. 1889; *Mail*, 12 Sept. 1890; *Mail*, 7 Sept. 1893; *Empire*, 11 Sept. 1888; *Mail*, 1 Sept. 1887; *Globe*, 1 Sept. 1887.

124 *Mail and Empire*, 29 Aug. 1901.

125 Hamilton *Spectator*, 11 Sept. 1883; *Globe*, 14 Sept. 1887; *Star*, 31 Aug. 1896.

126 *Globe*, 3 Sept. 1888; *Star*, 11 Sept. 1902.

127 *Mail*, 8 Sept. 1882; *Mail*, 12 Sept. 1888; *Mail*, 16 Sept. 1889; *News*, 9 Sept. 1896; *Mail*, 15 Sept. 1890.

128 *Mail*, 8 Sept. 1893. See also the case of George Musson, *News*, 11 and 18 Sept. 1883; *Mail*, 12 and 19 Sept. 1883.

129 *Globe*, 19 Sept. 1887.

130 *Labour Advocate*, 11 Sept. 1891; *Week* 5, 43 (20 Sept. 1888), 682.

131 CNEA, Industrial Exhibition Association, Annual Reports for 1879, Annual General Meeting, 17 Feb. 1880, 4; *Mail*, 6 Sept. 1881; *Globe*, 8 Sept. 1881; *Globe*, 10 Sept. 1887; *Globe*, 15 Sept. 1887; *Globe*, 12 Sept. 1903.

132 *Globe*, 6 Sept. 1880; *Globe*, 5 Sept. 1879; *Canadian Manufacturer* 1, 24 (8 Sept. 1882), 573; *Mail*, 16 Sept. 1891; *World*, 31 Aug. 1899.

133 *Globe*, 15 Sept. 1883; *Mail*, 11 Sept. 1885; *Mail*, 9 Sept. 1880. See also *Mail*, 6 Sept. 1882; *Mail*, 10 Sept. 1890.

134 *Mail*, 11 Sept. 1880; *Mail*, 6 Sept. 1881; *Globe*, 12 Sept. 1884; *Globe*, 11 Sept. 1885.

135 *Mail*, 14 Sept. 1880; *Mail*, 19 and 20 Sept. 1888; *Farming* 14, 2 (Oct. 1896), 110.

136 *News*, 8 Sept. 1891; *Mail*, 20 Sept. 1890.

137 CNEA, Industrial Exhibition Association, Annual Reports for 1883, President's Report, 12; *Mail*, 5 Sept. 1887; *Globe*, 3 Sept. 1887; *Telegram*, 1 Sept. 1887.

138 *News*, 16 and 17 Sept. 1886.
139 *Mail*, 4 Sept. 1880; *Telegram*, 10 Sept. 1881; *Mail*, 9 Sept. 1880; *Globe*, 13 Sept. 1881; *Mail*, 7 Sept. 1882; *Mail*, 13 Sept. 1882.
140 *Globe*, 3 Sept. 1887; *Globe*, 12 Sept. 1885. See also *Mail*, 14 Sept. 1891.
141 Sama [Emily Cummings], 'From a Woman's Standpoint,' *Globe*, 16 Sept. 1893; *Empire*, 15 Sept. 1894; letter of A.M. Regan, *Saturday Night*, 15 Sept. 1894, 1; *News*, 3 Sept. 1897; *Star*, 2 Sept. 1903. The piano industry was a significant part of the nineteenth-century Ontario economy. See Wayne Kelly, *Downright Upright: A History of the Canadian Piano Industry* (Toronto 1991), esp. 42–95.
142 Robert C. Allen, *Horrible Prettiness: Burlesque and American Culture* (Chapel Hill and London 1991), 32–6.

Chapter 2: Confidence

1 *World*, 31 Aug., 2, 4, and 5 Sept. 1882; *Telegram*, 2 Sept. 1882; *Globe*, 8 Sept. 1882.
2 *World*, 2 and 4 Sept. 1882; *Telegram*, 2 Sept. 1882.
3 *World*, 2 Sept. 1882; *Telegram*, 2 Sept. 1882; *World*, 31 Aug. 1882.
4 *World*, 1 and 2 Sept. 1882; Pickering *News*, 22 Sept. 1882; *Telegram*, 2 Sept. 1882.
5 See, for example, *Liberal* [Richmond Hill], 1 Sept. 1882; Elora *Express*, 7 Sept. 1882.
6 *World*, 1 and 4 Sept. 1882; *Telegram*, 4 Sept. 1882.
7 On quack nostrums in the nineteenth century, see James Harvey Young, *The Toadstool Millionaires: A Social History of Patent Medicines in America before Federal Regulation* (Princeton 1961).
8 *World*, 1 Sept. 1882; *Telegram*, 5 Sept. 1882.
9 *World*, 2 Sept. 1882, 5 Sept. 1882.
10 *World*, 1 Sept. 1882; *Telegram*, 18 Sept. 1882.
11 *World*, 4 Sept., 31 Aug., and 2 Sept. 1882.
12 *World*, 2 Sept. 1882; *Telegram*, 2 Sept. 1882.
13 *World*, 1 and 2 Sept. 1882; Pickering *News*, 22 Sept. 1882; *World*, 4 Sept. 1882.
14 *World*, 1 Sept. 1882; *Telegram*, 8 Sept. 1882.
15 *Telegram*, 4 Sept. 1882; *World*, 1 and 2 Sept. 1882.
16 *World*, 31 Aug. and 1 Sept. 1882; *Telegram*, 2 and 12 Sept. 1882.
17 Pickering *News*, 22 Sept. 1882; *World*, 2 Sept. 1882; *Telegram*, 2 Sept. 1882.
18 *Telegram*, 12 and 16 Sept. 1882.

19 *Telegram*, 16, 18, and 26 Sept. 1882.

20 On high rates of transiency in the nineteenth century, see Michael Katz, *The People of Hamilton, Canada West: Family and Class in a Mid-Nineteenth-Century City* (Cambridge, Mass. 1975), 94–175; Michael Katz, Michael Doucet, and Mark Stern, *The Social Organization of Early Industrial Capitalism* (Cambridge, Mass., and London 1982), 102–30.

21 John F. Kasson, *Rudeness and Civility: Manners in Nineteenth-Century Urban America* (New York 1990), 70; 'They Are a Joy Forever,' *Telegram*, 16 Sept. 1890. Even in a much smaller centre like Brantford, with a population of 10,555, according to the 1881 census, the long-serving Presbyterian minister William Cochrane insisted that 'young men coming from Christian homes to strange cities, lonely and friendless, should be introduced to good companions, invited to the homes of masters and made to feel that they are the objects of interest, beyond civil contract.' Quoted in David G. Burley, *A Particular Condition in Life: Self-Employment and Social Mobility in Mid-Victorian Brantford, Ontario* (Montreal and Kingston 1994), 193.

22 Karen Halttunen, *Confidence Men and Painted Women: A Study of Middle-Class Culture in America, 1830–1870* (New Haven and London 1982), 36; Richard Sennett, *The Fall of Public Man: On the Social Psychology of Capitalism* (1974; New York 1978), 39; Richard L. Bushman, *The Refinement of America: People, Houses, Cities* (New York 1992), 404; David Scobey, 'Anatomy of the Promenade: The Politics of Bourgeois Sociability in Nineteenth-Century New York,' *Social History* 17, 2 (May 1992), 212; Kasson, *Rudeness and Civility*, 96.

23 On the growth of the notion of the 'discontinuous self,' see Jackson Lears, *No Place of Grace: Antimodernism and the Transformation of American Culture, 1880–1920* (New York 1981), 36–40. For a discussion of how these concerns intruded in the life of a real person, see Susan Gillman, *Dark Twins: Imposture and Identity in Mark Twain's Identity* (Chicago 1989).

24 On changing relations between employers and employees, especially at the management level, see Alfred D. Chandler, *The Visible Hand: The Management Revolution in American Business* (Cambridge, Mass., 1977); Olivier Zunz, *Making America Corporate, 1870–1920* (Chicago 1990), passim. By the 1870s the credit-rating firm of R.G. Dun was processing five thousand queries daily. See James R. Beniger, *The Control Revolution: Technological and Economic Origins of the Information Society* (Cambridge, Mass., and London 1986), 257.

25 On declining self-sufficiency, see Susan Strasser, *Satisfaction Guaranteed: The Making of the American Mass Market* (New York 1989), 15–18.

26 This point is made by Peter J. Parish, 'Confidence and Anxiety in Victorian America,' in Steve Ickingrill and Stephen Mills, eds., *Victorianism in the United States: Its Era and its Legacy* (Amsterdam 1992), 1–18.

27 Halttunen, *Confidence Men and Painted Women*, 92–123.

28 See lists of fair dates in the *Empire*, 14 Sept. 1892, and *Mail and Empire*, 9 Sept. 1895, as well as Elwood Jones, *Winners: 150 Years of the Peterborough Exhibition* (Peterborough 1995), 215–16.

29 *Mail*, 15 Sept. 1881.

30 See, for example, *Mail*, 4 Sept. 1882; *Globe*, 11 Sept. 1885.

31 *Globe*, 7 Sept. 1891; *Globe*, 2 Sept. 1902; *Globe*, 19 Sept. 1888.

32 *Globe*, 8 Sept. 1891; *Mail*, 10 Sept. 1888. See also *Mail*, 8 Sept. 1880; *Mail*, 1 Sept. 1881; *Globe*, 3 Sept. 1887; *Globe*, 30 Aug. 1888.

33 *Mail*, 9 Sept. 1881. The first speaker quoted was the Honourable George W. Allan, a lawyer, senator, and central figure in many Toronto cultural organizations.

34 *Mail*, 15 Sept. 1881; *Globe*, 11 Sept. 1886; *Weekly Sun*, 2 Sept. 1896.

35 *Empire*, 18 Sept. 1889; *Mail and Empire*, 8 Sept. 1898.

36 *Mail*, 8 and 13 Sept. 1880.

37 'A Feature of the Toronto Exhibition – An Eloquent Exhibit,' *Saturday Night*, 17 Sept. 1892, 7. For a discussion of expansionist ideas on the Canadian West in this period, see Doug Owram, *Promise of Eden: The Canadian Expansionist Movement and the Idea of the West, 1856–1900* (Toronto 1980), 165–7.

38 'The Exhibition,' *Empire*, 8 Sept. 1891; *Globe*, 7 Sept. 1882; *Telegram*, 7 Sept. 1886.

39 'They Went to the City,' Port Hope *Guide*, 13 Sept. 1895.

40 On attitudes towards crowds in the nineteenth century, see Gregory W. Bush, *Lord of Attention: Gerald Stanley Lee and the Crowd Metaphor in Industrializing America* (Amherst 1991), 8–30; Richard Sennett, *Flesh and Stone: The Body and the City in Western Civilization* (New York and London 1994), 282–4; Susanna Barrows, *Distorting Mirrors: Visions of the Crowd in Late Nineteenth-Century France* (New Haven 1981); Robert Rutherdale, 'Canada's August Festival: Communitas, Liminality, and Social Memory,' *Canadian Historical Review* 77 (June 1996), 221–3.

41 *Mail*, 29 Aug. 1879.

42 The revolt of Ahmad Arabi al-Misri culminated in the Battle of Tel-el-Kebir on 13 September 1882. See P.J. Vatikiotis, *A History of Modern Egypt: From Muhammed Ali to Mubarak* (London 1991), 154–66.

43 *Mail*, 2, 6, and 12 Sept. 1882.

44 *Mail*, 12 and 14 Sept. 1882; *Globe*, 12 Sept. 1882.

45 *Mail*, 12 Sept. 1882; *Globe*, 12 Sept. 1882; *World*, 12 Sept. 1882.

46 *Globe*, 12 Sept. 1882; *Mail*, 12 and 2 Sept. 1882; 'From "What I Thought of the Bombardment" – by a Lady Spectator,' *Telegram*, 13 Sept. 1882.

47 *Mail*, 2 Sept. 1882; *World*, 12 Sept. 1882; *Mail*, 12 Sept. 1882; *Globe*, 12 Sept. 1882; *News*, 12 Sept. 1882.

48 *Globe*, 12 Sept. 1882; *World*, 13 Sept. 1882; *Mail*, 12 Sept. 1882.

49 *World*, 12 Sept. 1882; *Mail*, 12 Sept. 1882; *Globe*, 12 Sept. 1882.

50 'Scenes at the Fair,' *Mail*, 20 Sept. 1890. On increasingly favourable attitudes towards crowds, see Bush, *Lord of Attention*, 64–89.

51 *Mail*, 7 Sept. 1882; *Globe*, 16 Sept. 1884; *Canadian Manufacturer* 1, 24 (8 Sept. 1882), 573; 'Dingman's Soap,' *Mail*, 12 Sept. 1888; 'Comfort Soap,' *Mail and Empire*, 7 Sept. 1899.

52 'Just Fair,' *The Moon* 1, 15 (6 Sept. 1902), 215; 'Manufacturers Who Exhibit at the Fair,' *Canadian Manufacturer* 25, 6 (15 Sept. 1893), 223 ; 'Rubber Manufacture,' *News*, 16 Sept. 1886.

53 'Dominion Organ and Piano Company,' *News*, 17 Sept. 1886; *Globe*, 10 Sept. 1881; MTRL, Balwin Room, Ephemera Collection, BR 665. 352, Elliot and Co. pamphlet; *World*, 6 Sept. 1895; *Telegram*, 14 Sept. 1880; *Globe*, 13 Sept. 1886. On trade cards and other handouts in this period, see Strasser, *Satisfaction Guaranteed*, 163–202; Wayne Kelly, *Downright Upright: A History of the Canadian Piano Industry* (Toronto 1991), 32. On the popularity of perforated mottoes in the nineteenth century, see Kenneth L. Ames, *Death in the Dining Room, and Other Tales of Victorian Culture* (Philadelphia 1992), 97–149.

54 *Mail*, 5 Sept. 1891; *Empire*, 14 Sept. 1891; *Globe*, 7 Sept. 1899. See also *Globe*, 9 Sept. 1903.

55 *World*, 15 Sept. 1881; *Globe*, 11 Sept. 1886.

56 *Globe*, 12 Sept. 1903; *News* 3 Sept. 1903; *Mail*, 5 Sept. 1879; *Globe*, 4 Sept. 1896.

57 *Mail*, 8 Sept. 1879; *Globe*, 8 Sept. 1887; *Mail*, 16 Sept. 1884; *Mail*, 20 Sept. 1889.

58 *Mail*, 15 Sept. 1880; *Mail*, 21 Sept. 1883; *Mail*, 22 Sept. 1883; *Mail*, 24 Sept. 1880.

59 *Star*, 29 Aug. 1901; *Mail*, 9 Sept. 1890; *Telegram*, 9 Sept. 1881.

60 *Empire*, 7 Sept. 1892; *News*, 13 Sept. 1884.

61 'Reindeer' Brand ad, *Canadian Grocer*, 18 Oct. 1895, 59; University of Western Ontario, Weldon Library, Regional History Room, box 4043, file 108, Joseph Seymour Fallows Collection, booklet from Ontario Beekeepers' Supply Company; CNEA, miscellaneous artifacts box, R.W. King and Co. letterhead.

62 At the 1879 fair, almost all prizes for Industrial and Manufacturing

Classes were cash, ranging from $3 and $4 to a high of $50, though very few were more than $20. By 1883 the large majority of prizes, where they still existed, were medals and diplomas. See CNEA, Industrial Exhibition Association, Prize Lists for 1879 and 1883.

63 *Mail*, 15 Sept. 1880; Hamilton *Spectator*, 6 Sept. 1899.

64 *Telegram*, 9 Sept. 1880; *Telegram*, 16 Sept. 1880; letter from 'A Breeder,' *World*, 19 Sept. 1884.

65 Letter of 'Non-Exhibitor,' *Mail*, 15 Sept. 1880; *World*, 30 Aug. 1899.

66 See, for example, *Globe*, 10 Sept. 1881; *Mail*, 18 Sept. 1884.

67 'The Poultry at the Industrial Exhibition,' *Farmer's Advocate* Oct. 1882, 262; Hamilton *Spectator*, 24 Sept. 1884.

68 *World*, 17 Sept. 1892; *Globe*, 19 Sept. 1881; CNEA, Industrial Exhibition Association, Annual Report for 1883, 17–18.

69 Letter of Ed Shrapnel, *Mail*, 17 Sept. 1879; letter of V.E. Fuller, *Globe*, 14 Sept. 1886; Port Hope *Guide*, 24 Sept. 1880; F.C. Sibbald, 'Shorthorns at the Toronto Industrial,' *Farming* 13, 3 (Nov. 1895), 149; letter of Robert McAdam, *Farmer's Advocate*, 15 Oct. 1894, 413.

70 *Mail*, 9 Sept. 1881.

71 See, for example, 'The Fruit Exhibit at the Toronto Industrial,' *Canadian Horticulturist* 18, 9 (Oct. 1895), 349. Complaints about the quality of judging at fairs of all sizes seem to have been universal. See, for example, Chris Allen Rasmussen, 'State Fair: Culture and Agriculture in Iowa, 1854–1941' (PhD thesis, Rutgers University, The State University of New Jersey, 1992), 70–1, 156–60; David Jones, *Midways, Judges, and Sharp-Tongued Fakirs: The Illustrated Story of Country Fairs in the Prairie West* (Saskatoon 1983), 18–29; Elsbeth Heaman, 'Colonial Leviathan: Central Canadian Exhibitions at Home and Abroad during the Nineteenth Century' (PhD thesis, University of Toronto, 1995), 493–5.

72 *Globe*, 14 Sept. 1881; *Mail*, 18 Sept. 1888; *Mail*, 15 Sept. 1880.

73 *World*, 15 Sept. 1881; *Mail*, 9 Sept. 1881.

74 This request was made by manufacturers entering under the categories of 'stoves, grates and hollow-ware,' 'knitting and sewing machines,' and 'musical instruments.' See CNEA, Industrial Exhibition Association, Prize List for 1879.

75 CNEA, Industrial Exhibition Association, Annual Report for 1879, 10.

76 CNEA, Industrial Exhibition Association, Prize List for 1883; *Globe*, 13 Sept. 1881.

77 *Farmer's Advocate* Aug. 1883, 244–5; CNEA, Industrial Exhibition Association, Annual Report for 1888, 5–6; CNEA, Industrial Exhibition Association, Prize List for 1888.

78 *Industrial Canada*, Sept. 1900, 55.

79 At the Iowa State Fair, prizes for agricultural implements were done away with in the late 1870s when managers realized that incentives to the display of these goods were unnecessary. See Rasmussen, 'State Fair,' 81.

80 OA, Ontario Society of Artists Collection, MU 2254, Minute and Letter-book, March 1877–May 1881, motion passed 6 Sept. 1881; *Globe*, 10 Sept. 1880; *Mail*, 10 Sept. 1880.

81 *Mail*, 27 Aug. 1881; OA, Ontario Society of Artists Papers, MU 2254, Minute and Letterbook, March 1877–May 1881, Annual Report for year ending May 1, 1882, following page 67; *Mail*, 9 Sept. 1886.

82 On confidence criminals in nineteenth-century America and popular interest in them, see Kasson, *Rudeness and Civility*, 100–11; Halttunen, *Confidence Men and Painted Women*, 1–32, 198–205 and passim; Kathleen De Grave, *Swindler, Spy, Rebel: The Confidence Women in Nineteenth-Century America* (Columbia and London 1995); Hans Berg-mann, *God in the Street: New York Writing from the Penny Press to Melville* (Philadelphia 1995), 187–220; Earl W. Hayter, *The Troubled Farmer, 1850–1900: Rural Adjustment to Industrialism* (Dekalb 1968), 145–208; Allan Pinkerton, *Criminal Reminiscences and Detective Sketches* (1878; Freeport, NY, 1970), 138–53, 177–201; Edward Crapsey, *The Nether Side of New York or, the Vice, Crime and Poverty of the Great Metropolis* (1872; Montclair 1969), 21, 63–73. For a perceptive discussion of Canadian concerns about confidence crimes directed against rural resi-dents, see Kerry Badgley, '"Then I Saw I Had Been Swindled": Frauds and Swindles Perpetrated on Farmers in Late Nineteenth-Century Ontario,' in Donald H. Akenson, ed., *Canadian Papers in Rural History* 9 (Gananoque 1994), 337–54, as well as W.H. Graham, *Greenbank: Country Matters in nineteenth Century Ontario* (Peterborough 1988), 204–6. A more encyclopaedic survey of confidence crimes and well-known confi-dence criminals can be found in Carl Sifakis, *Hoaxes and Scams: A Com-pendium of Deceptions, Ruses and Swindles* (New York 1993).

83 *Globe*, 9 Sept. 1881; *Mail*, 11 Sept. 1880; *Mail and Empire*, 12 Sept. 1895; *Mail*, 14 Sept. 1881.

84 *Mail*, 11 Sept. 1882; *Mail*, 14 Sept. 1882.

85 Pickering *News*, 6 Sept. 1901; *Mail and Empire*, 29 Aug. 1901; *Mail*, 31 Aug. and 1 Sept 1893; *Globe*, 5 Sept. 1900. On the activities of some professional counterfeiters in 1880, see Victor Speer, ed., *Memoirs of a Great Detective: Incidents in the Life of John Wilson Murray* (Toronto 1905), 151–66.

86 *Mail*, 20 Sept. 1889; *World*, 19 Sept. 1892; *Mail*, 15 and 16 Sept. 1892; *Mail*, 11 and 12 Sept. 1883.

87 *World*, 25 Sept. 1901; *Empire*, 3 Sept. 1892. On similar schemes, see Larry K. Hartsfield, *The American Response to Professional Crime, 1870–1917* (Westport, Conn., and London 1985), 83.

88 *Mail*, 9 Sept. 1882; *News*, 10 Sept. 1884; *Mail*, 15 Sept. 1887; *Mail and Empire*, 2 Sept. 1897; *Mail*, 31 Aug. and 1 Sept. 1893.

89 *Telegram*, 6 Sept. 1886; Newmarket *Era*, 24 Sept. 1886; *Mail*, 3 Sept. 1887; *Globe*, 17 Sept. 1884; *World*, 17 Sept. 1884.

90 On the psychological importance of watches in the nineteenth century, see Michael O'Malley, *Keeping Watch: A History of American Time* (New York 1991), 174–99.

91 *Globe*, 10 Sept. 1887; *Telegram*, 14 Sept. 1886. See also *Mail*, 9 Sept. 1881; *Mail*, 18 Sept. 1891.

92 Aurora *Banner*, 8 Sept. 1893.

93 *News*, 14 Sept. 1891.

94 *Mail*, 13 Sept. 1882.

95 *Telegram*, 12 Sept. 1881; *Mail*, 7 Sept. 1882; *World*, 6 Sept. 1882.

96 See Thomas Byrnes, *Rogues' Gallery: 247 Professional Criminals of 19th Century America* (1886; Secaucus 1988), 41–2.

97 *Mail*, 10 Sept. 1880.

98 *Mail*, 24 Sept. 1880.

99 'Fake Sales,' *News*, 11 Sept. 1894; *News*, 11 Sept. 1895; *Telegram*, 13 Sept. 1890; 'Fraudulent Auctions,' *Dry Goods Review*, May 1896, 36.

100 *News*, 11 Sept. 1895.

101 *Mail*, 19 and 20 Sept. 1890; *World*, 19 Sept. 1890.

102 *News*, 11 Sept. 1895; *News*, 12 and 14 Sept. 1894.

103 'The Fake Auction Rooms,' Newmarket *Era*, 4 Sept. 1896. A similar ruse with horses instead of watches was practised at English country fairs. See Frances Brown, *Fairfield Folk: A History of the British Fairground and Its People* (Upton upon Severn 1988), 60.

104 'Mock Auctions and How They Injure Legitimate Trade,' *Telegram*, 13 Sept. 1890.

105 'The Fake Auction Rooms,' Newmarket *Era*, 4 Sept. 1896; *Telegram*, 7 Sept. 1895; *Mail and Empire*, 11 Sept. 1903. There was no Henry Hyman listed in the city directory for 1900. Nor was there a Henry Hyam listed in that volume. However, a Henry Hyam, auctioneer, did appear in directories through the 1890s, and he reappeared in the latter years of the first decade of the twentieth century, listed as a clerk.

106 *News*, 31 Aug. 1897.

107 *Christian Guardian*, 16 Sept. 1891, 583.

108 'A Social Misstep,' *Mail*, 4 Sept. 1893.

109 On advice literature dealing with confidence criminals, see Halttunen, *Confidence Men and Painted Women*, 6–32.
110 Badgley argues that the identification of confidence criminals with urban culture by rural folk was an important element in the fostering of late nineteenth-century agrarian protest. He also wonders whether urban confidence crimes differed from rural ones. It is significant, of course, that many of those victimized in Toronto at fairtime came from beyond the city, but my evidence suggests that urban schemes tended to rely on briefer interactions with dupes and that they used illiteracy far less as a tool of deception. See Badgley, 'Then I Saw,' 347–50.

Chapter 3: Display

1 Roland Barthes, *Mythologies* (New York 1972), 90. See also Martin Jay, 'Scopic Regimes of Modernity,' in Scott Lash and Jonathan Friedman, eds., *Modernity and Identity* (Oxford and Cambridge, Mass., 1992), 178–9; Walter Benjamin, *Charles Baudelaire: A Lyric Poet in the Era of High Capitalism*, English translation (London 1973), 38.
2 Miles Orvell, *The Real Thing: Imitation and Authenticity in American Culture, 1880–1940* (Chapel Hill 1989), 48–52; Richard L. Bushman, *The Refinement of America: People, Houses, Cities* (New York 1992). On the decoration of the Victorian parlour, see Katherine G. Grier, *Culture and Comfort: People, Parlors, and Upholstery, 1850–1930* (Amherst 1988), 81–102 and passim; Asa Briggs, *Victorian Things* (Chicago 1988), 245–9.
3 Neil Harris, *Cultural Excursions: Marketing Appetites and Cultural Tastes in Modern America* (Chicago 1990), 61.
4 See, for example, *Mail*, 17 Sept. 1879; *World*, 13 Sept. 1882; *Globe*, 29 Sept. 1884; *Mail*, 19 Sept. 1888.
5 *Mail*, 11 Sept. 1893; CNEA, Industrial Exhibition Association, Prize List for 1899, 14.
6 *Star*, 4 Sept. 1903; *Globe*, 16 Sept. 1894.
7 *Globe*, 9 Sept. 1880; *Globe*, 8 Sept. 1881; *Mail*, 12 Sept. 1881; *Mail*, 7 Sept. 1880; *Mail*, 11 Sept. 1884.
8 *Mail*, 8 Sept. 1881; *Telegram*, 10 Sept. 1881; *News*, 7 Sept. 1887. Robert Walker and Sons, proprietors of the Golden Lion, also manufactured ready-to-wear clothing. See Gerald Tulchinsky, 'Hidden among the Smokestacks: Toronto's Clothing Industry, 1871–1901,' in David Keane and Colin Read, eds., *Old Ontario: Essays in Honour of J.M.S. Careless* (Toronto 1990), 268.

9 *Telegram*, 23 Sept. 1889; *Canadian Manufacturer* 17, 7 (4 Oct. 1889), 225–6; *Star*, 8 Sept. 1900; *Mail*, 11 Sept. 1884.

10 *Globe*, 25 Aug. 1899; *World*, 31 Aug. 1899. On the influence of exhibitions on department stores, see Simon J. Bronner, 'Reading Consumer Culture,' in Bronner, ed., *Consuming Visions: Accumulation and Display of Goods in America, 1880–1920* (New York 1989), 26–28; Harris, *Cultural Excursions*, 65–6.

11 *Telegram*, 10 Sept. 1895.

12 *News*, 7 Sept. 1898; *News*, 6 Sept. 1899.

13 *Telegram*, 5 Sept. 1879; *Telegram*, 10 Sept. 1881. Suggestions by department stores that they were expositions in themselves probably were quite common. See Harris, *Cultural Excursions*, 65.

14 *World*, 11 Sept. 1884.

15 *Star*, 8 Sept. 1900; Whitby *Chronicle*, 16 Sept. 1892.

16 The literature in this subject is extensive, but my understanding is drawn especially from the following: David Hounshell, *From the American System to Mass Production, 1800–1930: The Development of Manufacturing Technology in the U.S.* (Baltimore 1984); Alfred D. Chandler Jr, *The Visible Hand: The Managerial Revolution in American Business* (Cambridge, Mass., 1977); Daniel Nelson, *Managers and Workers: Origins of the Factory System in the United States, 1880–1920* (Madison 1975); James R. Beniger, *The Control Revolution: Technological and Economic Origins of the Information Society* (Cambridge, Mass., 1986).

17 Daniel Horowitz, *The Morality of Spending: Attitudes toward the Consumer Society in America, 1875–1940* (Baltimore and London 1985), 1–12, 30–1; Michael Barton, 'The Victorian Jeremiad: Critics of Accumulation and Display,' in Bronner, *Consuming Visions*, 55–71, and William Leach, 'Strategists of Display and the Production of Desire,' in Bronner, *Consuming Visions*, 101–2; Orvell, *The Real Thing*, 41; Rachel Bowlby, *Just Looking: Consumer Culture in Dreiser, Gissing, and Zola* (New York and London 1985), 1–8.

18 Mary Douglas and Baron Isherwood, *The World of Goods: Towards an Anthropology of Consumption* (London 1978), 59; Orvell, *The Real Thing*, 40; Bronner, *Consuming Visions*, 13–14. On the feeling of 'weightlessness' in late nineteenth-century America, see T.J. Jackson Lears, *No Place of Grace: Antimodernism and the Transformation of American Culture, 1880–1920* (New York 1981), 32–47.

19 Jackson Lears, 'Beyond Veblen: Rethinking Consumer Culture in America,' in Bronner, *Consuming Visions*, 76, 84–5; Anne McClintock, *Imperial*

Leather: Race, Gender and Sexuality in the Colonial Conquest (New York 1995), 208–9.

20 See, for example, William Leach, 'Strategists of Display and the Production of Desire,' in Bronner, *Consuming Visions*, 99–132; William Leach, *Land of Desire: Merchants, Power, and the Rise of a New American Culture* (New York 1993), esp. 39–90; Keith Walden, 'Speaking Modern: Language, Culture, and Hegemony in Grocery Window Displays, 1887–1920,' *Canadian Historical Review* 70, 3 (Sept. 1989), 285–310; James M. Mayo, *The American Grocery Store: The Business Evolution of an Architectural Space* (Westport, Conn., and London 1993), 64–5, 69, 72; David Monod, *Store Wars: Shopkeepers and the Culture of Mass Marketing, 1890–1939* (Toronto 1996), 152–4.

21 James Gardner and Caroline Heller, *Exhibitions and Display* (London 1960), 8. Along the same lines, Jean Baudrillard has suggested that the most banal reality can become surreal, 'but only in certain privileged moments that nevertheless are still connected with art and the imaginary.' See *Simulations* (New York 1983), 147.

22 Thomas Richards, *The Commodity Culture of Victorian England: Advertising and Spectacle, 1851–1914* (Stanford 1990), 30–1, 39. See also Harris, *Cultural Excursions*, 184–5. As Linda Williams had pointed out, the industrial presentations at fairs, even large international expositions, increasingly involved goods directed at domestic consumers rather than productive tools intended for industry. See *Dream Worlds: Mass Consumption in Late Nineteenth Century France* (Berkeley 1982), 3.

23 Susan Strasser, *Satisfaction Guaranteed: The Making of the American Mass Market* (New York 1989), 163–202; Elizabeth Ewen and Stuart Ewen, *Channels of Desire: Mass Images and the Shaping of American Consciousness* (New York 1982), 62.

24 Peter Stallybrass and Allon White, *The Politics and Poetics of Transgression* (Ithaca 1986), 80. On the diversity of linguistic forms, see Walter Benjamin, 'On Language as Such and on the Language of Man,' in *One-Way Street and Other Writings* (London 1979), 107–23; Kenneth S. Greenberg, *Honor and Slavery: Lies, Duels, Noses, Masks, Dressing as a Woman, Gifts, Strangers, Humanitarianism, Death, Slave Rebellions, the Proslavery Argument, Baseball, Hunting and Gambling in the Old South* (Princeton 1996), xi–xiv.

25 *Canadian Grocer*, 11 Sept, 1903, 25. On 'dealer helps' provided to retailers by manufacturers, see Strasser, *Satisfaction Guaranteed*, 188–91.

26 Robert Rydell, 'The Culture of Imperial Abundance: World's Fairs in the Making of American Culture,' in Bronner, *Consuming Visions*, 202. On the relation between fairs and museums, see Neil Harris, 'Museums,

Merchandising, and Popular Taste: The Struggle for Influence,' in Ian M.B. Quimby, ed., *Material Culture and the Study of American Life* (New York 1978), 140–74, reprinted in *Cultural Excursions*, 56–81.

27 Ad for T. Thompson and Son, Mammoth House, *The Liberal* [Richmond Hill], 9 Sept. 1886; *Empire*, 17 Sept. 1891; ad for Oak Hall Clothiers, *World*, 12 Sept. 1894.

28 Letter of 'An Exhibitor,' *Canadian Manufacturer* 17, 7 (4 Oct. 1889), 225–6; *Globe*, 14 Sept. 1892.

29 Newmarket *Era*, 21 Sept. 1894; *Telegram*, 20 Sept. 1883; *News*, 17 Sept. 1894; *Star*, 14 Sept. 1895. The same sorts of complaints were voiced at the Minnesota State Fair. See Karal Ann Marling, *Blue Ribbon: A Social and Pictorial History of the Minnesota State Fair* (St Paul 1990), 274.

30 Letter of W.K. McNaught, *Canadian Grocer*, 29 Sept. 1899, 11; 'Mr. McNaught's Defence of Toronto Fair,' *Canadian Grocer*, 29 Sept. 1899, 17; 'Ellen Drew's Column,' *Star*, 1 Sept. 1900; 'The Weakness of the Toronto Exhibition,' *Canadian Grocer*, 14 Sept. 1900, 14.

31 Richards, *Commodity Culture*, 45.

32 For illustrations of the use of exotic imagery in traditional marketing, see Jackson Lears, 'American Advertising and the Reconstruction of the Body, 1880–1930,' in Kathryn Grover, *Fitness in American Culture: Images of Health, Sport, and the Body, 1830–1940* (Amherst and Rochester 1989), 54–55; Pasi Falk, *The Consuming Body* (London 1994), 162–8.

33 Williams, *Dream World*, 3; Hoh-Cheung Mui and Lorna H. Mui, *Shops and Shopkeeping in Eighteenth-Century England* (Montreal and Kingston, and London 1989), 226; Bronner, *Consuming Visions*, 26; Richards, *Commodity Culture*, 41–5; Leach, 'Strategists of Display,' 109, 119; Monod, *Store Wars*, 152.

34 Letter of Arthur Hemming, *Mail and Empire*, 4 Sept. 1899. See also letter of 'Tourist,' *Mail*, 18 Sept. 1885. More than a decade before Hemming, also commenting on public depredations of the statuary, the *Telegram* had suggested it would soon be necessary to rename the Apollo Belvedere as the Apollo with the Bevelled Ear. See *Telegram*, 16 Sept. 1887.

35 *News*, 29 Aug. 1903. For a recent assessment of the influence of the 1851 Crystal Palace Exhibition on display techniques, see Richards, *Commodity Culture*, 5, 17–71.

36 *Mail*, 2 Sept. 1879; *Mail*, 14 Sept. 1885; *Globe*, 5 Sept. 1894; *Mail*, 10 Sept. 1891.

37 David Dean, *The Architect as Stand Designer: Building Exhibitions, 1895–1983* (London 1985), 11. Dean suggests that in the case of British building-trade shows, most stands were not consciously designed until about 1925 (13).

38 *Globe*, 9 Sept. 1882; *Mail*, 8 Sept. 1894; *Mail*, 6 Sept. 1882; *Globe*, 12 Sept. 1884; *Globe*, 3 Sept. 1879; Whitby *Chronicle*, 14 Sept. 1883; *Star*, 9 Sept. 1904; Orvell, *The Real Thing*, 59.

39 See photo in *Canadian Grocer*, 11 Sept. 1903, 30.

40 Richards, *Commodity Culture*, 5.

41 *Canadian Grocer*, 11 Sept. 1903, 28.

42 *Mail*, 4 Sept. 1879; *Mail*, 8 Sept. 1881; *Globe*, 6 Sept. 1882.

43 *Globe*, 11 Sept. 1889; *Empire*, 19 Sept. 1889; *Mail*, 9 Sept. 1880; *Canadian Grocer*, 11 Sept. 1903, 23; *Globe*, 12 Sept. 1884. Stuart Ewen has emphasized efforts to obliterate the factory from public consciousness. See *Captains of Consciousness: Advertising and the Social Roots of the Consumer Culture* (New York 1976), 78.

44 *Mail*, 9 and 17 Sept. 1886.

45 *News*, 8 Sept. 1887; *Mail*, 12 and 14 Sept. 1888; *News*, 3 Sept. 1903. Katherine Grier has suggested that the model room originated at the 1876 Centennial Exhibition in Philadelphia. See 'Imagining the Parlor, 1830–1880,' in Gerald W.R. Ward, *Perspectives on American Furniture* (New York and London 1988), 210. On the general popularity of the goods-in-context approach to display, see Harris, *Cultural Excursions*, 184–5.

46 See, for example, *Farming* 14, 2 (Oct. 1896), 133.

47 *Mail*, 15 Sept. 1888; *Empire*, 19 Sept. 1890; *World*, 1 Sept. 1903; *Globe*, 11 Sept. 1889.

48 *Mail*, 18 Sept. 1888; *News*, 10 Sept. 1892.

49 *Mail*, 14 Sept. 1888; *Mail and Empire*, 5 Sept. 1895; *News*, 17 Sept. 1886; *Mail*, 20 Sept. 1889; *Canadian Grocer*, 11 Sept. 1903, 18; Orvell, *The Real Thing*, 43.

50 *Globe*, 11 Sept. 1889; *World*, 28 Aug. 1901.

51 Chatham *Weekly Planet*, 18 Sept. 1879; *Mail*, 3 Sept. 1879; Orillia *Packet*, 19 Sept. 1879; *Mail*, 13 Sept. 1883; *Globe*, 14 Sept. 1887; *World*, 6 Sept. 1894.

52 *Globe*, 12 Sept. 1884; *Empire*, 21 Sept. 1888; *News*, 3 Sept. 1903.

53 *World*, 8 Sept. 1886; *Mail*, 18 Sept. 1891. On the prevalence of this technique at nineteenth-century American exhibitions, see Roland Marchand, 'Corporate Imagery and Popular Education: World's Fairs and Expositions in the United States, 1893–1940,' in David E. Nye and Carl Pedersen, eds., *Consumption and American Culture* (Amsterdam 1991), 20–1.

54 *World*, 9 Sept. 1895; *Canadian Grocer*, 11 Sept. 1903, 28; *Mail*, 3 Sept. 1879; *Globe*, 12 Sept. 1883.

55 Richards, *Commodity Culture*, 40–1; *Globe*, 8 Sept. 1881.

56 *Empire*, 11 Sept. 1894; *Canadian Grocer*, 11 Sept. 1903, 16. For photos of the 1903 grocery exhibits, see the same issue of the *Canadian Grocer*, 16–30.

57 See Alan Trachtenberg, *The Incorporation of America: Culture and Society in the Gilded Age* (New York 1982), 231.

58 *Empire*, 11 Sept. 1894. On the recycling of displays, see Strasser, *Satisfaction Guaranteed*, 181–3.

59 Orvell, *The Real Thing*, 35.

60 *Globe*, 12 Sept. 1885; *News*, 7 Sept. 1887; *Mail*, 17 Sept. 1881.

61 *News*, 18 Sept. 1893; *Saturday Night*, 3 Sept. 1898, 9. See also *Globe*, 12 Sept. 1891.

62 Douglas and Isherwood, *The World of Goods*, 65. See, for example, Benjamin McArthur, *Actors and American Culture, 1880–1920* (Philadelphia 1984), 169–89; Mark Carnes, *Secret Ritual and Manhood in Victorian America* (New Haven 1989); David Cannadine, 'The Context, Performance and Meaning of Ritual: The British Monarchy and the "Invention of Tradition," c. 1820–1977,' in Eric Hobsbawm and Terrence Ranger, eds., *The Invention of Tradition* (Cambridge 1983), 101–64.

63 Most recent histories of the modern cemetery deal mainly with landscape rather than monuments, but see John Gary Brown, *Soul in the Stone: Cemetery Art from America's Heartland* (Lawrence 1994); Kenneth T. Jackson and Camilo Jose Vergara, *Silent Cities: The Evolution of the American Cemetery* (New York 1989); Ruth L. Bohan, 'A Home away from Home: Bellefontaine Cemetery, St. Louis, and the Rural Cemetery Movement,' *Prospects* 13 (1988), 135–79; Barbara Rotundo, 'Monumental Bronze: A Representative American Company,' in Richard E. Meyer, ed., *Cemeteries and Gravemarkers: Voices of American Culture* (Ann Arbor and London 1989), 263–91.

64 On these points, see Bronner, *Consuming Visions*, 51, and Rydell, 'The Culture of Imperial Abundance,' 204.

65 Lears, *No Place of Grace*, 85–6.

66 *Weekly Sun*, 9 Sept. 1896; Brampton *Conservator*, 8 Sept. 1896; Port Hope *Guide*, 11 Sept. 1896; *Christian Guardian*, 10 Sept. 1896. Chang's reputation did not save him from racist stereotyping. See Whitby *Chronicle*, 18 Sept. 1896.

67 Brampton *Conservator*, 8 Sept. 1896; *World*, 8 Sept. 1896.

68 In 1903 the formal opening was held in the lecture theatre of the new Dairy Building, where limited seating excluded those without invitations. Initially, the ceremony was conducted in the Main Building, and later was moved to the platform in front of the grandstand.

69 *Telegram*, 8 Sept. 1887. See also Markham *Economist*, 6 Sept. 1900, on the visit of Sidney Fisher, minister of agriculture.

70 Port Hope *Guide*, 28 Sept. 1881; *Globe*, 13 Sept. 1882; *Star*, 2 Sept. 1903; *Mail*, 20 Sept. 1890; *The Liberal* [York], 23 Sept. 1886.

71 See, for example, *Telegram*, 1 Sept. 1898; *Weekly Sun*, 9 Sept. 1897; *Globe*, 8 Sept. 1882. On the attraction of crowds at world's fairs, see Burton Benedict, 'Rituals of Representation: Ethnic Stereotypes and Colonized Peoples at World's Fairs,' in Robert W. Rydell and Nancy Gwinn, eds., *Fair Representations: World's Fairs and the Modern World* (Amsterdam 1994), 50; Fred Miller Robinson, *The Man in the Bowler Hat: His History and Iconography* (Chaple Hill and London 1993), 47.

72 See, for example, *Globe*, 12 Sept. 1891; *Saturday Night*, 2 Sept. 1899, 1.

73 John Kasson, *Rudeness and Civility: Manners in Nineteenth-Century America* (New York 1990), 96; Robinson, *Man in the Bowler Hat*, 46–51. There were occasions when respectable Victorians were not just permitted but expected to gaze. On the importance of the fashionable promenade, for example, see David Scobey, 'Anatomy of the Promenade: The Politics of Bourgeois Sociability in Nineteenth-Century New York,' *Social History* 17, 2 (1992), 203–27.

74 As Stallybrass and White have pointed out, these vantage points were especially esteemed because they minimized the potential for touching strangers while they maximized possibilities of seeing. Stallybrass and White, *Politics and Poetics of Transgression*, 136.

75 Mack [Joseph Thomas Clark], 'Folks at the Fair,' *Saturday Night*, 16 Sept. 1893, 7.

76 'Class 112 – Prizes for Types of Beauty,' CNEA, Industrial Exhibition Association, Prize List for 1884, 62; *Mail*, 12 Sept. 1884. Some American entrepreneurs, notably circus owner Adam Forepaugh in 1888, had more luck with photographic beauty contests, perhaps because his $10,000 prize was far more substantial. See Lois Banner, *American Beauty* (New York 1983), 256–7.

77 *News*, 8 Sept. 1893; *Mail*, 8 Sept. 1894.

78 *Globe*, 12 Sept. 1887. On the respectable anonymity of dress, especially male dress, in the nineteenth century, see Robinson, *Man in the Bowler Hat*, 43–6; Philippe Perrot, *Fashioning the Bourgeoisie: A History of Clothing in the Nineteenth Century* (Princeton 1994), 32–3; Jennifer Clark, *The Face of Fashion: Cultural Studies in Fashion* (London and New York 1994), 183–89; John Harvey, *Men in Black* (Chicago 1995), esp. 23–39.

79 'Sketches of Exhibition Week,' *Saturday Night*, 19 Sept. 1896, 7.

80 There is an extensive literature on the privileged nature of gazing. One of the first and most important discussions is M. Foucault, *The Birth of the Clinic: An Archaeology of Medical Perception* (New York 1973).

81 *Empire*, 6 and 11 Sept. 1893. On the exhibit of foreign peoples and cultures at fairs and exhibitions, see Robert Rydell, *All the World's a Fair: Visions of Empire at American International Expositions, 1876–1916* (Chicago 1984); Timothy Mitchell, *Colonising Egypt* (Berkeley 1991), 1–33; Curtis M. Hinsley, 'The World as Marketplace: Commodification of the Exotic at the World's Columbian Exposition, Chicago, 1893,' in Ivan Karp and Steven D. Lavine, eds., *Exhibiting Cultures: The Poetics and Politics of Museum Display* (Washington, DC, 1991), 344–65; Meg Armstrong, '"A Jumble of Foreignness": The Sublime Musayums of Nineteenth-Century Fairs and Expositions,' *Cultural Critique* 23 (winter 1992–3), 199–250; Benedict, 'Rituals of Representation.' On Western fantasies about Oriental sexuality, see Malek Alloula, *The Colonial Harem* (Minneapolis 1986); Rana Kabbani, *Europe's Myths of Orient: Devise and Rule* (London 1986).

82 *World*, 15 Sept. 1893. Bloom himself described the dance as a 'masterpiece of rhythm and beauty.' See *The Autobiography of Sol Bloom* (New York 1948), 135.

83 Stallybrass and White, *Politics and Poetics of Transgression*, 5.

84 *Canadian Grocer*, 18, 20 and 11 Sept. 1903.

85 *Canadian Grocer*, 11 Sept. 1903, 13.

86 *Globe*, 10 Sept. 1886; *Canadian Grocer*, 11 Sept. 1903, 19, 17, 21, 18.

87 *Mail*, 13 Sept. 1886.

88 *Mail and Empire*, 3 Sept. 1896; *Catholic Register*, 19 Sept. 1895; *Globe*, 12 Sept. 1879; *Mail*, 9 Sept. 1880; *Mail*, 10 Sept. 1891.

89 *Telegram*, 11 Sept. 1886; *Mail*, 14 Sept. 1891.

90 *News*, 5 Sept. 1900.

91 *Mail*, 13 and 17 Sept. 1890. Halil Yousef had guided Frederick Massey and his brother during the Middle Eastern portion of their world tour. When Frederick lay dying, he apparently wrote to Halil, expressing a desire to see him again. The Egyptian embarked for North America, but by the time he arrived, Massey had passed away. It seems likely that Massey's father hired the stranded tourist as part of a settlement to forestall a law suit. See *News*, 22 Aug. 1890.

92 *News*, 3 Sept. 1897.

93 Tony Bennett, 'The Exhibitionary Complex,' *New Formations* 4 (spring, 1988), 76.

94 On the power of spectacle environments to induce social regulation, see

Tony Bennett, *The Birth of the Museum: History, Theory, Politics* (London and New York 1995), 68; McClintock, *Imperial Leather*, 58–9.

Chapter 4: Identity

1 *Globe*, 9 Sept. 1882.
2 Elizabeth Wilson, *The Sphinx in the City* (London 1991), 50.
3 See, for example, *Discipline and Punish: The Birth of the Prison* (New York 1979).
4 For discussions of typing in the nineteenth century, see Miles Orvell, *The Real Thing: Imitation and Authenticity in American Culture, 1880–1940* (Chapel Hill 1989), 88; Meg Armstrong, '"A Jumble of Foreignness": The Sublime Musayums of Nineteenth-Century Fairs and Expositions,' *Cultural Critique* 23 (winter 1992–3), 199–250; Walter Benjamin, *Charles Baudelaire: A Lyric Poet in the Era of High Capitalism*, English translation (London 1973), 36, 54.
5 *News*, 1 Sept. 1887. For other examples of typing, see 'Ben,' 'Casual Comments,' *Labour Advocate*, 11 Sept. 1891, 328; 'Vagaries of a Vagrant,' *News*, 11 Sept. 1902; 'Troubles of a Hotel Clerk,' *Mail and Empire*, 14 Sept. 1903.
6 *Star*, 1 Sept. 1900.
7 *Globe*, 13 Sept. 1882.
8 Jonathan Raban, *Soft City* (London 1974), 30–2; Martha Banta, *Imaging American Women: Idea and Ideals in Cultural History* (New York 1987), 294, 328.
9 'Human Types at the Great Fair,' *Mail and Empire*, 5 Sept. 1903; *Star*, 5 Sept. 1896; *Mail*, 7 Sept. 1889.
10 *Mail*, 10 Sept. 1892; *World*, 30 Aug. 1900. David Nasaw has emphasized the importance of Black entertainers in unifying white audiences. See *Going Out: The Rise and Fall of Public Amusements* (New York 1993), 59.
11 *Mail*, 15 Sept. 1888; *Mail*, 16 Sept. 1890; *Mail*, 7 Sept. 1894. Racism was just as virulent off the grounds. When Haverly's Minstrels, a well-known troupe engaged in 1880, finally secured accommodation in a boarding house, white residents packed up and left. See *Mail*, 13 Sept. 1880.
12 *Mail*, 8 Sept. 1892; *News*, 5 Sept. 1903. On similar tendencies at American fairs, see Robert A. Trennert, 'Fairs, Expositions, and the Changing Face of Southwestern Indians, 1876–1904,' *New Mexico Historical Review* 62 (April 1987), 127–50, and 'Selling Indian Education at World's Fairs and Expositions, 1893–1904,' *American Indian Quarterly* 11, 3 (1987),

203–20. For a discussion of exhibitions sponsered by Canadian Native peoples themselves, see Elsbeth Heaman, Commercial Leviathan: Canadian Exhibitions at Home and Abroad during the Nineteenth Century' (PhD thesis, University of Toronto, 1995), 520–35.

13 *Globe*, 13 Sept. 1886; *World*, 2 Sept. 1901.

14 Robert W. Rydell, *All the World's a Fair: Visions of Empire at American International Expositions, 1876–1916* (Chicago 1984). During the first quarter-century of the Toronto fair, the most influential exhibits of racial hierarchy and white superiority were not pseudo-scientific ethnological displays but grandstand re-enactments of British and American battles in colonial realms.

15 On the use of feminine icons, see Mary P. Ryan, *Women in Public: Between Banners and Ballots, 1825–1880* (Baltimore and London 1990), 26–9, 35–6, 52–4; Angel Kwolek-Folland, *Engendering Business: Men and Women in the Corporate Office, 1870–1930* (Baltimore and London 1994), 131–3. On their use in connection with the Centennial Exposition, see David Scobey, 'What Shall We Do with Our Walls? The Philadelphia Centennial and the Meaning of Household Design,' in Robert W. Rydell and Nancy Gwinn, *Fair Representations: World's Fairs and the Modern World* (Amsterdam 1994), 93–5.

16 *Globe*, 11 Sept. 1893.

17 *Mail and Empire*, 2 Sept. 1895.

18 Paul Greenhalgh, *Ephemeral Vistas: The Expositions Universalles, Great Exhibitions and World's Fairs, 1851–1939* (Manchester 1988), 174. Elspeth Heaman has found that the success of smaller Canadian fairs depended heavily on the quality of the women's sections. See Heaman, 'Commercial Leviathan,' 409–54.

19 *Empire*, 16 Sept. 1891. The superintendent for many years was a Mrs Heaslip. See *Globe*, 14 Sept. 1883; *Mail*, 8 Sept. 1893.

20 *Mail*, 8 Sept. 1893; *Empire*, 16 Sept. 1891.

21 Jean Grant, 'Woman at the Fair,' *Saturday Night* 10 Sept. 1898, 9; *Globe*, 14 Sept. 1883.

22 *Star*, 9 Sept. 1900; *Globe*, 8 Sept. 1887; *Globe*, 6 Sept. 1901.

23 *Mail*, 12 Sept. 1890; *Empire*, 19 Sept. 1889; *Mail*, 7 Sept. 1882; *Mail*, 6 Sept. 1881; *Mail*, 12 Sept. 1884; *Mail*, 10 Sept. 1885; Katherine Leslie, 'Woman's World,' *World*, 1 Sept. 1900.

24 *Mail*, 7 Sept. 1882; *Mail*, 15 Sept. 1880; Katherine Leslie, 'Woman's World,' *World*, 1 Sept. 1900.

25 See, for example, CNEA, Industrial Exhibition Association of Toronto, *List of Premiums, Rules and Regulations for the Fifth Annual Exhibition,*

to be held in The Exhibition Park at the City of Toronto, from Tuesday,
11th September, to Saturday, 22nd September, 1883 (Toronto, 1883), 64.

26 Whitby *Chronicle*, 14 Sept. 1883; *Globe*, 14 Sept. 1883; Katherine Leslie,
'Woman's World,' *World*, 1 Sept. 1900.

27 *Mail*, 5 Sept. 1881.

28 On the cultural significance of the amount of time put into the creation of
handmade articles intended as gifts, see William B. Waits, *The Modern
Christmas in America: A Cultural History of Gift Giving* (New York and
London 1993), 20–1.

29 Mail, 5 Sept. 1881; Mail, 7 Sept. 1882; Whitby *Chronicle*, 14 Sept. 1883;
Katherine Leslie, 'Woman's World,' *World*, 1 Sept. 1900. Scobey suggests
that corresponding sentiments in the American context, though emerging
out of a critique of industrial production, ultimately served the acquisi-
tion of manufactured household goods. See 'What Shall We Do with Our
Walls?' 98–9, 114, 119–20. On Arts and Crafts ideology, see Jackson
Lears, *No Place of Grace: Antimodernism and the Transformation of
American Culture, 1880–1920* (New York 1981), 59–96. On design train-
ing for women in the Arts and Crafts Movement, see Anthea Callen,
Angel in the Studio: Women in the Arts and Crafts Movement, 1870–1914
(London 1979), 20–49; Eileen Boris, *Art and Labor: Ruskin, Morris, and
the Craftsman Ideal in America* (Philadelphia 1986), 91–138; Beverly
Gordon, 'The Fiber of our Lives: Trends and Attitudes about Women's
Textile Art as Reflected in the Literature in America, 1876–1976,' *Jour-
nal of Popular Culture* 10, 3 (winter 1976), 549–51.

30 Sama [Emily Cummings], 'From a Woman's Standpoint,' *Globe*, 16 Sept.
1893; Katherine Leslie, 'Woman's World,' *World*, 1 Sept. 1900.

31 *Mail and Empire*, 8 Sept. 1902; 'H. M. Q.,' 'Snap Shots,' *Mail and Empire*,
1 Sept. 1898; 'Doing the Exhibition,' *Globe*, 13 Sept. 1882; 'Rontgen Rae,'
'Exhibition Snap-Shots,' *Mail and Empire*, 3 Sept. 1896.

32 *Globe*, 10 Sept. 1897; *Globe*, 6 Sept. 1899; CNEA, Industrial Exhibition
Association, Prize List for 1900, 80; CNEA, Industrial Exhibition Association, Prize List for 1902, 89, 92. There were, of course, many other
changes to the Ladies Department Prize List. Most of these introduced
more specific criteria with respect to materials and designs to be used,
and to the ages of contestants. In 1883, for example, Class 113, 'Lace,
Wool Work, Embroidery, Painting, Etc.,' had included two prizes for
painting on china. By 1891 painting on china had become a separate class
with fourteen categories, eight specifying the type of dishes to be painted
and six specifying particular designs. In 1883 there were four knitting
categories, plain wool and cotton, and fancy wool and cotton. By 1890

there were thirteen categories, all of which specified type of clothing to be submitted, type of material to be used, and whether plain or fancy work was required. See Prize List for 1883, 66; Prize List for 1891, 67; Prize List for 1890, 69. Karal Ann Marling has suggested that women's prizes at the Minnesota State Fair were deliberately used to keep alive declining skills 'in order to counter the emergence of a new, undomesticated Minnesota female.' See Karal Ann Marling, *Blue Ribbon: A Social and Pictorial History of the Minnesota State Fair* (St Paul 1990), 95–6.

33 Grant, 'Women at the Fair,' 9.

34 Faith Fenton, 'Woman's Empire,' *Empire*, 7 Sept. 1894. On the history of woman's buildings, see Jeanne Madeline Weimann, *The Fair Women: The Story of The Woman's Building, World Columbian Exposition, Chicago, 1893* (Chicago 1981); Anne L. MacDonald, *Feminine Ingenuity: Women and Invention in America* (New York 1992), 76–97, 179–90; Heaman, 'Commercial Leviathan,' 7–17.

35 *World*, 7 Sept. 1894; 'Women and the Canadian National Exhibition,' *Woman's Century* 4, 3 (Sept. 1916); *Globe*, 6 Sept. 1897; CNEA, Industrial Exhibition Association, Annual Report for 1897, 6. On Mrs Cummings, see Henry James Morgan, ed., *Types of Canadian Women and of Women Who Are or Have Been Connected with Canada*, vol. 1 (Toronto 1903), 67; Henry James Morgan, ed., *The Canadian Men and Women of the Time: A Handbook of Canadian Biography* (Toronto 1898), 232. Many thanks to Donald Smith for bringing the *Woman's Century* article to my attention.

36 *World*, 6 Sept. 1898; *Star*, 9 Sept. 1900; *World*, 2 Sept. 1903. At the Iowa State Fair, agitation for a separate women's building began at roughly the same time as in Toronto, but an equivalent structure took a decade longer to materialize. See Chris Allen Rasmussen, 'State Fair: Culture and Agriculture in Iowa, 1854–1941' (PhD thesis, Rutgers University, The State University of New Jersey, 1992), 287–91.

37 *Mail and Empire*, 4 and 11 Sept. 1903; *Globe*, 10 Sept. 1903; 'Woman's Work at the Fair,' *Mail and Empire*, 2 Sept. 1903.

38 *World*, 3 Sept. 1903; *Star*, 9 Sept. 1900.

39 *Telegram*, 17 Sept. 1883; *Globe*, 17 Sept. 1883; *Mail*, 16 Sept. 1884; OA, MS 573, Fanny Marion Chadwick diaries, 12 Sept. 1894. Chadwick was especially taken with 'a petrified pussy' – 'the best thing of the whole show ... It had been dug up somewhere and was really most fascinating.'

40 On the role of women in the rural economy of nineteenth-century Ontario, see Marjorie Griffin Cohen, *Women's Work, Markets and Economic Development in Nineteenth-Century Ontario* (Toronto 1988), 74–5, 93–112, 155.

41 Kit Coleman, 'Woman's Kingdom,' *Mail*, 8 Sept. 1894.

42 Craig H. Roell, *The Piano in America, 1890–1940* (Chapel Hill and London 1989), 16. See also Julia Eklund Koza, 'Music and the Feminine Sphere: Images of Women as Musicians in *Godey's Lady's Book*, 1830–1877,' *Musical Quarterly* 75 (summer 1991), 103–29.

43 See, for example, *Telegram*, 9 Sept. 1881; *Globe*, 19 Sept. 1883.

44 *Telegram*, 6 Sept. 1879; *Globe*, 13 Sept. 1889.

45 Greenhalgh, *Ephemeral Vistas*, 190. See also Whitney Walton, *France at the Crystal Palace: Bourgeois Taste and Artisan Manufacture in the Nineteenth Century* (Berkeley 1992), 49–69.

46 On the role of the department store in expanding women's access to public space, see William R. Leach, 'Transformations in a Culture of Consumption: Women and Department Stores, 1890–1925,' *Journal of American History* 71 (Sept. 1984), 319–42; Susan Porter Benson, *Counter Cultures: Saleswomen, Managers and Customers in American Department Stores, 1890–1940* (Urbana and Chicago 1986), 75–123.

47 Aside from washrooms, perhaps the only area on the grounds that explicitly excluded women was an upper portion of the new grandstand opened in 1892 which was reserved for men. It may have been a smoking section. See *Star*, 12 Sept. 1895.

48 Coleman and Fenton both wrote for the *Mail and Empire* when the papers amalgamated in 1895. Details of their careers can be found in Jill Downie, *A Passionate Pen: The Life and Times of Faith Fenton* (Toronto 1996), and Barbara M. Freeman, *Kit's Kingdom: The Journalism of Kathleen Blake Coleman* (Ottawa 1989).

49 Kit Coleman, 'Woman's Kingdom,' *Mail*, 20 Sept. 1890. On proper female street behavior, see John F. Kasson, *Rudeness and Civility: Manners in Nineteenth-Century Urban America* (New York 1990), 128–32; Guy Szuberla, 'Ladies, Gentlemen, Flirts, Mashers, Snoozers, and the Breaking of Etiquette's Code,' *Prospects* 15 (1990), 171–2.

50 *Globe*, 15 Sept. 1880; *Mail*, 15 Sept. 1880; *Globe*, 17 Sept. 1883.

51 *Globe*, 13 Sept. 1887; 'Around Town,' *Saturday Night*, 17 Sept. 1892, 1; *World*, 30 Aug. 1902; *Mail*, 14 Sept. 1886; *Globe*, 14 Sept. 1885. Brief biographical remarks about Madame Carlotta can be found in MacDonald, *Feminine Ingenuity*, 157–60.

52 *Mail*, 9 Sept. 1893. On popular assumptions about gender and particular instruments, see Beth Abelson Macleod, '"Whence Comes the Lady Tympanist?" Gender and Instrumental Musicians in America, 1853–1990,' *Journal of Social History* 27 (winter 1993), 291–308.

53 'S.A.C.,' 'The Industrial Exhibition,' Orillia *Packet*, 21 Sept. 1888; Don

[E.E. Sheppard], 'Around Town,' *Saturday Night*, 17 Sept. 1892, 1. Sarah
Curzon was especially known for her writings on Canadian historical
subjects. She lived in Toronto. See Morgan, *Canadian Men and Women*,
235–6.

54 Faith Fenton, 'Exhibition Snapshots,' *Mail and Empire*, 3 Sept. 1897;
Globe, 21 Sept. 1883; Kit Coleman, 'Woman's Kingdom,' *Mail and
Empire*, 2 Sept. 1899; Faith Fenton, 'Exhibition Snapshots,' *Mail and
Empire*, 2 Sept. 1897.

55 Janet Davis has argued recently that semi-nude female circus performers
were not sexually transgressive, but rather represented contemporary
ideals of the athletic yet modest New Woman. Scanty dress, she suggests,
was understood by audiences to be a practical necessity for dangerous
physical activities. My evidence from the Toronto fair suggests that many
nineteenth-century viewers did see such female performers as transgressive. See Janet Davis, 'Walking the Tightrope of Propriety: Female Sexuality, and Community Disorder at the American Circus, 1890–1920,'
unpublished paper delivered to 1994 Canadian Historical Association
Meeting, Calgary.

56 Judith Fryer, 'Woman and Space: The Flowering of Desire,' *Prospects* 9
(1984), 191.

57 'S.A.C.,' 'Toronto Industrial Exhibition,' Orillia *Packet*, 9 Sept. 1892.

58 Greenhalgh, *Ephemeral Vistas*, 191.

59 Ryan, *Women in Public*, 73.

60 Janet Wolff has argued that the 'flaneuse' was 'rendered impossible by
the sexual divisions of the nineteenth century.' See *Feminine Sentences:
Essays on Women and Culture* (Berkeley and Los Angeles 1990), 47. See
also Anne McClintock, *Imperial Leather: Race, Gender and Sexuality in
the Colonial Conquest* (New York 1995), 81–2.

61 Ryan, *Women in Public*, 178.

62 Richard L. Bushman, *The Refinement of America: Persons, Houses, Cities*
(New York 1992), 353–4, 378, 400. On the persistence and meaning of
rural/urban distinctions in late nineteenth-century America, see also William Cronon, *Nature'e Metropolis: Chicago and the Great West* (New York
and London 1991), 357–69.

63 Markham *Economist*, 16 Sept. 1886; Elora *Express*, 15 Sept. 1892; letter
of 'Agricola,' Orillia *Packet*, 5 Sept. 1890.

64 University of Western Ontario, Weldon Library, Regional History Room,
B 4038, file 7, Joseph Seymour Fallows Collection, John Fallows to his
mother, 10 Sept. 1881; *Guelph Daily Mercury and Advertiser*, 7 Sept.
1887. See also 'The Industrial Exhibition,' Exhibition Supplement to the

Farmer's Advocate and Home Magazine, Sept./Oct. 1881, 3; *Dumfries Reformer* [Galt], 25 Sept. 1884 and 29 Sept. 1889; 'The Agricultural Shows,' Milton *Reformer*, 17 Sept. 1896.

65 Peterborough *Examiner*, 15 Sept. 1885; Orillia *Times and Expositor for East Simcoe and North Ontario*, 28 Sept. 1886; 'The Band at Toronto,' Chatham *Daily Planet*, 15 Sept. 1892.

66 'They Went to the City,' Port Hope *Guide*, 13 Sept. 1895. Some farmers who kept diaries were far more interested in what had gone on at home while they were away than in what had transpired at the fair. David Nelson, from Lang near Peterborough, left on 12 September for the 1882 show and came home on the 15th. His entries for the intervening days were 'plowing' and 'wind blew nearly all apples off trees.' These descriptions must have been written after he got home, but they suggest his emotional priorities while away. OA, MU 842, 1–N-2, David Nelson diary, 12 to 15 Sept. 1882. See also OA, MS 273, Joseph H. Wooley diaries, 13 Sept. 1894 and 5 Sept. 1896.

67 *Mail*, 10 Sept. 1881; *Empire*, 16 Sept. 1891.

68 *Empire*, 8 Sept. 1890; *Globe*, 6 Sept. 1894; CNEA, Industrial Exhibition Association, Report for 1894, 11. In 1879 the Grange had put up a tent on the grounds for the comfort of members, but there is no indication that the effort was repeated. See OA, MS 834, reel 5, A.J. Hughes diary, 17 and 18 Sept. 1879.

69 *News*, 15 Sept. 1894; *Mail and Empire*, 3 and 6 Sept. 1895; *World*, 11 Sept. 1896; *Mail and Empire*, 29 Aug. 1899; *Star*, 2 Sept. 1903. The fifteen organizations in 1895 included the WCTU, YMCA, and Ontario Veterinary Association. See *Mail and Empire*, 6 Sept. 1895.

70 *Mail and Empire*, 31 Aug. 1897; *Globe*, 2 Sept. 1897.

71 *Globe*, 2 Sept. 1897; *Mail and Empire*, 9 Sept. 1902.

72 *Star*, 2 Sept. 1903; Mary Ann Clawson, *Constructing Brotherhood: Class, Gender and Fraternalism* (Princeton 1989), 17; *Catholic Register*, 19 Sept. 1895.

73 *Canadian Statesman* [Bowmanville], 19 Sept. 1879.

74 Guelph *Daily Mercury and Advertiser*, 5 Sept. 1893; Guelph *Daily Mercury and Advertiser*, 19 Sept. 1890; Peterborough *Examiner*, 20 Sept. 1888.

75 *Canadian Champion and County of Halton Intelligencer*, 1 Sept. 1898; Orillia *Times*, 20 Sept. 1894; *Canadian Statesman* [Bowmanville], 29 Aug. 1900; *Ontario Gleaner* [Cannington], 30 Aug. 1900.

76 G.B. Ryan ad, Guelph *Daily Mercury and Advertiser*, 18 Sept. 1890; 'Buying at Toronto,' Guelph *Daily Mercury and Advertiser*, 18 Sept. 1890.

77 'Patronize Your Town,' Milton *Reformer*, 3 Sept. 1896; 'Spend Your Money at Home,' *Northern Advance* [Barrie], 2 Sept. 1897. On hostility to department stores in Toronto, see Joy L. Santink, *Timothy Eaton and the Rise of His Department Store* (Toronto 1990), 203–22.

78 *Star*, 10 Sept. 1897; Elaine S. Abelson, *When Ladies Go A-Thieving: Middle-Class Shoplifters in the Victorian Department Store* (New York 1989).

79 *Telegram*, 15 Sept. 1881.

80 OA, MS 185, Archibald Gillies diaries, 9 and 10 Sept. 1895.

81 *Mail*, 14 Sept. 1891.

82 MTRL, Baldwin Room, Helen Grant Macdonald diary, 16 Sept. 1891; *Globe*, 15 Sept. 1881; Kit Coleman, 'Woman's Kingdom,' *Mail*, 8 Sept. 1894; *Telegram*, 10 Sept. 1892; 'Human Types at the Great Fair,' *Mail and Empire*, 5 Sept. 1903.

83 *Telegram*, 15 Sept. 1881. On the rural myth, see W.L. Morton, 'Victorian Canada,' in W.L. Morton, *The Shield of Achilles: Aspects of Canada in the Victorian Age* (Toronto 1968), 312; Carl Berger, *The Sense of Power: Studies in the Ideas of Canadian Imperialism, 1867–1914* (Toronto 1970), 177–83.

84 'Crowding to the Cities,' *Mail*, 6 Sept. 1893; *Telegram*, 16 Sept. 1886; 'Our Exhibition,' *Mail*, 2 Sept. 1893. On ambivalent attitudes towards rural life, see Blaine A. Brownell, 'The Agrarian and Urban Ideals: Environmental Images in Modern America,' *Journal of Popular Culture* 5, 3 (winter 1971), 576–87; David B. Danbom, *The Resisted Revolution: Urban America and the Industrialization of Agriculture, 1900–1930* (Ames 1979), 24–36.

85 *Empire*, 14 Sept. 1893; Don [E.E. Sheppherd], 'Around Town,' *Saturday Night* 22 Sept. 1888, 1; *Telegram*, 10 Sept. 1881; Carolyn Strange, *Toronto's Girl Problem: The Perils and Pleasures of the City, 1880–1930* (Toronto 1995), 3–4 and passim.

86 *World*, 21 Sept. 1888; Madge Merton, 'Madge Merton's Page,' *Star*, 7 Sept. 1901; 'Human Types at the Fair,' *Mail and Empire*, 5 Sept. 1903; Don [E.E. Sheppard], 'Around Town,' *Saturday Night*, 20 Sept. 1890, 1. This assessment of the lot of the farm wife was not peculiar to Ontario. See Rasmussen, 'State Fair,' 284.

87 *World*, 21 Sept. 1888; *News*, 6 Sept. 1899; *News*, 16 Sept. 1886; 'Young Hayseed,' *Saturday Night*, 22 Sept. 1888, 6.

88 *Globe*, 14 Sept. 1882; *News*, 16 Sept. 1886; C.G. Porter, *World*, 9 Sept. 1903; Charles F. Raymond, 'Reuben,' *Star*, 3 Sept. 1903.

89 Swiz, 'At the Fair,' *Grip* 21, 13 (15 Sept. 1883), np; *Mail and Empire*, 2 Sept. 1899.

90 *News*, 6 Sept. 1899. See also 'The Impressionist,' 'Chromatics,' *Star*, 5 Sept. 1896.

91 On the popularity of 'hayseed acts' in vaudeville, see Nasaw, *Going Out*, 53.

92 Faith Fenton, *Mail and Empire*, 10 Sept. 1897; 'Sama' [Emily Cummings], *Globe*, 8 Sept. 1900; *Globe*, 6 Sept. 1901; 'Don' [E.E. Sheppard], 'Around Town,' *Saturday Night*, 20 Sept. 1890, 1.

93 *News*, 10 Sept. 1892.

94 'Chromatics,' *Star*, 10 Sept. 1898.

95 *World*, 17 Sept. 1884; *Mail*, 9 Sept. 1880; 'The Vagrant,' 'Vagaries of a Vagrant,' *News*, 11 Sept. 1902. David Danbom suggests that while negative rural stereotypes were not new in late nineteenth-century American society, their earlier gently mocking or patronizing tone was replaced by one that was 'almost savage.' See *Born in the Country: A History of Rural America* (Baltimore and London 1995), 151.

96 Whitby *Chronicle*, 9 Sept. 1892.

97 This is an example of what Dominick LaCapra calls the 'always already.' Categories used to describe the world or to organize existence inevitably embody opposite principles that are 'always already' present, whether acknowledged or not. See LaCapra, *Rethinking Intellectual History: Texts, Contexts, Language* (Ithaca 1983), 151–2; Lloyd S. Kramer, 'Literature, Criticism, and Historical Imagination: The Literary Challenge of Hayden White and Dominick LaCapra,' in Lynn Hunt, ed., *The New Cultural History* (Berkeley 1989), 112.

98 'Mack' [Joseph Thomas Clark], 'Folks at the Fair,' *Saturday Night*, 16 Sept. 1893, 7.

99 'Mack' [Joseph Thomas Clark], 'Around Town,' *Saturday Night*, 17 Sept. 1892, 1; 'Cousin Elsie,' *News*, 19 Sept. 1887; Madge Merton, *Globe*, 19 Sept. 1891; 'Ben,' 'Casual Comments,' *Labour Advocate*, 11 Sept. 1891, 324.

100 Kasson, *Rudeness and Civility*, 257–8; Raban, *Soft City*, 64. On changing notions of the self in the late nineteenth century, see Warren I. Susman, '"Personality" and the Making of Twentieth-Century Culture,' *Culture as History: The Transformation of American Society in the Twentieth Century* (New York 1984), 271–85. On the way in which nineteenth-century European urban bourgeoisies defined themselves in relation to groups and institutions representing otherness, see Scott Lash, *Sociology of Postmodernism* (London and New York 1990), 201–36.

101 This is not to deny the cultural influence of such manuals. See Kasson,

Rudeness and Civility, and Philippe Perrot, *Fashioning the Bourgeoisie: A History of Clothing in the Nineteenth Century* (Princeton 1994), 87–91.

102 University of Western Ontario, Weldon Library, Regional History Room, B 4038, file 7, Joseph Seymour Fallows Collection, John Fallows to his mother, 14 Sept. 1881.

103 On the complexity of multiple identities in modern society, see Douglas Kellner, 'Popular Culture and the Construction of Postmodern Identities,' in Scott Lash and Jonathan Friedman, eds., *Modernity and Identity* (Oxford and Cambridge, Mass., 1992), 141–2.

Chapter 5: Space

1 On various methods of illegal entry see *Mail*, 19 Sept. 1888; *Globe*, 7 Sept. 1882; Katherine Leslie, 'Woman's World,' *World*, 30 Aug. 1900. The misuse of passes got to be such a common occurrence that they were eventually marked with codes indicating prominent physical characteristics of the legitimate holder. On the poor quality of the fences see CNEA, Industrial Exhibition Association, Annual Report for 1891, 6; *Telegram*, 3 Sept. 1881. For examples of the apprehension of illegal entrants, see *Mail*, 9 and 16 Sept. 1880; *Globe*, 15 Sept. 1881; *News*, 11 Sept. 1891; *News*, 6 Sept. 1895.

2 See Peter Stallybrass and Allon White, *The Politics and Poetics of Transgression* (Ithaca 1986), 31–7. For a discussion of how liminality complicates the establishment of spatial identity, see Sharon Zukin, 'Postmodern Urban Landscapes: Mapping Culture and Power,' in Scott Lash and Jonathon Friedman, eds., *Modernity and Identity* (Oxford and Cambridge, Mass. 1992), 222.

3 'Scenes at the Fair,' *Mail*, 20 Sept. 1890.

4 *News*, 5 Sept. 1900.

5 As Richard Bushman has pointed out, most cities invested in a 'genteel architectural assemblage,' including concert halls, libraries, museums, colleges, and pleasure gardens, to establish and elevate urban refinement. A crystal palace, with its clear allusion to aristocratic antecedents, belonged to the same grouping. See *The Refinement of America: People, Houses, Cities* (New York 1992), 358.

6 John Withrow, 'Born Out of Protest,' *Once upon a Century: 100 Year History of the 'Ex'* (Toronto 1978), 14, 16; V.M. Roberts, *The Trail of the Canadian National Exhibition* (Toronto 1925), 32, 51.

7 On the domestic uses of glass and iron architecture, see Georg Kohl-

maier and Barna von Sartory, *Houses of Glass: A Nineteenth-Century Building Type* (Cambridge, Mass., and London 1986).

8 Johann Friedrich Geist, *Arcades: The History of a Building Type* (Cambridge, Mass., and London 1983); Pierre Missac, *Walter Benjamin's Passages* (Cambridge, Mass., and London 1995), 148–51.

9 Neil Harris, *Cultural Excursions: Marketing Appetites and Cultural Tastes in Modern America* (Chicago and London 1990), 115; Paul Greenhalgh, *Ephemeral Vistas: The Expositions Universalles, Great Exhibitions and World's Fairs, 1851–1939* (Manchester 1988), 15.

10 'On the Wing,' *Farmer's Advocate* June 1885, 162; *World*, 14 Sept. 1888; *Mail*, 29 Aug. 1879.

11 'Horticultural Hall,' *Mail*, 8 Sept. 1882.

12 *Canadian Statesman* [Bowmanville], 14 Sept. 1883; *West Durham News* [Bowmanville], 18 Sept. 1885; *Globe*, 4 Sept. 1886; *Globe*, 11 Sept. 1888.

13 *News*, 17 Sept. 1886; *Globe*, 14 Sept. 1887; *Globe*, 10 Sept. 1888.

14 M. Christine Boyer, *Dreaming the Rational City: The Myth of American City Planning* (Cambridge, Mass., and London 1983), 9.

15 Ian M. Drummond, *Progress without Planning: The Economic History of Ontario from Confederation to the Second World War* (Toronto 1987), 166–7.

16 David Schuyler, *The New Urban Landscape: The Redefinition of City Form in Nineteenth-Century America* (Baltimore and London 1986), 28–31; Galen Cranz, *The Politics of Park Design: A History of Urban Parks in America* (Cambridge, Mass., and London 1982), 3–7.

17 Paul Boyer, *Urban Masses and Moral Order in America, 1820-1920* (Cambridge, Mass., and London 1978), 131; Carl Smith, *Urban Disorder and the Shape of Belief: The Great Chicago Fire, the Haymarket Bomb, and the Model Town of Pullman* (Chicago and London 1995), 2–4, 6–9; Alan Trachtenberg, *The Incorporation of America: Culture and Society in the Gilded Age* (New York 1982), 103; David Scobey, 'Anatomy of the Promenade: The Politics of Bourgeois Sociability in Nineteenth-Century New York,' *Social History* 17, 2 (May 1992), 212. On the nineteenth-century literature of urban menace and secrecy, see Larry K. Hartsfield, *The American Response to Professional Crime, 1870-1917* (Westport, Conn., and London 1985), 77–104; Adrienne Siegel, *The Image of the American City in Popular Literature, 1820-1870* (Port Washington and London 1981), 13–60; Raymond Williams, *Country and City in the Modern Novel* (Swansea 1987), 10. On the compact nature of the pre-industrial city, see Stuart M. Blumin, *The Emergence of the Middle Class: Social Experience in the American City, 1760–1900* (Cambridge 1989), 21–52;

Bushman, *The Refinement of America*, 356; Peter Burke, 'We, the People: Popular Culture and Popular Identity in Modern Europe,' in Lash and Friedman, *Modernity and Identity*, 304. On the breakdown of the compact, heterogeneous character of activity in Toronto between 1860 and 1900, see Peter G. Goheen, *Victorian Toronto, 1850-1900: Pattern and Process of Growth* (Chicago 1970); Gunter Gad and Deryck W. Holdsworth, 'Streetscape and Society: The Changing Built Environment of King Street, Toronto,' in Roger Hall, William Westfall, and Laurel Sefton Mac-Dowell, eds., *Patterns of the Past: Interpreting Ontario's History* (Toronto and Oxford 1988), 178; Barbara Sanford, 'The Political Economy of Land Development in Nineteenth Century Toronto,' *Urban History Review / Revue d'histoire urbaine* 16, 1 (June 1987), 28–9; K.M. Campbell, 'The Changing Residential Patterns in Toronto, 1880–1910' (MA thesis, University of Toronto, 1971), 74–9.

18 Christine Boyer, *Dreaming the Rational City*, 18; Paul Boyer, *Urban Masses*, 175–80; Bushman, *The Refinement of America*, 421–2. On concerns about vice in late nineteenth-century Toronto and coercive responses to it, see Carolyn Strange, *Toronto's Girl Problem: The Perils and Pleasures of the City, 1880–1930* (Toronto 1995), 55–9, 96–109, and passim.

19 Gunther Barth, *Fleeting Moments: Nature and Culture in American History* (New York and Oxford 1990), 125–48; John Brinckerhoff Jackson, *Discovering the Vernacular Landscape* (New Haven and London 1984), 127–30; Ann Leighton, *American Gardens of the Nineteenth Century: 'For Comfort and Affluence'* (Amherst 1987), 138–42; Francesco Dal Co, 'From Parks to the Region: Progressive Ideology and the Reform of the American City,' in Giorgio Ciucci et al., *The American City: From the Civil War to the New Deal* (Cambridge, Mass., 1979), 154–61; Paul Boyer, *Urban Masses*, 236.

20 Roy Rosenzweig has pointed out that working people were not passive recipients of parks created by middle classes. When they had the opportunity, working people were determined to shape park spaces to suit their priorities. See *Eight Hours for What We Will: Workers and Leisure in an Industrial City, 1870–1920* (Cambridge 1983), 127–40. The same point is made in Robert A.J. McDonald, *Making Vancouver: Class, Status, and Social Boundaries, 1863–1913* (Vancouver 1996), 172–3.

21 Christine Boyer, *Dreaming the Rational City*, 34–8; Allan Smith, 'Farms, Forests and Cities: The Image of the Land and the Rise of the Metropolis in Ontario, 1860-1914,' in David Keane and Colin Read, *Old Ontario: Essays in Honour of J.M.S. Careless* (Toronto 1990), 83–5; Richard C. Foglesong, *Planning the Capitalist City: The Colonial Era to the 1920s*

(Princeton 1986), 90–2, 97–9, 115–17; Paul Rabinow, *French Modern: Norms and Forms of the Social Environment* (Cambridge, Mass., and London 1989), 256–60.

22 Leading park advocate Frederick Law Olmsted himself was well aware of the deficiencies of country life. See Susanna S. Zetzel, 'The Garden in the Machine: The Construction of Nature in Olmsted's Central Park,' *Prospects* 14 (1989), 310-11.

23 Cranz, *The Politics of Park Design*, 24–6. On the appeal of the pastoral landscape in American culture, see James L. Machor, *Pastoral Cities: Urban Ideals and the Symbolic Landscape of America* (Madison 1987), 5; Blaine A. Brownell, 'The Agrarian and Urban Ideals: Environmental Images in Modern America,' *Journal of Popular Culture* 5, 3 (winter 1971), 576–87.

24 Trachtenberg, *The Incorporation of America*, 108–12; Paul Boyer, *Urban Masses*, 241. On other aspects of the Victorians' manipulation of space for moral purposes, see James A. Schmiechin, 'The Victorians, the Historians, and the Idea of Modernism,' *American Historical Review* 93, 2 (April 1988), 312.

25 CTA, RG 17A, Exhibition Committee Minutes, box 4 (1878–88), 1878, minute 89, 10 Sept. 1878. Not long after this decision was made, a portion of Toronto Island was officially declared a park, ending years of newspaper and public agitation for the creation there of a landscaped resort. See Sally Gibson, *More than an Island: A History of the Toronto Island* (Toronto 1984), 88. There is little information about the history of the park movement in Toronto, but see David Bain, 'George Allen and the Horticultural Gardens,' *Ontario History* 87 (Sept. 1995), 231–52, as well as Alan Smith, 'Farms, Forests, and Cities,' 83–5; C. Pelham Mulvany, *Toronto: Past and Present* (Toronto 1884), 97–104, 263–6; C.S. Clark, *Of Toronto the Good: A Social Study. The Queen City of Canada as It Is* (1898; Montreal 1970), 77–9; J. Lawlor Woods, *Toronto Illustrated: Guidebook and Souvenir* (Toronto 1897), 96–104. On the park movement elsewhere in Canada, see Robert A.J. McDonald, '"Holy Retreat" or "Practical Breathing Spot"? Class Perceptions of Vancouver's Stanley Park, 1910–1913,' *Canadian Historical Review* 65 (June 1984), 127–53; Mary Ellen Cavett, H. John Selwood, and John C. Lehr, 'Social Philosophy and the Early Development of Winnipeg's Public Parks,' *Urban History Review / Revue d'histoire urbaine* 11, 1 (June 1982), 27–39.

26 On the presumed importance of trees to city parks and urban health, see Allan Smith, 'Farms, Forests, and Cities,' 84, and Mulvany, *Toronto*, 101.

27 CTA, RG 17A, Exhibition Committee Minutes, box 4 (1878–88), 1879,

minute 9; Greenhalgh, *Ephemeral Vistas*, 46–7. On standard features of urban parks, see Cranz, *The Politics of Park Design*, 32–56.

28 *Globe*, 12 Sept. 1883; *World*, 6 Sept. 1886; *Mail*, 1 Sept. 1881; *Mail*, 30 Aug. 1883.

29 *Mail*, 6 Sept. 1882; *Mail*, 30 Aug. 1883. See also the full-page illustration of the grounds in the *Canadian Illustrated News*, 18 Sept. 1880, 189.

30 *Globe*, 13 Sept. 1882; 'On the Fair Grounds,' *Globe*, 7 Sept. 1897.

31 Matthew Cooper, 'Access to the Waterfront: Transformations of Meaning on the Toronto Lakeshore,' in Robert Rotenberg and Gary McDonogh, eds., *The Cultural Meaning of Urban Space* (Westport and London 1993), 161.

32 *Mail*, 18 Sept. 1891; *Globe*, 9 Sept. 1882; 'The Lake and the Fair,' *Mail*, 5 Sept. 1899; 'The Exhibitions,' *Farmer's Advocate* Oct. 1882, 249. On the importance of the picturesque and sublime in nineteenth-century appreciation of landscape, see Patricia Jason, *Wild Things: Nature, Culture, and Tourism in Ontario, 1790–1914* (Toronto 1995), 7–13.

33 *Mail*, 29 Aug. 1888.

34 CTA, RG2 B2, Toronto Executive Committee Communications, box 7, Henry Scadding to Mayor Boswell, 3 May 1884; Mulvany, *Toronto*, 103.

35 CTA, RG2 B2, Toronto Executive Committee Communications, box 10, no. 381, Henry Scadding to Mayor and Corporation, 2 June 1886; CTA, Toronto City Council Minutes, 1887, appendix 70, Executive Committee Report no. 15, 2 June 1887, items 590 and 591. See also OA, Horwood Collection of Architectural Drawings, 474, Langley and Burke, 1884–5, Fort Rouille Monument, elevations and sections.

36 CTA, RG2 B2, Toronto Executive Committee Communications, box 10, no. 381, Henry Scadding to Mayor and Corporation, 2 June 1886; S.A.C. [Sarah Ann Curzon], 'Fort Toronto,' *Mail*, 6 Sept. 1887.

37 See Mulvany, *Toronto*, 101; Clark, *Of Toronto the Good*, 77–9.

38 On the importance of the promenade as a nineteenth-century social institution, see David Scobey, 'Anatomy of the Promenade: The Politics of Bourgeois Sociability in Nineteenth-century New York,' *Social History* 17, 2 (May 1992), 203–27.

39 William Lyon Mackenzie King, *The Mackenzie King Diaries, 1893–1931* (Toronto 1973), 13 Sept. 1895; *Empire*, 16 Sept. 1889. On the popularity of promenading, see also *Mail*, 8 Sept. 1882; 'Social and Personal,' *Saturday Night*, 11 Sept. 1897, 3; *Mail and Empire*, 1 Sept. 1898.

40 *Mail*, 17 Sept. 1885; *Globe*, 21 Sept. 1888; *World*, 14 Sept. 1888.

41 *Mail*, 9 Sept. 1892; *Globe*, 7 Sept. 1893; *Star*, 1 Sept. 1899.

42 *Mail*, 29 Aug. 1879; *Globe*, 6 and 7 Sept. 1880; *Globe*, 13 Sept. 1883.

43 *Globe*, 11 Sept. 1885; *Globe*, 3 Sept. 1888.

44 *Mail*, 6 and 12 Sept. 1883; *Mail*, 10 Sept. 1884; *Globe*, 10 and 12 Sept. 1884; *Canadian Manufacturer* 19, 6 (19 Sept. 1890), 193; *Mail*, 12 Sept. 1884; *Globe*, 9 Sept. 1886; CNEA, Industrial Exhibition Association of Toronto, Annual Report for 1886, 4. During the first exhibition, *Mail* staff had occupied a wooden 'kiosk' which may have been permanent. Notwithstanding its charming appearance in a drawing in the *Canadian Illustrated News*, it was probably quite small and dark. See the *Illustrated News* 20 (27 Sept. 1879), 208. On the development of private corporate pavilions at world's fairs, see Burton Benedict et al., *The Anthropology of World's Fairs: San Francisco's Panama Pacific International Exposition of 1915* (London and Berkeley 1983), 24.

45 See, for example, *News*, 15 Sept. 1883.

46 *Mail*, 10 Sept. 1884; *World*, 5 Sept. 1881; *Mail*, 6 and 8 Sept. 1886; *World*, 8 Sept. 1886; *Globe*, 28 Aug. 1899. See also *Telegram*, 5 Sept. 1887; *Globe*, 8 Sept. 1891.

47 Reid Badger estimated on the basis of paid admissions that 5 to 10 per cent of the American population visited the fair. A good number of those people undoubtedly came from southern Ontario and Toronto. See Badger, *The Great American Fair: The World's Columbian Exposition and American Culture* (Chicago 1979), 190.

48 Schuyler, *The New Urban Landscape*, 189. See also William R. Taylor, *In Pursuit of Gotham: Culture and Commerce in New York* (New York and Oxford 1992), 54–5.

49 On the architecture of the Chicago Exhibition and its influence on the City Beautiful Movement, see also William H. Wilson, *The City Beautiful Movement* (Baltimore and London 1989), 53–74; Neil Harris, 'Great American Fairs and American Cities: The Role of Chicago's Columbian Exposition,' in Harris, *Cultural Excursions: Marketing Appetites and Cultural Tastes in Modern America* (Chicago and London 1990), 115–19; Carl Smith, *Urban Disorder*, 224–6; Trachtenberg, *The Incorporation of America*, 212–14; Mario Manieri-Elia, 'Toward an "Imperial City": Daniel H. Burnham and the City Beautiful Movement,' in Ciucci, *The American City*, 1–142; Christine Boyer, *Dreaming the Rational City*, 46; Paul Boyer, *Urban Masses*, 182–3; James Gilbert, *Perfect Cities: Chicago's Utopias of 1893* (Chicago and London 1991), 75–130. Debora Silverman has suggested that the Chicago grounds were influenced significantly by the 1889 Paris Exhibition. See 'The 1889 Exhibition: The Crisis of Bourgeois Individualism,' *Oppositions* 8 (spring 1977), 75. Richard Foglesong has noted that the Chicago fair was an important influence on the City Beau-

tiful Movement, not just with respect to aesthetics but also in terms of its emphasis on expert planning, collaborative effort, and centralized administration. See Foglesong, *Planning the Capitalist City*, 134.

50 On the differences between the park movement and the City Beautiful Movement, see Schuyler, *The New Urban Landscape*, 190–5; Thomas Bender, *Toward An Urban Vision: Ideas and Institutions in Nineteenth Century America* (Baltimore and London 1975), 184–7.

51 Wilson, *The City Beautiful Movement*, 64–5; McDonald, *Makaing Vancouver*, 169–73; Walter Van Nus, 'The Plan-Makers and the City: Architects, Engineers, Surveyors and Urban Planning in Canada, 1890–1939' (PhD thesis, University of Toronto, 1975), 134–5, 138.

52 *Empire*, 15 Sept. 1894; *Mail and Empire*, 14 Sept. 1895. See also *Globe*, 5 Sept. 1894.

53 *The Trader and Canadian Jeweller*, Oct. 1900, 6.

54 *Globe*, 1 Sept. 1903. Priorities and plans for the new buildings had been decided by the Exhibition Association in the spring of 1901. See *Mail and Empire*, 3 and 4 May 1901.

55 For one example of the growing middle-class appreciation of art in Toronto, see OA, MU 1292, M.O. Hammond Papers, Diary, 5 Sept. 1903.

56 OA, MU 2251, Ontario Society of Artists, *Reasons for a New Art Gallery at the Industrial Exhibition with Designs: A Report from the Ontario Society of Artists to the Industrial Exhibition Association* (Toronto 1899); *News*, 3 Sept. 1897.

57 On the role of art in progressive ideology, see Helen Lefkowitz Horowitz, *Culture and the City: Cultural Philanthropy in Chicago from the 1880s to 1917* (Lexington 1976), x, 6–7; Lawrence W. Levine, *Highbrow / Lowbrow: The Emergence of Cultural Hierarchy in America* (Cambridge, Mass., and London 1988), 177; Harris, *Cultural Excursions*, 19–21.

58 *Mail and Empire*, 2 Sept. 1902.

59 *Star*, 2 Sept. 1902; *Globe*, 4 Sept. 1902.

60 OA, Ontario Society of Artists Collection, MU 2252, anonymous notebook with information relating to relationship between the society and the Exhibition Association, 33, 38. The first gallery was given over to Natural History in 1905.

61 On the establishment of a regular gallery in Toronto, see David Kimmel, 'Toronto Gets a Gallery: The Origins and Development of the City's Permanent Public Art Museum,' *Ontario History* 84, 3 (Sept. 1992), 195–210.

62 *News*, 28 Aug. 1903; OA, MU 1292, M.O. Hammond Papers, Diary, 5 Sept. 1903.

63 *Mail and Empire*, 26 Aug. 1903.

64 *Mail and Empire*, 2 Sept. 1902; *Star*, 13 Sept. 1902.
65 'Displays of Dry Goods at the Dominion Exhibition,' *Dry Goods Review*, Oct. 1903, 69–70.
66 *Mail and Empire*, 29 Aug. 1903.
67 OA, Horwood Collection, 1684, Plans for suggested improvements to the Exhibition Grounds.
68 On the shift from appeariential to spatial ordering, see Lyn H. Lofland, *A World of Strangers: Order and Action in Urban Public Space* (New York 1973).
69 Richard Sennett, *Flesh and Stone: The Body and the City in Western Civilization* (New York and London 1994), 276–8; Blumin, *The Emergence of the Middle Class*, 21–5.
70 Christine Boyer, *Dreaming the Rational City*, 33; Edward W. Soja, *Postmodern Geographies: The Reassertion of Space in Critical Social Theory* (London and New York 1989), 34.
71 As Derek Gregory has suggested, urban modernization in late nineteenth-century Europe, like the 'Hausmannization' of Paris, frequently involved the imposing of domestic standards of interior order on savage 'exterior' streets. See *Geographical Imaginations* (Cambridge, Mass., and Oxford 1994), 244.
72 On the increasing sharpness of social boundaries in nineteenth-century Toronto, see Goheen, *Victorian Toronto*, 220 and passim.
73 On interest in introducing park and City Beautiful elements to Toronto, see Van Nus, 'The Plan-Makers and the City,' 134–140; J.M.S. Careless, *Toronto to 1918: An Illustrated History* (Toronto 1984), 193; Byron E. Walker, 'A Comprehensive Plan for Toronto (1906),' in Paul Rutherford, ed., *Saving the Canadian City: The First Phase, 1880–1920* (Toronto and Buffalo 1974), 222–25; John C. Weaver, 'The Modern City Realized: Toronto Civic Affairs, 1880–1915,' in Alan F.J. Artibise and Gilbert A. Stelter, eds., *The Usable Urban Past: Planning and Politics in the Modern Canadian City* (Toronto 1979), 60-2; Douglas Richardson, ed., *Beaux-Arts Toronto: Permanence and Change in Early 20th Century Architecture* (Toronto 1973).

Chapter 6: Entertainment

1 Quoted in the *World*, 24 Sept. 1888; *Mail*, 12 Sept. 1884.
2 Peter Stallybrass and Allon White, *The Politics and Poetics of Transgression* (Ithica 1986), 30. On the proliferation of entertainment at a major American agricultural fair, see Chris Allen Rasmussen, 'State Fair: Cul-

ture and Agriculture in Iowa, 1854–1941' (PhD thesis, Rutgers University, The State University of New Jersey, 1992), passim.

3 For an excellent survey of the spectrum of leisure attractions in this era, see David Nasaw, *Going Out: The Rise and Fall of Public Amusements* (New York 1993); on Toronto specifically, see Carolyn Strange, *Toronto's Girl Problem: The Perils and Pleasures of the City, 1880-1930* (Toronto 1995), 116–24.

4 For discussions of campaigns for rational leisure, see Peter Bailey, *Leisure and Class in Victorian England: Rational Recreation and the Contest for Control, 1830–1885* (London and New York 1987); Hugh Cunningham, *Leisure in the Industrial Revolution, c. 1780-c. 1880* (London 1980), 76–109; Roy Rosenzweig, *Eight Hours for What We Will: Workers and Leisure in an Industrial City, 1870-1920* (Cambridge 1983); Dominic Cavallo, *Muscles and Morals: Organized Playgrounds and Urban Reform, 1880–1920* (Philadelphia 1981).

5 *Globe*, 13 Sept. 1882; *News*, 15 Sept. 1882.

6 Gerald Lenton, 'The Development and Nature of Vaudeville in Toronto from 1899 to 1915' (PhD thesis, University of Toronto, 1983), 177; *Dominion Review* 1, 8 (Oct. 1896), 321–2.

7 *Saturday Night*, 8 Sept. 1894, 6. Small, who began his career as an usher, eventually bought the Grand. Popular interest in him now relates more to his disappearance without a trace in 1919.

8 The most useful discussion of sporting male culture is Timothy J. Gilfoyle, *City of Eros: New York City, Prostitution, and the Commercialization of Sex, 1790–1920* (New York 1992), 92–116. Also helpful are Richard B. Stott, *Workers in the Metropolis: Class, Ethnicity, and Youth in Antebellum New York City* (Ithaca and London 1990), 212–35, 251–6; Lynne Marks, 'Religion, Leisure, and Working-Class Identity,' in Paul Craven, ed., *Labouring Lives: Work and Workers in Nineteenth-Century Ontario* (Toronto 1995), 304–7; Colin Howell, *Northern Sandlots: A Social History of Maritime Baseball* (Toronto 1995), 63–4, 70-1.

9 For discussions of the recreational character of pool halls and saloons, see Donald G. Wetherell and Irene Kmet, *Useful Pleasures: The Shaping of Leisure in Alberta, 1896–1945* (Regina 1990), 345–60, and Peter de Lottinville, 'Joe Beef of Montreal: Working Class Culture and the Tavern, 1869–1889,' *Labour / Le Travailleur* 8 / 9 (autumn/spring 1981–2), 9–40.

10 *Mail*, 1 Oct. 1879. Another *Mail* article on 25 Sept. 1879 referred to the 'notorious' dance hall of Bob Berry. Anxieties surrounding pool halls and saloons are revealed in the report on a sermon of Reverend W.F. Wilson, *Empire*, 12 Sept. 1892. See also Strange, *Toronto's Girl Problem*, 59, 149–

50, 157–8, and Kathy Peiss, *Cheap Amusements: Working Women and Leisure in Turn-of-the-Century New York* (Philadelphia 1986), 88–114.

11 See, for example, Richard Butsch, 'Bowery B'hoys and Matinee Ladies: The Re-gendering of Nineteenth Century American Theater Audiences,' *American Quarterly* 46, 3 (Sept. 1994), 374–405; Lawrence W. Levine, *Lowbrow / Highbrow: The Emergence of Cultural Hierarchy in America* (Cambridge, Mass., and London 1986), 195–200; Robert W. Snyder, *The Voice of the City: Vaudville and Popular Culture in New York* (New York and Oxford 1989), 22–5.

12 Carolyn Strange describes these suspicions in the context of concerns about single working women. See Strange, *Toronto's Girl Problem*, esp. 117–18.

13 *News*, 17, 22, and 23 Sept. 1885; *Telegram*, 22 Sept. 1885; *Mail and Empire*, 2 Sept. 1899. Prize fighting had been banned by the federal government in 1881. In the incident mentioned above, the boxers were eventually released on bail, to appear for sentencing when called. George Fulljames, one of the contestants, was killed three years later in a fight in Grand Forks, North Dakota. See *News*, 29 Sept. 1885 and *Telegram*, 25 Sept. 1888. On the popularity of boxing in nineteenth-century America, see Elliott Gorn, *The Manly Art: Bare-Knuckle Prize Fighting in America* (Ithaca and London 1986). On illegal boxing in nineteenth-century Britain, see Kellow Chesney, *The Victorian Underworld* (New York 1972), 267–78. Reform interest in sport as a moral instrument is discussed in Mark Dyreson, 'The Emergence of Consumer Culture and the Transformation of Physical Culture: American Sport in the 1920s,' in David K. Wiggins, ed., *Sport in America: From Wicked Amusement to National Obsession* (Champaign 1995), 207–23; Nancy B. Bouchier, 'Idealized Middle-Class Sport for a Young Nation: Lacrosse in Nineteenth-Century Ontario Towns, 1871–1891,' *Journal of Canadian Studies* 29 (summer 1994), 89–110; Howell, *Northern Sandlots*, passim.

14 On Toronto theatres in this period, see Robert Fairfield, 'Theatres and Performance Halls,' in Ann Saddlemyer, ed., *Early Stages: Theatre in Ontario, 1800–1914* (Toronto 1990), 221–32; Richard Plant, 'Chronology: Theatre in Ontario to 1914,' ibid., 288–346; Joan P. Baillie, *Look at the Record* (Oakville 1985). On the history of theatre in Ontario, see Gerald Lenton-Young, 'Variety Theatre,' in Saddlemyer, *Early Stages*, 166–213; Lenton, 'The Development and Nature of Vaudeville in Toronto,' 59–137; James Russell Aikens, 'The Rival Operas: Toronto Theatre, 1874–84' (PhD thesis, University of Toronto, 1975).

15 *Mail and Empire*, 30 Aug. 1899.

16 *Mail*, 13 Oct. 1879; *World*, 16 Sept. 1881; *Mail*, 15 Sept. 1881. On the

traditionally disreputable nature of the theatre, see Robert C. Allen, *Horrible Prettiness: Burlesque and American Culture* (Chaple Hill and London 1991), 46–61.

17 *Under the Gaslight* played at the Royal Opera House in 1879; *Later On* at the Grand in 1890. See *Mail*, 16 Sept. 1879, and *Empire*, 9 Sept. 1890. William Lyon Mackenzie King, *The Mackenzie King Diaries, 1893–1931* (Toronto 1973), 8 Sept. 1898; OA, MS 573 reel 3, Fanny Marion Chadwick diaries, 9 Sept. 1903. Theatre offerings in late nineteenth-century Pittsburgh were very similar. See Francis G. Couvares, 'The Plebian Moment: Theatre and Working-Class Life in Late Nineteenth-Century Pittsburgh,' in Bruce A. McConachie and Daniel Friedman, eds., *Theatre for Working-Class Audiences in the United States, 1830-1980* (Westport and London 1985), 47–60.

18 *Globe*, 10 Sept. 1887; *Telegram*, 13 Sept. 1887; *Mail*, 13 Sept. 1887; *Globe*, 14 Sept. 1887. Paid admissions on a single day of the 1888 exhibition totalled $2898, indicating an attendance of well over six thousand people. See *Empire*, 22 Sept. 1888; *Mail*, 20 Sept. 1888. The Cyclorama was initially managed by C.A. Shaw, who also ran the Toronto Opera House, an indication of the close link between variety theatre and dime museum attractions. On the popularity of panoramas in the nineteenth century, see Miles Orvell, *The Real Thing: Imitation and Authenticity in American Culture, 1880–1940* (Chaple Hill 1989), 21; Norman Altick, *The Shows of London* (Cambridge, Mass., 1978), 117–210 and 464–82.

19 *Newmarket Era*, 16 Sept. 1887; *World*, 12 Sept. 1889; *Globe*, 19 Sept. 1889; *Mail*, 11 Sept. 1890; *World*, 7 Sept. 1892; *Mail*, 2 Sept. 1893; *Mail*, 20 Aug. 1897. The Cyclorama building was sold to a machinery dealer, who used it as a showroom. See *Canada Lumberman* 23, 8 (Aug. 1903), 22–3.

20 *World*, 17, 23, and 29 Sept. 1884.

21 On the background of the nineteenth-century museum, see Altick, *The Shows of London*, 5–33 and passim; Neil Harris, *Humbug: The Art of P.T. Barnum* (Boston and Toronto 1973). The dime museum eventually evolved into vaudeville, on the one hand, and the movie theatre, on the other.

22 On the history of dime museums in Toronto, see Lenton-Young, 'Variety Theatre,' 190–3.

23 *News*, 22 Aug. 1891; *News*, 5 Sept. 1891; *Mail*, 5 Sept. 1891. Overlap between the museum and the regular theatre was highlighted by the case of Henry and Ann Fitkins, a city couple who put their new triplets on display in 1894. They initially agreed to show the babies at the Toronto Opera House, but reneged, supposedly on moral grounds. When the chil-

dren turned up soon after at the Musée, the Opera House started legal proceedings. The matter was eventually settled out of court, but it underscores that both types of business employed similar acts. See *News*, 11 Sept. 1894; *Empire*, 12 Sept. 1894. On the history of the Toronto Musée, see also Peter Stevens, '"Living Pictures": When the Movies Came to Canada,' *Beaver* 76 (April/May 1996), 32–40.

24 Robinson had been involved with the Musée when it first opened in 1890. See *World*, 29 Aug. and 1 Sept. 1896; *News*, 5 Sept. 1896; News, 30 Aug. 1899. For an earlier example of a profession of respectability, see the Wonderland ad, *Empire*, 9 Sept. 1890.

25 *Globe*, 24 Aug. 1901; *Star*, 31 Aug. 1895; *World*, 14 Sept. 1889.

26 *World*, 17 Sept. 1890.

27 Mark Judd, '"The Oddest Combination of Town and Country": Popular Culture and the London Fairs, 1800–60,' in John K. Walton and James Wolvin, eds., *Leisure in Britain, 1780–1939* (Manchester 1983), 26; Joel B. Goldsteen and Cecil D. Elliott, *Designing America: Creating Urban Identity* (New York 1994), 95–6; Alan Delgado, *Victorian Entertainment* (Newton Abbot 1971), 29–33; Judith A. Adams, *The American Amusement Park Industry: A History of Technology and Thrills* (Boston 1991), 1–9; Altick, *The Shows of London*, 317–31. On the early history of pleasure gardens in Paris, see Gilles-Antoine Langlois, *Folies, Tivolis, et Attractions: Les premiers parc de loisirs parisiens* (Paris 1991). A similar kind of space in Montreal is the focus of Yvan Lamonde and Raymond Montpetit, *Le Parc Sohmer de Montreal, 1889–1919: Un lieu populaire de culture urbaine* (Quebec 1986).

28 See, for example, CTA, RG 2 B2, box 9, no. 162, Toronto Executive Committee, Communications, Statement of Receipts from Entertainments at Horticultural Gardens, for the year ending 1st March, 1886. See also Fairfield, 'Theatres and Performance Halls,' 228.

29 *News*, 9 Sept. 1884; *World*, 9 Sept. 1884; *Mail*, 11 Sept. 1882. Brief descriptions of several other nineteenth-century Toronto amusement parks can be found in Mike Filey, *I Remember Sunnyside: The Rise and Fall of a Magical Era* (Toronto 1981), 11–31, and Mary Campbell and Barbara Myrvold, *The Beach in Pictures, 1793–1932* (Toronto 1988), 34–5.

30 *Mail*, 30 Aug. 1879; *News*, 5 Sept. 1891; *Mail and Empire*, 9 Sept. 1899; Sally Gibson, *More Than an Island: A History of Toronto Island* (Toronto 1984), 64–119; Elizabeth Wakeford, unpublished undergraduate essay, Trent University, 1990.

31 *Globe*, 7 Sept. 1881; *World*, 12 Sept. 1884; *News*, 7 Sept. 1898; *News*, 26 Sept. 1885.

32 *Saturday Night*, 15 Sept. 1900, 1; *Empire*, 3 and 4 Sept. 1891. See also C.S. Clark, *Of Toronto the Good: A Social Study. The Queen City of Canada as It Is* (1898; Montreal 1970), 93–6; Strange, *Toronto's Girl Problem*, 95, 119–20.

33 Paul Greenhalgh, *Ephemeral Vistas: The Expositions Universalles, Great Exhibitions and World's Fairs, 1851–1939* (Manchester 1988), 41–5; Charles Rearick, *Pleasures of the Belle Epoque: Entertainment and Festivity in Turn-of-the-Century France* (New Haven and London 1985), 119; Reid Badger, *The Great American Fair: The World's Columbian Exposition and American Culture* (Chicago 1979), 20.

34 On the history of American amusement parks, see *The American Amusement Park Industry*, Adams; John F. Kasson, *Amusing the Million: Coney Island at the Turn of the Century* (New York 1978); Nasaw, *Going Out*, 80–95.

35 *Globe*, 3 Sept. 1881; CTA, City Council Minutes for 1882, minute no. 82, 23 Jan. 1882; *Globe*, 18 Sept. 1883. The zoo probably was also anxious to move from its downtown location because of persistent complaints about its smell. See CTA, City Council Minutes for 1883, item 528, Appendix, Report No. 15 of the Committee on Markets and Health, 24 July 1883, 338.

36 CTA, City Council Minutes for 1885, Appendix, Report of the Exhibition Committee, 13 April 1885, 189; OA, MU 3810, no. 94, Prospectus of the Zoological and Acclimatization Society of Ontario, nd; *Globe*, 4 and 8 Sept. 1885; *Globe*, 4 Sept. 1886; *Mail*, 13 Sept. 1886.

37 *World*, 20 Sept. 1886; *Mail*, 10 Sept. 1887; CNEA, Industrial Exhibition Association, Annual Report for 1887, receipts, 14; *News*, 19 Sept. 1888; *Mail*, 18 Sept. 1888.

38 CTA, Executive Committee / Board of Control Communications, RG 2 B2, box 9, nos. 166–9, Petition of Toronto Zoological and Acclimatization Society, 1 March 1886; CTA, City Council Minutes for 1888, Appendix, no. 1004, results of plebiscite, 17 Aug. 1888, 287; letter of H. Piper, *Mail*, 3 Sept. 1888; CNEA, Industrial Exhibition Association, *Reports for 1889*, 5; CTA, City Council Minutes for 1889, Appendix, no. 1083, Report no. 12 of the Committee on Parks and Gardens, 195; *Mail*, 12 Sept. 1890; *News*, 11 Sept. 1891. Most of the animals ended up a small city-run zoo in High Park.

39 The Toronto Industrial was not the first fair to introduce new transportation technology in the guise of amusement. The first Austrian railway was constructed in 1823 to carry visitors around the Prater, a Viennese pleasure garden. See Adams, *The American Amusement Park Industry*, 8.

40 *Mail*, 12 Sept. 1893; James W. Easton, 'The Pioneer Electric Railway Of Canada,' *Canadian Electrical News* (March 1896), 43; *Globe*, 12 Sept. 1894; *Globe*, 4 Sept. 1885; *Mail*, 15 Sept. 1885; 'Our First Electric Railway,' *Canadian Electrical News* (Sept. 1890), 129. The railway was closed after 1889, possibly because of intense political pressures on the association to dismantle it. The Toronto Street Railway Company had earlier failed to shut the line through legal proceedings. See *Globe*, 5 Sept. 1885; CNEA, Industrial Exhibition Association, Annual Report for 1886, 7.

41 *News*, 12 Sept. 1885; *Globe*, 4 and 16 Sept. 1885. The first mechanical ride at Coney, a merry-go-round, appeared in the 1870s. The first tracked ride, also called the switchback, appeared in 1884. See Robert E. Snow and David E. Wright, 'Coney Island: A Case Study in Popular Culture and Technological Change,' *Journal of Popular Culture* 9, 4 (spring 1976), 966. On the history of rides, see also David Braithwaite, *Fairground Architecture* (London 1976), 34–65; Ian Starsmore, *English Fairs* (London 1975), 16, 46–8; Robert Cartmell, *The Incredible Scream Machine: A History of the Roller Coaster* (Bowling Green 1987); Norman Anderson, *Ferris Wheels: An Illustrated History* (Bowling Green 1992); Frederick Fried, *A Pictorial History of the Carousel* (New York and London 1964); Adams, *The American Amusement Park Industry*, 9–18, 31–5.

42 *Mail*, 21 Sept. 1888; *Mail*, 12 Sept. 1889; *News*, 12 Sept. 1888.

43 *Empire*, 11 Sept. 1894; *Mail*, 15 Sept. 1894; *World*, 2 Sept. 1897; *Mail and Empire*, 1 Sept. 1897.

44 Snippets of evidence suggest that a few small museum-type attractions operated independently on the grounds. In 1886, for example, the *News* referred to the presence of a fat lady. Two years later the *World* mentioned that a boat recently used to navigate the Niagara rapids was on display in a tent charging ten cents admission. At the 1892 show, 'one of the museum tents' housed an elderly Black man covered with white spots. It is not clear what, if any, arrangement existed between them and the Exhibition Association. See *News*, 14 Sept. 1886; *World*, 22 Sept. 1888; *World*, 9 Sept. 1892.

45 Chatham *Weekly Planet*, 18 Sept. 1879; *Mail*, 29 Aug. 1879.

46 *Mail*, 18 Sept. 1879; *Telegram*, 8 and 11 Sept. 1879; *Globe*, 9 and 8 Sept. 1880; *Mail*, 5 Sept. 1881. The attendance calculation is based on figures found in Oswald C.J. Withrow, *The Romance of the Canadian National Exhibition* (Toronto 1936), 100.

47 *Empire*, 11 Sept. 1891; *News*, 3 Sept. 1896; *Globe*, 5 Sept. 1899.

48 *Globe*, 11 Sept. 1886; *News*, 11 Sept. 1886. On Japanese exhibits at nineteenth-century American fairs, see Neil Harris, *Cultural Excursions:*

Marketing Appetites and Tastes in Modern America (Chicago 1990), 29–55.

49 *News*, 14 Sept. 1886; Orillia *Packet*, 17 Sept. 1886; *World*, 7 Sept. 1887; *Mail*, 8 Sept. 1888; *Globe*, 7 Sept. 1889; *Mail*, 19 Sept. 1889. In this period, the fair entertainment business was becoming more organized. Not much is yet known about this process, but see Rasmussen, 'State Fair,' 243–6, 341; Karal Ann Marling, *Blue Ribbon: A Social and Pictorial History of the Minnesota State Fair* (St Paul 1990), 186.

50 *Star*, 7 and 1 Sept. 1900; *News*, 6 Sept. 1900.

51 *News*, 6 Sept. 1900; *World*, 30 Aug. 1900; *Mail and Empire*, 8 Sept. 1900.

52 *Mail and Empire*, 8 Sept. 1900; *World*, 30 Aug. 1900; *Star*, 6 Sept. 1900.

53 *News*, 6 Sept. 1900; *Star*, 6 and 7 Sept. 1900.

54 *Globe*, 1 Sept. 1900; *Star*, 1 Sept. 1900; *World*, 1 Sept. 1900; *Mail and Empire*, 29 Aug. 1900; *World*, 29 Aug. 1900.

55 CNEA, Industrial Exhibition Association, Annual Report for 1900, 10. The association normally took about 20 to 30 per cent of sideshow receipts. See *Star*, 24 Nov. 1900.

56 CNEA, Industrial Exhibition Association, Annual Report for 1902, 22, and *Annual Report for 1901*, 11.

57 *Globe*, 16 Sept. 1889; *Empire*, 19 Sept. 1889; *Globe*, 15 Sept. 1885; *News*, 15 Sept. 1885; *Empire*, 10 Sept. 1891.

58 *Mail*, 9 and 11 Sept. 1880; CNEA, Industrial Exhibition Association, Prize List for 1884, 6–7.

59 *Globe*, 5 Sept. 1883; *Globe*, 14 Sept. 1885; *World*, 14 Sept. 1888.

60 Alan Metcalfe, *Canada Learns to Play: The Emergence of Organized Sport, 1807–1914* (Toronto 1987), 153–4; *Mail*, 13 Sept. 1880; *Mail*, 14 Sept. 1881; *Mail*, 10 Sept. 1894; *Mail*, 9 Sept. 1880; *Globe*, 11 Sept. 1885; *Globe*, 9 Sept. 1886.

61 *Empire*, 7 Sept. 1893; *News*, 2 Sept. 1897; Metcalfe suggests the 1870s slump was related to the departure from Canada of British garrisons. See *Canada Learns to Play*, 148–55.

62 CNEA, Toronto Exhibition Prize List for 1896, 23–4; *News*, 2 Sept. 1897; *Saturday Night*, 8 Sept. 1900, 2; CNEA, Industrial Exhibition Association, Minutes for 1903, Board of Directors Meeting, Recommendations of Executive Committee no. 3, 12 May 1903.

63 *Mail*, 15 Sept. 1882; *Globe*, 19 and 21 Sept. 1883.

64 *Telegram*, 15 Sept. 1883; *World*, 20 Sept. 1883; CNEA, Industrial Exhibition Association, Annual Report for 1883, 8; *Mail*, 12 Sept. 1884.

65 Three times as long as the old one, with two tiers of galleries, the new grandstand had a seating capacity of twelve thousand. Civic boosters

bragged it was the largest such facility on any exhibition ground in the world, but it still proved inadequate on occasion. See *Empire*, 7 Sept. 1892; *Globe*, 7 Sept. 1899.

66 *Empire*, 7 Sept. 1892; *Empire*, 5 Sept. 1894; *News*, 2 Sept. 1897; *News*, 9 Sept. 1902; *Mail*, 10 Sept. 1890; *Mail*, 9 Sept. 1891; Orillia *Packet*, 9 Sept. 1892; *Mail*, 1 Sept. 1893. On the origins of the Wild West show, see William Brasmer, 'The Wild West Exhibition: A Fraudulent Reality,' in Myron Matlaw, ed., *American Popular Entertainment: Papers and Proceedings of the Conference on the History of American Popular Entertainment* (Westport and London 1979), 207–14. L.G. Moses, *Wild West Shows and the Images of American Indians, 1883–1933* (Albuquerque 1996), is based largely on the Buffalo Bill Cody Show.

67 Whitby *Chronicle*, 23 Sept. 1892; *Saturday Night*, 17 Sept. 1892, 1. See also *Mail*, 13 Sept. 1887; *Telegram*, 23 Sept. 1889; *Star*, 11 Sept. 1897.

68 *World*, 7 Sept. 1900; *Globe*, 13 Sept. 1887; *Globe*, 6 Sept. 1898. Those caught in the crush sometimes had to be inventive to protect their lines of sight. Kit Coleman described one man who had a pocketful of paper balls to throw at people who stood up in front of him. See *Mail*, 20 Sept. 1890. At the Iowa State Fair, the evening spectacle was also the main attraction. See Rasmussen, 'State Fair,' 369.

69 *The Liberal* [Richmond Hill], 17 Sept. 1891; MTRL, Baldwin Room, Larratt Smith diaries, 9 Sept. 1896; OA, MU 4451, Ardagh Family Papers, Edward G.R. Ardagh diaries, 6 Sept. 1898; *Mail*, 8 Sept. 1893; *Mail and Empire*, 31 Aug. 1899. Fanny Chadwick was one of the few who found the spectacles disappointing. See OA, MS 573, Fanny Marion Chadwick diaries, 10 Sept. 1895 and 7 Sept. 1899.

70 *Mail,* 18 Sept. 1883; *News*, 18 Sept. 1884; Delgado, *Victorian Entertainment*, 31–3; Alan St. H. Brock, *A History of Fireworks* (London 1949), 56, 62, 105–6; Rearick, *Pleasures of the Belle Epoque*, 208; Harris, *Humbug*, 245.

71 OA, MU 2314, Seymour Richard George Penson Memoires.

72 *Globe*, 11 Sept. 1891; *Mail and Empire*, 7 Sept. 1896; *Telegram*, 9 Sept. 1892. See also *Globe*, 9 Sept. 1887; *Empire*, 14 Sept. 1888.

73 Penson Memoires; *Mail and Empire*, 4 Sept. 1895; *Star*, 26 Aug. 1901; *Mail and Empire*, 6 Sept. 1895; *Empire*, 11 Sept. 1891; *News*, 1 Sept. 1898.

74 *Mail*, 9 Sept. 1892; *World*, 30 Aug. 1900; *Mail and Empire*, 26 Aug. 1902. On civic pageants and their relation to spectacle theatre, see David Glassberg, *American Historical Pageantry: The Uses of Tradition in the Early Twentieth Century* (Chaple Hill and London 1990), 26–7.

75 *Mail*, 18 Sept. 1888; *Mail*, 8 Sept. 1893.

76 See, for example, *World*, 1 Sept. 1897; William Lyon Mackenzie King diaries, 31 Aug. 1897. A list of spectacle themes can be found in Withrow, *The Romance of the Canadian National Exhibition*, 122–3.

77 Penson Memoires; Barbara M. Barker, ed., *Bolossy Kiralfy, Creator of Great Musical Spectacles: An Autobiography* (Ann Arbor and London 1988), 187, 203, 254. Some productions that originated in Toronto were afterwards exported to other fairs and exhibitions. See Marling, *Blue Ribbon*, 129.

78 Judd, 'The Oddest Combination,' 18–20. See also Douglas A. Reid, 'Interpreting the Festival Calendar: Wakes and Fairs as Carnivals,' in Robert D. Storch, ed., *Popular Culture and Custom in Nineteenth-Century England* (London/Canberra and New York 1982), 125–6, 140-1.

79 In 1899, for example, the barker at the Oriental Theatre intimated that while women were not expressly forbidden from seeing the Coochee Coochee dance inside, none were expected to request admission. His remarks quickly 'sifted all the women out of the crowd.' The booking of such an attraction perhaps indicates the association's confidence that it could contain disreputable behaviour, but it was seen by many as an unnecessary experiment. *Saturday Night* columnist 'Mack,' for one, pounced on General Manager Hill. This was not the kind of speech fair visitors 'have been accustomed to,' he suggested, and its presence threatened the success of future shows. See 'Mack' [Joseph Thomas Clark], 'The Toronto Fair,' *Saturday Night*, 9 Sept. 1899, 7.

80 *Star*, 30 Aug. 1900; *Mail and Empire*, 1 and 8 Sept. 1900.

81 T.J. Jackson Lears, 'Some Versions of Fantasy: Towards a Cultural History of American Advertising, 1880–1930,' *Prospects* 9 (1984), 354.

82 Orvell, *The Real Thing*, 55; *Mail*, 9 Sept. 1891; *Mail*, 13 Sept. 1892; *Mail*, 20 Sept. 1890; Harris, *Humbug*, 77.

83 *Mail and Empire*, 8 Sept. 1900; *Star*, 26 Aug. 1901.

84 *World*, 7 Sept. 1894; *News*, 17 Sept. 1894. The best source on the history of living pictures is Jack W. McCullough, *Living Pictures on the New York Stage* (Ann Arbor 1983), but also see Allen, *Horrible Prettiness*, 92–4 and Lois Banner, *American Beauty* (New York 1983), 185. On earlier presentations of living pictures in Toronto, see Lenton-Young, 'Variety Theatre,' 189 and 193–4.

85 *News*, 9 Sept. 1902; *Saturday Night*, 16 Sept. 1893, 7; *Empire*, 12 Sept. 1893.

86 *Empire*, 9 Sept. 1892; *Empire*, 15 Sept. 1894; *Mail and Empire*, 6 Sept. 1895.

87 *Globe*, 17 Sept. 1883; *Mail*, 17 and 18 Sept. 1883.

88 *Globe*, 21, 22, and 24 Sept. 1883.

89 *Mail*, 18 Sept. 1888; *Mail and Empire*, 12 Sept. 1903; *Globe*, 12 Sept. 1903; *Mail*, 2 and 11 Sept. 1891.

90 *News*, 15 Sept. 1883; *Globe*, 15 Sept. 1883.

91 Electric current was supplied to the train in 1884 by a copper strip laid in a wooden box on the ground. Patronage was so far below expectation that the price was reduced from ten to five cents a ride. The design was changed the following year to an overhead wire. See 'Our First Electric Railway,' 129; *Mail*, 20 and 15 Sept. 1884; *Globe*, 4 Sept. 1895; *Globe*, 3 Sept. 1897.

92 *Star*, 9 Sept. 1900; *Star*, 29 Aug. 1900; *World*, 30 Aug. 1900; Rearick, *Pleasures of the Belle Epoque*, 200, 202, 207; *Saturday Night*, 22 Sept. 1888, 1.

93 *Globe*, 11 Sept. 1885; *Mail*, 20 Sept. 1883; *Dumfries Reformer* [Waterloo], 22 Sept. 1887; *Dominion Churchman*, 9 Sept. 1886, 556; *Farmer's Advocate*, Oct. 1886, 290; *Empire*, 13 Sept. 1888.

94 *World*, 13 Sept. 1889; *Empire*, 12 Sept. 1889; *News*, 16 Aug. 1889; *Globe*, 13 and 12 Sept. 1889.

95 *Globe*, 13 Sept. 1889.

96 *World*, 13 Sept. 1889; *Empire*, 17 Sept. 1889; *Mail*, 17 Sept. 1889; *World*, 17 Sept. 1889; *Globe*, 17 Sept. 1889.

97 Pickering *News*, 20 Sept. 1889; *Globe*, 14 Sept. 1889; *Saturday Night*, 21 Sept. 1889, 1; *World*, 17 Sept. 1889; *Empire*, 8 Sept. 1893.

98 *Empire*, 7 and 15 Sept. 1894.

99 *News*, 17 Sept. 1894; *Empire*, 17 Sept. 1894; *News*, 19 Sept. 1894.

100 *Saturday Night*, 15 Sept. 1894, 7; *Globe*, 8 Sept. 1894; *Mail*, 6 Sept. 1894; *World*, 17 Sept. 1894.

101 *Mail and Empire*, 12 Sept. 1896; *News*, 5 Sept. 1896.

102 *Telegram*, 8 Sept. 1896; *Christian Guardian*, 10 Sept. 1896, 600; *Saturday Night*, 19 Sept. 1896, 2.

103 CNEA, Industrial Exhibition Association, Annual Report for 1896, 10; *Saturday Night*, 11 Sept. 1897, 1; *News*, 31 Aug. 1898.

104 *World*, 9 Sept. 1902; *Star*, 9 Sept. 1902.

105 OA, MU 1292, M.O. Hammond Papers, Diary, 5 Sept. 1903. For biographical detail on Hammond, see Sandra Gwyn, *The Private Capital: Ambition and Love in the Age of Macdonald and Laurier* (Toronto 1984), 389–430.

106 For other examples of changing criteria of middle-class identity, see Kenneth Cmiel, *Democratic Eloquence: The Fight over Popular Speech*

in Nineteenth-Century America (New York 1990), 251; Lewis Erenberg, *Steppin' Out: New York Nightlife and the Transformation of American Culture, 1890-1930* (Westport 1981); Stuart Blumin, *The Emergence of the Middle Class: Social Experience in the American City, 1760-1900* (Cambridge 1989).

107 R.D. Gidney and W.P.J. Millar, *Professional Gentlemen: The Professions in Nineteenth-Century Ontario* (Toronto 1994), 277–82; Warren I. Susman, '"Personality" and the Making of Twentieth-Century Culture,' in John Higham and Paul K. Conkin, eds., *New Directions in American Intellectual History* (Baltimore and London 1979), 212–26.

108 Rasmussen has constructed much of his study of the Iowa State Fair around this issue. See 'State Fair,' 8–9 and passim.

109 Galt *Reformer*, 8 Sept. 1881; Newmarket *Era,* 16 Sept. 1881; *World*, 19 Sept. 1884; *Telegram*, 17 Sept. 1886; *Labour Advocate*, 18 Sept. 1886.

110 *Saturday Night*, 17 Sept. 1892, 1; Markham *Economist*, 2 Sept. 1880; London *Free Press*, quoted in *Week* 1, 41 (11 Sept. 1884), 652.

111 *Empire*, 15 Sept. 1894; Bobcaygeon *Independent*, quoted in Port Hope *Weekly Guide*, 30 Sept. 1892; Whitby *Chronicle*, 16 Sept. 1892.

112 'On the Wing,' *Farmer's Advocate*, Oct. 1885, 290. See also Orillia *Times*, 17 Sept. 1891; remarks of W.C. Edwards, member of parliament for Russel, at directors' luncheon, *World*, 8 Sept. 1897; 'The Toronto Fair,' *Saturday Night*, 9 Sept. 1899, 7.

113 'The Toronto Exhibition,' *Farmer's Advocate*, March 1883, 73.

114 *Globe*, 14 Sept. 1887; *Globe*, 13 Sept. 1888. See also *Globe*, 29 Aug. 1896.

115 CNEA, Industrial Exhibition Association, Annual Report for 1891, 5; *Empire*, 21 Sept. 1889.

116 *Canadian Manufacturer* 2, 20 (21 Sept. 1883), 375; *World*, 20 Sept. 1883; *Globe*, 8 Sept. 1888; Whitby *Chronicle*, 16 Sept. 1892; Whitby *Chronicle,* 13 Sept. 1895.

117 *Mail*, 12 Sept. 1892.

118 *News*, 2 Sept. 1897; *Saturday Night*, 9 Sept. 1899, 7; 'Reform the Toronto Exhibition,' *Canadian Grocer*, 27 April 1900, 15.

119 *Star*, 5 Sept. 1900; *News*, 6 Sept. 1900.

120 *Star*, 7 and 8 Sept. 1900. Similar comments can be found in the *Star* throughout the period from 5 to 11 September.

121 See, for example, the comments of C.H. Botsford and H. Ryrie, *Star*, 5 Sept. 1900.

122 *Star*, 7 Sept. 1900. See also comments of L.B. Moore, *Star*, 5 Sept. 1900 and A.E. Huestle, *Star*, 6 Sept. 1900.

123 *Mail*, 5 Sept. 1893; *Mail and Empire*, 26 Aug. 1899. The concentration of

amusements along a 'Rue de Caire' originated at the 1878 Paris fair, and by 1880 the foreign street was a regular feature at exhibitions. See Greenhalgh, *Ephemeral Vistas*, 102. On the Chicago midway and Sol Bloom, see James Gilbert, *Perfect Cities: Chicago's Utopias of 1893* (Chicago and London 1991), 75–130.

124 *Star*, 11 Sept. 1900.

125 *Star*, 5 and 6 Sept. 1900.

126 *Star*, 8 Sept. 1900. Not surprisingly, the same strategy was common at many other exhibitions and fairs. See Greenhalgh, *Ephemeral Vistas*, 42; Roland Marchand, 'Corporate Imagery and Popular Education: World's Fairs and Expositions in the United States, 1893–1940,' in David Nye and Carl Pedersen, eds., *Consumption and American Culture* (Amsterdam 1991), 21.

127 The *Star*'s critique stimulated city council to conduct a special inquiry into the management of the exhibition, during which similar complaints and defences were voiced. As well as confirming the strategy for change, the inquiry resulted in manufacturers having more clout within the Exhibition Association, and city council more representation on the board of directors. See *Mail and Empire*, 24 Nov. 1900; *Star*, 24 Nov. 1900; *Mail and Empire*, 19 Dec. 1900; *Star*, 19 Dec. 1900; *Mail and Empire*, 19 and 22 Feb. 1901; *Mail and Empire*, 6 March 1901.

128 *Globe*, 30 Aug. 1902; CNEA, Industrial Exhibition Association, Annual Report for 1902, 15.

129 *World*, 29 Aug. 1903; CNEA, Industrial Exhibition Association, Board Meeting Minutes, 11 Aug. 1903; CNEA, Industrial Exhibition Association, Annual Report for 1900 and Annual Report for 1903; *World*, 28 Aug. 1903.

130 CNEA, Industrial Exhibition Association, *Annual Report for 1902*; *Mail and Empire*, 26 Aug. 1902; *Mail and Empire*, 29 Aug. 1903.

131 Chatham *Weekly Planet*, 18 Sept. 1879; *News*, 18 Sept. 1893; *Globe*, 14 Sept. 1881; *Star*, 1 Sept. 1899; *Mail*, 18 Sept. 1883.

132 *Mail and Empire*, 29 Aug. 1903; *Globe*, 1 Sept. 1903; *Star*, 2 Sept. 1903; *Mail and Empire*, 5 Sept. 1903.

133 *Globe*, 31 Aug. 1900.

134 Folke T. Kihlstedt, 'Utopia Realized: The World's Fairs of the 1930s,' in Joseph J. Corn, ed., *Imagining Tomorrow: History, Technology, and the American Future* (Cambridge, Mass., and London 1987), 97–118; Robert W. Rydell, *World of Fairs: The Century of Progress Expositions* (Chicago and London 1993), 116; Marchand, 'Corporate Imagery,' 19.

135 *World*, 10 Sept. 1903.

136 *World*, 29 Aug. 1903.

137 'The Best Shows Outside,' *Star*, 5 Sept. 1903. In 1902 a *Mail and Empire* reporter noted that barkers had trouble being heard above the noise of children. See 3 Sept. 1902.

138 Katherine Leslie, 'Woman's World,' *World*, 1 Sept. 1899; 'Echos of the Midway,' *News*, 3 Sept. 1903; 'Woman's Kingdom,' *Mail and Empire*, 1 Sept. 1900.

139 Katherine Leslie, 'Woman's World,' *World*, 1 Sept. 1899; *Globe*, 31 Aug. 1900.

140 The vogue for process exhibits hit the Minnesota State Fair in the same period. According to Karal Ann Marling, businesses that installed them there soon discovered they were an expensive form of advertising and, despite public interest, the number declined very quickly. See Marling, *Blue Ribbon*, 275–6.

141 In 1898 midway concessionaires in Omaha who tried to extend their success for another year after the close of an exhibition discovered that a midway without a fair was a financial disaster. See Nasaw, *Going Out*, 69.

Chapter 7: Carnival

1 OA posters, P1850, 1895, Toronto Exhibition poster. In 1890 an event explicitly called a 'Summer Carnival' was inaugurated in the city, perhaps in counterpoint to Montreal's Winter Carnival. A dismal failure, it was never mounted again. See *Globe*, 4 July and 7 July 1890.

2 Peter Burke, *Popular Culture in Early Modern Europe* (New York 1981), 182–204; Robert W. Malcolmson, *Popular Recreations in English Society, 1700–1850* (Cambridge 1973), 19–25, 30–3, 76–88; Michael D. Bristol, *Carnival and Theatre: Plebeian Culture and the Structure of Authority in Renaissance England* (New York and London 1985), 40–4; David Cressy, *Bonfires and Bells: National Memory and the Protestant Calendar in Elizabethan and Stuart England* (London 1989), 18–19, 21–24, 67–8.

3 Mikhail Bakhtin, *Rabelais and His World* (Bloomington 1984), 4–12; Renate Lachmann, 'Bakhtin and Carnival: Culture as Counter Culture,' *Cultural Critique* 11 (winter 1988–9), 130; Samuel Kinser, *Carnival, American Style: Mardi Gras at New Orleans and Mobile* (Chicago and London 1990), xv.

4 Bakhtin, *Robelais and His World*, 7. The similarity between Bakhtin's understanding of carnival and Victor Turner's concept of liminality has not gone unnoticed. See, for example, C. Clifford Flanigan, 'Liminality,

Carnival, and Social Structure: The Case of Late Medieval Drama,' in Kathleen M. Ashley, ed., *Victor Turner and the Construction of Cultural Criticism* (Bloomington and Indianapolis 1990), 42–63.

5 On the displacement of carnival into literature, see Mike Featherstone, 'Postmodernism and the Aestheticization of Everyday Life,' in Scott Lash and Jonathan Friedman, eds., *Modernity and Identity* (Oxford and Cambridge, Mass., 1992), 284. Jackson Lears has recently applied the concept to modern advertising. See *Fables of Abundance: A Cultural History of Advertising in America* (New York 1994).

6 Peter Stallybrass and Allon White, *The Politics and Poetics of Transgression* (Ithaca 1986), 13–19, 30–1; Teofilo F. Ruiz, 'Elite and Popular Culture in Late Fifteenth-Century Castilian Festivals: The Case of Jaen,' in Barbara A. Hanawalt and Kathryn L. Reyerson, eds., *City and Spectacle in Medieval Europe* (Minneapolis and London 1994), 307.

7 Gerard Nijsten, 'The Duke and His Towns: The Power of Ceremonies, Feasts, and Public Amusement in the Duchy of Guelders (East Netherlands) in the Fourteenth and Fifteenth Centuries,' in Hanawalt and Reyerson, *City and Spectacle*, 238; Ruiz, 'Elite and Popular Culture,' 315.

8 Emmanuel Le Roy Ladurie, *Carnival in Romans* (New York 1979); Natalie Z. Davis, *Society and Culture in Early Modern France* (Stanford 1975), 97–123, 137–42; Reid Mitchell, *All on a Mardi Gras Day: Episodes in the History of New Orleans Carnival* (Cambridge, Mass., and London 1995).

9 Leslie Fiedler, *Freaks: Myths and Images of the Secret Self* (New York 1993), 43, 107; Robert Bogdan, *Freak Show: Presenting Human Oddities for Amusement and Profit* (Chicago and London 1988), 12, 98–9, 161.

10 'A Two Mouthed Lion,' *The Critic* 1, 4 (8 Sept. 1883), 60.

11 *World*, 9 Sept. 1895; *Globe*, 10 Sept. 1883; *Weekly Sun*, 2 Sept. 1896. John Weldon Eaton, a nephew of Timothy Eaton, was a minority shareholder in The John Eaton Company, which failed after a fire in 1897. See Joy L. Santink, *Timothy Eaton and the Rise of His Department Store* (Toronto 1990), 209–11.

12 *World*, 11 Sept. 1884; *Globe*, 7 Sept. 1896; *World*, 11 Sept. 1888; *Mail and Empire*, 11 Sept. 1896; 'Machinery Exhibit,' *The Canada Lumberman*, Aug. 1903, 22.

13 *Empire*, 24 Sept. 1888; *Liberal* [Richmond Hill], 16 Sept. 1897.

14 Touchstone, 'Some Old Friends Back Again,' *Saturday Night*, 12 Sept. 1891, 6; 'Fakir and His Fakes,' *World*, 17 Sept. 1890; 'Toronto,' *Port Hope Weekly Guide*, 18 Sept. 1891. For additional examples of complaints, see 'Grumbler's Corner,' *News*, 8 and 15 Sept. 1887; *Star*, 12 Sept. 1894.

15 'The Fakirs,' *Globe*, 11 Sept. 1882.

16 Peter G. Goheen, 'Parading: A Lively Tradition in Early Victorian Toronto,' in Alan R.H. Baker and Gideon Biger, eds., *Ideology and Landscape in Historical Perspective* (Cambridge 1992), 332. See also Peter G. Goheen, 'Negotiating Access to Public Space in Mid-Nineteenth Century Toronto,' *Journal of Historical Geography* 20, 4 (1994), 430-49; P.G. Goheen, 'The Ritual of the Streets in Mid-19th-Century Toronto,' *Environment and Planning D: Society and Space* 11 (1993), 127–45; Peter G. Goheen, 'Symbols in the Streets: Parades in Victorian Urban Canada,' *Urban History Review* 18, 3 (Feb. 1990), 237–43; Mary Ryan, 'The American Parade: Representations of the Nineteenth-Century Social Order,' Lynn Hunt, ed., *The New Cultural History* (Berkeley 1989), 132; Bonnie Huskins, 'The Ceremonial Space of Women: Public Processions in Victorian St. John and Halifax,' in Janet Guildford and Suzanne Morton, *Separate Spheres: Women's Worlds in the Nineteenth-Century Maritimes* (Fredericton 1994), 145–59.

17 *Globe*, 12 Sept. 1887; *News*, 7 Sept. 1897; 'The Labour Demonstration,' *Labour Reformer*, 18 Sept. 1886, 5; *Mail*, 13 Sept. 1886.

18 *Mail*, 13 Sept. 1883; *Globe*, 20 Sept. 1883.

19 'The Vice-Regal Reception at Toronto,' *Canadian Illustrated News*, 14 Sept. 1879, 166.

20 *Mail*, 11 Sept. 1885; *Mail*, 7 Sept. 1892; *Globe*, 25 Aug. 1900; *News*, 8 Sept. 1893; *Mail and Empire*, 12 Sept. 1892.

21 OA, MU 2215, A-vi-1, Scrapbook Volume 2, Independent Order of Oddfellows: Grand Lodge of Canada West and Ontario Records and Papers, Print Materials Relating to 1880 Grand Lodge Meeting, ii) Sovereign Grand Lodge Reception, 3 Sept. 1880; *Globe*, 16 Sept. 1884. On the popularity of fire companies, see, for example, *News*, 7 Sept. 1897; *Mail and Empire*, 2 Sept. 1902.

22 *News*, 10 Sept. 1892. Labour Day parades in Vancouver were similar to ones in Toronto. See Robert A.J. McDonald, *Making Vancouver: Class, Status, and Social Boundaries, 1863–1913* (Vancouver 1996), 79–85.

23 *News*, 8 Sept. 1893; *News*, 10 Sept. 1892; *News*, 13 Sept. 1886.

24 OA, MU 2214, A-iv-4, Independent Order of Oddfellows: Grand Lodge of Canada West and Ontario, Records and Papers, Letterbook, Committee on Reception, 1880, John Donogh to Chief Constable Draper, 18 Aug. 1880, and J.B. King to S.F. Eddy, 23 Aug. 1880; OA, MU 2215, A-vi-1, Scrapbook Volume 2, Independent Order of Oddfellows: Grand Lodge of Canada West and Ontario Records and Papers, Print Materials Relating to 1880 Grand Lodge Meeting, ii) Sovereign Grand Lodge Reception,

3 Sept. 1880; *World*, 13 Sept. 1886; *World*, 12 Sept. 1892; *Globe*, 7 Sept. 1897. For some indication of the range of the nineteenth century North American parade repertoire, see Susan Davis, *Parades and Power: Street Theatre in Nineteenth-Century Philadelphia* (Berkeley 1988). She suggests (167) that after the Civil War in the United States, memories of 'the wild disorder of festivals and holidays and the sense that festivity expresses parts of an oppositional working class culture' disappeared. Until further research is done, it is impossible to say whether a similar tradition existed in Ontario.

25 *World*, 13 Sept. 1886.

26 *Globe*, 7 Sept. 1897; *News*, 8 Sept. 1893. In 1886 a contingent of ladies representing the female assembly of the Knights of Labor did participate in the labour parade. They were carried in 'pleasure vans,' muting any symbolic assertion of a right to occupy the public street. In 1892 there seems to have been no female participation. See *Telegram*, 11 Sept. 1886; *News*, 10 Sept. 1892. Mary Ryan has suggested that in this period, women began to be more active participants in American parades. See *Women in Public: Between Banners and Ballots, 1825–1880* (Baltimore and London 1990), 42–57.

27 On the traditional festive use of bonfires, see Cressy, *Bonfires and Bills*, 80–7.

28 Neil Baldwin, *Edison: Inventing the Century* (New York 1995), 102–14; Robert M. Stamp, *Bright Lights, Big City: The History of Electricity in Toronto* (Toronto 1991), 11–12.

29 'Gas v. Electricity,' *Mail*, 3 Sept. 1883; *Globe*, 15, 17, and 22 Sept. 1883; *News*, 15 Sept. 1883; MTRL, Baldwin Room, Denison Papers, Diary of Frederick C. Denison, 19 Sept. 1883. On the competition in Toronto between gas and electric utility companies, see Christopher Armstrong and H.V. Nelles, *Monopoly's Moment: The Organization and Regulation of Canadian Utilities, 1830-1930* (Toronto 1986), 77–80.

30 George McConkey had inaugurated electric light in Toronto in 1879 by running two arc lamps in his restaurant from a portable steam engine. Obviously, his experiments continued to be commercially successful. Stamp, *Bright Lights*, 11–12; *Telegram*, 9 Sept. 1882; *World*, 8 and 9 Sept. 1882.

31 *Globe*, 13 Sept. 1889; *Mail and Empire*, 3 Sept. 1902; *World*, 4 Sept. 1902; *News*, 30 Aug. 1899. There were precedents going back a decade and a half for draping actors and dancers with lights. See Carolyn Marvin, *When Old Technologies Were New: Thinking about Electric Communication in the Late Nineteenth Century* (New York and Oxford 1988), 176–7.

32 *Mail*, 6 Sept. 1879; *Globe*, 13 Sept. 1879; 'Exhibition at Toronto,' Peterborough *Review*, 8 Sept. 1879.

33 Details for this account were taken from *Globe*, 2, 7, and 8 Sept. 1887; *Telegram*, 7 Sept. 1887; 'Stella's Toronto Letter,' *Northern Advance* [Barrie], 15 Sept. 1887; 'Illuminate the Streets,' *News*, 4 Sept. 1895.

34 *Mail*, 10 Sept. 1880. David E. Nye has pointed out that 'while isolated illuminations only dotted the landscape, visions of a fully electrified world emerged at world's fairs and expositions.' See *Electrifying America: Social Meanings of a New Technology, 1880-1940* (Cambridge, Mass., and London 1990), 33.

35 *Globe*, 5 Sept. 1882; *Mail*, 5 and 7 Sept. 1882.

36 *Mail*, 7 Sept. 1882; Guelph *Daily Mercury and Advertiser*, 9 Sept. 1882; *Mail*, 9 Sept. 1882; *Globe*, 2 Sept. 1882; *Mail*, 11 Sept. 1882. A device similar to the electro-hydraulic fireworks was already operating at Prospect Park, Niagara Falls, and the effect remained one of the standard spectacles of light in the late nineteenth century. See *Mail*, 4 Sept. 1882, and Marvin, *When Old Technologies Were New*, 167.

37 'The Electric Light,' *Globe*, 11 Sept. 1882; *Mail*, 9 Sept. 1882; *Globe*, 9 Sept. 1882; *Telegram*, 9 Sept. 1882; *Mail*, 7 Sept. 1882. On the use of electric light at world's fairs to create dream landscapes, see Nye, 'Electrifying Expositions, 1880–1939,' in Robert W. Rydell and Nancy Gwinn, eds., *Fair Representations: World's Fairs and the Modern World* (Amsterdam 1994), 140–56, 152.

38 *Mail*, 8 Sept. 1883; CNEA, Industrial Exhibition Association of Toronto, Report for 1883, 9; *Globe*, 18 Sept. 1883; *Mail*, 13 Sept. 1883.

39 *Mail*, 3 Sept. 1883; *Mail*, 12 Sept. 1883; *Globe*, 14 Sept. 1883; *Mail*, 14 Sept. 1883.

40 CNEA, Industrial Exhibition Association of Toronto, Reports for 1883, 18; *Mail*, 12 Sept. 1884; *Globe*, 12 Sept. 1884; *Canadian Electrical News* 9, 9 (Sept. 1899), 12. On the concept of tower lighting, see Wolfgang Schivelbusch, *Disenchanted Night: The Industrialization of Night in the Nineteenth Century* (Berkeley/Los Angeles/London 1988), 128–34.

41 *Empire*, 17 Sept. 1888; *Mail*, 18 Sept. 1888; *Mail*, 9 Sept. 1892; *Globe*, 28 Aug. 1897; *Mail and Empire*, 27 Aug. 1897; *Mail and Empire*, 24 Aug. 1903.

42 *World*, 28 Aug. 1882; *World*, 14 Sept. 1887. On the repertoire of spectacle effects with electric light, see Marvin, *When Old Technologies Were New*, 158–79.

43 See, for example, *Globe*, 12 Sept. 1887; *Mail*, 18 Sept. 1888.

44 Umberto Eco, for example, has written, 'Carnival, in order to be enjoyed,

requires that rules and rituals be parodied, rules and rituals that are already recognized and respected ... Without a valid law to break, carnival is impossible.' See 'The Frames of Comic "Freedom,"' in Umberto Eco, V.V. Ivanov, and Monica Rector, *Carnival!* (Berlin and New York 1984), 6.

45 'The Exhibition,' *World*, 10 Sept. 1898; MTRL, Baldwin Room, Henry Scadding diaries, 16 Sept. 1880; 'Letter from Toronto,' Peterborough *Review*, 12 Sept. 1881; *Mail and Empire*, 27 Aug. 1903; *Globe*, 25 Aug. 1900.

46 *Mail*, 17 Sept. 1883; 'Toronto Exhibition,' Orillia *Packet*, 26 Sept. 1890; *Mail*, 16 Sept. 1881; *Mail*, 12 Sept. 1893; MTRL, Baldwin Room, Percy Beale diaries, 9 Sept. 1886; *Globe*, 17 Sept. 1887; *Mail and Empire*, 9 Sept. 1898; *Globe*, 20 Sept. 1884.

47 'Meet Me at the Station,' *Star*, 3 Sept. 1903.

48 CTA, Council Minutes for 1880, Appendix 4, Report of the Chief Constable, 26; CTA, Council Minutes for 1881, Appendix 7, Report of the Chief Constable; *Mail*, 15 Sept. 1881; *Globe*, 15 Sept. 1881; *Mail*, 1 Sept. 1881. On late nineteenth-century concerns in New York City about the lack of comfort stations for visitors, see William R. Taylor, *In Pursuit of Gotham: Culture and Commerce in New York* (New York and Oxford 1992), 42–3.

49 Letter of 'Humanity,' *Mail*, 11 Sept. 1886; letter of Kate Eunice Watts, *World*, 11 Sept. 1889; *Mail*, 18 Sept. 1889; *Mail*, 13 Sept. 1894; *Empire*, 8 Sept. 1894.

50 'Why Ma Is Going Batty,' *World*, 29 Aug. 1899; 'From "The Advantages of Country Cousins" – by a Householder,' *Telegram*, 16 Sept. 1882. See also 'His Visitors,' *Star*, 7 Sept. 1901; 'Stacked,' *Saturday Night*, 5 Sept. 1903, 7.

51 Ad for P. Patterson and Son, *Telegram*, 7 Sept. 1881; ad for Charles Rogers and Sons, *Empire*, 5 Sept. 1894; *News*, 30 Aug. 1902.

52 NA, MG 29 A 52, Radcliff Family Papers, Memoirs of Stephen Radcliff, 105; 'H.A.H.,' 'Welcome to Our Country Cousins,' *Mail and Empire*, 31 Aug. 1901; *Telegram*, 16 Sept. 1892; letter of 'Paterfamilias,' *Telegram*, 5 Sept. 1879; *Dominion Churchman*, 6 Sept. 1883, 558; *British Whig* [Kingston], 22 Sept. 1881.

53 *Star*, 5 Sept. 1896; *Globe*, 31 Aug. 1895; *Mail*, 10 Sept. 1881; *Globe*, 2 Sept. 1901.

54 Ad for Arlington Hotel, *Mail*, 17 Sept. 1889; *World*, 29 Aug. 1900.

55 See, for example, *World*, 9 Sept. 1886; *Mail and Empire*, 2 Sept. 1896.

56 'Letter from Toronto,' Peterborough *Review*, 12 Sept. 1881; *Mail*, 5 Sept. 1881; *Mail and Empire*, 4 Sept. 1902; *Globe*, 13 Sept. 1895; *News*, 12 Sept. 1884; *Globe*, 15 Sept. 1885.

57 *News*, 10 Sept. 1887; *Mail and Empire*, 14 Sept. 1903; *Star*, 10 Sept. 1903.

58 *Globe*, 10 Sept. 1890; *Empire*, 13 Sept. 1894; *Mail and Empire*, 7 Sept. 1898; *Empire*, 20 Sept. 1888; *Mail and Empire*, 2 Sept. 1898.

59 *Globe*, 2 Sept. 1903; 'Letter from Toronto,' Peterborough *Review*, 12 Sept. 1881.

60 Markham *Economist*, 14 Sept. 1882; Port Hope *Weekly Guide and News*, 16 Sept. 1887; *Mail*, 20 Sept. 1890.

61 *Globe*, 2 Sept. 1879; *World*, 8 Sept. 1902; *Mail*, 5 Sept. 1881.

62 'The Exhibition,' *The Critic*, 1, 4 (8 Sept. 1883), 53; *Globe*, 6 and 8 Sept. 1884; *Mail*, 17 Sept. 1884; *Globe*, 12 Sept. 1903. These sorts of problems were not peculiar to Toronto's fair. See Anne Lincoln Fitzpatrick, *The Great Russian Fair: Nizhnii Novgorod, 1840-1890* (Oxford 1990), 172.

63 'Our Toronto Letter,' *The Witness and South Simcoe News* [Bradford], 21 Sept. 1893; *Mail*, 17 Sept. 1880; University of Western Ontario, Weldon Library, Regional History Room, B 4038, file 7, Joseph Seymour Fallows Collection, John Fallows to his mother, 14 Sept. 1881; *Globe*, 13 Sept. 1882; *Mail*, 19 Sept. 1889; *Mail and Empire*, 7 Sept. 1898.

64 Bakhtin, *Rabelais and His World*, 7.

65 *Mail*, 29 Aug. 1879; *Mail*, 10 Sept. 1879; *Telegram*, 21 Sept. 1883. On management's efforts to provide more facilities, see, for example, *Globe*, 3 Sept. 1881; *Globe*, 11 Sept. 1885; *Globe*, 7 Sept. 1895; *Mail and Empire*, 29 Aug. 1903. On complaints about inadequacies, see, for example, *Mail*, 17 Sept. 1880; *News*, 13 Sept. 1888; *Star*, 14 Sept. 1895; 'Social and Personal,' *Saturday Night*, 11 Sept. 1897, 3. For another interpretation of the nineteenth-century fair-going experience, see Elsbeth Heaman, 'Colonial Leviathan: Central Canadian Exhibitions at Home and Abroad during the Nineteenth Century' (PhD thesis, University of Toronto, 1995), 466–515.

66 'Faith at the Show,' *Empire*, 19 Sept. 1889; *Mail*, 17 Sept. 1880; *Empire*, 18 Sept. 1890.

67 *News*, 11 Sept. 1884; CNEA, Industrial Exhibition Association of Toronto, Report for 1882, 6; MTRL, Baldwin Room, Henry Scadding diaries, 17 Sept. 1880.

68 *Globe*, 14 Sept. 1882; *Globe*, 15 Sept. 1888; Scadding diaries, 16 Sept. 1884.

69 *Globe*, 12 Sept. 1882; *Mail*. 19 Sept. 1889; *Canadian Manufacturer* 21, 6 (18 Sept. 1891), 185–6; *Globe*, 20 Sept. 1890. From 1885 to 1890 an electric trolley running from the grounds to the end of the streetcar line had technical problems, but was heavily used. It seems to have been discon-

tinued under pressure from the regular streetcar company. See *Globe*, 4 Sept. 1885; *Mail*, 5 Sept. 1891; 'Our First Electric Railway,' *Canadian Electrical News* 1, 9 (Sept. 1891), 129.

70 *West Durham News* [Bowmanville], 18 Sept. 1885; OA, MU 4451, Ardagh Family papers, Henry Ardagh diary, 5 Sept. 1898; *Star*, 8 Sept. 1903; *World*, 8 Sept. 1903; *Globe*, 8 Sept. 1903; *World*, 9 Sept. 1898.

71 See, for example, *World*, 15 Sept. 1881; *News*, 14 Sept. 1888; *Globe*, 12 Sept. 1889.

72 *News*, 19 Sept. 1888; *Globe*, 4 Sept. 1900; *Daily Telegraph* [Berlin], 2 Sept. 1899; Madge Merton, 'Woman's Work and Ways,' *Globe*, 19 Sept. 1891.

73 'Toronto Exhibition,' Orillia *Packet*, 26 Sept. 1890; *Globe*, 13 Sept. 1879; *News*, 3 Sept. 1903; *Globe*, 12 Sept. 1882; The Gossip, 'Topics for the Tea Table,' *Star*, 1 Sept. 1899; Faith Fenton, 'Faith at the Show,' *Empire*, 19 Sept. 1889; *Mail*, 14 Sept. 1885.

74 *Mail*, 29 Aug. 1879; CNEA, Industrial Exhibition Association of Toronto, Report for 1881, 7; CNEA, Industrial Exhibition Association of Toronto, Report for 1883, 14; Peterborough *Examiner*, 14 Sept. 1885; *Globe*, 11 Sept. 1885; *Mail*, 19 Sept. 1885; *Mail*, 6 Sept. 1887; CNEA, Industrial Exhibition Association, Prize List for 1896, Plan of the Toronto Exhibition Grounds, np; *Mail and Empire*, 29 Aug. 1903; *Mail and Empire*, 8 Sept. 1902.

75 *Farmers' Sun*, 16 Sept. 1896; *Mail*, 29 Aug. 1879; *Mail*, 14 Sept. 1889; letter of T.C. Mewburn, *Globe*, 25 Sept. 1883; *Mail*, 12 Sept. 1884; Lady Gay [Grace Elizabeth Denison], 'Between You and Me,' *Saturday Night*, 19 Sept. 1891, 3.

76 *News*, 2 Sept. 1898; *News*, 3 Sept. 1896; *News*, 31 Aug. 1900; *Globe*, 14 Sept. 1886; *Mail*, 8 Sept. 1887;

77 *Globe*, 9 Sept. 1881; *News*, 15 Sept. 1887; Jean Grant, 'Woman at the Fair,' *Saturday Night*, 10 Sept. 1898, 9.

78 *Star*, 9 Sept. 1902.

79 Letter from 'One That Was Victimized,' *Telegram*, 12 Sept. 1879; *Saturday Night*, 19 Sept. 1891, 3; 'Abe Loner at the Fair,' *Star*, 4 Sept. 1900. See also *Telegram*, 10 Sept. 1903.

80 *Globe*, 14 Sept. 1881; *News*, 13 Sept. 1887; *Telegram*, 22 Sept. 1888.

81 *Mail*, 18 Sept. 1888; *Globe*, 12 Sept. 1882; MTRL, Baldwin Room, Larratt Smith diaries, 11 Sept. 1893; *Mail*, 15 Sept. 1887. The directors avoided inconvenient delays by establishing in 1889 a separate dining hall for their luncheons, which were amply provided. The fare at an 1898 banquet included soup, Newfoundland cod, steak and kidney pie, hot roasts of

beef, lamb, chicken, and pork, cold boiled ham, roast beef, and roast lamb, apple, and raspberry pies, three kinds of pudding, and cheese. See *Mail*, 7 Sept. 1889; *World*, 9 Sept. 1898.

82 *Globe*, 15 Sept. 1885; 'The Exhibition,' *World*, 10 Sept. 1898. See also *Globe*, 18 Sept. 1888; *News*, 16 Sept. 1890.

83 Letter of 'A Lady Victim,' *Telegram*, 11 Sept. 1879; *Globe*, 12 Sept. 1882; Madge Merton, 'Woman's Work and Ways,' *Globe*, 19 Sept. 1891.

84 *Mail*, 16 Sept. 1890; *Empire*, 12 Sept. 1893; Mack [Joseph Thomas Clark], 'Around Town,' *Saturday Night*, 19 Sept. 1896, 2; *Mail and Empire*, 12 Sept. 1895; *Globe*, 18 Sept. 1888; *Star*, 12 Sept. 1895; exhibition advertisement, *Mail and Empire*, 2 Sept. 1902. Poor F.W. Choate in 1889 was not only unable to get into the grandstand but could not see anything else for the crowd. See OA, MU 7247, F.W. Choate diaries, 19 Sept. 1889.

85 *Star*, 12 Sept. 1895; *Mail*, 13 Sept. 1890; *World*, 21 Sept. 1888; OA, MS 573, Fanny Marion Chadwick diaries, 10 Sept. 1895; Mail, 18 Sept. 1890; '"Teresa" Sees the Show,' *Catholic Register*, 16 Sept. 1897.

86 Newmarket *Era*, 17 Sept. 1886; Elora *Express*, 9 Sept. 1897.

87 NA, MG 30, C 97, J.J. Kelso Papers, diary, 15 Sept. 1885; OA, MU 4451, Ardagh Family Papers, Henry H. Ardagh diaries, 8 and 9 Sept. 1894; William Lyon Mackenzie King, *The Mackenzie King Diaries, 1893–1931* (Toronto 1973), 13 and 14 Sept. 1895.

88 Kit Coleman, 'Gossip of the Fair,' *Mail*, 13 Sept. 1894; Frances Burton Clare, 'At The Exhibition,' *Saturday Night*, 21 Sept. 1889, 3.

89 *Empire*, 21 Sept. 1889.

90 Readers who object to my grinch-like interpretation of the fair experience can find a corrective in Karal Ann Marling's loving descriptions of the attractions at the Minnesota State Fair. See *Blue Ribbon: A Social and Pictorial History of the Minnesota State Fair* (St Paul 1990).

91 Charles Rearick, *Pleasures of the Belle Epoque: Entertainment and Festivity in Turn-of-the-Century France* (New Haven and London 1985), 199; Markham *Sun*, 14 Sept. 1900.

92 Letter of 'Grumbler,' *Empire*, 25 Sept. 1888.

93 In the late Victorian era, there seem to have been two peak periods in hotel construction: from 1889 to 1891, when twenty construction permits were issued, including five for new structures, and from 1898 to 1901, when sixteen permits were issued, five for new buildings. See CTA, RG 13 B4, Toronto Building Permits, Hotels, 1882–1903.

94 *Globe*, 20 Sept. 1887. See also *Globe*, 1 and 5 Sept. 1882; *Mail*, 27 Sept. 1889; letter of 'W.S.,' *Mail*, 2 Sept. 1892; *Saturday Night*, 14 Sept. 1895, 1.

95 CTA, Council Minutes for 1892, 10 Oct. 1892, no. 944; *Canadian Contract Record*: 5 April 1894, 2; 1 Nov. 1894, 2; 20 Dec. 1894, 2; 14 March 1895, 3; 9 April 1896, 3; 30 April 1896, 3. On Frank Smith, see Christopher Armstrong and H.V. Nelles, *The Revenge of the Methodist Bicycle Company: Sunday Streetcars and Municipal Reform in Toronto, 1888–1897* (Toronto 1977), 29–34.

96 'Toronto's Long Felt Want,' *Canadian Grocer*, 25 Jan. 1895, 28; 'The Proposed New Hotel,' *The Week*, 1 Feb. 1895, 222; *Canadian Contract Record*, 16 May 1895, 3; *Canadian Contract Record*, 2 April 1896, 3; Hamilton *Spectator*, 10 Sept. 1896; *Canadian Contract Record*, 19 Aug. 1897; *Canadian Contract Record*, 25 Nov. 1897; CTA, RG 2 B3, Board of Control Communications, 1898, no. 710, 8 Oct. 1898.

97 *Canadian Contract Record*: 29 June 1898, 3; 28 Sept. 1898, 3; 5 Oct. 1898, 2; 9 Nov. 1898, 3; 18 Jan. 1899, 3; *Mail and Empire*, 10 and 15 May 1900; *Canadian Contract Record*, 7 June 1899, 3; *Canadian Contract Record*, 23 May 1900, 3; *Mail and Empire*, 6 July 1900; *Canadian Contract Record*, 11 July 1900, 3; *Mail and Empire*, 8 and 29 Oct. 1900; *Canadian Contract Record*, 26 Dec. 1900, 3; *Mail and Empire*, 7 Feb. 1901; *Canadian Contract Record*, 10 April 1901, 3; *Canadian Contract Record*, 25 Dec. 1901, 3. In the course of construction, another addition costing $150,000 was incorporated into the design. See *Canadian Contract Record*, 9 April 1902, 6. Initial design was by architect Henry Ives Cobb of Chicago, modified by E.J. Lennox of Toronto. See Marilyn M. Litvak, *Edward James Lennox: 'Builder of Toronto'* (Toronto and Oxford 1995), 52–4, 63–5.

98 *Mail and Empire*, 9 Sept. 1902; *Mail and Empire*, 25 Aug. 1903.

99 On the development of the palace hotel in America, see Katherine Grier, 'Imagining the Parlor, 1830–1880,' in Gerald W.R. Ward, *Perspectives on American Furniture* (New York and London 1988), 219–30.

100 Samuel Kinser, *Carnival American Style: Mardi Gras at New Orleans and Mobile* (Chicago 1990), xx–xxi.

101 Sylvie Dufresne, 'Le Carnaval d'hiver de Montreal, 1803–1889,' *Urban History Review / Revue d'histoire urbaine* 11, 3 (Feb. 1983), 25–45; Frank Abbott, 'Cold Cash and Ice Palaces: The Quebec Winter Carnival of 1894,' *Canadian Historical Review* 69 (June 1988), 167–202.

Epilogue: Modernity

1 One of the best descriptions of modern change can be found in Allen Pred's study of Stockholm between 1880 and 1900. See *Lost Words and*

Lost Worlds: Modernity and the Language of Everyday Life in Late Nineteenth-Century Stockholm (Cambridge 1990), xiii–xiv. See also Ben Singer, 'Modernity, Hyperstimulus, and the Rise of Popular Sensationalism,' in Leo Charney and Vanessa R. Schwartz, eds., *Cinema and the Invention of Modern Life* (Berkeley 1995), 72–99.

2 Dana Brand, *The Spectator and the City in Nineteenth-Century American Literature* (Cambridge 1991), 1–2. See also Adrian Forty, 'The City without Qualities,' in Iain Borden and David Dunster, *Architecture and the Sites of History: Interpretations of Buildings and Cities* (Oxford 1995), 304–11; Scott Lash and Jonathan Friedman, 'Introduction: Subjectivity and Modernity's Other,' in Lash and Friedman, eds., *Modernity and Identity* (Oxford and Cambridge, Mass., 1992), 1; Peter Fritzsche, *Reading Berlin 1900* (Cambridge, Mass., and London 1966), 131–2, 147–69.

3 Tony Bennett, 'The Exhibitionary Complex,' in Nicholas B. Dirks, Geoff Eley, and Sherry B. Ortner, eds., *Culture / Power / History: A Reader in Contemporary Social Theory* (Princeton 1994), 126; David Scobey, 'What Shall We Do with Our Walls? The Philadelphia Centennial and the Meaning of Household Design,' in Robert W. Rydell and Nancy Gwinn, eds., *Fair Representations: World's Fairs and the Modern World* (Amsterdam 1994), 26.

4 Lash and Friedman, *Modernity and Identity*, 2.

5 NA, MG 30, C 97, vol. 1, John Joseph Kelso Papers, Diary 1885–1891, 16 Sept. 1888.

6 Brand, *The Spectator and the City*, 6–9; Charles Rearick, *Pleasures of the Belle Epoque: Entertainment and Festivity in Turn-of-the-Century France* (New Haven and London 1985), 176–7.

7 On the figure of the *flâneur* in American literature, see Brand, 9–13, 64–78; Hans Bergmann, *God in the Street: New York Writing from the Penny Press to Melville* (Philadelphia 1995), 53–62.

8 Fred Miller Robinson, *The Man in the Bowler Hat: His History and Iconography* (Chapel Hill and London 1993), 49–51; Walter Benjamin, *Charles Baudelaire: A Lyric Poet in the Era of High Capitalism*, English translation (London 1973), 69; Rearick, *Pleasures of the Belle Epoque*, 177–81.

9 Philippe Perrot, *Fashioning the Bourgeoise: A History of Clothing in the Nineteenth Century* (Princeton 1994), 57.

Illustration Credits

Chang,' AO 3474; 'Fort Rouillé,' ACC 13222-25; 'Suggested Improvements,' Horwood Collection no. 1684, AO 2220; 'Illumination of the Temple,' ACC 14053-32

Thomas Fisher Rare Book Library, University of Toronto: *Canadian Grocer*: 'Lever Brothers' Sunlight,' 11 September 1903, 28; 'Exhibit of McLaren's Imperial Cheese,' 11 September 1902, 18; 'John Taylor & Co.,' 21 September 1894, 36; 'Bensdorp display,' 2 October 1891, 66; 'Edwardsburg and St. Lawrence Starch Co.,' 11 September 1903, 21 and 24; 'The Metallic Roofing Co.,' 18 September 1903, 20; 'Blue Ribbon Tea Exhibit,' 11 September 1903, 17; 'Appleton's Display,' 26 June 1896, 8; *Grip*: 'Representative Exhibitors,' 18 September 1880, 676; 'Short-Horns,' 15 September 1888, 3; 'Some Hard Cases,' 9 September 1882, 672; 'The Greatest Wonder,' 14 September 1889, cover; 'At the Industrial,' 29 September, 1888, 7; 'Revenge Is Sweet,' 11 September 1880

Index